T0192014

Lecture Notes in Computer Science   12553

More information about this subseries at http://www.springer.com/series/7410

Salil Kanhere · Vishwas T Patil ·
Shamik Sural · Manoj S Gaur (Eds.)

Information Systems Security

16th International Conference, ICISS 2020
Jammu, India, December 16–20, 2020
Proceedings

 Springer

Editors
Salil Kanhere
UNSW Sydney
Sydney, NSW, Australia

Vishwas T Patil
IIT Bombay
Mumbai, India

Shamik Sural
IIT Kharagpur
Kharagpur, West Bengal, India

Manoj S Gaur
IIT Jammu
Jammu, India

ISSN 0302-9743   ISSN 1611-3349   (electronic)
Lecture Notes in Computer Science
ISBN 978-3-030-65609-6   ISBN 978-3-030-65610-2   (eBook)
https://doi.org/10.1007/978-3-030-65610-2

LNCS Sublibrary: SL4 – Security and Cryptology

This Springer imprint is published by the registered company Springer Nature Switzerland AG
The registered company address is: Gewerbestrasse 11, 6330 Cham, Switzerland

Preface

This volume contains the papers selected for presentation and publication at the 16th International Conference on Information Systems Security (ICISS 2020), held during December 16–20, 2020, at IIT Jammu, India.

In response to the call for papers of this edition of ICISS, 52 submissions were received from all the continents, except Antarctica! All the submissions underwent a blind-review process by the Technical Program Committee of 67 researchers from industry and academia. The papers were reviewed and then discussed online by the members of the Technical Program Committee and 22 external reviewers.

Out of 52 submissions, the conference accepted 16 papers (comprising 11 regular papers, 2 short papers, and 3 work-in-progress papers), resulting in an acceptance rate of 30%. The papers were evaluated for their significance, novelty, technical quality, and relevance to the current trends in the field of systems security. Each paper received three or more reviews. The accepted papers cover a wide range of topics in security and privacy, including access control, information flow control, authentication, forensics, Android, IoT, applications of AI/ML, and cryptography to network/application/systems security.

In addition to the accepted papers, the conference program also featured five keynote talks by eminent speakers working in the field of security. The keynote speakers, in alphabetical order of their last names, were Omar Chowdhury from the University of Iowa, USA, Sanjam Garg from the University of California, Berkeley, USA, Peng Liu from the Penn State University, USA, Surya Nepal from CSIRO, Australia, and Ravi Sandhu from The University of Texas at San Antonio, USA. A tutorial by Balaji Palanisamy from the University of Pittsburgh, USA, and Chao Li from Beijing Jiaotong University, China, preceded the main program of the conference.

ICISS 2020 would not have been possible without the contributions of the many volunteers who devoted their time and energy to the success of the conference. We would like to thank the Program Committee and the external reviewers for their diligence and timely submission of the reviews of the papers. We would also like to thank the ICISS Steering Committee, the general chair, the publicity chairs, and the Local Arrangement Committee for virtual organization of this year's conference due to the COVID-19 pandemic. We are grateful to the EasyChair conference management service for carrying out the tasks of scrutinizing submissions, evaluating the papers, and notifying the authors of the status of their papers. We also thank Springer for helping us disseminate these papers as a LNCS proceeding to a wider scientific community.

We hope that you find the proceedings of ICISS 2020 inspiring for your future research. And we look forward to your contributions to the future editions of the conference.

December 2020

Salil Kanhere
Vishwas T Patil
Shamik Sural
Manoj S Gaur

Preface

Organization

General Chair

Manoj S Gaur   IIT Jammu, India

Program Committee Chairs

Salil Kanhere	UNSW, Australia
Vishwas T Patil	IIT Bombay, India
Shamik Sural	IIT Kharagpur, India

Workshop and Tutorial Co-chairs

Venkata Badarla	IIT Tirupati, India
Jimson Mathew	IIT Patna, India
Somnath Tripathy	IIT Patna, India

Publicity Co-chairs

Deepak Garg	Max Planck, Germany
N. V. Narendra Kumar	IDRBT Hyderabad, India

Local Organizing Committee

Vinit Jakhetiya	IIT Jammu, India
Preeti Kapahi	IIT Jammu, India
Harkeerat Kaur	IIT Jammu, India
Sumit Pandey	IIT Jammu, India
Yamuna Prasad	IIT Jammu, India
Gaurav Varshney	IIT Jammu, India

Steering Committee

Aditya Bagchi	ISI Kolkata, India
Venu Govindaraju	University at Buffalo SUNY, USA
Sushil Jajodia	George Mason University, USA
Somesh Jha	University of Wisconsin Madison, USA
Arun Majumdar	IIT Kharagpur, India
Chandan Mazumdar	Jadavpur University, India
Atul Prakash	University of Michigan, USA

A. S. Ramasastri	IDRBT Hyderabad, India
Pierangela Samarati	University of Milan, Italy
R. K. Shyamasundar	IIT Bombay, India

Technical Program Committee

Claudio Ardagna	University of Milan, Italy
Vijay Atluri	Rutgers University, USA
Venkata Ramana Badarla	IIT Tirupati, India
Arati Baliga	Persistent Systems, India
Anirban Basu	Hitachi R&D, Japan
Sang Kil Cha	KAIST, South Korea
Sambuddho Chakravarty	IIIT Delhi, India
Donghoon Chang	IIIT Delhi, India
Ayantika Chatterjee	IIT Kharagpur, India
Sanjit Chatterjee	IISc Bangalore, India
Mauro Conti	University of Padua, Italy
Frederic Cuppens	IMT Atlantique, France
Manik Lal Das	DA-IICT Gandhinagar, India
Lorenzo DeCarli	Worcester Polytechnic Institute, USA
Rinku Dewri	University of Denver, USA
Roberto Di Pietro	HBKU Qatar, Qatar
Changyu Dong	Newcastle University, UK
Yanick Fratantonio	Eurecom, France
Chaya Ganesh	IISc Bangalore, India
Deepak Garg	Max Planck Institute – SWS, Germany
Murtuza Jadliwala	The University of Texas at San Antonio, USA
Aniket Kate	Purdue University, USA
Hyoungshick Kim	Sungkyunkwan University, South Korea
Ram Krishnan	The University of Texas San Antonio, USA
Peng Liu	Penn State University, USA
Haibing Lu	Santa Clara University, USA
Pratyusa Manadhata	Micro Focus, USA
Luigi V. Mancini	Università di Roma – Sapienza, Italy
Debadatta Mishra	IIT Kanpur, India
Samrat Mondal	IIT Patna, India
Debdeep Mukhopadhyay	IIT Kharagpur, India
Toby Murray	The University of Melbourne, Australia
Adwait Nadkarni	College of William and Mary, USA
N. V. Narendra Kumar	IDRBT Hyderabad, India
Michele Nati	IOTA, UK
Alwyn Roshan Pais	NIT Suratkal, India
Balaji Palanisamy	University of Pittsburgh, USA
Phu Phung	University of Dayton, USA
Atul Prakash	University of Michigan, USA
Sanjiva Prasad	IIT Delhi, India

R. Ramanujam	IMSc Chennai, India
Silvio Ranise	Fondazione Bruno Kessler, Italy
Kai Rannenberg	Goethe University Frankfurt, Germany
Sanjay Rawat	Vrije University, The Netherlands
Indrakshi Ray	Colorado State University, USA
Chester Rebeiro	IIT Madras, India
Sushmita Ruj	Data61 CSIRO, Australia
Giovanni Russello	The University of Auckland, New Zealand
Somitra Sanadhya	IIT Ropar, India
R. Sekar	Stony Brook University, USA
Arash Shaghaghi	Deakin University, Australia
Shweta Shinde	University of California, Berkeley, USA
Anoop Singhal	NIST, USA
Scott Stoller	Stony Brook University, USA
Rajat Subhra	IIT Kharagpur, India
Pramod Subramanyan	IIT Kanpur, India
S. P. Suresh	Chennai Mathematical Institute, India
Laszlo Szekeres	Google, USA
Somnath Tripathy	IIT Patna, India
V. N. Venkatakrishnan	University of Illinois at Chicago, USA
Hayawardh Vijayakumar	Samsung Research, USA
Stijn Volckaert	KU Leuven, Belgium
Stefano Zanero	Politecnico di Milano, Italy

Additional Reviewers

Debopriyo Banerjee
Stefano Berlato
Anirban Chakraborty
Saptarshi Das
Deepak D'Souza
Alberto Giaretta
Hajar Homayouni
Ramamohanarao Kotagiri
Vireshwar Kumar
Prabhat Kushwaha
Yi Lu

Mohammad Nur Nobi
Raghavendra K. R.
Rajat Sadhukhan
Bharath K. Samanthula
Rijurekha Sen
Mehrnoosh Shakarami
Hossein Shirazi
Priyanka Singh
Alessandro Tomasi
Pier Paolo Tricomi
Yevhen Zolotavkin

Abstracts of Keynote Talks

On Adversarial Testing of Cellular Network Protocols

Omar Chowdhury

The University of Iowa, USA

Abstract. Cellular networks are an indispensable part of a nation's critical infrastructure enabling global-scale communication and a wide range of novel applications and services, including earthquake and tsunami warning system (ETWS), telemedicine, and smart-grid electricity distribution. Cellular networks thus have been an attractive target of adversaries ranging from rogue individuals to more resourceful adversaries such as foreign intelligence agencies. Unfortunately, security- and privacy-enhancing considerations, however, have often played second fiddle to quality-of-service, interoperability, and bandwidth concerns during cellular protocol design. As a consequence, cellular protocols, including the most recent generation, have been often plagued with debilitating attacks due to design weaknesses and deployment slip-ups. In this talk, I will start by discussing an automated analysis approach to reason about the security and privacy properties of cellular network protocol. Next, I will discuss several side-channel attacks that can give away a victim's geographical location as well as its persistent identifier, when the adversary only knows the victim's phone number. I will conclude the talk by discussing several low-cost defense mechanisms whose inclusion can raise the bar for the attackers.

Formalizing Data Deletion in the Context of the Right to be Forgotten

Sanjam Garg

University of California, Berkeley, USA

Abstract. The right of an individual to request the deletion of their personal data by an entity that might be storing it – referred to as the right to be forgotten – has been explicitly recognized, legislated, and exercised in several jurisdictions across the world, including the European Union, Argentina, and California. However, much of the discussion surrounding this right offers only an intuitive notion of what it means for it to be fulfilled – of what it means for such personal data to be deleted. In this work, we provide a formal definitional framework for the right to be forgotten using tools and paradigms from cryptography. In particular, we provide a precise definition of what could be (or should be) expected from an entity that collects individuals' data when a request is made of it to delete some of this data. Our framework captures several, though not all, relevant aspects of typical systems involved in data processing. While it cannot be viewed as expressing the statements of current laws (especially since these are rather vague in this respect), our work offers technically precise definitions that represent possibilities for what the law could reasonably expect, and alternatives for what future versions of the law could explicitly require. Finally, with the goal of demonstrating the applicability of our framework and definitions, we consider various natural and simple scenarios where the right to be forgotten comes up. For each of these scenarios, we highlight the pitfalls that arise even in genuine attempts at implementing systems offering deletion guarantees, and also describe technological solutions that provably satisfy our definitions. These solutions bring together techniques built by various communities. (Based on joint work with Shafi Goldwasser and Prashant Nalini Vasudevan)

Insecurity Analysis of the IoT Platforms and Systems

Peng Liu

Penn State University, USA

Abstract. In this talk, I present our findings of two new families of security vulnerabilities associated with IoT platforms and systems. (Family 1) state out-of-sync vulnerabilities; and (Family 2) privilege separation vulnerabilities. In addition, I will provide a systematic classification of the recently identified security-related logic bugs in IoT platforms and systems. Our study shows that new kinds of security vulnerabilities indeed exist in emerging IoT applications and platforms. I also comment on the difficulties of removing these vulnerabilities.

A Defense Against Trojan Attacks on Deep Neural Networks

Surya Nepal

Data61, CSIRO, Australia

Abstract. Backdoor attacks insert hidden associations or triggers to the deep learning models to override correct inference such as classification and make the system perform maliciously according to the attacker-chosen target while behaving normally in the absence of the trigger. As a new and rapidly evolving realistic attack, it could result in dire consequences, especially considering that the backdoor attack surfaces are broad. This talk first provides a brief overview of backdoor attacks, and then present a countermeasure, STRong Intentional Perturbation (STRIP). STRIP intentionally perturbs the incoming input, for instance by superimposing various image patterns, and observe the randomness of predicted classes for perturbed inputs from a given deployed model – malicious or benign. A low entropy in predicted classes violates the input-dependence property of a benign model and implies the presence of a malicious input.

Access Control Convergence: Challenges and Opportunities

Ravi Sandhu

The University of Texas at San Antonio, USA

Abstract. There have been a handful of ground-breaking concepts in access control over the past half century which have received significant traction in practical deployments. These include the fundamental policy-mechanism and operational-administrative distinctions, along with the authorization models of discretionary access control (DAC), mandatory access control (MAC), role-based access control (RBAC), attribute-based access control (ABAC), and relationship-based access control (ReBAC). In this talk we will argue that modern cyber systems require an effective convergence of these concepts, in that they must coexist in mutually supportive synergy. We will highlight some challenges and opportunities in making this vision a practical reality.

Contents

Access Control

A Unified Access Control Model for Calibration Traceability in Safety-Critical IoT

Ryan Shah[✉] and Shishir Nagaraja

University of Strathclyde, Glasgow, Scotland
ryan.shah@strath.ac.uk

Abstract. Accuracy (and hence calibration) is a key requirement of safety-critical IoT (SC-IoT) systems. Calibration workflows involve a number of parties such as device users, manufacturers, calibration facilities and NMIs who must collaborate but may also compete (mutually untrusting). For instance, a surgical robot manufacturer may wish to hide the identities of third-parties from the operator (hospital), in order to maintain confidentiality of business relationships around its robot products. Thus, information flows that reveal *who-calibrates-for-whom* need to be managed to ensure confidentiality. Similarly, meta-information about *what-is-being-calibrated* and *how-often-it-is-calibrated* may compromise operational confidentiality of a deployment. We show that the challenge of managing information flows between the parties involved in calibration cannot be met by any of the classical access control models, as any one of them, or a simple conjunction of a subset such as the lattice model, fails to meet the desired access control requirements. We demonstrate that a new unified access control model that combines BIBA, BLP, and Chinese Walls holds rich promise. We study the case for unification, system properties, and develop an XACML-based authorisation framework which enforces the unified model. We show that upon evaluation against a baseline simple-conjunction of the three models individually, our unified model outperforms with authorisation times at least 10ms lower than the baseline. This demonstrates it is capable of solving the novel access control challenges thrown up by digital-calibration workflows.

1 Introduction

Many safety-critical IoT (SC-IoT) systems, such as surgical robots, are employed to address the need for automation, accuracy and precision. For example, the Robodoc surgical robot has shown a decrease in the number of complications in hip surgeries by providing higher accuracy for implant sizing and positioning within the bone compared to traditional surgery [5]; and in autonomous vehicles, a variety of sensor devices are heavily relied on to provide assistance for real-time decision making [27]. This has led to an increased desire in the adoption of

© Springer Nature Switzerland AG 2020
S. Kanhere et al. (Eds.): ICISS 2020, LNCS 12553, pp. 3–22, 2020.
https://doi.org/10.1007/978-3-030-65610-2_1

such systems in high-assurance environments, where the system can outperform traditional methods whilst lowering risk of complications.

While IoT device security and privacy has received a lot of attention [1,11,17], the security of calibration has received little attention. There are a number of safety-critical IoT systems in the industrial landscape, such as surgical robotics, where one of the key safety requirements is to ensure valid calibration of all its components before deployment and operation. To ensure valid calibration, there are calibration processes which involve many parties. These parties form a hierarchy of other calibrated devices within which they interact (Fig. 1). First, at the field level we have device operators who control, interact with and maintain the system and its components. Second, we have one or more intermediary calibration facilities who employ technicians which interact with other calibrated devices within the hierarchy. Finally, we have National Measurement Institutes (NMIs) at the highest level, such as NIST (USA) and NPL (UK), who maintain homeostatic control within the hierarchy.

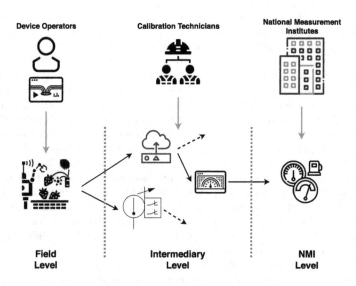

Fig. 1. Calibration hierarchy for an SC-IoT system

While many of these parties do cooperate in harmony, for example NMIs who manage publicly available calibration information and act as the root of trust, a subset of them may share an adversarial relationship (in direct competition, or *conflict*, with one another). Consider a surgical robot which employs a number of sensors (among other components) that require valid calibration to ensure all sensed data is accurate and reliable. While the calibration of these devices may be performed in-house, some system-level organisations make use of third-party calibration service providers (i.e. an intermediary calibration facility) who may wish to remain confidential – for example, to show responsibility for calibrating their own devices and helping to maintain business relationships. By revealing this information to parties in competition, in this case to other hospitals, the confidentiality among the participants (*who-calibrates-for-whom*) would be compromised, possibly hindering potential investor engagements. As well as this, by allowing a calibration technician to calibrate a system for an organisation in conflict with another that the same technician calibrates for, the potential for the collection and leakage of sensitive business secrets is of significant concern. Furthermore, while protecting the confidentiality of business relationships among organisations with conflicts of interest, the information regarding the frequency of calibration and what is being calibrated can lead to the compromise of operational confidentiality of SC-IoT deployments. For instance, by monitoring the calibration processes and collecting calibration offsets and other meta-data, it is possible to reveal how system components are used.

Ultimately, we observe that the potential compromise of calibration integrity and confidentiality, and the adversarial relationships (conflict) between a subset of interacting parties in the calibration ecosystem, presents us with a unique set of information flows where meta-information such as what is calibrated, how often it is calibrated and who calibrates for who, need to be managed. This presents us with an interesting access control challenge, to which an effective solution to adderss this should satisfy the following requirements:

(R_1) How can we manage the adversarial relationships between a subset of interacting parties in the calibration ecosystem, to avoid unintended disclosure of information?

(R_2) How can we protect the confidentiality of business relationships (*who-calibrates-for-whom*) whilst providing transparency for calibration processes?

(R_3) How can we ensure operational confidentiality of SC-IoT deployments by protecting *what-is-being-calibrated* and *how-often-it-is-calibrated*?

(R_4) As many SC-IoT systems are time-critical, how can we support calibration processes to be carried out efficiently (*on-the-fly*) whilst ensuring R_1–R_3?

We propose the case for the unification of three classical access control models: BIBA, BLP and Chinese Walls models; propose a conjunction; and evaluate an efficient implementation of the unified model. Upon evaluation using an attribute-based authorisation framework, we observe that our unified model outperforms the baseline authorisation times by at least 10 ms, which in the context of safety-critical IoT systems, where time-critical operation is key to adhere to, suggests that it can adequately solve the access control challenges which arise from digital-calibration workflows.

The rest of the paper is organised as follows. In Sect. 2, we further detail the inadequacies of the current state-of-the-art in calibration and access control, and discuss the observed information flow constraints pertaining to multi-level integrity and confidentiality and compartmentation of conflicts of interest, which demands a novel unification of BIBA, BLP and Chinese Walls. Following this, we detail our unified access control model in Sect. 3 and evaluate its performance using an attribute-based authorisation mechanism in Sect. 4. In Sect. 5, we provide a discussion of the presented work, provide related work in Sect. 6 and conclude in Sect. 7.

2   Calibration Traceability and Access Control: A Case for Unification

Calibration is a key factor which contributes to the accuracy and reliability of our devices, such as the readings produced from sensing equipment. Simply put, the process of calibration is a comparison of a given device, such as a sensor in an SC-IoT system, with a more accurate (parent) device. Specifically, the accuracy and reliability of our device's output is derived from its parent. Whilst it is important to maintain calibration of our devices, ensuring valid calibration is key [26]. An important requirement for valid calibration is having an unbroken chain of traceable calibration to a trustworthy source [7, 26] (Fig. 2). This means that valid calibration requires a complete trace of calibration, starting with a comparison between our device and a more accurate parent device. The parent will then be compared against an even more accurate device, and so forth until we compare against a device that is as accurate as possible (where the accuracy and uncertainty of output meets national standards), typically maintained by National Measurement Institutes (NMIs).

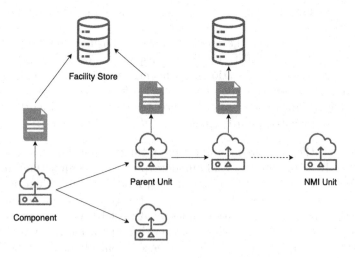

Fig. 2. Traceability chain

With the considerations of SC-IoT systems, we observe several inadequacies with the current state-of-the-art in calibration traceability.

First, current calibration traceability processes are inefficient. As an output of calibration, a report (hereafter refered to as a calibration report) is produced, which details the information used in traceability verification (such as calibration offsets, uncertainty measurements, operating ranges, etc.). Furthermore, these are stored centrally within the organisation who carried out the calibration of the associated device. For example, a device calibrated by a technician at some intermediary calibration facility will typically have its report stored locally. To carry out verification checks (Fig. 2), a subject (device owner, technician performing calibration, etc.) must first request the device's report from the holding organisation. Once access is granted, the parent units of the device can be identified from the report and the reports for these devices must also be accessed, and so forth to national standards. While the process is relatively trivial to conduct, many SC-IoT systems are comprised of large numbers of devices, each of them having their own individual traceability chains. With this in mind, a verification process which ensures there is a complete chain of calibration for a single device in the current state-of-the-art could take a few hours but for an entire SC-IoT system, verification time would increase significantly.

Second, given that calibration reports are stored in different organisations for a single device's traceability chain, each organisation could have their own security requirements to grant access to reading a report. For example, test and measurement equipment used to calibrate military equipment could have their reports classed as confidential, heavily restricting who can gain access to the information within the report. Further, an organisation who employs calibration services from a third-party provider may wish to not reveal this relationship to other parties related to the organisation (for example stakeholders). If this information was revealed, it would compromise the confidentiality of business relationships. By verifying calibration along each step in a device's chain could leak confidential information about how the device is used (i.e *what-is-calibrated* and *how-often-it-is-calibrated*) and the parties involved with its calibration (*who-calibrates-for-whom*).

Third, we consider insider attacks. It is entirely possible that a technician at the field level in the chain could fabricate reports for (potentially non-existent) devices further up the chain, such as for intermediary calibration facilities or National Measurement Institutes (NMIs). As the calibration status of downstream equipment is dependent on upper levels, the integrity of calibration traceability and ultimately the device itself could be compromised. Furthermore, it is important to allow subjects conducting traceability verification checks at lower levels (i.e. the field level) to access reports at each upper level for completeness, while disallowing those operating at the field level to write reports for upper levels, and vice-versa.

Finally, the potential for conflicts of interest between competing calibration facilities arise. For example, a calibration technician who calibrates devices for one organisation, should not be allowed to calibrate devices for another, to avoid leaking potentially sensitive information about the device and the organisation's internal calibration processes.

Upon observation of the problem space surrounding the current state-of-the-art and the considerations surrounding SC-IoT, we can see that the key failures are provoked by varying access control requirements for verifying calibration traceability within a multi-level hierarchy.

2.1   Information Flow Constraints

An important requirement for designing an effective solution that meets our requirements is to define the information flow constraints which should be enforced. For subsequent discussion, we refer to the information flow model depicted in Fig. 3.

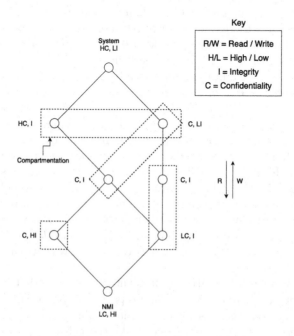

Fig. 3. Information flow model

Multi-level Integrity. Our first requirement is to maintain the integrity of calibration. By maintaining the integrity of calibration reports at the root level, we can reduce the damage inflicted to intermediate levels between the root level and the components which make up a safety-critical system. As a reminder, if compromise occurs at the root level in a traceability chain, then the validity of all subsequent levels towards the field level is questionable. By maintaining the integrity of calibration, we can limit any damage to its immediate locality, as opposed to inflicting widespread damage.

Overall, we observe that with respect to traceability, information flows from a high integrity source, the root calibration units at NMIs, to a low integrity destination, the components at the field level.

Multi-level Confidentiality. The second requirement is maintaining confidentiality among participants whilst enabling transparency in traceability chains. Interestingly, we observe that it is relatively trivial to map components in traceability chains to real actors. For example, a component's calibration report could reveal the facility at which calibration was carried out, as well as information that denotes a facility's internal calibration processes. With consideration to NMIs where the information is globally available, the mapping of equipment at this level does not succumb to confidentiality concerns. However, in the case of intermediate levels, who do not wish to reveal information to other levels above or below them, the possibility of such a mapping becomes of real concern.

Additionally, the timing of traceability verification checks could reveal information about system operations. For example, in the context of surgical robots, the timing of surgical procedures could be leaked, as a result of monitoring verification checks. When combined with other sources of information such as patient admission and exit times, a violation of patient confidentiality is possible. It is also important that the verification process does not reveal information about the deployment to intermediaries involved between the deployed system and the public-facing NMI at the highest level. The reason for this is simple: calibration traffic could leak information to parties further down the chain. For example, a device manufacturer may employ the services of a third-party calibration facility to calibrate the system's sensors, but may not want to reveal who the third party is. Thus, the traceability chain should be verifiable in a manner, such that information about the setting where the system is deployed is not leaked to other facilities, and likewise from these facilities to the NMIs.

Overall, we note that the field level, where systems are deployed, must retain the highest level of confidentiality, whilst calibration present at the public-facing root level are found to have the lowest confidentiality requirements.

Conflicts of Interest. The last requirement for an appropriate solution is to prevent unintended disclosure of information, specifically relating to the nature of conflicts between calibration providers that manage the systems. For example, a hospital which employs a number of surgical robots may wish to hide the identity of the calibration service provider who calibrates the robot's sensors. A technician from this company should not be allowed to calibrate surgical robots for other hospitals, to avoid the leakage of sensitive business information to competitors, and protect confidential business relationships. As such, it is vital that we compartmentalise those in competition into conflict of interest sets, such that this sensitive information cannot flow between them.

2.2 Existing Access Control Models and Calibration Traceability

Naturally, given the information flow contraints which arise from calibration traceability, one would consider the adoption of existing access control models. To this, we will refer to the requirements of multi-level confidentiality and integrity, as well as the conflicts of interest among calibration providers. The existing BLP model provides confidentiality, most prominently for military applications, preventing unauthorised disclosure from an object. The existing model matches our information flow from high confidentiality (system) to low confidentiality (NMIs at the root level), however while BLP address confidentiality, by itself it does not satisfy our integrity requirements. Similarly, the existing BIBA model prevents unauthorised modification where integrity flows from low to high are prevented. While BIBA can satisfy our integrity requirements, similar to BLP itself alone cannot satisfy our confidentiality requirements. Unfortunately, neither model alone will prevent the undesirable information flows described in Sect. 2.1 and both are required. Notably, while BIBA and BLP address integrity and confidentiality, respectively, neither address both concerns and although it is ideal to join together concerns of confidentiality and integrity in security systems, there is no previously proposed conjunction. Finally, with regard to conflicts of interest, the Chinese Wall model (albeit refers equally to integrity and confidentiality) mandates that access to data is constrained by what data the subject already holds access rights to and not just by attributes of the data in question [6]. In contrast to this, BLP and BIBA place no constraints on the interrelationships between objects and structure is defined by the security attributes of the data.

Ultimately, while each of the existing models could potentially satisfy *some* of the information flow requirements individually, none alone can meet our requirements. Thus, the unification of the BLP, BIBA and Chinese Wall models is necessary. The model rules are presented in Sect. 3

3   A Unified Access Control Model for Calibration Traceability

In current calibration-related business practices, we identified that these models are loosely implemented. Within calibration facilities, the notions of confidentiality set forth in the BLP model is exercised on calibration reports. Specifically, some calibration reports may have a degree of confidentiality, or the technicians calibrating equipment may do so under a non-disclosure agreement, and it is likely that internal systems and individuals maintain these levels of confidentiality. As for the notions of integrity handled by BIBA, we observe this is inherent to the calibration ecosystem but is not rigorously enforced. Instead, it is implied that integrity must be maintained at all levels, specifically at the root level, but any problems are not discovered until the annual cycle of traceability verification, at which point the liabilities that arise due to invalid calibration may not be settled easily.

For subsequent discussion of the unification of the three models, we define the terminology using notation based on the work of Sandhu [24].

(Definition) Conflict of Interest Set. A Conflict of Interest (COI) set is defined as the set of conflict of interest classes, that contains all calibration reports (objects) whose providers are in direct competition with each other. Following standard notation, we denote the set of n COI sets as

$\{COI_1, COI_2, \ldots, COI_n\}$, where each set $COI_i = \{P_1, P_2, \ldots, P_k\}$ and P_k is the group of calibration reports which concern the same provider k.

(Definition) Set of Integrity Labels. The set of integrity labels is denoted as $\Omega = \{\omega_1, \omega_2, \ldots, \omega_q\}$, where each label corresponds to a unique integrity level. In accordance with our information flows, each integrity label also constitutes a unique confidentiality level.

(Definition) Security Label. A security label is defined as a set of two n-sized vectors $\{[i_1, i_2, \ldots, i_n], [p_1, p_2, \ldots, p_n]\}$, where $i_j \in \{COI_j \cup \perp \cup T\}$, $p_j \in \Omega$ and $1 \leq j \leq n$.

- Where $i_j = \perp$, the calibration traceability chain does not contain information from any provider in COI_j.
- Where $i_j = T$, the calibration traffic contains information from *at least* two facilities who are in a conflict of interest set COI_j.
- Where $i_j \in COI_j$, the calibration traffic contains information from the corresponding calibration facility in COI_j.

(Definition) Dominance Relations. We define the (transitive) dominance relations between security labels as follows, where the notation $l_j[i_k]$ denotes the i_k^{th} element of the label l_j. We say that a security label l_1 dominates a label l_2, denoted by $l_1 \geq l_2$, where $l_1 \geq l_2 \iff \forall i_k, p_k = (1, 2, \ldots, n)[((l_1[i_k] = l_2[i_k]) \vee (l_2[i_k] = \perp) \vee (l_1[i_k] = T)) \wedge (l_1[p_k] \leq l_2[p_k])]$.

- A label l_1 dominates a label l_2, provided that l_1 and l_2 agree whenever l_2 is not public or in conflict, and the integrity level of l_2 is higher than that of l_1.
- The security label corresponding to an NMI at the root level, $\{[\perp, \perp, \ldots, \perp], [\omega_q]\}$, is **dominated by** all other levels.
- The system high, denoted by $\{[T, T, \ldots, T], [\omega_1]\}$, **dominates** all other levels.
- The dominance relation defines a lattice structure, where the NMI label appears at the bottom and the level trusted appears at the top. Incomparable levels are not connected in this lattice structure.

In accordance with our proposed access control model, the rules for information flow as they apply to it are as follows:

1. Simple Property: A calibration technician (S), may read a calibration report (O), only if the label, $L(S) \geq L(O)$.
2. * (Star) Confinement Property: A calibration technician (S) can only calibrate (write) a system component or unit (O), if the label of the component dominates that of the technician, i.e. if $L(O) \geq L(S)$. Specifically, write corresponds to the production of a calibration report.

4   Evaluation

While our unified model may be theoretically sound, it is vital to evaluate whether or not such a model is practically efficient for enforcing constraints in a real application. In this section, we first describe a case example for which our model could be applied, and follow on to evaluate the performance of our model as a practical solution for authorising traceability verification checks.

4.1   Case Example: Calibration Traceability for a Sensor Device

To describe a case as to how our proposed model can be applied, we take the example of an infrared thermometer sensor. To keep within scope of this paper, we will discount the uncertainty calculations that make part of the traceability verification process, as the primary concern is with the authorisation time for enforcing our model rather than the overall time to complete calibration itself.

In order to calibrate an infrared thermometer, we need: (1) a thermal radiation source, (2) a transfer standard (an intermediate device when comparing other devices in calibration), (3) an ambient temperature thermometer, and (4) a distance measuring device. In some cases, for example where an aperture is part of its calibration, additional equipment may be required. However, we will consider the more general case described. As shown in Fig. 4, we can see an example scheme for tracing the infrared thermometer to national standards.

To discuss our model in this case setting, we will assume the following:

– The calibration facilities $O1 - O3$ are classed as intermediary calibration facilities, and $O4$ is a National Measurement Institute (NMI)
– The infrared thermometer sensor is calibrated by technician $T1$ at calibration facility $O1$
– The transfer standard used in calibrating the sensor is itself, calibrated by a technician $T2$ at organisation $O2$
– The facilities $O2$ and $O3$ are in direct competition with one another
– The traceability chain information flows from the sensing device to $O1$, to the transfer standard calibrated by a technician at $O2$, towards the NMI ($O4$)

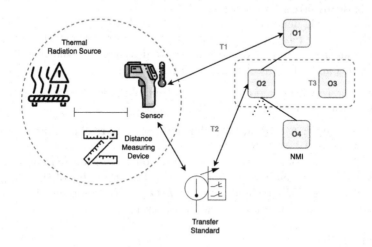

Fig. 4. Traceability chain for infrared thermometer

Given the assumptions above, we now describe the calibration traceability lifecycle for our infrared thermometer sensor and how our proposed unified model can be applied.

Initial Calibration

Inspired by biology, we refer to the initial calibration of a system component, or test and measurement equipment, as the *birth* of the device, representing the behaviour which implements its secure initialisation. For all devices, there is always an initial calibration step which commences the start of its lifecycle and inaugurates them into the calibration ecosystem. After manufacturing, there are three primary methods of initial calibration: (a) by the manufacturer; (b) by a third-party intermediary calibration facility; and (c) at a National Measurement Institute (NMI).

In accordance with our model, and taking our case example, the sensor's initial calibration will be conducted by the technician $T1$ at the facility $O1$. This process will output a calibration report for the sensor and this will be given the security label assigned to the technician: $\{[\perp, \perp, \perp], [\omega_1]\}$. Similarly, the transfer standard is calibrated by the technician $T2$ at facility $O2$ and will have the security label: $\{[\perp, COI_1, \perp], [\omega_2]\}$, where $COI_1 = \{O2, O3\}$ contains the group of calibration reports which concern both the providers $O2$ and $O3$ that are in conflict.

In most cases, there will be no conflicts that arise as part of a device's initial calibration, however some devices such as those created for military or other government organisations may be classified in nature. Thus, if the organisation previously used a calibration facility for calibrating a set of other devices, the new facility to be contracted could be in competition/conflict with the other and thus the labels would indicate a conflict in the chain.

Verifying Traceability

Traceability plays a key role in verifying a newly calibrated device, as well as determining whether it needs to be recalibrated; ultimately being at the heart of on-the-fly calibration. As the traceability verification process first involves retrieving the report of the device being traces, followed by its parents' reports, until the root level, the party who carries out the verification check must first satisfy a set of conditions set out by the unified model.

In accordance with our access control model, the security label of the device being traced must dominate the label of the party carrying out the verification check. For example, in the case of recalibration which first involves a traceability check, the label for a device must dominate that of the verifier. As we are required to read all the reports of all parents at each step in the chain, up to national standards, the label of each parent should also dominate that of the verifying party, such that for a traceability chain $C = \{L(O_1), L(O_2), \ldots, L(O_n)\}, \forall c \in C$, $L(S) \geq c_i$, where $i, n \geq 1$ and $L(S)$ is the label of the party carrying out the verification.

Recalibration

The process of recalibration is one that is carried out either: (a) when the expiry date of a component/unit's calibration report has been exceeded, (b) when critical measurements are taken, (c) if the accuracy or measurement uncertainty of the equipment has noticeably degraded or drifted before the expiry period, or (d) if any parent unit in the chain does not have valid calibration. In any case, recalibration first involves performing a traceability verification check, to ensure that the component/unit has unbroken traceability and valid calibration. The technician performing calibration must first be allowed to carry out the traceability check, such that the label of the component or unit being calibrated dominates that of the technician, $L(O) \geq L(S)$. Specifically, this dominance relation is satisfied when the technician is not in conflict; i.e. if the technician is the same as the one who performed the initial calibration or previous recalibration, then they will be allowed to do so. Similarly, if not then the model would verify that the new technician performing recalibration is not in conflict with the previous, or others in the chain. That is, the traceability chain of the equipment being recalibrated does not contain information from both technicians in a conflict of interest set COI_j.

4.2   Performance Evaluation

As well as discussing how the model will be applied in a real-world case, it is vital to determine its practicality. We mention that the individual access control models, or a simple conjunction of them, may not be suitable or efficient compared to the unified model. In this evaluation, we determine whether our unified model can be enforced in a practical setting to support efficient calibration verification *on-the-fly* and scale well with large, complex calibration hierarchies.

Setup
To evaluate our model, we made use of an attribute-based authorisation framework, following the XACML standard [21] and structured as shown in Fig. 5. The framework provides standards for access requests and policy specification, where a client program acts as a Policy Enforcement Point (PEP) which sends access requests to and enforced responses given by the server running a Policy Decision Point (PDP). The experiments on the authorisation framework to evaluate our model were performed on a virtual machine running Ubuntu 14.04 LTS allocated with 64 GB of RAM.

Baseline Model
To provide a more in-depth comparison on how our access control model performs, we conducted the evaluation starting with a *simple conjunction* of the three models (BLP, Reverse BIBA (RBIBA) and Chinese Walls), as a **baseline model** to compare our unified model against. Specifically, to create the baseline model we made use of the XACML *PolicySet*, where policies for each model can be combined into a policy set and enforced together using a *PolicyCombiningAlgorithm*. As the policy set contains multiple policies (one for each model), with each returning different decisions, the question remains as to what the policy combination should return. To combine the policies for our baseline, we used the *permit-unless-deny* algorithm, which only allows a Permit or Deny response, and will deny access if any one of the combined policies produce a Deny result. In comparison, our unified model is a single policy which makes use of the *deny overrides* rule combining algorithm, such that if any rule results in a Deny response, then this decision wins.

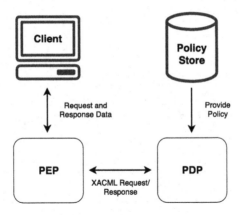

Fig. 5. XACML authorisation architecture

Authorising Traceability Verification

For the first part of our evaluation, we measured the time taken to authorise access requests for calibration traceability verification using our unified model. As a point of comparison, we also measure this time for the baseline model. To recall, traceability verification involves verifying the calibration at each level in the chain of calibrations for some equipment, up to national standards.

Naturally, in the calibration hierarchy, there are several levels for a single traceability chain. A simple temperature sensor, for example, could be calibrated with a platinum resistance thermometer, which in turn is calibrated by a more accurate reference thermometer, and finally calibrated by a helium gas thermometer (primary reference standard) [20]. However, with the consideration of SC-IoT systems, where devices could be off-the-shelf components, the length of traceability chains could be much larger than 4 levels. Thus for completeness, we conduct our experiment measuring the authorisation time for traceability verification up to 50 levels.

For the first experiment, we measured the time to authorise traceability verification up to 50 levels, with only a single parent (reference device) at each level. As shown in Fig. 6, we observe that across the board, the unified model is significantly faster compared to the baseline simple conjunction, with authorisation times not exceeding 11 ms on average in the worst case, compared to roughly 30 ms for the baseline model.

In realistic traceability chains, some devices are calibrated with more than one reference (parent) device. For example, an infrared temperature sensor is calibrated with a distance gauge, infrared source (i.e. hotplates) and reference thermometer [18]. Each of these parent devices will have their own parents, meaning that instead of having a single chain, we now have a chain that branches off several times. Hence, our next experiment involves measuring the authorisation time for traceability verification for 2 and 4 branches per level, such that we can observe the impact of realistically complex chains. As shown in Fig. 7(a) and Fig. 7(b), we see a similar pattern to a single branch for a chain, with our

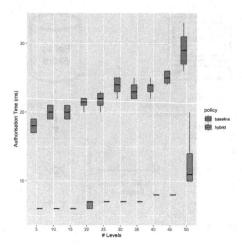

Fig. 6. Authorisation time for single traceability chain

unified model outperforming the baseline model by at least 15 ms in the worst case. Furthermore, we can also observe an increase in the authorisation time as the number of branches per level also increases, as authorisations for each parent device and so forth in their branches also need to be made.

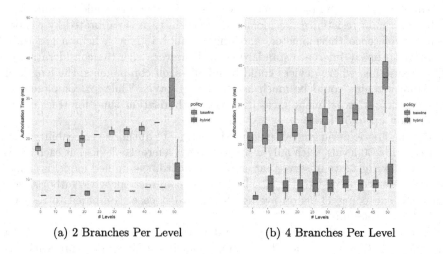

(a) 2 Branches Per Level   (b) 4 Branches Per Level

Fig. 7. Authorisation times for branching traceability chains

Across all test cases, while the unified model does outperform (significantly) the baseline simple conjunction, the authorisation time does increase as the number of levels increases. However, in the case of our unified model, the increase of just a few milliseconds as the number of levels or branches increase is considered a reasonable wait on the device prep-cycle or if a measurement was to be taken [10].

Conflict Management

Pertaining to the conflict component of security labels, we note that it is in fact the size of conflict sets, rather than the number of them, which needs to be considered, as some sets may only contain two members, whilst others could contain more. Thus, we evaluated the effect of the size of conflict sets on authorisation time in traceability verification, for our unified model.

For our calibration traceability dataset, we generated a set of calibration reports which contained real calibration data. Each of which were assigned a security label, where the integrity component of the label corresponded with the level at which calibration was conducted, and the conflict component of the label was generated using a $G(n, p)$ variant of the Erdös–Rényi random graph model, where n is the number of potential competitors and p is the probability of conflict. Specifically, the cliques of the random graph represented conflict sets, which for each node n_i was assigned a set of conflict sets.

To evaluate the impact of the size of conflict sets, we increase the number of potential competitors n and probability of potential competitors being in conflict p, such that we get a range of conflict set sizes from 1 member in the set to 50. As shown in Fig. 8, we observe an increase in the time taken to authorise traceability verification requests as the size of the conflict sets increase. Our experiment here shows the effect on authorisation time for a single conflict set, however, we can see clearly that as the number of conflict sets increase, so will the authorisation time; but impressive yet the increase is fairly minimal and as previously stated is considered a reasonable wait on the device prep-cycle.

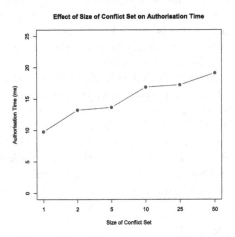

Fig. 8. Effect of conflict set size on authorisation time

5   Discussion and Limitations

Within the calibration hierarchy, we observe a unique set of information flows which we hypothesised could not be effectively met by classical access control models, as any one of them or a simple conjunction of a subset such as the lattice model, fails to meet the desired access control requirements for compartmental-ising conflicts of interest, integrity and confidentiality. To this, we propose an efficient conjunction of three existing models: BLP, BIBA and Chinese Walls, which significantly outperforms our baseline simple conjunction, with authori-sation times for the unified model being at least 10 ms lower in all cases.

With some key players (device operators, calibration facilities, etc.) in the calibration ecosystem sharing an adversarial relationship with a subset of others, we observe a unique set of information flows. First, we observe that calibration traceability checks could reveal *who-calibrates-for-whom*, which can ultimately compromise the confidentiality of business relationships surrounding SC-IoT sys-tems. With the adoption of our unified model, we constrain these information flows such that the field level where systems are deployed retain the highest level of confidentiality and calibration meta-information such as *what-is-being-calibrated* and *how-often-it-is-calibrated* cannot be revealed to levels above the field level (i.e. intermediary facilities). While the model does protect this infor-mation from being leaked from information flows arising from traceability checks, other side channels such as insider technicians could reveal *who-calibrates-for-whom* and thus are not protected by the access control model alone. Upon eval-uation, we show that in comparison with a baseline simple conjunction of the three models, our unified model not only meets these requirements but improves authorisation times roughly ten-fold. This result demonstrates that our unified model meets our requirement for efficiency ($R4$) as SC-IoT systems are time-critical. Specifically, in the context of calibration, it is important that calibration can be verified *on-the-fly*. Consider a surgical robot which employs a number of sensing devices. During secure boot, or before conducting a surgical operation on a patient where critical measurements are made, the calibration needs to be verified quickly to minimise any disruption to the start of the procedure.

One limitation of this work, is that policies and calibration reports are stored centrally. We assume that encryption mechanisms are in place, however we do not consider the impact of security mechanisms such as TLS and PKI on authorisa-tion times in our evaluation. In any case, added security presents overheads that would need to be considered, and in certain cases (i.e. critical liabilities resulting from calibration checks before system operation can continue) the addition of such security measures could increase the low authorisation times observed from evaluation of our unified model.

6   Related Work

The security surrounding time- and safety-critical IoT systems is an active research area [8], with the main focus pertaining to attacks in the cyber domain (i.e. control system security [2, 14]) and the physical domain (i.e. physical compromise of sensors [3, 9] and physical safety of devices and surrounding environment [9, 23]). However, with the calibration of such systems contributing highly to system accuracy and precision, the compromise of its calibration can ultimately impact the ability to operate safely. Quarta et al. describe calibration parameters of robotics systems to be an essential construct used to compensate for known measurement errors [22]. They demonstrated that by manipulating calibration parameters, an adversary could cause the robot to operate unsafely, such as affecting the servo motor causing the robot to move erratically. Consider a temperature sensor mounted on a needle driver in a surgical robot, which is calibrated in a manner such that it provides accurate and reliable readings for temperatures between 0–50 °C. If these calibration parameters are modified to state that it is accurate up to 100 °C, then the system would accept this at face value, and any sensed data cannot be trusted.

Existing access control literature for safety-critical IoT systems focus on various aspects of the system itself, ranging from securing control systems (i.e. access to actuators) to the validation/enforcement of security policies. Hasan and Mohan [14] propose a framework based on the Simplex architecture, commonly used for time-critical cyberphysical systems for fault-tolerance, which makes use of a rule-based invariant and access control mechanism to ensure the timing and safety requirements of IoT cyberphysical systems (i.e. ensure some task can only access a given actuator if the task has the required permission given a set of invariant conditions). Frank et al. [12] describe a combination of both logical and physical access control – explain each, respectively. He describes that the most widely used multi-level security models are inadequate when logical resources obtain a physical form, that makes use of both mandatory and discretionary access control. While not directly applicable to calibration traceability, one must also consider the access constraints to the physical process of calibration which traceability verification is a key part of. Compared to our work, we make use of attribute-based access control (ABAC) due to its flexibility, limited only by the computational language when implementing policies to enforce access control models. Specifically, it allows greater breadth for access relationships (subjects to access objects) without the need to specify the individual relationships between them. Compared to other traditional approaches such as rule-based access control, this makes its use ideal for dynamic environments such as SC-IoT [16].

In this work, we focus on the calibration angle which has been paid little attention to. Specifically, we focus on the unification of three classical access control models (namely BLP, BIBA and Chinese Walls) which is required to solve the novel set of information flows which arise from calibration traceability. Yang et al. [28] state that while BLP is widely used to enforce multi-level confidentiality, it lacks flexibility due to strict confidentiality rules. Furthermore, they describe that BLP poorly controls integrity and that BLP is commonly combined with BIBA for increased integrity control [15, 25, 29]. In their work, they propose an improved BLP model to manage multi-level security, where the security of each level is distinguished by the security level of the accessed content itself (subjects are defined as a multi-level entity and objects are defined as a single-level entity). With regard to BIBA, Liu et al. [19] note that BIBA can possibly deny non-malicious access requests made by subjects, ultimately reducing the availability to a system. To this, they propose the integration of notions from Break The Glass (BTG) strategies – a set of (efficient) strategies used to extend subject access rights in exceptional cases (i.e. irregular system states) – with the existing BIBA model (BTG-BIBA). They show that with the proposed BTG-BIBA model, it can now provide more fine-grained access control that is context-aware for dynamic situations. In this work, we take into account the traditional BIBA and BLP models in our case for unification, however one can question the applicability of improvements made to these models over recent years. While attribute-based access control provides key advantages to earlier forms of access control, such as ACLs and role-based access control, and having a well-maintained policy declaration language and authorisation framework (XACML) for practical solutions, other forms of access control have been proposed which may also be suitable for enforcing our unified model. For example, capability-based access control has been shown to perform well in highly scalable and distributed environments, such as IoT. Similarly, like attribute-based access control, capability-based mechanisms can also be enforced in a fine-grained manner [4,13], where tokens can be given to subjects on-the-fly containing the appropriate security label, and also be verifiable and unlinkable to preserve privacy [30]. Ultimately, it would be interesting to observe the difference in enforcement when using other approaches, such as capability-based access control, and the impact on authorisation times and efficiency.

7   Conclusion

We have highlighted the shift towards a digital calibration paradigm presents us with a novel access control challenge when we consider the calibration of rapidly adopted safety-critical IoT systems. Upon discussion of the current state-of-the-art in calibration traceability, we observe the information flow through a systems calibration hierarchy and present an access control model which uniquely unifies the BLP, BIBA and Chinese Wall models. Furthermore, we have developed an authorisation framework to evaluate the performance of our model for safety-critical IoT systems, and have shown that authorisation times can suitably enforce restrictions that enable efficient, safe calibration traceability.

Acknowledgements. The authors are grateful for the support by Engineering and Physical Sciences Research Council (11288S170484-102), UKIERI-2018-19-005, and the support of the National Measurement System of the UK Department of Business, Energy & Industrial Strategy, which funded this work as part of NPL's Data Science program.

References

1. Abomhara, M., Køien, G.M.: Security and privacy in the internet of things: current status and open issues. In: 2014 International Conference on Privacy and Security in Mobile Systems (PRISMS), pp. 1–8. IEEE (2014)
2. Alemzadeh, H., Chen, D., Li, X., Kesavadas, T., Kalbarczyk, Z.T., Iyer, R.K.: Targeted attacks on teleoperated surgical robots: dynamic model-based detection and mitigation. In: 2016 46th Annual IEEE/IFIP International Conference on Dependable Systems and Networks (DSN), pp. 395–406. IEEE (2016)
3. Ali, B., Awad, A.I.: Cyber and physical security vulnerability assessment for IoT-based smart homes. Sensors 18(3), 817 (2018)
4. Anggorojati, B., Mahalle, P.N., Prasad, N.R., Prasad, R.: Capability-based access control delegation model on the federated IoT network. In: 2012 15th International Symposium on Wireless Personal Multimedia Communications (WPMC), pp. 604–608. IEEE (2012)
5. Bargar, W.L., Bauer, A., Börner, M.: Primary and revision total hip replacement using the ROBODOC (R) system. Clin. Orthop. Relat. Res. **1976–2007**(354), 82–91 (1998)
6. Brewer, D.F., Nash, M.J.: The Chinese wall security policy. In: null, p. 206. IEEE (1989)
7. de Castro, C.N., Lourenço, M., Sampaio, M.: Calibration of a DSC: its importance for the traceability and uncertainty of thermal measurements. Thermochim. Acta **347**(1–2), 85–91 (2000)
8. Chen, C.Y., Hasan, M., Mohan, S.: Securing real-time internet-of-things. Sensors **18**(12), 4356 (2018)
9. Chowdhary, S., Som, S., Tuli, V., Khatri, S.K.: Security solutions for physical layer of IoT. In: 2017 International Conference on Infocom Technologies and Unmanned Systems (Trends and Future Directions) (ICTUS), pp. 579–583. IEEE (2017)
10. Chu, M., et al.: Respiration rate and volume measurements using wearable strain sensors. NPJ Digit. Med. **2**(1), 1–9 (2019)
11. Dabbagh, M., Rayes, A.: Internet of things security and privacy. Internet of Things From Hype to Reality, pp. 211–238. Springer, Cham (2019). https://doi.org/10.1007/978-3-319-99516-8_8
12. Frank, K., Willemoes-Wissing, I.C.: Combining logical and physical access control for smart environments. Master's thesis, Technical University of Denmark, DTU, DK-2800 Kgs. Lyngby, Denmark (2004)
13. Gusmeroli, S., Piccione, S., Rotondi, D.: A capability-based security approach to manage access control in the internet of things. Math. Comput. Modell. **58**(5–6), 1189–1205 (2013)
14. Hasan, M., Mohan, S.: Protecting actuators in safety-critical IoT systems from control spoofing attacks. In: Proceedings of the 2nd International ACM Workshop on Security and Privacy for the Internet-of-Things, pp. 8–14 (2019)
15. He, J.B., Qing, S.H., Wang, C.: Analysis of two improved BLP models. Ruan Jian Xue Bao (J. Softw.) **18**(6), 1501–1509 (2007)
16. Hu, V.C., Kuhn, D.R., Ferraiolo, D.F., Voas, J.: Attribute-based access control. Computer **48**(2), 85–88 (2015)
17. Hwang, Y.H.: IoT security & privacy: threats and challenges. In: Proceedings of the 1st ACM Workshop on IoT Privacy, Trust, and Security, p. 1 (2015)
18. Liebmann, F.: Infrared thermometer calibration. Cal. Lab. Int. J. Metrol. 20–22 (2011)

19. Liu, G., Wang, C., Zhang, R., Wang, Q., Song, H., Ji, S.: BTG-BIBA: a flexibility-enhanced BIBA model using BTG strategies for operating system. Int. J. Comput. Inf. Eng. 11(6), 765–771 (2017)
20. Morris, A.S., Langari, R.: Measurement and Instrumentation: Theory and Application. Academic Press, Cambridge (2012)
21. OASIS: extensible access control markup language (XACML) version 3.0. https://docs.oasis-open.org/xacml/3.0/xacml-3.0-core-spec-os-en.html
22. Quarta, D., Pogliani, M., Polino, M., Maggi, F., Zanchettin, A.M., Zanero, S.: An experimental security analysis of an industrial robot controller. In: 2017 IEEE Symposium on Security and Privacy (SP), pp. 268–286. IEEE (2017)
23. Salmi, T., Ahola, J.M., Heikkilä, T., Kilpeläinen, P., Malm, T.: Human-robot collaboration and sensor-based robots in industrial applications and construction. In: Bier, H. (ed.) Robotic Building. SSAE, pp. 25–52. Springer, Cham (2018). https://doi.org/10.1007/978-3-319-70866-9_2
24. Sandhu, R.S.: Lattice-based access control models. Computer 11, 9–19 (1993)
25. Shi, W.: Research on and enforcement of methods of methods of secure operating systems development. Ph.D thesis, Institute of Software, The Chinese Academy of Sciences, Beijing (2001)
26. Vim, I.: International vocabulary of basic and general terms in metrology (VIM). Int. Org. 2004, 09–14 (2004)
27. Yağdereli, E., Gemci, C., Aktaş, A.Z.: A study on cyber-security of autonomous and unmanned vehicles. J. Defense Model. Simul. 12(4), 369–381 (2015)
28. Yang, P., Wang, Q., Mi, X., Li, J.: An improved BLP model with more flexibility. In: 2016 13th International Conference on Embedded Software and Systems (ICESS), pp. 192–197. IEEE (2016)
29. Zhang, J., Yun, L.J., Zhou, Z.: Research of BLP and BIBA dynamic union model based on check domain. In: 2008 International Conference on Machine Learning and Cybernetics, vol. 7, pp. 3679–3683. IEEE (2008)
30. Zhang, R., Zhang, Y., Ren, K.: Dp^{2}ac: Distributed privacy-preserving access control in sensor networks. In: IEEE INFOCOM 2009, pp. 1251–1259. IEEE (2009)

Learning Attribute-Based and Relationship-Based Access Control Policies with Unknown Values

Thang Bui and Scott D. Stoller[✉]

Department of Computer Science, Stony Brook University, Stony Brook, USA
stoller@cs.stonybrook.edu

Abstract. Attribute-Based Access Control (ABAC) and Relationship-based access control (ReBAC) provide a high level of expressiveness and flexibility that promote security and information sharing, by allowing policies to be expressed in terms of attributes of and chains of relationships between entities. Algorithms for learning ABAC and ReBAC policies from legacy access control information have the potential to significantly reduce the cost of migration to ABAC or ReBAC.

This paper presents the first algorithms for mining ABAC and ReBAC policies from access control lists (ACLs) and incomplete information about entities, where the values of some attributes of some entities are unknown. We show that the core of this problem can be viewed as learning a concise three-valued logic formula from a set of labeled feature vectors containing unknowns, and we give the first algorithm (to the best of our knowledge) for that problem.

1 Introduction

Relationship-based access control (ReBAC) extends the well-known attribute-based access control (ABAC) framework by allowing access control policies to be expressed in terms of chains of relationships between entities, as well as attributes of entities. This significantly increases the expressiveness and often allows supporting more natural policies. High-level access control policy models such as ABAC and ReBAC are becoming increasingly widely adopted, as security policies become more dynamic and more complex, and because they promise long-term cost savings through reduced management effort. ABAC is already supported by many enterprise software products. Forms of ReBAC are supported in popular online social network systems and are being studied and adapted for use in more general software systems as well.

The up-front cost of developing an ABAC or ReBAC policy can be a significant barrier to adoption. *Policy mining* (a.k.a. policy learning) algorithms have the potential to greatly reduce this cost, by automatically producing a draft

This material is based on work supported in part by NSF grant CCF-1954837 and ONR grant N00014-20-1-2751.

© Springer Nature Switzerland AG 2020
S. Kanhere et al. (Eds.): ICISS 2020, LNCS 12553, pp. 23–44, 2020.
https://doi.org/10.1007/978-3-030-65610-2_2

high-level policy from existing lower-level data, such as access control lists or access logs. There is a substantial amount of research on role mining and a small but growing literature on ABAC policy mining, surveyed in [10], and ReBAC policy mining [2–6,15,16].

The basic ABAC (or ReBAC) policy mining problem is: Given information about the attributes of entities in the system, and the set of currently granted permissions; Find an ABAC (or ReBAC) policy that grants the same permissions using concise, high-level ReBAC rules. Several papers consider a variant of this problem where the information about permissions is incomplete [5,9,16,18,21]. However, all existing works on ABAC and ReBAC policy mining assume that the attribute (and relationship) information is complete, i.e., all attributes of all entities have known values. Unfortunately, in most real-world data, some attribute values are unknown (a.k.a. missing). Bui et al. [3–6] allow an attribute to have the special value "bottom", which is analogous to None in Python. It is different from unknown. For example, for a field Student.advisor with type Faculty, bottom (or None) means the student lacks an advisor, while unknown means we don't know whether the student has an advisor or, if they have one, who it is. Xu and Stoller [22] consider ABAC mining from noisy attribute data, where some of the given attribute values are incorrect; this is also different, because the input does not specify which ones are incorrect.

This paper proposes the first algorithms for mining ABAC or ReBAC policies when some attribute values are unknown. We present our algorithm in the context of ReBAC mining because ReBAC is more general than ABAC. Our algorithm can easily be restricted to mine ABAC policies instead, simply by limiting the length of path expressions that it considers.

Our main algorithm, called DTRMU$^-$ (Decision-Tree ReBAC Miner with Unknown values and negation), produces policies in ORAL2$^-$, an object-oriented ReBAC language introduced by Bui and Stoller [2]. We chose ORAL2$^-$ because it is more expressive than other policy languages that have been used in work on ReBAC mining. In ORAL2$^-$, relationships are expressed using object attributes (fields) that refer to other objects, and chains of relationships between objects are described by *path expressions*, which are sequences of attribute dereferences. A policy is a set of rules. A rule is essentially a conjunction of conditions on the *subject* (an object representing the issuer of the access request), conditions on the *resource* (an object representing the resource to be accessed), and constraints relating the subject and resource; the subject may perform a specified action on the resource if the conditions and constraints are satisfied. An example of a condition is subject.employer = LargeBank; an example of a constraint is subject.department ∈ resource.project.departments. ORAL2$^-$ also supports negation, so conditions and constraints can be negated, e.g., subject.employer ≠ LargeBank. We also give an algorithm, called DTRMU, that mines policies in ORAL2, which is the same as ORAL2$^-$ except without negation. Deciding whether to include negation in the policy language involves a trade-off between safety and conciseness, as discussed in [2]; different organizations might make different decisions, and we support both.

A policy can be viewed, roughly speaking, as a logical formula in disjunctive normal form (DNF), namely, the disjunction of the conjunctions (of conditions and constraints) in the rules. Bui and Stoller [2] exploited this view to reduce the core of the ReBAC policy mining problem to decision-tree learning; note that a decision tree compactly represents a logical formula in DNF, where each conjunction contains the conditions labeling the nodes on a path from the root to a leaf labeled "true" (corresponding to "permit").

Our algorithms are built on the insight that the core of the ReBAC policy mining problem in the presence of unknown attribute values can be reduced to the general problem of *learning a formula in Kleene's three-valued logic* [17,20], rather than traditional Boolean logic. Three-valued logic allows three truth values: true (T), false (F), and unknown (U). With three-valued logic, we can assign the truth value U to conditions and constraints involving unknown attribute values. Could the need for three-valued logic be avoided by regarding them as false instead? No, because if we stick with Boolean logic, and declare that (say) the condition subject.employer = LargeBank is false when the employer is unknown, then we are forced to conclude that its negation, ¬(subject.employer = LargeBank), is true when the employer is unknown, and this is clearly unsafe. Note that SQL uses three-valued logic to deal with null (i.e., missing) values for similar reasons.

Surprisingly, we could not find an existing algorithm for learning a concise three-valued logic formula from a set of labeled feature vectors containing unknowns. Therefore, we developed an algorithm to solve this general problem, based on learning multi-way decision trees, and then adapted Bui and Stoller's Decision-Tree ReBAC Mining algorithms (DTRM and DTRM⁻) to use that algorithm. We adopted their decision-tree based approach, because their algorithms are significantly faster, achieve comparable policy quality, and can mine policies in a richer language than other ReBAC mining algorithms such as FS-SEA* [3] and Iyer et al.'s algorithm [15], as demonstrated by their experiments [2].

We performed two series of experiments on several ReBAC policies. The first series of experiments compares our algorithms with Bui and Stoller's DTRM and DTRM⁻ algorithms, and shows that, *on policies where all attribute values are known, our algorithms are equally effective at discovering the desired ReBAC rules, produce policies with the same quality, and have comparable running time.* The second series of experiments, on policies containing a varying percentage of unknown values, shows that *our algorithms are effective at discovering the desired ReBAC rules, even when a significant percentage of attribute values are unknown.*

In summary, the main contributions of this paper are the first ABAC and ReBAC policy mining algorithms that can handle unknown attribute values, and, to the best of our knowledge, the first algorithm for learning a concise three-valued logic formula from a set of labeled feature vectors containing unknowns. Directions for future work include extending our algorithms to deal with incomplete information about permissions and extending them to "fill in" missing attribute values, guided by the permissions. Another is developing incremental algorithms to efficiently handle policy changes. Note that, as usual in ABAC and ReBAC policy mining, changes to attribute data (known values changing, or unknown values becoming known) do not require learning a new policy, except in the infrequent case that the current policy does not grant the desired permissions.

2   Learning Three-Valued Logic Formulas

2.1   Problem Definition

We consider the problem of learning a formula in Kleene's three-valued logic from a set of labeled feature vectors. The feature values and the labels are truth values in three-valued logic, namely, true (T), false (F), and unknown (U). In this setting, the features would usually be called "propositions", and the feature vectors would usually be called "interpretations", but we prefer to use more general terminology. The conjunction, disjunction, and negation operators are extended to handle unknown, in a natural way [17,20]. For example, $T \vee U$ evaluates to T, while $T \wedge U$ evaluates to U.

We require that the set of labeled feature vectors is monotonic, in the sense defined below, otherwise there would be no three-valued logic formula that represents it. For a feature vector v and feature f, let $v(f)$ denote the value of feature f in v. For a formula ϕ, let $\phi(v)$ denote the truth value of ϕ for v, i.e., the result of evaluating ϕ using the truth values in v.

For truth values t_1 and t_2, $t_1 \leq t_2$ iff $t_1 = t_2$ or $t_1 = U$. This is sometimes called the *information ordering*; it captures the idea that U provides less information than T and F. For feature vectors v_1 and v_2, $v_1 \leq v_2$ iff $v_1(f) \leq v_2(f)$ for every feature f. A basic fact of three-valued logic is that every formula, regarded as a function from feature vectors to truth values, is monotonic with respect to the information ordering, i.e., for all feature vectors v_1 and v_2, if $v_1 \leq v_2$ then $\phi(v_1) \leq \phi(v_2)$.

A set S of labeled feature vectors is *monotonic* iff, for all (v_1, ℓ_1) and (v_2, ℓ_2) in S, if $v_1 \leq v_2$ then $\ell_1 \leq \ell_2$. This ensures S can be represented by a formula.

The *three-valued logic formula learning problem* is: given a monotonic set S of labeled feature vectors, where the feature values and labels are truth values in three-valued logic, find a three-valued logic formula ϕ in disjunctive normal form (DNF) that exactly characterizes the feature vectors labeled T, i.e., for all (v, ℓ) in S, $\phi(v) = T$ iff $\ell = T$.

A stricter variant of this problem requires that ϕ preserve all three truth values, i.e., for all (v, ℓ) in S, $\phi(v) = \ell$. We adopt the looser requirement above, because when a formula ultimately evaluates to unknown, this outcome is conservatively treated the same as false in many application domains including security policies and SQL queries, and adopting the looser requirement allows smaller and simpler formulas. Note that distinguishing U and F is still critical during evaluation of formulas and their subformulas, for the reasons discussed in Sect. 1. The stricter variant of the problem would be relevant in a security policy framework, such as XACML, that allows policies to return indeterminate results; this is relevant mainly when composing policies, since an indeterminate result typically still results in a denial at the top level.

2.2   Learning a Multi-way Decision Tree

Since we are dealing with three truth values, we need multi-way decision trees, instead of binary trees. Each internal node is labeled with a feature. Each outgoing edge of an internal node corresponds to a possible value of the feature. Each leaf node is labeled with a classification label, which in our setting are also truth values. A feature vector is classified by testing the feature in the root node, following the edge corresponding to the value of the feature to reach a subtree, and then repeating this procedure until a leaf node is reached. A sample decision tree is shown in Sect. 5.

Our algorithm uses C4.5 [7], a well-known decision tree learning algorithm, to build a multi-way decision tree that correctly classifies a given set S of labeled feature vectors. It builds a decision tree by recursively partitioning feature vectors in the dataset S, starting from a root node associated with the entire dataset. It chooses (as described below) a feature to test at the root node, creates a child node for each possible outcome of the test, partitions the set of feature vectors associated with the root node among the children, based on the outcome of the test, and recursively applies this procedure to each child. The recursion stops when all of the feature vectors associated with a node have the same classification label or when there is no feature vector associated with a node (the leaf node is labeled with False in this case). At each node n, the algorithm evaluates a scoring criteria for each of the remaining features (i.e., features that have not been used for splitting at an ancestor of n) and then chooses the top-ranked feature. C4.5 uses information gain as the scoring criteria.

2.3   Algorithm for Learning a Three-Valued Logic Formula

The algorithm is presented as pseudocode in Fig. 1, with explanations inlined in comments. It iterates to build a formula D in DNF satisfying the requirements. For convenience, we represent D as a set of conjunctions; the desired formula is the disjunction of the conjunctions in D. For a path p through a decision tree from the root to a leaf, let conj(p) be a conjunction of conditions on the features associated with internal nodes on that path; specifically, if the path passes through a node labeled with feature f and follows the out-edge labeled T, F or U, then f, $\neg f$, or $f = U$, respectively, is included as a conjunct. Although the algorithm uses conditions of the form $f = U$ in intermediate conjunctions, they need to be eliminated, because $f = U$ is not a formula in three-valued logic; furthermore, three-valued logic does not contain any formula equivalent to $f = U$, because this condition is not monotonic (in other words, it does not satisfy the monotonicity property of formulas stated above). A formula ϕ is *valid* with respect to a set S of labeled feature vectors, denoted valid(ϕ, S), if it does not mis-evaluate any feature vectors as true, i.e., for every feature vector v in S labeled F or U, $\phi(v)$ is F or U. A formula ϕ *covers* S if $\phi(v)$ is T for every feature vector in S labeled T. An example of how the algorithm works appears in Sect. 5.

3   Policy Language with Unknown Attribute Values

We adopt Bui et al.'s ORAL2⁻ [2] ReBAC policy language and modify it to handle unknown attribute values. It contains common ABAC constructs, similar to those in [22], plus path expressions. ORAL2⁻ can easily be restricted to express ABAC policies by limiting the maximum length of path expressions to 1. We give a brief overview of the language (for details, see [2]) and focus on describing the changes to handle unknown values. The largest changes are to the definitions of path dereferencing (see the definition of nav) and the definitions of truth values of conditions and constraints.

A *ReBAC policy* is a tuple $\pi = \langle CM, OM, Act, Rules \rangle$, where CM is a class model, OM is an object model, Act is a set of actions, and $Rules$ is a set of rules.

A *class model* is a set of class declarations. Each field has a *type*, which is a class name or "Boolean", and a *multiplicity*, which specifies how many values may be stored in the field and is "one" (also denoted "1"), "optional" (also denoted "?"), or "many" (also denoted "*", meaning any number). Boolean fields always have multiplicity 1. Every class implicitly contains a field "id" with type String and multiplicity 1.

An *object model* is a set of objects whose types are consistent with the class model and with unique values in the id fields. Let type(o) denote the type of object o. The value of a field with multiplicity "many" is a set of values. The value of a field with multiplicity "one" or "optional" is a single value. The value of a field with multiplicity "optional" is a value of the specified type or **None** (called "bottom" in [2]). The value of any field can also be the special value **unknown**, indicating that the actual value is unknown (missing). The difference between **None** and **unknown** is explained in Sect. 1. **unknown** cannot appear in a set of values in the object model, but it may appear in sets of values constructed by our algorithm. Note that we distinguish **unknown** (a placeholder used in object models) from U (a truth value in three-valued logic).

A *path* is a sequence of field names, written with "." as a separator. A *condition* is a set, interpreted as a conjunction, of atomic conditions or their negations. An *atomic condition* is a tuple $\langle p, op, val \rangle$, where p is a non-empty path, op is an operator, either "in" or "contains", and val is a constant value, either an atomic value (if op is "contains") or a set of atomic values (if op is "in"). For example, an object o satisfies $\langle$dept.id, in, {CompSci}$\rangle$ if the value obtained starting from o and following (dereferencing) the dept field and then the id field equals CompSci. In examples, conditions are usually written using mathematical notation as syntactic sugar, with "$\in$" for "in" and "$\ni$" for "contains". For example, $\langle$dept.id, in, {CompSci}$\rangle$ is more nicely written as dept $\in$ {CompSci}. Note that the path is simplified by omitting the "id" field since all non-Boolean paths end with "id" field. Also, "=" is used as syntactic sugar for "in" when the constant is a singleton set; thus, the previous example may be written as dept = CompSci.

S = the given set of labeled feature vectors
$D = \emptyset$ // the desired formula in DNF, represented as a set of conjunctions
$B = \emptyset$ // set of black-listed features
$iter = 0$ // number of iterations of tree learning
while D does not cover S and $iter < max\_iter$
  // add disjuncts until D covers S or max_iter is reached
  $S' = S \setminus \{(v, T) \mid D(v) = T\}$ // remove feature vectors covered by D
  Use C4.5 to learn a multi-way decision tree dt for S', without using features in B
  D' = set containing conj(p) for each path p through dt from the root to a leaf labeled T
  // eliminate conjuncts of the form $f = U$
  for each conjunction c in D' that contains a condition of the form $f = U$
    $c' = c$; remove c from D'
    for each condition f_u of the form $f = U$ in c'
      $c'' =$ formula obtained from c' by removing f_u
      if valid(c'', S) **then** $c' = c''$ // successfully removed f_u
      else
        // f_u cannot simply be removed; try to replace it with another condition
        F_r = set containing features not used in c, and the negations of those features
        for each f_1 in F_r
          $c'' =$ formula obtained from c' by replacing f_u with f_1
          if valid(c'', S) $\wedge$ ($D' \cup \{c''\}$ covers S')
            $c' = c''$ // successfully replaced f_u with f_1
            break
    if c' does not contain any conditions of the form $f = U$ **then** add c' to D'
    else
      // some $f = U$ conditions in c couldn't be eliminated or replaced.
      // discard c, and blacklist features used in its $f = U$ conditions.
      for each condition of the form $f = U$ in c
        add f to B
  $D = D \cup D'$
  $iter = iter + 1$
if D does not cover S
  // max iterations was exceeded. cover the remaining feature vectors one at a time.
  $uncov = \{v \mid (v, T) \in S \wedge D(v) \neq T\}$ // uncovered feature vectors
  for each feature vector v **in** $uncov$
    c = conjunction containing the conjunct f for each feature f s.t. $v(f) = T$
    and the conjunct $\neg f$ for each feature f s.t. $v(f) = F$
    // note that $c(v) = T$, and monotonicity of S ensures valid(c, S) holds
    add c to D
// remove redundant disjuncts from D
for each conjunction c in D
  if the set of conjuncts in c is a superset of the set of conjuncts in another element of D
  remove c from D

Fig. 1. Algorithm for learning a three-valued logic formula.

A *constraint* is a set, interpreted as a conjunction, of atomic constraints or their negations. Informally, an atomic constraint expresses a relationship between the requesting subject and the requested resource, by relating the values of paths starting from each of them. An *atomic constraint* is a tuple $\langle p_1, op, p_2 \rangle$, where p_1 and p_2 are paths (possibly the empty sequence), and op is one of the following five operators: equal, in, contains, supseteq, subseteq. Implicitly, the first path is relative to the requesting subject, and the second path is relative to the requested resource. The empty path represents the subject or resource itself. For example, a subject s and resource r satisfy $\langle \text{specialties}, \text{contains}, \text{topic} \rangle$ if the set s.specialties contains the value r.topic. In examples, constraints are written using mathematical notation as syntactic sugar, with "=" for "equal", "⊇" for "supseteq", and "⊆" for "subseteq".

A *rule* is a tuple $\langle subjectType, subjectCondition, resourceType, resourceCondition, constraint, actions \rangle$, where *subjectType* and *resourceType* are class names, *subjectCondition* and *resourceCondition* are conditions, *constraint* is a constraint, *actions* is a set of actions. A rule must satisfy several well-formedness requirements [6]. For a rule $\rho = \langle st, sc, rt, rc, c, A \rangle$, let $\text{sCond}(\rho) = sc$, $\text{rCond}(\rho) = rc$, $\text{con}(\rho) = c$, and $\text{acts}(\rho) = A$.

In the example rules, we prefix paths in conditions and constraints that start from the subject and resource with "subject" and "resource", respectively, to improve readability. For example, the e-document case study [6,11] involves a bank whose policy contains the rule: A project member can read all sent documents regarding the project. Using syntactic sugar, this is written as ⟨ Employee, subject.employer = LargeBank, Document, true, subject.workOn.relatedDoc ∋ resource, {read}⟩, where Employee.workOn is the set of projects the employee is working on, and Project.relatedDoc is the set of sent documents related to the project.

The *type of a path* p is the type of the last field in the path. The *multiplicity of a path* p is "one" if all fields on the path have multiplicity one, is many if any field on the path has multiplicity many, and is optional otherwise. Given a class model, object model, object o, and path p, let $\text{nav}(o, p)$ be the result of navigating (a.k.a. following or dereferencing) path p starting from object o. If the navigation encounters **unknown**, the result is **unknown** if p has multiplicity one or optional, and is a set of values containing **unknown** (and possibly other values) if p has multiplicity many. Otherwise, the result might be **None**, an atomic value, or (if p has multiplicity many) a set of values. Aside from the extension to handle unknown, this is like the semantics of path navigation in UML's Object Constraint Language[1].

The truth value of an atomic condition $ac = \langle p, op, val \rangle$ for an object o, denoted $\text{tval}(o, ac)$, is defined as follows. If p has multiplicity one (or optional) and $\text{nav}(o, p)$ is **unknown**, then $\text{tval}(o, ac) = U$. If p has multiplicity one (or optional) and $\text{nav}(o, p)$ is known, then $\text{tval}(o, ac) = T$ if $\text{nav}(o, p) \in val$, and $\text{tval}(o, ac) = F$ otherwise. If p has multiplicity many, then $\text{tval}(o, ac) = T$ if $\text{nav}(o, p) \ni val$; otherwise, $\text{tval}(o, ac) = F$ if $\text{nav}(o, p)$ does not contain **unknown**,

---

[1] http://www.omg.org/spec/OCL/.

and $\mathrm{tval}(o, ac) = U$ if it does. Note that the operator op is not used explicitly in this definition, because op is uniquely determined by the multiplicity of p. Next, we define tval for negated atomic conditions. If $\mathrm{tval}(o, ac) = T$ and $\mathrm{nav}(o, p)$ is a set containing **unknown**, then $\mathrm{tval}(o, \neg ac) = U$; otherwise, $\mathrm{tval}(o, \neg ac) = \neg \mathrm{tval}(o, ac)$, where $\neg$ denotes negation in three-valued logic [20].

The truth value of an atomic constraint $ac = \langle p_1, op, p_2 \rangle$ for a pair of objects o_1, o_2, denoted $\mathrm{tval}(o_1, o_2, ac)$, is defined as follows. If no **unknown** value is encountered during navigation, then $\mathrm{tval}(o_1, o_2, ac) = T$ if $(op = \mathrm{equal} \wedge \mathrm{nav}(o_1, p_1) = \mathrm{nav}(o_2, p_2)) \vee (op = \mathrm{in} \wedge \mathrm{nav}(o_1, p_1) \in \mathrm{nav}(o_2, p_2)) \vee (op = \mathrm{contains} \wedge \mathrm{nav}(o_1, p_1) \ni \mathrm{nav}(o_2, p_2)) \vee (op = \mathrm{supseteq} \wedge \mathrm{nav}(o_1, p_1) \supseteq \mathrm{nav}(o_2, p_2)) \vee (op = \mathrm{subseteq} \wedge \mathrm{nav}(o_1, p_1) \subseteq \mathrm{nav}(o_2, p_2))$, otherwise $\mathrm{tval}(o_1, o_2, ac) = F$. If $\mathrm{nav}(o_1, p_1)$ and $\mathrm{nav}(o_2, p_2)$ both equal **unknown**, then $\mathrm{tval}(o_1, o_2, ac) = U$. If either of them is **unknown** and $op \in \{\mathrm{equal}, \mathrm{subseteq}, \mathrm{supseteq}\}$, then $\mathrm{tval}(o_1, o_2, ac) = U$. If either of them is **unknown** and $op \in \{\mathrm{in}, \mathrm{contains}\}$ (hence the other one is a set possibly containing **unknown**), the truth value is defined similarly as in the corresponding case for atomic conditions. The truth value of negated atomic constraints is defined similarly as for negated atomic conditions.

We extend tval from atomic conditions to conditions using conjunction (in three-valued logic): $\mathrm{tval}(o, \{ac_1, \ldots, ac_n\}) = \mathrm{tval}(o, ac_1) \wedge \cdots \wedge \mathrm{tval}(o, ac_n)$. We extend tval from atomic constraints to constraints in the same way. An object or pair of objects *satisfies* a condition or constraint if c has truth value T for it.

An *SRA-tuple* is a tuple $\langle s, r, a \rangle$, where the subject s and resource r are objects, and a is an action, representing (depending on the context) authorization for s to perform a on r or a request to perform that access. An SRA-tuple $\langle s, r, a \rangle$ *satisfies* a rule $\rho = \langle st, sc, rt, rc, c, A \rangle$ if $\mathrm{type}(s) = st \wedge \mathrm{tval}(s, sc) = T \wedge \mathrm{type}(r) = rt \wedge \mathrm{tval}(r, rc) = T \wedge \mathrm{tval}(\langle s, r \rangle, c) = T \wedge a \in A$. The *meaning* of a rule ρ, denoted $[\![\rho]\!]$, is the set of SRA-tuples that satisfy it. The *meaning* of a ReBAC policy π, denoted $[\![\pi]\!]$, is the union of the meanings of its rules.

4   The Problem: ReBAC Policy Mining with Unknowns

We adopt Bui et al.'s definition of the ReBAC policy mining problem and extend it to include unknown attribute values. The ABAC policy mining problem is the same except it requires the mined policy to contain paths of length at most 1.

An *access control list (ACL) policy* is a tuple $\langle CM, OM, Act, AU \rangle$, where CM is a class model, OM is an object model that might contains unknown attribute values, Act is a set of actions, and $AU \subseteq OM \times OM \times Act$ is a set of SRA tuples representing authorizations. Conceptually, AU is the union of ACLs. An ReBAC policy π is *consistent* with an ACL policy $\langle CM, OM, Act, AU \rangle$ if they have the same class model, object model, actions, and $[\![\pi]\!] = AU$.

Among the ReBAC policies consistent with a given ACL policy π_0, the most desirable ones are those that satisfy the following two criteria. (1) The "id" field should be used only when necessary, i.e., only when every ReBAC policy consistent with π_0 uses it, because uses of it make policies identity-based and less general. (2) The policy should have the best quality as measured by a given policy quality metric Q_{pol}, expressed as a function from ReBAC policies to natural numbers, with small numbers indicating high quality.

The *ReBAC policy mining problem with unknown attribute values* is: given an ACL policy $\pi_0 = \langle CM, OM, Act, AU \rangle$, where the object model OM might contain unknown attribute values, and a policy quality metric Q_{pol}, find a set *Rules* of rules such that the ReBAC policy $\pi = \langle CM, OM, Act, Rules \rangle$ is consistent with π_0, uses the "id" field only when necessary, and has the best quality, according to Q_{pol}, among such policies.

The policy quality metric that our algorithm aims to optimize is *weighted structural complexity* (WSC), a generalization of policy size [6]. WSC is a weighted sum of the numbers of primitive elements of various kinds that appear in a rule or policy. It is defined bottom-up. The WSC of an atomic condition $\langle p, op, val \rangle$ is $|p| + |val|$, where $|p|$ is the length of path p, and $|val|$ is 1 if val is an atomic value and is the cardinality of val if val is a set. The WSC of an atomic constraint $\langle p_1, op, p_2 \rangle$ is $|p_1| + |p_2|$. The WSC of a negated atomic condition or constraint c is $1 + \text{WSC}(c)$. The WSC of a rule ρ, denoted $\text{WSC}(\rho)$, is the sum of the WSCs of the atomic conditions and atomic constraints in it, plus the cardinality of the action set (more generally, it is a weighted sum of those numbers, but we take all of the weights to be 1). The WSC of a ReBAC policy π, denoted $\text{WSC}(\pi)$, is the sum of the WSC of its rules.

5   ReBAC Policy Mining Algorithm

This section presents our ReBAC policy mining algorithms, DTRMU⁻ and DTRMU. They have two main phases. The first phase learns a decision tree that classifies authorization requests as permitted or denied, and then constructs a set of candidate rules from the decision tree. The second phase improves the policy by merging and simplifying the candidate rules and optionally removing negative atomic conditions/constraints from them.

5.1   Phase 1: Learn Decision Tree and Extract Rules

Problem Decomposition. We decompose the problem based on the subject type, resource type, and action. Specifically, for each type C_s, type C_r, and action a such that AU contains some SRA tuple with a subject of type C_s, a resource of type C_r, and action a, we learn a separate DNF formula $\phi_{C_s, C_r, a}$ to classify SRA tuples with subject type C_s, resource type C_r, and action a. The decomposition by type is justified by the fact that all SRA tuples authorized by a rule contain subjects with the same subject type and resources with the same resource type. Regarding the decomposition by action, the first phase of our algorithm generates rules that each contain a single action, but the second phase merges similar rules and can produce rules that authorize multiple actions.

Construct Labeled Feature Vectors. To apply our formula-learning algorithm, we first need to extract sets of features and feature vectors from an input ACL policy. We use the same approach as described in [2].

A *feature* is an atomic condition (on the subject or resource) or atomic constraint satisfying user-specified limits on lengths of paths in conditions and constraints. We define a mapping from feature vectors to three-valued logic labels: given an SRA tuple $\langle s, r, a \rangle$, we create a feature vector (i.e., a vector of the three-valued logic truth values of features evaluated for subject s and resource r) and map it to T if the SRA tuple is permitted (i.e., is in AU) and to F otherwise. We do not label any feature vector with U, since the set of authorizations AU in the input ACL policy is assumed to be complete, according to the problem definition in Sect. 4.

Table 1. Extracted features and feature vectors for the sample policy. FV_id is a unique ID assigned to the feature vector. sub_id and res_id are the subject ID and resource ID, respectively. Features that are conditions on sub_id or res_id are not shown. The labels specify whether a student has permission to read a document (T = permit, F = deny).

FV_id	sub_id	res_id	Features				Label
			sub.dept = res.dept	sub.dept = CS	res.dept = CS	res.type = Handbook	
1	CS-student-1	CS-doc-1	U	T	U	T	T
2	CS-student-1	CS-doc-2	T	T	T	U	T
3	CS-student-1	CS-doc-3	U	T	U	U	F
4	EE-student-1	CS-doc-1	U	U	U	T	T
5	EE-student-1	CS-doc-2	U	U	T	U	F
6	EE-student-1	CS-doc-3	U	U	U	U	F

Table 1 shows a set of labeled feature vectors for our running example, which is a ReBAC policy containing two student objects, with IDs CS-student-1 and EE-student-1, and three document objects, with IDs CS-doc-1, CS-doc-2 and CS-doc-3. Each student object has a field "dept" specifying the student's department. Each document object has a field "dept" specifying which department it belongs to, and a field "type" specifying the document type. The field values are CS-student-1.dept = CS, EE-student-1.dept = unknown, CS-doc-1.dept = CS-doc-3.dept = unknown, CS-doc-2.dept = CS, CS-doc-1.type = Handbook, and CS-doc-2.type = CS-doc-3.type = unknown. The labels are consistent with the ReBAC policy containing these two rules: (1) A student can read a document if the document belongs to the same department as the student, and (2) every student can read handbook documents. Formally, the rules are (1) ⟨ Student, true, Document, true, subject.dept = resource.dept, {read}⟩, and (2) ⟨ Student, true, Document, resource.type = Handbook, true, {read}⟩. Note that this is also an ABAC policy, since all paths have length 1.

The feature vectors constructed to learn $\phi_{C_s,C_r,a}$ include only features appropriate for subject type C_s and resource type C_r, e.g., the path in the subject condition starts with a field in class C_s. The set of labeled feature vectors used to learn $\phi_{C_s,C_r,a}$ contains one feature vector generated from each possible combination of a subject of type C_s (in the given object model) and a resource of type C_r. We also use the optimizations described in [2, Section 5.1] to discard some "useless" features, namely, features that have the same value in all feature vectors, and sets of features equivalent to simpler sets of features. For the running example, Table 1 shows the feature vectors for $C_s = $ Student, $C_r = $ Document, $a = $ read.

Learn a Formula. After generating the labeled feature vectors, we apply the formula-learning algorithm in Sect. 2.3. We do not explicitly check the monotonicity of the set of labeled feature vectors. Instead, after constructing each formula, we directly check whether it is valid (it will always cover the given set of labeled feature vectors); this is necessary because, if the set of labeled feature vectors is not monotonic, disjuncts added by the loop over *uncov* might be invalid. This approach has two benefits: it is computationally cheaper because it requires iterating over feature vectors (or, equivalently, subject-resource-action tuples) individually, whereas monotonicity requires considering pairs of feature vectors; and it provides an end-to-end correctness check as well as an implicit monotonicity check.

To help the formula-learning algorithm produce formulas that lead to rules with lower WSC, we specialize the scoring metric used to choose a feature to test at each node. Specifically, we use information gain as the primary metric, but we extend the metric to use WSC (recall that WSC of atomic conditions and atomic constraints is defined in Sect. 4) as a tie-breaker for features that provide the same information gain.

Specialized treatment of conditions on the "id" attribute, e.g., subject.id = CS-student-1 is also beneficial. Recall from Sect. 4 that such conditions should be used only when needed. Also, we expect that they are rarely needed. We consider two approaches to handling them. In the first approach, we first run the formula-learning algorithm on feature vectors that do not contain entries for these conditions; this ensures those conditions are not used unnecessarily, and it can significantly reduce the running time, since there are many such conditions for large object models. That set of feature vectors is not necessarily monotonic, so the learned formula might not be valid; this will be detected by the validity check mentioned above. If it is not valid, we generate new feature vectors that include these conditions and run the formula-learning algorithm on them.

In the second approach, we run a modified version of the formula-learning algorithm on feature vectors that do not contain entries for these conditions. The modification is to the loop over *uncov*: for each feature vector v in *uncov*, it adds the conjunction subject.id = id_s $\wedge$ resource.id = id_r to D, where s and r are the subject and resource, respectively, for which v was generated, and id_s and id_r are their respective IDs. The disadvantage of this approach is that it can sometimes use conditions on *id* when they are not strictly needed; the advantage of this approach is that it can sometimes produce policies with smaller WSC, because the modified version of the loop over *uncov* produces conjunctions with few conjuncts, while the original version of the loop over *uncov* produces conjunctions with many conjuncts (though some conjuncts may be removed by simplifications in phase 2).

In practice, both approaches usually produce the same result, because, even when conditions on "'id" are omitted, the first top-level loop in the formula-learning algorithm usually succeeds in covering all feature vectors.

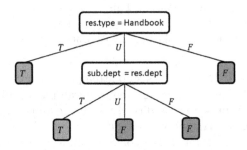

Fig. 2. Multi-way decision tree for the running example.

Figure 2 shows the learned multi-way decision tree for the set of labeled feature vectors in Table 1. Internal nodes and leaf nodes are represented by unfilled and filled boxes, respectively. The conjunctions $\text{conj}(p)$ generated from paths from the root to a leaf labeled T are (1) res.type = Handbook and (2) $\langle \text{res.type} = \text{Handbook} \rangle = U \wedge \text{sub.dept} = \text{res.dept}$. Note that, for convenience, a formula containing a single condition is considered to be a (degenerate) kind of conjunction.

The algorithm tries to eliminate the condition $\langle \text{res.type} = \text{Handbook} \rangle = U$ in conjunction (2). Removing that condition leaves the (one-element) conjunction sub.dept = res.dept, which is still valid WRT to the set of feature vectors in Table 1, so the algorithm replaces conjunction (2) with sub.dept = res.dept in D. The first top-level loop in the algorithm succeeds in covering all feature vectors in S. Thus, the learned formula $\phi_{\text{Student,Document,read}}$ is (res.type = Handbook) $\vee$ (sub.dept = res.dept).

Extract Rules. We convert the formula into an equivalent set of rules and add them to the candidate mined policy. For each conjunction c in the formula $\phi_{C_s,C_r,a}$, we create a rule with subject type C_s, resource type C_s, action a, and with c's conjuncts as atomic conditions and atomic constraints. For the running example, the formula $\phi_{\text{Student,Document,read}}$ has two (degenerate) conjunctions, and the algorithm successfully extracts the two desired rules given above in the description of Table 1.

5.2   Phase 2: Improve the Rules

Phase 2 has two main steps: eliminate negative features, and merge and simplify rules. We adopt these steps from DTRM. We give brief overviews of these steps in this paper, and refer the reader to [2] for additional details.

Eliminate Negative Features. This step is included only in DTRMU, in order to mine rules without negation. This step is omitted from DTRMU⁻. It eliminates each negative feature in a rule ρ by removing the negative feature (if the resulting rule is valid) or replacing it with one or more positive feature(s).

Merge and Simplify Rules. This step attempts to merge and simplify rules using the same techniques as [2] (e.g., removing atomic conditions and atomic constraints when this preserves validity of the rule, eliminating overlap between rules, and replacing constraints with conditions), extended with one additional simplification technique: If an atomic condition on a Boolean-valued path p has the form $p \neq F$ or $p \neq T$, it is replaced with $p = T$ or $p = F$, respectively.

Naively Applying DTRM. One might wonder whether DTRM⁻ can be used to mine policies, by assuming that features involving unknown attribute values evaluate to F (instead of U). Although there is no reason to believe that this will work, it is easy to try, so we did. For the running example, DTRM⁻ produces two rules:⟨Student, true, Document, res.type = Handbook, true, {read}⟩ and ⟨Student, true, Document, res.type $\neq$ Handbook, sub.dept = res.dept, {read}⟩. This policy is incorrect, because it does not cover feature vector 2 in Table 1, i.e., it prevents CS-student-1 from reading CS-doc-2.

6   Evaluation Methodology

We adopt Bui et al.'s methodology for evaluating policy mining algorithms [3]. It is depicted in Fig. 3. It takes a class model and a set of ReBAC rules as inputs. The methodology is to generate an object model based on the class model (independent of the ReBAC rules), compute the authorizations AU from the object model and the rules, run the policy mining algorithm with the class model, object model, and AU as inputs, and finally compare the mined policy rules with the simplified original (input) policy rules, obtained by applying the simplifications in Sect. 5.2 to the given rules. Comparison with the simplified original policy is a more robust measure of the algorithm's ability to discover high-level rules than comparison with the original policy, because the original policy is not always the simplest. If the mined rules are similar to the simplified original rules, the policy mining algorithm succeeded in discovering the desired ReBAC rules that are implicit in AU.

Policy_N	#obj	#field	#FV	#rule
EMR_15	353	877	4134	6
healthcare_5	736	1804	42121	8
healthcare_5⁻	736	1875	42121	8
project-mgmt_5	179	296	4080	10
project-mgmt_10⁻	376	814	23627	10
university_5	738	926	83761	10
e-document_75	284	1269	31378	39
eWorkforce_10	412	1124	14040	19

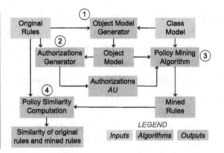

Fig. 3. Left: Policy sizes. For the given value of the object model size parameter N (after the underscore in the policy name), #obj is the average number of objects in the object model, and #field is the average number of fields in the object model, i.e., the sum over objects o of the number of fields in o. #FV is the number of feature vectors (i.e., labeled SRA tuples) that the algorithms generate to learn a formula. Averages are over 5 pseudorandom object models for each policy. "healthcare_5⁻" and "project-mgmt_10⁻" are the policies with negations that we generated. Right: Evaluation methodology; reproduced from [2].

6.1 Datasets

We use four sample policies developed by Bui et al. [6]. One is for electronic medical records (EMR), based on the EBAC policy in [1], translated to ReBAC; the other three are for healthcare, project management, and university records, based on ABAC policies in [22], generalized and made more realistic, taking advantage of ReBAC's expressiveness. These policies are non-trivial but relatively small.

We also use Bui et al.'s translation into ORAL2⁻ [2] of two large case studies developed by Decat, Bogaerts, Lagaisse, and Joosen based on the access control requirements for Software-as-a-Service (SaaS) applications offered by real companies [12,13]. One is for a SaaS multi-tenant e-document processing application; the other is for a SaaS workforce management application provided by a company that handles the workflow planning and supply management for product or service appointments (e.g., install or repair jobs).

More detailed descriptions of these policies are available in [2]. The ABAC or ReBAC versions of these policies, or variants of them, have been used as benchmarks in several papers on policy mining, including [2,5,14,15,19].

These sample policies and the case studies do not include any rules with negations. Therefore, we created modified versions of the healthcare and project management policies that include some rules with negation; the names of the modified version end with "⁻". For the healthcare policy, we add a new attribute "COIs" in the Patient class to specify the physicians or nurses who have a conflict of interest with the patient, and in the rules that give any permission on a patient's record to a physician or nurse, we add the constraint subject $\notin$ resource.patient.COIs. For the project management policy, we add a new attribute "status" in the Task class with possible values not_started, in_progress, and completed. In the rules that give permission to change the cost, schedule, or status of a task, we add the condition resource.status $\neq$ completed.

The object models are generated by policy-specific pseudorandom algorithms designed to produce realistic object models, by creating objects and selecting their attribute values using appropriate probability distributions. These algorithms are parameterized by a size parameter N; for most classes, the number of instances is selected from a normal distribution whose mean is linear in N. We use the same object model generators as Bui and Stoller [2], which are slightly modified versions of the object model generators described and used in [3,6], which are available online.[2] Note that, in these object models, all attribute values are known. The table in Fig. 3 shows several metrics of the size of the rules, class model, and object model in each policy.

6.2   Policy Similarity Metrics

We evaluate the quality of the generated policy primarily by its *syntactic similarity* and *policy semantic similarity* to the simplified original policy. These metrics are first defined in [5,22] and adapted in [2] to take negation into account. They are normalized to range from 0 (completely different) to 1 (identical). They are based on Jaccard similarity of sets, defined by $J(S_1, S_2) = |S_1 \cap S_2| / |S_1 \cup S_2|$. For convenience, we extend J to apply to single values: $J(v_1, v_2)$ is 1 if $v_1 = v_2$ and 0 otherwise.

Syntactic similarity of policies measures the syntactic similarity of rules in the policies, based on the fractions of types, conditions, constraints, and actions that rules have in common. The *syntactic similarity of rules* is defined bottom-up as follows. For an atomic condition ac, let sign(ac), path(ac), and val(ac) denote its sign (positive or negative), its path, and its value (or set of values), respectively. Syntactic similarity of atomic conditions ac_1 and ac_2, $\text{syn}_{ac}(ac_1, ac_2)$, is 0 if they contain different paths, otherwise it is the average of $J(\text{sign}(ac_1), \text{sign}(ac_2))$, $J(\text{path}(ac_1), \text{path}(ac_2))$, and $J(\text{val}(ac_1), \text{val}(ac_2))$); we do not explicitly compare the operators, because atomic conditions with the same path must have the same operator, since the operator is uniquely determined by the multiplicity of the path. For a set S of atomic conditions, let paths(S) = {path(ac) | $ac \in S$}. For sets S_1 and S_2 of atomic conditions,

$$\text{syn}(S_1, S_2) = |\text{paths}(S_1) \cup \text{paths}(S_2)|^{-1} \sum_{ac_1 \in S_1, ac_2 \in S_2} \text{syn}_{ac}(ac_1, ac_2)$$

The *syntactic similarity of rules* $\rho_1 = \langle st_1, sc_1, rt_1, rc_1, c_1, A_1 \rangle$ and $\rho_2 = \langle st_2, sc_2, rt_2, rc_2, c_2, A_2 \rangle$ is syn(ρ_1, ρ_2) = average($J(st_1, st_2)$, syn(sc_1, sc_2), $J(rt_1, rt_2)$, syn(rc_1, rc_2), $J(c_1, c_2)$, $J(A_1, A_2)$). The *syntactic similarity of policies* π_1 and π_2, denoted syn(π_1, π_2), is the average, over rules ρ in π_1, of the syntactic similarity between ρ and the most similar rule in π_2.

The *semantic similarity of polices* measures the fraction of authorizations that the policies have in common. Specifically, the *semantic similarity* of policies π_1 and π_2 is $J(\llbracket \pi_1 \rrbracket, \llbracket \pi_2 \rrbracket)$.

---

[2] https://www.cs.stonybrook.edu/~stoller/software/.

7   Evaluation Results

We performed two series of experiments. The first series of experiments compares our algorithms with Bui and Stoller's DTRM and DTRM$^-$ algorithms (which are state-of-the-art, as discussed in Sect. 1), and shows that, *on policies where all attribute values are known, our algorithms are equally effective at discovering the desired ReBAC rules, produce policies with the same quality, and have comparable running time.* The second series of experiments, on policies containing a varying percentage of unknown values, shows that *our algorithms are effective at discovering the desired ReBAC rules, even when a significant percentage of attribute values are unknown.*

We implemented our formula-learning algorithm in Python, on top of Esmer's implementation of the C4.5 decision-tree learning algorithm[3]. Bui and Stoller's implementation of DTRM$^-$ [2] uses the optimized version of the CART decision-tree learning algorithm provided by the scikit-learn library[4]; we could not use it, because it supports only binary trees. Since Esmer's implementation of C4.5 supports only information gain as the feature scoring metric, we chose it as the scoring metric in scikit-learn when running DTRM and DTRM$^-$, which originally used the default scoring metric, which is gini index. This change had a negligible effect on the algorithms' output (no effect for all policies except e-document_75, for which it improved the results slightly) and allows a fairer comparison of DTRM and DTRM$^-$ with DTRMU and DTRMU$^-$. We re-used Bui and Stoller's implementation of Phase 2, with the small extension in Sect. 5.1. When generating feature vectors, we use the same path length limits (*cf.* Sect. 5.1) as in [3,6] for all algorithms. We set the value of the *max_iter* parameter in the formula-learning algorithm to 5. We ran DTRM$^-$ and DTRMU$^-$ on the policies containing rules with negation (healthcare_5$^-$ and project-mgmt_10$^-$), and we ran DTRM and DTRMU on the other policies. All experiments were run on Windows 10 on an Intel i7-6770HQ CPU.

7.1   Comparison with DTRM and DTRM$^-$

We compared our algorithms with DTRM and DTRM$^-$ using the datasets described in Sect. 6.1. We ran experiments on five object models for each policy and averaged the results. The standard deviations (SD) are reasonable, indicating that averaging over five object models for each data point is sufficient to obtain meaningful results.

All of these algorithms always mine policies that grant the same authorizations as the input ACL policies and thus achieve perfect *semantic similarity* for all datasets. Our algorithms achieve almost exactly the same *syntactic similarity* as DTRM and DTRM$^-$ when comparing mined rules with simplified original rules, as explained in Sect. 6. DTRM and DTRMU both achieve the same results for average syntactic similarity: 1.0 (SD = 0) for healthcare_5, project-mgmt_5,

---

[3] https://github.com/barisesmer/C4.5.
[4] https://scikit-learn.org/stable/modules/tree.html.

and university_5; 0.99 (SD = 0.01) for EMR_15; 0.98 (SD = 0.01) for eWork-force_10; and 0.92 (SD = 0.02) for e-document_75. DTRMU⁻ and DTRM− both achieve 1.0 (SD = 0) average syntactic similarity for healthcare_5⁻ and project-mgmt_10⁻. For all of the datasets, our algorithms and theirs mine policies with the same average WSC.

The running times of DTRM and DTRM⁻ are somewhat faster than our algorithms. Averaged over all policies, DTRM is 1.53 (SD = 0.20) times faster than DTRMU, and DTRM⁻ is 1.72 (SD = 0.05) times faster than DTRMU⁻. The difference in the running time comes mostly from the decision-tree learning step. When there are no unknown values, our algorithms and DTRM and DTRM⁻ are essentially the same at the algorithm level, aside from our algorithms having a very small overhead to check for unknowns. Therefore, we attribute the difference in running time primarily to the use of different tree-learning libraries—Esmer's straightforward implementation of C4.5 used by our algorithms vs. the optimized version of CART in scikit-learn used by DTRM and DTRM⁻. Furthermore, C4.5 and CART are similar algorithms and should construct the same binary trees when applied to boolean feature vectors labeled with booleans (they handle continuous data differently), so the difference in running time is mainly due to implementation-level differences.

7.2   Experiments with Unknown Attribute Values

We generated datasets with unknown attribute values by changing the values of pseudorandomly chosen fields to **unknown** in the datasets used for the experiments in Sect. 7.1. We introduce a scaling factor s to vary how many **unknown** values are introduced. In each policy, for most fields f of each class C, we pseudorandomly choose a probability p in the range $[0.02s, 0.05s]$, and then, for each instance o of C, we change the value of f to **unknown** with probability p. This is done for all fields except a few manually classified as *required* or *important*. For a required field, we take $p = 0$, i.e., no instances are changed to unknown. For an important field (i.e., one whose value is more likely to be known), we take $p = 0.01s$. For example, the university policy has one required field, Transcript.student (the student whose transcript it is), and one important field, Faculty.department. For all policies, the number of required or important fields is less than 15% of the total number of fields in the class model.

We ran experiments with $s = 0$ (i.e., all attribute values are known, same datasets as in Sect. 7.1), 1, 2, and 3. Averaged over all policies, the percentages of field values in the object model that are changed to **unknown** are 3%, 6%, and 8% for $s = 1$, 2, and 3, respectively. Experimental results appear in Table 2 and are discussed below.

Policy Similarity and WSC. Our algorithms always mine policies that grant exactly the same authorizations as the input ACL policies and thus achieve perfect *semantic similarity* for all datasets.

For the sample policies (including the variants with negation), our algorithms achieve 0.99 or better average syntactic similarity for all four values of s. For

Table 2. Experimental results for our algorithms on datasets with different values of scaling factor s. "Syn. Sim" is the average syntactic similarity achieved on each policy. "Run time" is measured in seconds. For $s > 0$, we report the slowdown relative to $s = 0$, i.e., the ratio of the running time to the running time on the same policy with $s = 0$.

Policy	$s = 0$		$s = 1$		$s = 2$		$s = 3$	
	Syn. Sim	Run time	Syn. Sim	Slowdown	Syn. Sim	Slowdown	Syn. Sim	Slowdown
EMR_15	0.99	76.19	0.99	2.28	1.00	9.52	0.99	6.46
healthcare_5	1.00	129.50	1.00	1.24	1.00	1.25	0.99	1.23
project-mgmt_5	1.00	3.81	1.00	1.08	1.00	1.21	1.00	1.45
university_5	1.00	266.29	1.00	1.07	1.00	1.03	1.00	1.07
eWorkforce_10	0.98	96.40	0.96	11.88	0.93	8.41	0.94	9.13
e-document_75	0.92	420.27	0.93	8.03	0.93	15.77	0.91	9.41
healthcare_5⁻	1.00	171.95	1.00	1.38	0.99	1.38	0.99	1.34
project-mgmt_10⁻	1.00	38.04	1.00	1.39	0.99	1.71	0.99	1.74

the case studies, DTRMU achieves 0.96, 0.93, and 0.94 syntactic similarity for eWorkforce_10 with $s = 1$, 2, and 3, respectively; for e-document_75, the results are 0.93, 0.93, and 0.91, respectively. The standard deviations are less than 0.02 for all results, except for eWorkforce_10 with $s = 2$, where $SD = 0.04$. In short, we see that *unknown attribute values cause a small decrease in policy quality, but policy quality remains high* even with up to 8% of field values set to **unknown** (with $s = 3$), and trend downward slowly as the percentage of unknowns increases.

Our algorithms generate policies with *the same or better (smaller) average WSC than the simplified input policies* for all datasets except e-document_75, for which the average WSC of the mined policy is 20%, 14%, and 15% higher in experiments with $s = 1$, 2, and 3, respectively. The standard deviations (over the 5 object models) for each policy are between 5% and 9% of the averages for EMR_15, eWorkforce_10, and e-document_75; for other policies, the standard deviations are 0.

Running Time. Table 2 reports our algorithms' running times for $s = 0$ and the slowdown (relative to $s = 0$) for larger values of s. This slowdown reflects the additional processing needed to handle unknown values. Averaged over all policies, the average slowdown is 3.5, 5.0, and 4.0 for $s = 1$, 2, and 3, respectively. The median slowdown is 1.4, 1.5, and 1.6 for $s = 1$, 2, and 3, respectively.

Our algorithms spend most of the time in phase 1, to learn decision trees and extract rules. The slowdown on a few policies is notably larger than the others, and the standard deviations in running time for those policies are also high, indicating that, for each of those policies, the algorithms take much longer on a few object models than on the others. The larger slowdown for these object models is caused by additional time spent eliminating features involving the unknown. In particular, several of the features involving unknown cannot be eliminated by *max_iter* iterations of the top-level **while** loop, so the **for** loop over *uncov* is executed to eliminate them; we use the second approach in Sect. 5.1, generating rules that use "id". On the positive side, these low-quality rules are removed in phase 2, and the algorithms still succeed in mining high-quality policies.

8   Related Work

We discuss related work on policy mining. As mentioned in Sect. 1, the primary distinction of our work is that *no related work on ReBAC or ABAC policy mining considers unknown attribute values.* We are not aware of related work on learning concise formulas in three-valued logic.

Related Work on ReBAC Policy Mining. Bui et al. developed several ReBAC policy mining algorithms [2–6], the most recent and best of which are DTRM and DTRM⁻ [2]. Our algorithms modify them to handle unknown attribute values. Bui et al.'s algorithms in [5] can mine ReBAC policies from incomplete and noisy information about permissions [5].

Iyer et al. present algorithms, based on ideas from rule mining and frequent graph-based pattern mining, for mining ReBAC policies and graph transition policies [15]. Their policy mining algorithm targets a policy language that is less expressive than ORAL2⁻, because it lacks set comparison operators and negation; furthermore, unlike ORAL2, it does not directly support Boolean attributes, and encoding them may be inefficient [2]. Also, in Bui and Stoller's experiments, DTRM is faster and more effective than their algorithm [2].

Iyer et al. [16] present an algorithm for active learning of ReBAC policies from a black-box access control decision engine, using authorization queries and equivalence queries. The algorithm is assumed to have access to complete information about attributes and relationships.

Related Work on ABAC Policy Mining. Xu et al. proposed the first algorithm for ABAC policy mining [22] and a variant of it for mining ABAC policies from logs [21]. Medvet et al. developed the first evolutionary algorithm for ABAC policy mining [19]. Iyer et al. developed the first ABAC policy mining algorithm that can mine ABAC policies containing deny rules as well as permit rules [14]. Cotrini et al. proposed a new formulation of the problem of ABAC mining from logs and an algorithm based on APRIORI-SD, a machine-learning algorithm for subgroup discovery, to solve it [9]. Cotrini et al. also developed a "universal" access control policy mining algorithm framework, which can be specialized to produce policy mining algorithms for a wide variety of policy languages [8]; the downside, based on their experiments, is that the resulting algorithms achieve lower policy quality than customized algorithms for specific policy languages. Law et al. present a scalable inductive logic programming algorithm and evaluate it for learning ABAC rules from logs [18].

References

1. Bogaerts, J., Decat, M., Lagaisse, B., Joosen, W.: Entity-based access control: supporting more expressive access control policies. In: Proceedings of 31st Annual Computer Security Applications Conference (ACSAC), pp. 291–300. ACM (2015)
2. Bui, T., Stoller, S.D.: A decision tree learning approach for mining relationship-based access control policies. In: Proceedings of the 25th ACM Symposium on Access Control Models and Technologies (SACMAT 2020), pp. 167–178. ACM Press (2020)
3. Bui, T., Stoller, S.D., Le, H.: Efficient and extensible policy mining for relationship-based access control. In: Proceedings of the 24th ACM Symposium on Access Control Models and Technologies (SACMAT 2019), pp. 161–172. ACM (2019)
4. Bui, T., Stoller, S.D., Li, J.: Mining relationship-based access control policies. In: Proceedings of 22nd ACM Symposium on Access Control Models and Technologies (SACMAT), pp. 239–246 (2017)
5. Bui, T., Stoller, S.D., Li, J.: Mining relationship-based access control policies from incomplete and noisy data. In: Zincir-Heywood, N., Bonfante, G., Debbabi, M., Garcia-Alfaro, J. (eds.) FPS 2018. LNCS, vol. 11358, pp. 267–284. Springer, Cham (2019). https://doi.org/10.1007/978-3-030-18419-3_18
6. Bui, T., Stoller, S.D., Li, J.: Greedy and evolutionary algorithms for mining relationship-based access control policies. Comput. Secur. **80**, 317–333 (2019). Preprint: http://arxiv.org/abs/1708.04749. An earlier version appeared as a short paper in ACM SACMAT 2017
7. C4.5 algorithm. https://en.wikipedia.org/wiki/C4.5_algorithm
8. Cotrini, C., Corinzia, L., Weghorn, T., Basin, D.: The next 700 policy miners: a universal method for building policy miners. In: Proceedings of 2019 ACM Conference on Computer and Communications Security (CCS 2019), pp. 95–112 (2019)
9. Cotrini, C., Weghorn, T., Basin, D.: Mining ABAC rules from sparse logs. In: Proceedings of 3rd IEEE European Symposium on Security and Privacy (EuroS&P), pp. 2141–2148 (2018)
10. Das, S., Mitra, B., Atluri, V., Vaidya, J., Sural, S.: Policy engineering in RBAC and ABAC. In: Samarati, P., Ray, I., Ray, I. (eds.) From Database to Cyber Security. LNCS, vol. 11170, pp. 24–54. Springer, Cham (2018). https://doi.org/10.1007/978-3-030-04834-1_2
11. Decat, M., Bogaerts, J., Lagaisse, B., Joosen, W.: The e-document case study: functional analysis and access control requirements. CW Reports CW654, Department of Computer Science, KU Leuven, February 2014
12. Decat, M., Bogaerts, J., Lagaisse, B., Joosen, W.: The e-document case study: functional analysis and access control requirements. CW Reports CW654, Department of Computer Science, KU Leuven, February 2014. https://lirias.kuleuven.be/handle/123456789/440202
13. Decat, M., Bogaerts, J., Lagaisse, B., Joosen, W.: The workforce management case study: functional analysis and access control requirements. CW Reports CW655, Department of Computer Science, KU Leuven, February 2014. https://lirias.kuleuven.be/handle/123456789/440203
14. Iyer, P., Masoumzadeh, A.: Mining positive and negative attribute-based access control policy rules. In: Proceedings of 23rd ACM on Symposium on Access Control Models and Technologies (SACMAT), pp. 161–172. ACM (2018)
15. Iyer, P., Masoumzadeh, A.: Generalized mining of relationship-based access control policies in evolving systems. In: Proceedings of 24th ACM on Symposium on Access Control Models and Technologies (SACMAT), pp. 135–140. ACM (2019)

16. Iyer, P., Masoumzadeh, A.: Active learning of relationship-based access control policies. In: Lobo, J., Stoller, S.D., Liu, P. (eds.) Proceedings of the 25th ACM Symposium on Access Control Models and Technologies, SACMAT 2020, Barcelona, Spain, 10–12 June 2020, pp. 155–166. ACM (2020). https://doi.org/10.1145/3381991.3395614

17. Kleene, S.C.: Introduction to Metamathematics. D. Van Nostrand, Princeton (1950)

18. Law, M., Russo, A., Bertino, E., Broda, K., Lobo, J.: FastLAS: scalable inductive logic programming incorporating domain-specific optimisation criteria. In: Thirty-Fourth AAAI Conference on Artificial Intelligence (AAAI 2020), pp. 2877–2885. AAAI Press (2020)

19. Medvet, E., Bartoli, A., Carminati, B., Ferrari, E.: Evolutionary inference of attribute-based access control policies. In: Gaspar-Cunha, A., Henggeler Antunes, C., Coello, C.C. (eds.) EMO 2015. LNCS, vol. 9018, pp. 351–365. Springer, Cham (2015). https://doi.org/10.1007/978-3-319-15934-8_24

20. Three-valued logic. https://en.wikipedia.org/wiki/Three-valued_logic

21. Xu, Z., Stoller, S.D.: Mining attribute-based access control policies from logs. In: Atluri, V., Pernul, G. (eds.) DBSec 2014. LNCS, vol. 8566, pp. 276–291. Springer, Heidelberg (2014). https://doi.org/10.1007/978-3-662-43936-4_18. Extended version available at http://arxiv.org/abs/1403.5715

22. Xu, Z., Stoller, S.D.: Mining attribute-based access control policies. IEEE Trans. Depend. Secure Comput. 12(5), 533–545 (2015)

Reliability and Security
for Safety-Critical Service Compositions

Kevin Theuermann[(✉)]

Institute of Applied Information Processing and Communications,
Graz Technical University, 8010 Graz, Austria
kevin.theuermann@egiz.gv.at

Abstract. Service composition represents the combination of individual distributed services, which are operated by different organizations. A composite service may include security or safety-critical services, which could have a serious impact on individuals and thus, require correctness of generated outputs as a crucial property. For this reason, service composition systems must avoid a manipulation of critical services and have to guarantee high reliability of computed outputs as well as availability. Secure multiparty computation and verifiable secret sharing enables a privacy-preserving computation of service outputs jointly generated by several parties, which makes it possible to prevent a single point of failure for critical services and guarantees correctness of a generated output. In this work, we introduce a concept for privacy-preserving and reliable service compositions through the application of secure multiparty computation in combination with threshold signatures. Threshold signatures make it possible to define a maximum number of allowed unavailable actors, which do not participate in the mulitparty computation protocol. This mechanism enables a flexible definition of security or safety requirements for critical services. The feasibility of the proposed solution is demonstrated by an implemented proof-of-concept for a composite medical alert service.

Keywords: Reliability · Availability · Privacy · Safety

1 Introduction

With the emergence of Service-Oriented Computing [1], a promising paradigm to perform service compositions has been introduced. Service composition represents the cross-organizational combination of distributed services to enhance reusability and to enable a flexible combination of atomic services to form a more complex and innovative application. There is a growing reliance on online composite services, which turns them into an attractive target for malicious attacks. Some composite services may require special focus on the correctness of execution outputs, as they could have a critical impact and cause serious political, economic or health-related consequences [2]. For instance, let's assume a composite medical service for an automatic insulin injection system similarly like

© Springer Nature Switzerland AG 2020
S. Kanhere et al. (Eds.): ICISS 2020, LNCS 12553, pp. 45–65, 2020.
https://doi.org/10.1007/978-3-030-65610-2_3

introduced by Changyong and Suk Jin [3]. This system consists of two atomic services; one service provided by a hospital, validating the blood glucose level of a patient and a second service running inside a wearable control device, receiving the validation result and transmitting commands to an insulin pump, which automatically injects a required insulin dose. In this example, the output of the first service may have a critical impact, as a wrong insulin dose could harm the patient's health. Thus, services computing a critical output require special mechanisms against adversarial attacks.

In the past, Formal Description Techniques [4–6] have been introduced to verify, validate or refining service compositions, which is particularly important for safety-critical systems [7]. While these techniques provide verifications against formal properties or semantic aspects, they do not focus on the detection of incorrect execution outputs during a process. Adversaries can use diverse attack vectors to have different influences on a service. For instance, an adversary could aim to cause a complete failure of a service or may aim to manipulate the processing to cause a wrong output. Both cases must be taken into account for security or safety-critical services.

Blockchain-based service composition systems have been introduced recently [8,9], which use consensus protocols to ensure correctness of transactions. Consensus protocols are one of the core elements of blockchain systems, which are used to reach a consensus regarding information sharing or generating a correct execution result. However, to integrate the blockchain into existing service composition systems still represents a challenge, as synchronization processes between nodes in widely distributed systems are complex. Furthermore, private or sensitive data also requires special focus in blockchain systems. Most of the existing blockchain-based service composition systems do not consider the privacy of sensitive user data shared in a consensus protocol. Carminati et al. [10] proposes a concept for a business process execution on a blockchain, which guarantees confidentiality of sensitive data through homomorphic encryption. However, homomorphic encryption schemes suffers from poor performance, restricted functionality and requires a high memory capacity [11].

To our best knowledge, there is no service composition system, which particularly aims on the correctness of execution outputs, reliability and availability to guarantee high security for safety-critical composite services. In this paper, we propose a solution for high reliability and trustworthiness of execution outputs in service compositions, particularly aiming on safety-critical systems and programs. This concept includes the usage of secure multiparty computation, which enables a privacy-preserving computation of processes in a distributed system. This solution do not only provide means to protect security or safety critical services from several attack vectors, but also considers the privacy of the data inputs against actors, who perform the multiparty computation protocol. Additionally, it is possible to adjust the required level of availability regarding the number of participating actors in the protocol according to the outgoing risk of a respective service through an adjustable security level determined by the required number of reconstruction shares to create a valid threshold signature.

An implemented proof-of-concept demonstrates the feasibility of our proposed solution.

The remainder of this paper is structured as follows. Section 2 provides information about the cryptographic background applied in our proposed concept. Section 3 describes the system model including the involved actors and our defined security objectives. The privacy-preserving service composition protocol for critical services is introduced by Sect. 4. Section 5 provides an evaluation by introducing the proof of concept of a case study followed by a discussion. Finally, Sect. 6 provides related work, followed by a conclusion in Sect. 7.

2 Background

This section provides background information regarding the applied cryptographic primitives used in this work to be able to understand the proposed solution thoroughly.

2.1 Secure Multiparty Computation

Secure Multiparty Computation (SMPC) represents a cryptographic protocol, in which a number of actors can jointly compute a public function without revealing their private input values. Therefore, every actor only learns the result of the given public function, preventing all actors from learning other private input values. This goal can be accomplished through the execution of an interactive protocol between all actors involved [12]. This cryptographic method enables the execution of a function in a privacy-preserving manner without involving a trusted third party.

Definition 1 (Secure Multiparty Computation). We recall the definition of SMPC as suggested by Cramer et al. [13]. Let $(A_1, ..., A_n)$ be a number of actors participating in the computation, where $n > 2$. For each actor A_i let X_i be a private input value. The n actors agree on a public function:

$$F : X_i \times ... \times X_n \to Y$$

For simplicity, we consider the case where a function takes multiple values as input and only generates a single output. Let $(x_1, ..., x_n) \in X_i \times ... \times X_n$ be the private input vector of the involved actors $(A_1, ..., A_n)$. Finally, the goal of the actors represents the computation of $Y = (x_1, ..., x_n)$ in order to satisfy a correct computation of Y and simultaneously preserving the privacy, such that Y is the only new information any participating actor A_i retrieves.

It is important to define a desired security model for the SMPC protocol, since the output correctness depends on the actor's inputs, which may be corrupted. In our work, we aim to guarantee *Malicious (Active) Security* [14]. This

security model considers adversaries, who may arbitrarily deviate from the protocol execution trying to manipulate the final output. In case of malicious actors
involved in a SMPC who try to manipulate a value, the honest actors detect the
cheating, abort the process and restart without this adversary.

2.2   Secret Sharing

Typically, SMPC is accomplished by dividing an input value considered as secret,
into multiple secret shares, which are distributed to the group of participating
actors and processed afterwards. Any group of actors of a certain threshold or
more can jointly reconstruct the secret, whereas no group of fewer actors can
perform a reconstruction. The number of the tolerated adversaries t out of n
actors participating in a SMPC varies depending on the used secret sharing
scheme.

Definition 2 (Secret Sharing). We recall the definition of secret sharing
as suggested by Chor and Kushilevitz [15]. Let K be a finite set of secrets
$\{k_1, ..., k_n\}$, where $|K| \geq 2$. A distribution scheme $\langle \Pi, \mu \rangle$, where μ is a probability distribution on a finite set of random strings $R = \{r_1, ..., r_n\}$ and Π is a
mapping from $K \times R$ to a domain of n-tuples $K_1 \times K_2 \times ... \times K_j$, where K_j is
called the domain of shares of p_j. The domain of secrets K is considered as a
secret sharing scheme, which realizes an access structure A if these requirements
hold:

Correctness. The secret k can be reconstructed by any authorized set of parties.
That is, for any set $B \in A$ (where $B = \{pi_1, ..., pi_{|B|}\}$ there exists a reconstruction
function $RECON_B : Ki_1 \times ... \times Ki_{|B|} \rightarrow K$ such that for every $k \in K$:

$$Pr[RECON_B(\Pi(k,r)_B) = k] = 1$$

Perfect Privacy. Every unauthorized set cannot learn anything about the secret
from their shares. Formally, for any set $T \in A$, for every two secrets $a, b \in K$,
and for every possible vector of shares $\langle s_j \rangle_{pj \in T}$:

$$Pr[\Pi(a,r)_T = \langle s_j \rangle_{pj \in T}] = Pr[\Pi(b,r)_T = \langle s_j \rangle_{pj \in T}]$$

In our work, we want to avoid any adversary deviating from the protocol by
manipulating secret shares to guarantee highest security. Thus, we use verifiable
secret sharing in our concept.

Verifiable Secret Sharing. Verifiable Secret Sharing (VSS) represents a fundamental building block for SMPC, as it provide means to verify the output of
a SMPC regarding correctness of the jointly generated result. This scheme provides means for every participant of a SMPC to verify the secret shares, which
are transmitted during the protocol. This prevents active adversaries, participating in the SMPC protocol or controlling internal parties, from manipulating
the secret shares to cause a wrong output [16]. The VSS protocol consists of two
phases:

1. **Sharing:** Initially, a dealer (data input provider) holds a secret and generates n secret shares. Next, he distributes one share to each of the actors conducting the SMPC, which simultaneously generate an independent random input. The sharing phase may include several rounds, where one actor transmits private messages to other actors or broadcasts a message. The message depends on a randomly generated input, a secret share and messages received in previous rounds.

2. **Reconstruction:** Every actor provides the entire view resulting from the sharing phase. Finally, they perform a reconstruction function to generate the output by adding the secret shares homomorphically.

For an extended definition of VSS, we refer to the scheme proposed by Patra et al. [17]. Even if a group of adversaries out of n actors exceeding a certain threshold t would work according to the protocol, they could still collude and try to reconstruct the secret. A *Perfectly Secure SMPC* protocol, which does not allow do involve any errors in the computation, is only possible if $n \geq 4t + 1$.

2.3   Threshold Signatures

Threshold Signature Scheme (TSS) enables the definition of a flexible threshold policy. This technology replaces traditional central signature creation with a distributed computation, in which multiple actors jointly perform the signature creation. Every actor participating in the signature creation holds a share of a private signing key. Through the determination of a desired threshold, it is possible to define the number of required actors, which at least have to create a signature jointly [18]. In our solution, it allows us to define a maximum amount of unavailable actors, who are not participating in processing a critical function through secure multiparty computation, by determining the minimum number of actors needed to create a valid signature.

Definition 3 (Threshold Signatures). We recall the definition of threshold signatures as suggested by Stathakopoulou et al. [19]. The Threshold Signature Scheme (TSS) consists of several algorithms (ThreshKeyGen, ThreshSig, SigShareComb, Ver) which are defined as follows:

$ThreshKeyGen() \rightarrow (PubKey, PrivKey, S_{1-n}, VerKey)$: This algorithm generates an asymmetric keypair *(PubKey,Privkey)*, a set of n private key shares $S_{1-n} = \{S_1, S_2, ..., S_n\}$ as well as a set of verification keys $V_{1-n} = \{V_1, V_2, ..., V_n\}$, which are necessary to verify a private key share.

$ThreshSig(m, S_i) \rightarrow \sigma_i$: This signing algorithm takes as input a given message m as well as a private key share S_i and outputs a signature share σ_i.

$SigShareComb(\sigma_{k-n}) \rightarrow \sigma$: This algorithm takes at least k valid signature shares $\{\sigma_1, \sigma_2, ..., \sigma_k\}$ as input and outputs the signature σ.

$Ver(\sigma) \rightarrow valid/invalid$: This algorithm takes as input a signature σ for verification and succeeds if the signature is valid.

3 System Model

This section describes the involved actors including their related trust assumptions as well as the data flow of a composite service in our service composition architecture. Based on this trust model, we derive several security objectives, which serve as motivation for our proposed solution.

3.1 Security Objectives

This section summarizes our defined security objectives, which are based on our system model and explained in the following paragraphs.

Objective 1: Correct Service Execution. The output of a security or safety-critical service may have serious consequences, especially in service compositions, where the output of one service may serve as input for another service. This is even more important, e.g. when a service could raise issues related to the safety of users and may cause health-related problems. Thus, the first security objective is to achieve correctness of service outputs of critical services. For reasons of traceability and to ensure the correctness of the results in service compositions, actors must be able to check whether the result of a critical service has possibly been changed by other actors in the process sequence. For this reason, service compositions require a runtime verification, which makes it possible to identify process participants and a comprehensible verification enabling traceability regarding the emergence of a process state.

Objective 2: Distributed Execution of Critical Services. Since security or safety-critical services have a serious impact on individuals or systems, they represent an attractive target for attackers. If the processing of a critical service is performed centrally, the composite service suffers from a single point of failure, which is a problem, e.g. when an attacker compromises this service. For this purpose, the second security objective represents a distributed execution of critical services.

Objective 3: Privacy-Preserving Service Execution. Service compositions may deal with highly sensitive data. For instance, electronic health services often process personalized information, which require special data protection. Besides a reliable and correct service execution, we want to protect the confidentiality of data. Hence, our third security objective represents a reliable and privacy-preserving computation of services.

Objective 4: Adjustable Level of Security for Critical Services. Security objective 4 represents an adjustable level of security for critical services, since not every service poses the same risk. Service providers should be able to define a required number of parties jointly processing a critical service and a maximum number of unavailable parties, which enables an optimization of the overall performance.

3.2   Actors and Data Flow

The system architecture for our reliable and privacy-preserving service composition system consists of the actors explained in the following paragraphs. Figure 1 illustrates the overall architecture.

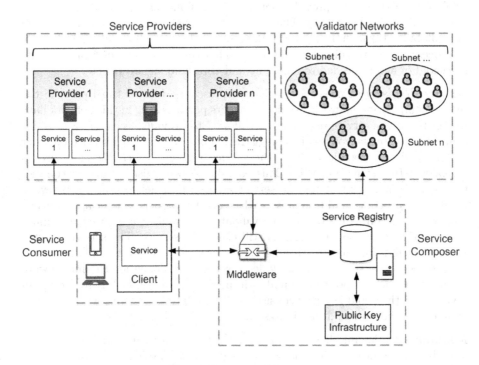

Fig. 1. System architecture

Client: The client represents a device (e.g. smartphone or laptop) of the service consumer, with which a composite service is used. This composite service comprises various atomic services that are combined to fulfill a desired use-case. As the client starts a service composition, he transfers necessary data to the middleware and encrypts sensitive data parts for privacy-protection reasons, if necessary. Furthermore, the client does not need to know anything about participating actors providing a service for the required composite service, because the whole composition is coordinated by a middleware.

Service Providers: A service provider represents an actor providing one or more services in the service composition network. In order to participate in this network, each service provider has to perform an initial registration. However, an exact authentication procedure is not in the scope of this work. If a service provider provides a security or safety-critical service, he determines the required level of security for the provided service by announcing a set of actors for the creation of a validator subnet. The service provider also defines the required level of availability through a required minimum number of actors, who jointly have to process the output of a critical service. This minimum number represents the threshold of actors needed to create a valid threshold signature.

Service Registry: The service registry represents a trusted third party in the service composition network. Service providers participating in this network have to register at the service registry to be allowed to provide electronic services for compositions. In the course of the registration of a service, each service provider obtains a digital certificate from the service registry, which therefore uses a Public Key Infrastructure (PKI). This way, the service registry is able to conduct the identity management for the service composition network and can revoke certificates centrally. Additionally, each service provider registering a critical service has to announce the service validators as well as a allowed maximum number of unavailable validators to still execute a service. The service registry stores the validators and the threshold, creates a corresponding validator subnet for the respective service and provides a service catalogue for the middleware taking over the composition. Finally, it performs the algorithm to create an asymmetric threshold key pair consisting of n private key shares, where n is the number of validators and distributes one share to each validator.

Middleware: The middleware runs in the trusted third party environment and directly communicates with the service registry. It represents an orchestration service coordinating incoming service requests. To avoid a single-point-of-failure, a service composition system should not rely on a single middleware and should provide more service orchestrators.

Validator Network: The validation network consists of multiple actors (e.g. different service providers), who jointly perform a critical service execution and generate a reliable and correct result. This validation is conducted in a sub-net within the service composition network, which is only accessible by autho-rized actors. All the information shared in the validation network is transmitted securely via TLS channels. The number of actors in a validation network varies depending on the risk of a processed service. Thus, for every service comput-ing a critical process, an own validation subnet is created, only including actors authorized to read the respective input data. When a service provider registers a critical service at the service registry, he announces the required validators as well as the allowed maximum number of unavailable actors. Each validator of a subnet receives a private key share transmitted by the service registry. This private key share has to be used by the validators to create a valid signature. An invalid threshold signature indicates that the number of unavailable actors exceeds the specified threshold determined by the service provider and thus, does not offer a satisfying security regarding the output correctness.

3.3 Creation of a Validator Subnet

This section describes the creation of validator subnets in more detail. Figure 2 illustrates the processes.

Creation of a Validator Subnet:

1. In a first step, a service provider registers the critical *service X* at the service registry. For this purpose, he transmits a list of all actors that are part of the validator subnet for this service including their corresponding digital certificates. If any validator does not possess a certificate issued by the service registry, he has to register at the service registry. Additionally, the service provider sends a threshold policy, which defines the minimum number of actors required to create a valid signature.
2. The service registry creates a threshold keypair *ThreshKeyGen()* for the validators *1-n* consisting of a public key and *1-n* private key shares.
3. Next, the service registry sends one private key share via secure TLS channels to every validator, which is part of the respective subnet.
4. The validators answer with a confirmation of the received private key share. The creation of a validator subnet for *service X* is completed after this step.

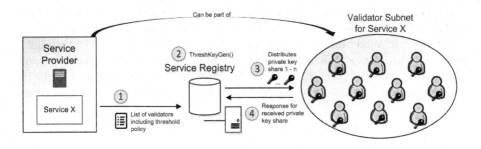

Fig. 2. System architecture

4   Reliable Service Composition Protocol

This section describes the reliable service composition protocol in detail. The following paragraph explain the process for the execution of a critical service on a generic level. The whole process is summarized by Protocol 1.

Critical Service Execution: The sender starts the execution of a critical service by transmitting a service request for a critical *service X* to the middleware. The middleware forwards the request to the service registry in order to obtain the registered validators for this service. The service registry answers with a list of validators containing their endpoints and public keys. The middleware relays the information to the sender, who creates a challenge (random nonce) for the generation of a threshold signature. Afterwards, the sender passes the challenge to the middleware, which forwards it to the validators. Each available validator in the subnet signs the challenge with his private key share and returns the threshold signature share back to the middleware. The middleware again relays the signatures shares to the sender, who combines the shares to verify, if the signature is valid and the amount of available validators fulfills the required threshold. In case of an invalid signature, the sender is aware that fewer validators would perform the critical service jointly via SMPC than initially required to achieve a certain security level defined by the service provider. In case of a valid signature, the sender divides the input data for *service X*, signs it and encrypts these parts for the validators using their public keys. The way, how the input is split depends on the used secret sharing scheme for the SMPC. Afterwards, the sender transmits the signatures and ciphertexts for every validator to the middleware, which broadcasts the encrypted inputs to the validators. The validators jointly generate the result for the critical service. If any corrupted validator deviates from the protocol, the honest validators cancel the process and report it to the middleware, which restarts the computation of the function without the corrupted validator, if the number of remaining validators is not below the minimum number of required validators, determined by the threshold policy for this service. Finally, they return the result to the sender via the middleware. Alternatively, the middleware forwards the result to the next actor in a service composition, if a composite service has not been finished at this time.

Critical Service Execution

Repeat these steps for every safety/security-critical process, assuming the *client* initially verifies the availability of necessary validators through a threshold signature. Afterwards, the client starts the critical service execution by sending multiple message parts msg_{1-j} to the middleware, which serve as input for a public function $f(msg_{(i)})$ processed via SMPC:

① **Sender$_{(i)}$ (client or service provider)**
1. Sends service request for *service X* to middleware via TLS

② **Middleware**
1. Forwards service request to service registry

③ **Service Registry**
1. Identifies *service X* from request
2. Queries validator list from database: $validator_{(1-j)} \leftarrow getValidators$ $(serviceX)$
3. Sends $validator_{(1-j)}$ to middleware

④ **Middleware**
1. Relays public keys of $validator_{(1-j)}$ to service consumer

⑤ **Sender$_{(i)}$ (client or service provider)**
1. Stores public keys of $validator_{(1-j)}$ for later
2. $challenge \leftarrow generateRandomNonce()$
3. Sends $challenge$ to the middleware

⑥ **Middleware**
1. Relays $challenge$ to the $validators_{(1-j)}$

⑦ **Validator$_{(1-j)}$**
1. $\sigma_{ThreshSigShare_{(1-j)}} \leftarrow ThreshSig(challenge, S_i) \quad \forall \quad validators_{(1-j)}$
2. Returns $\sigma_{ThreshSigShare_{(1-j)}}$ to middleware

⑧ **Middleware**
1. Forwards $\sigma_{ThreshSigShare_{(1-j)}}$ to sender

⑨ **Sender$_{(i)}$ (client or service provider)**
1. $\sigma_{ThreshSig} \leftarrow SigShareComb(\sigma_{ThreshSigShare_{(1-j)}})$
2. $valid/invalid \leftarrow Ver(\sigma_{ThreshSig})$
3. $msg_{(1-j)} \leftarrow Split(msg)$
4. $\sigma_{(1-j)} \leftarrow Sign(SK_{client}, msg_{(i)}) \quad \forall \quad msg_{(1-j)}$
5. $CT_{(1-j)} \leftarrow Enc(PK_{validator_{1-j}}, msg_{(i)}) \quad \forall \quad msg_{(1-j)}$
6. Send $CT_{(1-j)}, and \sigma_{(1-j)}$ to the middleware

⑩ **Middleware/Orchestrator**
1. Transmits $CT_{(1-j)}, \sigma_{(1-j)} and PK_{sender_{(i)}}$ to the corresponding validators

⑪ **Validator$_{(1-j)}$**
1. $msg_{(1-j)} \leftarrow Dec(CT, SK_{(validator)}) \quad \forall \quad validator_{(1-j)}$
2. $valid/invalid_{(1-j)} \leftarrow Ver(\sigma, PK_{(sender_{(i)})}) \quad \forall \quad validator_{(1-j)}$
3. $result \leftarrow f(msg) \quad \forall \quad msg_{(1-j)}$ via SMPC
4. If receiver is the client: $CT_{(result)} \leftarrow Enc(PK_{(client)}, result)$
5. If receiver is a service provider $sp_{(i+1)} : CT_{(result)} \leftarrow Enc(PK_{(sp_{i+1})}, result)$
6. Send $CT_{(result)}$ to the middleware

⑫ **Middleware/Orchestrator**
1. Forwards $PK_{(TS)}$ and $CT_{(result)}$ to the next $receiver_{(i+1)}$ in the composition

⑬ **Receiver$_{(i+1)}$ (service provider or finally the client)**
1. If receiver is the client: $result \leftarrow Dec(CT_{(result)}, SK_{(client)})$
2. If receiver is a service provider $sp_{(i+1)} : result \leftarrow Dec(CT_{(result)}, SK_{(sp(i+1))})$
3. Start again at $receiver_{(i+1)}$ to act as sender, if the process has not been finished

Protocol 1: Critical Service Execution Protocol

5   Evaluation

This section illustrates a case study for a medical alert service, presents a proof-of-concept implementation and discusses various aspects.

5.1   Case Study

To demonstrate the feasibility of our proposed solution, let us assume an example use-case representing a medical alert service, as shown in Fig. 3. In this use-case, a patient records his vital signs via a heart rate monitor, which is connected to a smartphone application via Bluetooth. Besides the heart rate, the smartphone also monitors the motion of the patient via sensors. The smartphone application starts a telemedical composite service, either automatically if the motion of the patient is conspicuous (e.g. patient fell down) or manually, if the patient clicks on an emergency button when he does not feel well. In both cases, the smartphone application summarizes the last 30 pulse rates that were recorded in a request and transmits it to the middleware, which coordinates the process flow according to a specified sequence. The represented use-case thus consists of 5 individual services, which conduct the following actions:

- **Service ①:** This service represents the heart rate monitor considered as an IoT device, which measures the heart rate as well as the motion of the patient via sensors. The device connects to a telemedical alert smartphone app via Bluetooth. Since IoT devices still have limited functionality and computing power, it only transmits the vital signs together with a hash-value calculated from these values.
- **Service ②:** The telemedical alert service represents the second service provided by a smartphone app. This app receives the vital signs and verifies the hash value to avoid adversarial modifications during the transmission. Besides, this service adds a digital signature as well as a use-case identifier, which is necessary to enable a verification against the authenticity of the sender at the middleware and an identification of the required process sequence. Unauthenticated requests are ignored by the middleware.
- **Service ③:** This service represents a secure multiparty computation including several validators that perform the creation of a threshold signature as well as a function to validate the heart rate of the patient. As the output of this service may have a critical impact on the health of the patient (e.g. if a heart attack is not detected), it is registered as a critical service and requires a validator network.
- **Service ④:** This alert service is operated by a hospital that receives the validated heart rates and acts accordingly. If the result indicates a heart attack, the service searches for any available emergency doctor to send an emergency call including the validated heart rate, the firstname and surname of the patient as well as his location.
- **Service ⑤:** This service runs on any end-device of an emergency doctor. If a doctor receives an emergency call, he has to confirm on receiving the

message by pressing a button. Afterwards, an acknowledgment of the received emergency call is returned to the client device, indicating that an emergency doctor is on the way.

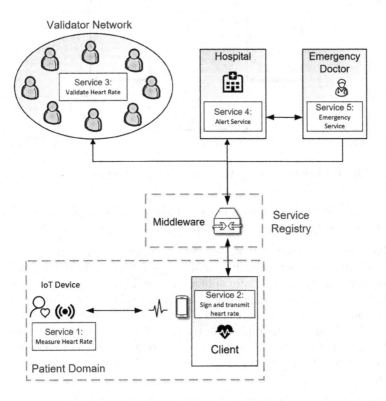

Fig. 3. Use-case of a medical alert service

5.2 Implementation

We have implemented the introduced use-case with Java-based web services as well as an Android app, which starts the process. The interaction between all services is based on JSON Web Tokens (JWT), as it enables a lightweight communication. For the creation of JWT, we have used Java JWT[1] as it represents a stable and mature release. To simulate a medical alert, first the smartphone app generates a signed JWT containing the following data:

– *Challenge:* Any nonce randomly generated by the smartphone app.

---

[1] https://github.com/jwtk/jjwt.

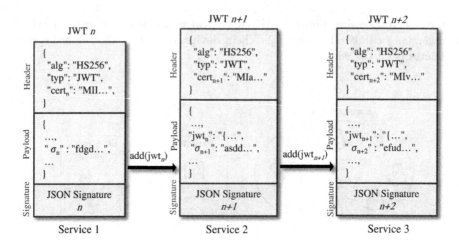

Fig. 4. Chaining of JWT transmitted during a service composition

- *Public key:* A string representing the public key of the sender, needed for verifying the signature of the JWT to ensure integrity.

This JWT is transmitted to another service, acting as service orchestrator. This service coordinates the process flow and forwards the received JWT to 30 web services representing the validator subnet. The validators verify the signature of the JWT and sign the challenge with their private key share. For the creation of threshold signatures, we have used the platform PROTECT[2] (Platform for Robust Threshold Cryptography) designed and implemented by a team that includes experts from the fields of threshold cryptography and Byzantine fault tolerant systems. Every service creates a signed JWT containing the following information:

- *Challenge:* The challenge initially transmitted by the sender.
- *Signature:* A string representing a signature share of the received challenge.
- *Public key:* A string representing the public key of the respective validator.

All JWT are returned to the service orchestrator, which relays the information to the smartphone app. After verifying the signature of each JWT and combining the threshold signature shares, the generated threshold signature is also verified. For this use case, we have defined a minimum threshold of 26 validator services that have to be available. Next, the smartphone app creates an integer array consisting of 30 values, which are randomly generated integers in a range between 0 and 200. For every validator an own JWT is created containing the public key of the sender and an integer value representing one heart rate of the sender encrypted with the public key of a validator. These JWT are transmitted to the validators via the service orchestrator. To implement SMPC including verifiable secret sharing, we have used the secret sharing library Archistar-SMC[3] (Secure

[2] https://github.com/jasonkresch/protect.
[3] https://github.com/Archistar/archistar-smc.

Multi-Cloud Prototype) framework, which was published in [29]. The validators perform two public functions via SMPC. One function to compute the lowest and one function to compute the highest heart rate:

$$int \leftarrow maxValue() \quad \& \quad int \leftarrow minValue()$$

The result processed by SMPC is returned back to the sender via the orchestrator. Finally, the smartphone app creates a JWT and sends it to the orchestrator containing the lowest and highest heart rate, the location, public key and name of the user. The orchestrator forwards the information to another web service, which validates the minimum and maximum heart rate and sends an emergency call to a web service representing any emergency doctor.

Runtime Verification: To enable a runtime verification of outputs during a service composition, the messages represented as JWT are cryptographically chained. Everyone except the starting actor, adds the JWT of the previous actor to the payload of the JWT generated by themselves like illustrated by Fig. 4. This makes it possible to optionally trace back all previous participating actors by verifying the digital certificates and to verify the correctness of a process state, since a JWT also ensures integrity. For privacy reasons, only encrypted values are included in the payloads. Additionally, actors can verify, if data has been modified by any unauthorized actor in the process sequence, since JWT also ensure integrity of transmitted messages.

5.3   Performance

Test Setup. The Verifiable Secret Sharing algorithms are performed by a service considered as the dealer of a validator network running on a Lenovo Thinkpad T460s, which has an Intel i5-6200U dual-core processor and 12 GB RAM. To provide reliable results, we have conducted each test 50 times and used the median of these performance values.

Performance of Rabin-Ben-Or Verifiable Secret Sharing. We have tested our use-case with several settings, where the number of shares in total n, as well as the number of shares required to reconstruct a secret k varies. Since we want to guarantee a Perfectly Secure SMPC protocol, we have to consider that this is only possible if $n \geq 4t + 1$. Therefore we consider a certain minimum ratio between n and k. We have tested the performance of the Rabin-Ben-Or Verifiable Secret Sharing with the following ratio between n and k, denoted as $(n|k)$: $(7|8), (10|12), (20|16), (30|23), (40|31)$. Figure 5 provides the performance values in milliseconds for sharing and reconstruction phase with a message size of 1MB. The results demonstrate that the processing time does not raise significantly for the sharing phase with a chosen $(n|k)$ ratio of $(8|7)$ to $(30|23)$. Similarly, the processing time for reconstructing a secret for a ratio of $(8|7)$ to $(20|13)$ does not increase. The performance value for the ratio of $(30|23)$ representing the amount of shares for our use-case demonstrates an practically-efficient execution with a processing time of 87 [ms] for the sharing- and 128 [ms] for the reconstruction phase.

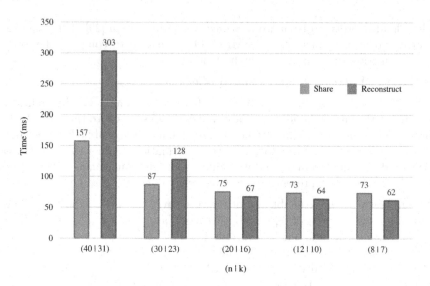

Fig. 5. Execution time in milliseconds [ms] for Rabin-Ben-Or Verifiable Secret Sharing

Performance for the Generation of Threshold Signatures. We have split the evaluation of the generation of a threshold signature into a key creation phase and a threshold signature creation phase. The service registry performs the key creation when registering a validator network. Table 1 summarizes the execution time for the generation of private key shares for 30 validators as well as the time needed for sharing these keys provided by the key-creation phase. The threshold signature creation phase provides the execution time for generating and verifying the signature shares as well as recovering of the secret. Evidently, the execution time for generating and verifying a threshold signature takes about 3 s, which might be acceptable to provide high security for critical services.

Table 1. Execution time in milliseconds for algorithms of Threshold Signatures

Key-Creation Phase		Threshold Signature-Creation Phase			
ThreshKey Generation	Key Sharing	Signature Share Creation	Signature Share Verification	Recovering Secret	Verifying Signature
1307 [ms]	1299 [ms]	10 [ms]	8 [ms]	3028 [ms]	7 [ms]

5.4 Discussion and Future Work

Reliability and Availability: Through the application of SMPC, it is possible to perform a distributed computation of a function, which avoids a single point of failure in case of a malicious or compromized service provider. Service providers can determine a required number of actors processing a function through threshold signatures, as the amount of parties participating in the computation influences the security.

The application of verifiable secret sharing guarantees the detection of adversaries participating in the SMPC, who try to deviate from the protocol and manipulate the output. This cryptographic mechanism is highly important for safety-critical systems. However, the number of adversaries must not exceed $n \geq 4t + 1$ to avoid colluding. This means that the required threshold of parties to create a valid threshold signature to start the SMPC, indirectly also determines the number of required actors, who take part in the SMPC. A higher number of actors results in a higher number of required adversaries, to be able to reconstruct a secret by colluding. However, the execution time for the sharing as well as the reconstruction phase increases with a higher number of participating actors as demonstrated in our performance tests. Thus, the outgoing risk of a critical service must be evaluated and to find an acceptable trade-off between the required execution time and the desired security.

To further increase reliability and availability of a critical service, service providers might determine additional validators, which only be included in a validation, if the validator network would not provide enough participants to fulfill a required ratio of $(n|k)$ for instance, in case of adversaries compromising several validators.

Privacy: SMPC limits to amount of sensitive data that is transmitted to the validators in a way that each validator only learns about the input and output of the respective critical function. Nevertheless, the proposed concept does not guarantee full privacy against service validators, because they may learn from data inputs and outputs over time, which represents a limitation that has to be mentioned. This problem can be reduced in a way that validators only learn the output by dividing the input through secret sharing already when the data provider disseminates the input to the validators. However, we did not consider this approach due to performance issues.

The use of homomorphic encryption represents an option to guarantee full privacy against the validators, which we did not consider, because of a higher computation effort as well. However, this is something we want to investigate in our future work.

Flexible Security or Safety Policies: By including threshold signatures, it is possible to define an allowed number of unavailable validators. This mechanism makes it possible to react on the outgoing risk of a service and enables a specific level of availability for every individual service. Also the number of required adversaries needed to reconstruct a secret can be indirectly defined by threshold signatures, which enables a flexible definition of a required security level.

Flexible Service Composition Properties: Our proposed solution ensures the inclusion of critical services into a composite service and offers a solution to guarantee correctness of generated outputs. Every actor providing a critical service is able to define a desired network of validators on his own. This mechanism makes our concept more practical and increases trust of the service provider. The system model of the proposed concept ensures high reusability and an easy exchange of individual services.

Runtime Verification: To provide a means for verification of the authenticity of participating actors in service compositions, as well as a verification of the integrity of messages processed by previous actors, we have defined an approach to cryptographically chain messages in JWT data formant. This mechanism enables a backwards validation for actors in service composition, provides high transparency and thus also high accountability that might be fundamental to clarify liabilities especially for critical services. Nevertheless, it is important to note that the message size increases linearly, which might be problematic for composite service that include a large number of individual services. Especially in this case, backwards validations might be expensive and raise performance issues. However, not every actor participating in a service compositions necessarily needs to perform a backwards validation, which only represents an additional security feature.

This work introduces a concept, which is able to fulfill the security objectives defined in Sect. 3.1. In our future work we will investigate the overall performance of the proposed concept by a comprehensive evaluation. The importance of the performance of security or safety-critical systems must not be neglected.

6   Related Work

Reliability in service executions has not been investigated intensively, although it represents a widely recognized aspect in service compositions. Most of the existing research only considers the availability or selection of a service on investigating reliability [22–24] and does not consider compromized services, which may compute a wrong output. Especially for security or safety-critical systems, correctness of a service output is a crucial requirement. Thus, we have investigated a lot of research that was conducted in the area of verifiable computing [20,21]. This approach aims on a remote execution of functions on untrusted servers and also enables a verification of the generated output. While verifiable computing offers means to outsource the computation of a function, it still requires an expensive pre-processing phase by the sender particularly in schemes, where the privacy of the input data must be preserved. Castro and Liskov [27] introduced a Byzantin fault-tolerant system, which provides proactive recovery. This work describes an asynchronous state-machine replication system is able to detect and respond to denial of service attacks and recovers faulty replicas proactively. While this work offers no privacy protection, the recovery mechanism only works, if the number of malicious replicas is below 1/3. To ensure correctness of services in distributed systems, intensive research was conducted in recent years on Paxos protocols [30–32], which aim to achieve a consensus in a network including unreliable or fallible processors. Our concept does not include a Paxos protocol, as Verifiable Secret Sharing enables the identification of incorrect results generated by participants in a distributed calculation. Viriyasitavat et al. [28] highlight benefits of consensus protocols for modern business process execution, particularly providing high safety and fault-tolerance. Distributed consensus ensures correctness of service executions and thus, collaborations among different organizations. Carminati et al. [10,25] proposes concepts for an inter-organizational and confidential process execution using the blockchain. These concepts rely on homomorphic encryption, which we did not include in our concept, because it is expensive and still suffers from various limitations [26].

7 Conclusion

In this paper, we have introduced a concept that guarantees high reliability, availability and a correct computation of service outputs for service composition systems, which include security or safety critical services. The combination of secure multiparty computation and threshold signatures enable a flexible adaptation of a required security level for a specific use-case. Additionally, this concept protects the privacy of input data of a critical function by secure multiparty computation. The proposed solution makes it possible to securely integrate services that pose an increased risk and potentially cause a system damage or harm an individual. The feasibility of this concept is demonstrated by a proof-of-concept implementation representing a telemedical alert service.

References

1. Papazoglou, M.P., Traverso, P., Dustdar, S., Leymann, F.: Service-oriented computing: state of the art and research challenges. In: IEEE Computer Society Press Los Alamitos, vol. 40, pp. 38–45 (2007)
2. Baum, C., Damgård, I., Orlandi, C.: Publicly auditable secure multi-party computation. In: Abdalla, M., De Prisco, R. (eds.) SCN 2014. LNCS, vol. 8642, pp. 175–196. Springer, Cham (2014). https://doi.org/10.1007/978-3-319-10879-7_11
3. Jung, C., Lee, S.J.: Design of automatic insulin injection system with Continuous Glucose Monitoring (CGM) signals, pp. 102–105 (2016)
4. Fokkink, W.: Introduction to Process Algebra. Springer, New York (2000). https://doi.org/10.1007/978-3-662-04293-9
5. Reisig, W.: Petri Nets: An Introduction. Springer, Heidelberg (2012). https://doi.org/10.1007/978-3-642-69968-9
6. Hopcroft, J.E., Motwani, R., Ullman, J.D.: Introduction to Automata Theory, Languages, and Computation. Adison Wesley Publishing Company, Boston (1979)
7. Campos, G.M.M., Rosa, N.S., Pires, L.F.: A survey of formalization approaches to service composition. In: IEEE International Conference on Services Computing (2014)

8. Viriyasitavat, W., Da Xu, L., Bi, Z., Sapsomboon, A.: Blockchain-based business process management (BPM) framework for service composition in industry 4.0. J. Intell. Manuf. **31**, 1737–1748 (2018). https://doi.org/10.1007/s10845-018-1422-y

9. Yu, C., Zhang, L., Zhao, W., Zhang, S.: A blockchain-based service composition architecture in cloud manufacturing. Int. J. Comput. Integr. Manuf. 1–11 (2019)

10. Carminati, B., Rondanini, C., Ferrari, E.: Confidential business process execution on blockchain. In: IEEE International Conference on Web Services (ICWS), pp. 58–65 (2018)

11. Song, X., Wang, Y.: Homomorphic cloud computing scheme based on hybrid homomorphic encryption. In: International Conference on Computer and Communications (2017)

12. Bogetoft, P., et al.: Secure multiparty computation goes live. In: Dingledine, R., Golle, P. (eds.) FC 2009. LNCS, vol. 5628, pp. 325–343. Springer, Heidelberg (2009). https://doi.org/10.1007/978-3-642-03549-4_20

13. Cramer, R., Damgard, I., Nielsen, J.P.: Secure Multiparty Computation and Secret Sharing. Cambridge University Press (2015). https://www.cambridge.org/de/academic/subjects/computer-science/cryptography-cryptology-and-coding/secure-multiparty-computation-and-secret-sharing?format=HB%5C&isbn=9781107043053

14. Genkin, D., Ishai, Y., Polychroniadou, A.: Efficient multi-party computation: from passive to active security via secure SIMD circuits. In: Gennaro, R., Robshaw, M. (eds.) CRYPTO 2015. LNCS, vol. 9216, pp. 721–741. Springer, Heidelberg (2015). https://doi.org/10.1007/978-3-662-48000-7_35

15. Chor, B., Kushilevitz, E.: Secret sharing over infinite domains. J. Cryptol. **6**(2), 87–95 (1993). https://doi.org/10.1007/BF02620136

16. Rabin, T., Ben-Or, M.: Verifiable secret sharing and multiparty protocols with honest majority (extended abstract). In: STOC 1989: Proceedings of the Twenty-First Annual ACM Symposium on Theory of Computing, pp. 73–85 (1989)

17. Patra, A., Choudhury, A., Rangan, P.C.: Efficient asynchronous verifiable secret sharing and multiparty computation. J. Cryptol. **28**, 49–109 (2015). https://doi.org/10.1007/s00145-013-9172-7

18. Wiener, F.: Threshold Signatures: Security for the Libra Digital Asset Era. Whitepaper (2019)

19. Stathakopoulou, C., Cachin, C.: Threshold Signatures for Blockchain Systems. IBM Computer Science Research Report (2017)

20. Demirel, D., Schabhueser, L., Buchmann, J.: Privately and Publicly Verifiable Computing Techniques. SpringerBriefs in Computer Science. Springer, Cham (2017). https://doi.org/10.1007/978-3-319-53798-6

21. Gennaro, R., Gentry, C., Parno, B.: Non-interactive verifiable computing: outsourcing computation to untrusted workers. In: Rabin, T. (ed.) CRYPTO 2010. LNCS, vol. 6223, pp. 465–482. Springer, Heidelberg (2010). https://doi.org/10.1007/978-3-642-14623-7_25

22. Gaaloul, W., Bhiri, S., Rouchached, M.: Event-based design and runtime verification of composite service transactional behavior. IEEE Trans. Serv. Comput. **3**, 32–45 (2010)

23. Hamel, L., Graiet, M., Gaaloul, W.: Event-B formalisation of web services for dynamic composition. In: International Conference on Semantics, Knowledge and Grids (2012)

24. Graiet, M., Abbassi, I., Hamel, L.: Event-B based approach for verifying dynamic composite service transactional behavior. In: IEEE 20th International Conference on Web Services (2013)

25. Carminati, B., Ferrari, E. Rondanini, C.: Blockchain as a platform for secure inter-organizational business processes. In: IEEE 4th International Conference on Collaboration and Internet Computing (2018)
26. Kogos, K.G., Filippova, K.S., Epishkina, A.V.: Fully homomorphic encryption schemes: the state of the art. In: IEEE Conference of Russian Young Researchers in Electrical and Electronic Engineering (EIConRus) (2017)
27. Castro, M., Liskov, B.: Proactive recovery in a Byzantine-fault-tolerant system. In: OSDI 2000: Proceedings of the 4th Conference on Symposium on Operating System Design & Implementation (2000)
28. Viriyasitavat, W., Hoonsopon, D.: Blockchain characteristics and consensus in modern business processes. J. Ind. Inf. Integr. **13**, 32–39 (2018)
29. Loruenser, T., Happe, A., Slamanig, D.: ARCHISTAR: towards secure and robust cloud based data sharing. In: IEEE Cloud Computing Technology and Science, CloudCom 2015, pp. 371–378 (2016)
30. Dang, H.T., Canini, M., Pedone, F., Soule, R.: Paxos Made Switch-y. In: ACM SIGCOMM Computer Communication Review, pp. 18–24 (2016)
31. Renesse, R.V., Altinbuken, D.: Paxos made moderately complex. In: ACM Computing Surveys (2015)
32. Padon, O., Losa, G., Sagiv, M., Shoham, S.: Paxos made EPR: decidable reasoning about distributed protocols. In: Proceedings of the ACM on Programming Languages (2017)

AI/ML in Security

A Defence Against Input-Agnostic Backdoor Attacks on Deep Neural Networks

Yansong Gao[1] and Surya Nepal[1,2]($\boxtimes$)

[1] Data61, CSIRO, Syndey, Australia
{garrison.gao,surya.nepal}@data61.csiro.au
[2] Cyber Security Cooperative Research Centre, Joondalup, Australia

Abstract. Backdoor attacks insert hidden associations or triggers to the deep neural network (DNN) models to override correct inference such as classification. Such attacks perform maliciously according to the attacker-chosen target while behaving normally in the absence of the trigger. These attacks, though new, are rapidly evolving as a realistic attack, and could result in severe consequences, especially considering that backdoor attacks can be inserted in variety of real-world applications. This paper first provides a brief overview of backdoor attacks and then presents a countermeasure, STRong Intentional Perturbation (STRIP). STRIP intentionally perturbs the incoming input, for instance by superimposing various image patterns, and observes the randomness of predicted classes for perturbed inputs from a given deployed model – malicious or benign. STRIP fundamentally relies on the entropy in predicted classes; for example, a low entropy violates the input-dependence property of a benign model and implies the presence of a malicious input. We demonstrate the effectiveness of our method through experiments on two public datasets, MNIST and CIFAR10.

Keywords: Backdoor attack · Backdoor countermeasure · Deep learning · Adversarial attack

1 Introduction

Deep learning, in particular those builds upon deep neural network (DNN), has achieved superior performance in a wide range of real-world applications such as computer vision, speech recognition, natural language processing [26,41,45]. While it is undeniable that the DNN models are 'smart', they have also shown to be 'fragile' in front of adversarial attacks. The adversarial example has been extensively studied to fool the DNN model [17]. Herein, an imperceptible or semantically consistent manipulation of inputs, that could be image, text or audio, can make DNN models to make attacker-intended decisions [17].

Recently, a new security threat, called backdoor attacks, on DNN model has been revealed [18]. The backdoored model behaves correctly for normal inputs

© Springer Nature Switzerland AG 2020
S. Kanhere et al. (Eds.): ICISS 2020, LNCS 12553, pp. 69–80, 2020.
https://doi.org/10.1007/978-3-030-65610-2_4

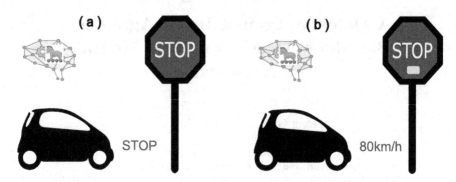

Fig. 1. (a) The backdoored model makes stop decision when seeing STOP traffic sign in normal cases. (b) The backdoored model makes decision of 'speed with 80 km/h' when seeing STOP traffic sign stamped with a trigger that is a yellow color post-it-note.

but misbehaves once the input contains a trigger. Such a trigger fires the backdoor to hijack the model, making a wrong decision [7,12,18,30]. Figure 1 illustrates the effect of a backdoor attack on the model's decision. As shown in the figure, the backdoored traffic recognition model can correctly make a stop decision when encountering the stop traffic sign in normal cases. However, the model misbehaves when the stop traffic sign is stamped with the attacker-set trigger—here, the post-it-note in yellow colour. The backdoored model is hijacked to make a decision of 'speed of 80 km/h' instead of "stop" [18]. Such a backdoor attack could cause dire or catastrophic consequences, especially in security-critical scenarios such as security surveillance, self-driving car and medical diagnosis.

The backdoored model is infeasible to be detected by simply checking the testing accuracy with held-out validation dataset. The backdoor attack is stealthy because it has a similar testing accuracy to that of a clean model whenever the secret backdoor trigger is absent. Besides, it is impossible to guess what the trigger looks like, and where it is placed. An attacker can arbitrarily choose the trigger and its position. Even worse, there are many means of implanting a backdoor into the DNN model, which will be discussed in the next section.

This article first provides an overview of when and how backdoor attacks can be inserted in real-world scenarios. We then present a simple but effective defense against the input-agnostic backdoor attacks, called STRIP, which detects trigger inputs online when the DNN model is deployed. Such a defense can be plugged with any DNN models.

2   Backdoor Attacks

There are several phases in building and using the DNN models. The backdoor can be inserted exploiting the vulnerabilities existed in those phases. For example, the attacker can manipulate or poison the data used to train the model to insert a backdoor. The attacker can also tamper the model directly to inject backdoor. In real-world scenarios, the backdoor attacks can occur when (a) the model is outsourced [18], (b) the model is trained over a pre-trained model [23], (c) the model is trained with collaborative learning techniques [3], and (d) the model is trained with data collected from untrusted parties [38]. We next describe how the backdoor is introduced under each of these scenarios.

Outsourcing. Many model users opt for outsourcing the DNN model training to a third-party [18]. Some of the reasons to use third-party services include users not having in-house machine learning (ML) expertise or lack of availability of computational resources internally. For example, training a 50 layer residual network [20] (ResNet-50) on the ImageNet-1K dataset takes around 10 days using an NVIDIA P100 GPU card. Training a larger ResNet-152 in the same setting would take roughly more than 3 weeks. It would take roughly one year to train a ResNet-152 model using the full ImageNet-22K dataset, which is about one order of magnitude larger than ImageNet-1K (around 14 million images split across 21841 different image categories) [8]. Besides, users could also rent a cloud server to increase available computational resources and train their model on the cloud server, which is usually referred to as Machine Learning as a Service (MLaaS) [36]. However, users cannot fully trust both third-party and cloud service providers because they can access the training process and insert a backdoor.

The outsourcing attack scenario is the most straightforward to implant a backdoor attack. Early backdoor attacks are performed under this threat model [7,18]. The most adopted attack technique is to change the label of a small fraction of training sample x to the targeted label c_t to create poisoned data points $x^a = x + t$, where each data point x^a is stamped with an attacker-chosen secret trigger t. Once the model is trained over the collection of the poisoned data and normal data, the backdoored model f_{bd} will have an association between the presence of the trigger and the targeted class. Therefore, given any input with the trigger, the backdoored model f_{bd} will classify the input to the attacker-targeted class c_t, accomplishing the backdoor attack effect set by the attacker. However, the backdoored model f_{bd} still correctly recognizes any input x, in the absence of the trigger, to its corresponding normal class c. Such a backdoor attack thus cannot be detected by simply checking the test accuracy, e.g., via held-out test dataset.

It is not unexpected that under such an attack setting, the attack success rate (ASR) is very high, e.g., could be as high as 100%. Because the attacker has full control of the training process, Also, given the control over the training process, the attacker can take the evasion-of-the-defense objectives into the loss function to adaptively bypass existing countermeasures [2,3,9,40].

Pretrained. There are many pretrained models publicly available, e.g., from the model zoo [29]. These pretrained models have been trained on a large dataset and have complex model architectures. For example, the model has more than hundred convolutional layers to gain enhanced performance, such as ResNet-152 [20].

The model user may customize their model through transfer learning [23]. Transfer learning is a common practice to obtain a down-stream model with limited data. It also significantly reduces the computational cost. There is two impetus behind using transfer learning. Firstly, it may not be realistic to acquire a huge amount of data, given the data collection is expensive in many cases. For example, the data usually needs to be labelled to fit supervised learning; such a labelling process could entail high cost and even require domain expertise, e.g., medical image, malware [42]. Secondly, transfer learning also reduces the computational cost because the customized model does not need to be trained from scratch. Essentially, the pretrained model functions as a feature extractor.

The attacker can insert a backdoor into the pretrained model. The downstream model builds upon such a pretrained model will be affected. In other words, the backdoor could be inherited by the down-stream model [22,23,29,37, 48]. Generally, the pretrained attack impacts a broad set of victims as employing a pretrained model to customize the user's downstream task is now recognized as a good practice. Besides vision tasks, such attacks have also been demonstrated to affect natural language processing models [25,37]. However, the attacker usually has limited control over the downstream user tasks and with limited knowledge of the transfer learning strategies adopted by the user. For example, after the user replaces the dense layers, she/he can opt to retain the convolutional layers completely or fine-tune it, which results in two different transfer learning strategies [48]. Due to these limitations, the ASR for such an attack is usually not as high as backdoor attacks introduced by outsourcing. The ASR may be easily disrupted in certain attacks, e.g., the latent backdoor [48] where the transfer learning strategy deployed is fine-tuning the early convolutional layers. It is worthwhile to mention that the pretrained backdoor attack, more or less, needs to have some knowledge of the downstream tasks and a small set of data for the downstream tasks—though such data may be easily available from the public sources.

Data Collection. The DNN model needs a large volume of data to achieve high accuracy. The data generation is expensive if this is done in-house by the model users. Hence, there is a practice to curate data from public or multiple sources. For instances, some popular and publicly available dataset essentially depend on data contributed from individual volunteers [11,32]. Some datasets are crawled data from the Internet, e.g., ImageNet [10]. For example, the OpenAI trains a GPT-2 model on all webpages where at least three users on Reddit have interacted [35].

However, data collection is usually error-prone and susceptible to untrusted sources [21]. If the data contributors are malicious, the collected data could be already poisoned. Manual checking of the collected data appears unrealistic; hence, the poisoned data can be hardly detected and removed before it is used to train the model. In addition, the poisoned data can be tampered in a way that the content is visually, e.g., for images, consistent with the label to evade strict integrity check. For example, clean-label poisoning attacks [38,50] and image-scaling poisoning attacks [34,46] lie under such poison strategies to maintain the consistency between the contents and corresponding labels. Such data poisoning attacks keep consistency between labels and data values, thus bypassing manual or visual inspections. As a consequence, the backdoor can be inserted when the model is trained over those poisoned data.

The data collection attack can impact a wide range of users or victims as discussed above. As a consequence, not only the end-to-end trained model but also the transfer learning could be infected. Feature collision is a common mean of crafting label-consistent poisonous inputs to inject backdoors. However, in some cases, some knowledge of the infected model architecture is needed to determine a proper latent representation. Therefore, the label-consistent attack to poison data may require a specific understanding of the downstream tasks. From the attacker perspective, to ensure the stealthiness, he/she needs to keep the poisonous data rate as small as possible, because the defender now is assumed to have access to the poisoned data for carrying out detection.

Collaborative Learning. In many cases, the data is very sensitive, and there is a privacy concern if the data is aggregated into a centralized server. Hence, such a centralised solution does not work and remains undesirable. In this context, collaborative learning is attractive to train a joint model by harnessing data from participants without direct access to the local data. This greatly eliminates the privacy concern from the participants. Federated learning and split learning are two popular collaborative or distributed learning techniques [1,3,13,43,49]. Collaborative learning has been employed in commercial environments to enhance privacy preservation. For example, Google trains word prediction models from localised data on users' phone [19].

However, as the data is obscured and not allowed to be accessed, collaborative learning is vulnerable to various attacks [5] that include the backdoor attack. Even when a small fraction of participants are malicious or compromised by the attacker, the joint model can be infected by a backdoor because both localized data and local model uploaded to the server could be easily manipulated [3,4,33,39]. From a similar perspective, we can also think that the privacy-preserving DNN learning frameworks, in particular, using data encryption such as CryptoNet [16], SecureML [31] and CryptoNN [47] are indeed susceptible to backdoor attacks. These frameworks aim to train the model over encrypted data in order to preserve data privacy. Such a situation, in particular, arises in the cases where the data are contributed from different clients, and it is impossible to check whether the data has been poisoned for implanting backdoor attack.

As a matter of fact, defending backdoor attacks under collaborative learning is more challenging because training data is not allowed to be accessed by the defender, including the server or the model aggregator. However, most backdoor countermeasures do require a (small) set of held-out validation samples to assist the backdoor detection.

3   A Plug-In Backdoor Defense: STRIP

Considering the potential dire consequence caused by backdoor attacks on DNN models, we have observed that significant efforts have been invested in developing countermeasures [6,28,44]. However, a one-to-all defense is yet an open research challenge. Each countermeasure has strengths and limitations. Generally, most countermeasures are specifically designed for image classifications, i.e., the countermeasures are usually domain-specific. In addition, most countermeasures focus on the input-agnostic backdoor attacks, where the backdoor effect solely depends on the presence of the trigger. Furthermore, most countermeasures require certain ML expertise or/and computational resources, which somehow is less attractive in some application scenarios such as outsourcing and usage of pretrained model. We refer interesting readers to [12] for a detailed analysis and comparison of countermeasures. This paper details a simple yet efficient defense against input-agnostic backdoor attacks, which is also generic to different domain tasks.

3.1   Overview

In this paper, we use an image classification task in computer vision to explain our proposed defense technique, called STRIP. It can be easily extended to text and audio domain; we refer readers to [14] for further details. STRIP [15] exploits the input-agnostic characteristic of the trigger, which is essentially regarded as the main strength of input-agnostic backdoor attacks. In essence, we turn the attacker's strength—ability to set up a robust and effective input-agnostic trigger—into an asset for the defender to counter against the backdoor attack. In essence, predictions of perturbed trigger inputs are invariant to different perturbing patterns, whereas predictions of perturbed normal inputs vary greatly. In this context, we introduce an entropy measure to quantify the prediction randomness. We hypothesis that a trigger input always exhibits low entropy, and a clean input consistently exhibits high entropy.

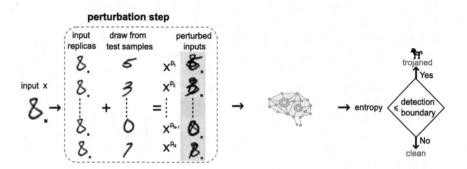

Fig. 2. Run-time STRIP backdoor attack detection system overview [15].

The STRIP backdoor detection system is depicted in Fig. 2. It follows the following steps:

1. The perturbation step generates N perturbed inputs $\{x^{p_1}, \ldots\ldots, x^{p_N}\}$ corresponding to **one** given incoming input x. Specifically, each perturbed input is a superimposed image of both the input x (replica) and an image randomly drawn from the user held-out dataset, $\mathcal{D}_{\text{test}}$.
2. All the perturbed inputs along with x itself are concurrently fed into the deployed DNN model, $f(x_i)$. According to the input x, the DNN model predicts its label. At the same time, the DNN model determines whether the input x is trigger input or not based on the observation on predicted classes to all N perturbed inputs $\{x^{p_1}, \ldots\ldots, x^{p_N}\}$ that forms a perturbation set $\mathcal{D}_p$.

In particular, the randomness—quantified by entropy—of the predicted classes is used to facilitate the judgment on whether the input is adversarial or not. The entropy is defined as:

$$\mathbb{H}_n = -\frac{1}{N} \sum_{n=1}^{n=N} \sum_{i=1}^{i=M} y_i \times \log_2 y_i \tag{1}$$

where y_i is the probability of being predicted as the i_{th} class. There are M classes. N is the number of perturbed samples and $\frac{1}{N}$ is used for normalization.

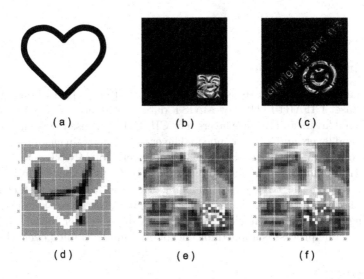

Fig. 3. Triggers (top) used for experimental validations. Bottom row shows the trigger stamped input samples.

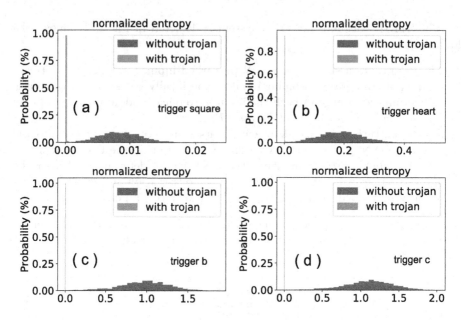

Fig. 4. Entropy distribution of normal and trigger inputs. The trigger input shows a small entropy, which can be winnowed given a proper detection boundary (threshold). Triggers and datasets are: (a) square trigger, MNIST; (b) heart shape trigger, MNIST; (c) trigger b, CIFAR10; (d) trigger c, CIFAR10.

3.2   Results

3.3   Experimental Setup

We use hand-written digit recognition dataset MNIST [27] and image classification dataset CIFAR10 [24]. For MNIST dataset, the used DNN model has 2 convolutional layers and 2 dense layers. For CIFAR10, the used DNN model has 8 convolutional layers and 2 fully connected layers. We first train clean model showing the accuracy of 98.62% and 88.27%, respectively, for MNIST and CIFAR10. Then we train backdoored models by poisoning 10% of training samples, in particular, stamping the trigger and changing the label to the target class. For MNIST, the backdoored model has 98.86% accuracy for normal inputs, which is indistinguishable from the clean model. Its ASR on trigger inputs is close to 100%. The same process is applied for backdoored model trained over CIFAR10.

3.4   MNIST

For MNIST dataset, the square trigger and heart trigger (Fig. 3(a)) are used, where the square trigger is a 3 × 3 black pixels localized at the bottom-right corner that is used in [18,44]. The former stands for small trigger size, while the latter stands for large trigger size to show that STRIP is independent on the trigger size.

Here, 2000 normal digit images and 2000 trigger images are tested. Given each incoming image x, $N = 100$ different images randomly drawn from the held-out samples are linearly blended with x to generate $N = 100$ perturbed images. Then an entropy of input x is calculated according to Eq. 1. The entropy distribution of tested 2000 normal and 2000 trigger digit images are detailed in Fig. 4(a) (with the square trigger) and Fig. 4(b) (with the heart trigger). We can see that there a gap between the normal input entropy distribution and the trigger input entropy distribution. In other words, the entropy of a normal input is always large, while the trigger input is much small. Thus, the trigger input can be easily differentiated.

3.5   CIFAR10

For CIFAR10 dataset, triggers shown in Fig. 3(b) and (c) are used (referred to as trigger b and c hereafter.). Note that the former is a small trigger size, while the later is a large trigger size. We also tested 2000 benign and trojaned input images, respectively. The entropy distribution of tested 2000 benign and 2000 trigger input images are detailed in Fig. 4(c) (with trigger b) and Fig. 4(d) (with trigger c), respectively. We can see that the entropy of benign input is always large, while the entropy of the trojaned input is always small.

3.6   Discussion

In practice, the entropy distribution of the normal inputs can be determined offline. Then, the user can choose a threshold, where for example 99% normal input entropy is larger than this threshold. This equally means that there will be a preset false rejection rate—falsely reject normal inputs as trigger input—of 1% as an acceptable trade-off. During the online detection phase, the input with entropy lower than the threshold will be detected as trigger input and rejected, thus defeating the backdoor attack.

STRIP is not limited for vision domain that is the focus of the work presented here. It is also applicable to text and speech domains. In those domains, instead of linear image blend used in this work, other perturbing methodologies need be considered. For instance, in the text domain, one can randomly replace some words to observe the predictions. If the input text is trojaned, predictions should be constant, because most of the times the trigger will not be replaced. For speech recognition, two audio samples can be added, similar to the image perturbation, to form perturbing replicas. Details of STRIP on text and audio domains can be found in [14].

4   Conclusion

This paper has provided an overview of backdoor attacks on DNN models. We explain four practical scenarios that could be exploited by attackers to insert backdoors to demonstrate that the backdoor is a realistic security threat. We then introduce an easy-to-deploy defense, namely STRIP, that is efficacious against input-agnostic backdoor attacks.

References

1. Abuadbba, S., et al.: Can we use split learning on 1D CNN models for privacy preserving training? In: The 15th ACM ASIA Conference on Computer and Communications Security (AsiaCCS) (2020)
2. Bagdasaryan, E., Shmatikov, V.: Blind backdoors in deep learning models. arXiv preprint arXiv:2005.03823 (2020)
3. Bagdasaryan, E., Veit, A., Hua, Y., Estrin, D., Shmatikov, V.: How to backdoor federated learning. In: International Conference on Artificial Intelligence and Statistics (AISTATS), pp. 2938–2948 (2020). https://github.com/ebagdasa/backdoor_federated_learning
4. Bhagoji, A.N., Chakraborty, S., Mittal, P., Calo, S.: Analyzing federated learning through an adversarial lens. In: International Conference on Machine Learning (ICML), pp. 634–643 (2019)
5. Bonawitz, K., et al.: Towards federated learning at scale: system design. arXiv preprint arXiv:1902.01046 (2019)
6. Chen, H., Fu, C., Zhao, J., Koushanfar, F.: DeepInspect: a black-box Trojan detection and mitigation framework for deep neural networks. In: International Joint Conference on Artificial Intelligence, pp. 4658–4664 (2019)
7. Chen, X., Liu, C., Li, B., Lu, K., Song, D.: Targeted backdoor attacks on deep learning systems using data poisoning. arXiv preprint arXiv:1712.05526 (2017)
8. Codreanu, V., Podareanu, D., Saletore, V.: Scale out for large minibatch SGD: residual network training on Imagenet-1k with improved accuracy and reduced time to train. arXiv preprint arXiv:1711.04291 (2017)
9. Costales, R., Mao, C., Norwitz, R., Kim, B., Yang, J.: Live Trojan attacks on deep neural networks. arXiv preprint arXiv:2004.11370 (2020). https://github.com/robbycostales/live-trojans
10. Deng, J., Dong, W., Socher, R., Li, L.J., Li, K., Fei-Fei, L.: ImageNet: a large-scale hierarchical image database. In: 2009 IEEE Conference on Computer Vision and Pattern Recognition, pp. 248–255. IEEE (2009)
11. Freesound: Freesound dataset. https://annotator.freesound.org/. Accessed 14 July 2020
12. Gao, Y., et al.: Backdoor attacks and countermeasures on deep learning: a comprehensive review. arXiv preprint arXiv:2007.10760 (2020)
13. Gao, Y., et al.: End-to-end evaluation of federated learning and split learning for Internet of Things. In: The 39th International Symposium on Reliable Distributed Systems (SRDS) (2020)
14. Gao, Y., et al.: Design and evaluation of a multi-domain Trojan detection method on deep neural networks. arXiv preprint arXiv:1911.10312 (2019)
15. Gao, Y., Xu, C., Wang, D., Chen, S., Ranasinghe, D.C., Nepal, S.: STRIP: a defence against Trojan attacks on deep neural networks. In: Proceedings of the Annual Computer Security Applications Conference (ACSA), pp. 113–125 (2019). https://github.com/garrisongys/STRIP
16. Gilad-Bachrach, R., Dowlin, N., Laine, K., Lauter, K., Naehrig, M., Wernsing, J.: CryptoNets: applying neural networks to encrypted data with high throughput and accuracy. In: International Conference on Machine Learning, pp. 201–210 (2016)
17. Goodfellow, I.J., Shlens, J., Szegedy, C.: Explaining and harnessing adversarial examples. arXiv preprint arXiv:1412.6572 (2014)
18. Gu, T., Dolan-Gavitt, B., Garg, S.: BadNets: identifying vulnerabilities in the machine learning model supply chain. arXiv preprint arXiv:1708.06733 (2017)

19. Hard, A., et al.: Federated learning for mobile keyboard prediction. arXiv preprint arXiv:1811.03604 (2018)
20. He, K., Zhang, X., Ren, S., Sun, J.: Deep residual learning for image recognition. In: Proceedings of the IEEE Conference on Computer Vision and Pattern Recognition (CVPR), pp. 770–778 (2016)
21. Jagielski, M., Severi, G., Harger, N.P., Oprea, A.: Subpopulation data poisoning attacks. arXiv preprint arXiv:2006.14026 (2020)
22. Ji, Y., Liu, Z., Hu, X., Wang, P., Zhang, Y.: Programmable neural network Trojan for pre-trained feature extractor. arXiv preprint arXiv:1901.07766 (2019)
23. Ji, Y., Zhang, X., Ji, S., Luo, X., Wang, T.: Model-reuse attacks on deep learning systems. In: Proceedings of the ACM SIGSAC Conference on Computer and Communications Security (CCS), pp. 349–363. ACM (2018)
24. Krizhevsky, A., Hinton, G.: Learning multiple layers of features from tiny images. Technical report. Citeseer (2009)
25. Kurita, K., Michel, P., Neubig, G.: Weight poisoning attacks on pre-trained models. arXiv preprint arXiv:2004.06660 (2020). https://github.com/neulab/RIPPLe
26. LeCun, Y., Bengio, Y., Hinton, G.: Deep learning. Nature **521**(7553), 436 (2015)
27. LeCun, Y., Bottou, L., Bengio, Y., Haffner, P.: Gradient-based learning applied to document recognition. Proc. IEEE **86**(11), 2278–2324 (1998)
28. Liu, Y., Lee, W.C., Tao, G., Ma, S., Aafer, Y., Zhang, X.: ABS: scanning neural networks for back-doors by artificial brain stimulation. In: The ACM Conference on Computer and Communications Security (CCS) (2019)
29. Liu, Y., et al.: Trojaning attack on neural networks. In: Network and Distributed System Security Symposium (NDSS) (2018)
30. Liu, Y., Xie, Y., Srivastava, A.: Neural Trojans. In: 2017 IEEE International Conference on Computer Design (ICCD), pp. 45–48. IEEE (2017)
31. Mohassel, P., Zhang, Y.: SecureML: a system for scalable privacy-preserving machine learning. In: 2017 IEEE Symposium on Security and Privacy (SP), pp. 19–38. IEEE (2017)
32. Mozilla: Common voice dataset. https://voice.mozilla.org/cnh/datasets. Accessed 14 July 2020
33. Nguyen, T.D., Rieger, P., Miettinen, M., Sadeghi, A.R.: Poisoning attacks on federated learning-based IoT intrusion detection system. In: NDSS Workshop on Decentralized IoT Systems and Security (2020)
34. Quiring, E., Rieck, K.: Backdooring and poisoning neural networks with image-scaling attacks. arXiv preprint arXiv:2003.08633 (2020). https://scaling-attacks.net/
35. Radford, A., Wu, J., Child, R., Luan, D., Amodei, D., Sutskever, I.: Language models are unsupervised multitask learners. OpenAI Blog **1**(8), 9 (2019)
36. Ribeiro, M., Grolinger, K., Capretz, M.A.: MLaaS: machine learning as a service. In: 2015 IEEE 14th International Conference on Machine Learning and Applications (ICMLA), pp. 896–902. IEEE (2015)
37. Schuster, R., Schuster, T., Meri, Y., Shmatikov, V.: Humpty dumpty: controlling word meanings via corpus poisoning. In: IEEE Symposium on Security and Privacy (SP) (2020)
38. Shafahi, A., et al.: Poison frogs! Targeted clean-label poisoning attacks on neural networks. In: Advances in Neural Information Processing Systems (NIPS), pp. 6103–6113 (2018). https://github.com/ashafahi/inceptionv3-transferLearn-poison
39. Sun, Z., Kairouz, P., Suresh, A.T., McMahan, H.B.: Can you really backdoor federated learning? arXiv preprint arXiv:1911.07963 (2019)

40. Tan, T.J.L., Shokri, R.: Bypassing backdoor detection algorithms in deep learning. In: IEEE European Symposium on Security and Privacy (EuroS&P) (2020)
41. Tang, T.A., Mhamdi, L., McLernon, D., Zaidi, S.A.R., Ghogho, M.: Deep learning approach for network intrusion detection in software defined networking. In: International Conference on Wireless Networks and Mobile Communications (WIN-COM), pp. 258–263. IEEE (2016)
42. Veldanda, A.K., et al.: NNoculation: broad spectrum and targeted treatment of backdoored DNNs. arXiv preprint arXiv:2002.08313 (2020). https://github.com/akshajkumarv/NNoculation
43. Vepakomma, P., Gupta, O., Swedish, T., Raskar, R.: Split learning for health: distributed deep learning without sharing raw patient data. arXiv preprint arXiv:1812.00564 (2018)
44. Wang, B., et al.: Neural cleanse: identifying and mitigating backdoor attacks in neural networks. In: Proceedings of the IEEE Symposium on Security and Privacy (SP) (2019). https://github.com/bolunwang/backdoor
45. Wang, Q., et al.: Adversary resistant deep neural networks with an application to malware detection. In: Proceedings of the ACM SIGKDD International Conference on Knowledge Discovery and Data Mining (SIGKDD), pp. 1145–1153. ACM (2017)
46. Xiao, Q., Chen, Y., Shen, C., Chen, Y., Li, K.: Seeing is not believing: camouflage attacks on image scaling algorithms. In: {USENIX} Security Symposium ({USENIX} Security 19), pp. 443–460 (2019). https://github.com/yfchen1994/scaling_camouflage
47. Xu, R., Joshi, J.B., Li, C.: CryptoNN: training neural networks over encrypted data. In: 2019 IEEE 39th International Conference on Distributed Computing Systems (ICDCS), pp. 1199–1209. IEEE (2019)
48. Yao, Y., Li, H., Zheng, H., Zhao, B.Y.: Latent backdoor attacks on deep neural networks. In: Proceedings of the 2019 ACM SIGSAC Conference on Computer and Communications Security (CCS), pp. 2041–2055 (2019)
49. Zhou, C., Fu, A., Yu, S., Yang, W., Wang, H., Zhang, Y.: Privacy-preserving federated learning in fog computing. IEEE Internet Things J. **7**, 10782–10793 (2020)
50. Zhu, C., et al.: Transferable clean-label poisoning attacks on deep neural nets. In: International Conference on Learning Representations (ICLR) (2019). https://github.com/zhuchen03/ConvexPolytopePosioning

An Overview of Cyber Threat Intelligence Platform and Role of Artificial Intelligence and Machine Learning

Abir Dutta[✉] and Shri Kant[✉]

Research and Technology Development Center, Sharda University, Noida, UP, India
abir_wbsetcl@yahoo.com, shrikant.ojha@gmail.com

Abstract. Ever enhancing computational capability of digital system along with upgraded tactics, technology and procedure (TTPs) enforced by the cybercriminals, does not match to the conventional security mechanism for detection of intrusion and prevention of threat in current cyber security landscape. Integration of artificial intelligence, machine learning and cyber threat intelligence platform with the signature-based threat detection models like intrusion detection system (IDS), SNORT, security information and event management (SIEM) which are being primarily implemented in the network for continuous analysis of the indicator of compromise (IoC) becomes inevitable, for prompt identification of true events and subsequent mitigation of the threat. In this paper, author illustrated the approach to integrate artificial intelligence and machine learning with the cyber threat intelligence for the collection of actionable threat intelligence from various sources like dark web, hacker's forum, hacker's assets, honeypot, etc. Furthermore, the application of threat intelligence in the aspect of cyber security has been discussed in this paper. Finally, a model has been proposed for generating actionable threat intelligence implementing a supervised machine learning approach employing Naïve Bayes classifier.

Keywords: Cyber threat intelligence · Artificial intelligence · Machine learning · Cyber security · Threat

1 Introduction

According to the recent survey of IT Governance of UK, around 6 billion data security breach has been recorded in the first quarter of 2020 and in the recent COVID-19 pandemic outburst this figure is boosting significantly due to espousing of "work from home" model by the organizations without implementing sufficient counter measures to deceive the attacks. Threat changes its nature of function and the structure very frequently in the domain of cyber security and advanced attack technique such as advanced persistent threats (combining both "multi-vector" and "multi-staged"), are adopted by the cyber criminals to attack the victim continuously in order to infiltrate the network and remains undetected for a period of time and finally filtrate out the targeted information without causing mutilation of the network. However, integration of artificial

© Springer Nature Switzerland AG 2020
S. Kanhere et al. (Eds.): ICISS 2020, LNCS 12553, pp. 81–86, 2020.
https://doi.org/10.1007/978-3-030-65610-2_5

intelligence, machine learning and deep leaning with cyber threat intelligence generates an automated framework to extract intelligence from various sources and blending this actionable threat intelligence to existing security mechanism to perform quickly, accurately, effectively and efficiently.

Residue of this paper is structured as follows. Section 2 specify the survey of present cyber threat intelligence status, Sect. 3 demonstrates the GAP identified in the literature review, Sect. 4 describes the Role of AI, ML and DL in cyber threat intelligence, while Sect. 5 illustrate author's proposal for implementation of AI and ML in cyber threat intelligence platform, Sect. 6 represents the future scope of work and finally, Sect. 7 provides the conclusion of the research.

2   Overview of Cyber Threat Intelligence

Several definitions of cyber threat intelligence have been exposition across the literature. However, the most comprehensive definition of CTI is "cyber threat intelligence is any evidence-based knowledge about threats that can inform decisions, with the aim of preventing an attack or shortening the window between compromise and detection".

Radical shift of attack technology placed the traditional signature based threat detection model into severe challenging position, which generates the necessity of combining of cyber threat intelligence platform and existing communication methodology. Jorge Buzzio Garcí et al. 2019 focuses on implementation of actionable threat data feed collected from CTI to enhance the software defined networks (SDN) security. Threat Intelligence are gathered by commissioning collective intelligence framework (CIF version 3) which receives "feed" type from internal or external sources of known attacks and CIF primarily stored the information like IP addresses, domains and URLs, of suspected activities and elaborate the way of preventing malicious traffic using physical testbed consisting of five components such as CIF server, SDN controller and application, OpenFlow switch and hosts.

In cyber threat intelligence platform STIX format has been extended [1] to facilitate the interpretation of critical patterns. Extension of STIX allows marking the feature of an object and these features represents relationship among various objects.

3   GAP Identified

Scope of experiment is still expected in this domain such as- manual labelling of information is error prone and time consuming activity that can be replaced by providing an automated window to upload the relevant intelligence [2], so that the portal will automatically sense the threat intelligence and tag appropriate information to minimize the effort of incident responder and extract the optimal combat mechanism. Furthermore, developing a multi-layer cyber threat intelligence ontology can be explored in future studies. Multilayer CTI ontology can be constructed by explaining formal definition and lexicon; inclusion of abstract layer of CTI in the ontology, constraints must be exposition properly to facilitate underlying Web Ontology Language (OWL) with the analytical capabilities.

4 Role of AI and ML in CTI Platform

Integration of machine learning in cyber security domain helps to build a superior and reliable model [3–7] pertaining to the malware detection, spam classification and network intrusion identification. Implementation of artificial intelligence at various phase of cyber threat intelligence like tactical intelligence and operational intelligence describe that, tactical threat intelligence is suitable for "Multi-Agent" system where as operational CTI is applicable for "Recurrent Neural Network".

To transform the overwhelming threat intelligence generated by structured and unstructured sources to actionable data feed is an utmost crucial aspect of CTI perspective. At the same time eradication of spurious threat intelligence is also expected for building an effective and accurate intelligence platform.

5 Proposed Model for Using AI and ML with Cyber Threat Intelligence Domain

5.1 Outline of the Proposed Model

In this section we proposed a machine learning approach to extract actionable threat intelligence from various sources. Phases of the model generation is depicted in Fig. 1.

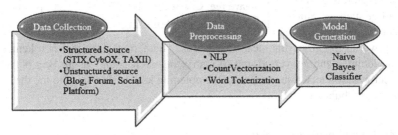

Fig. 1. Depicts various phases of proposed architecture

5.2 Data Accumulation

Cyber threat intelligence is generated from various sources like structured sources (STIX, CybOX, TAXII) as well as from unstructured sources (hacker's forum, Blog, blacklists). In this experiment we have collected latest CVE entries of 2020 and CWE list v4.1 along with malware dataset and Goodware dataset from 'kaggle' web portal to construct our dataset. In CVE list, entries are in.xml format and we have filtered the "title' and "description" attributes merely under the 'vulnerability" tag by using ElementTree XML API of python discarding all other attributes like header, references etc. from the intended dataset and converted the extracted information of CVE list into CSV format. In addition to that we have downloaded the latest CWE list version 4.1 in and extracted the "description" attribute from the CWE list. Furthermore, we have collected few malware description as well as few benign descriptions from 'kaggle' web portal to construct our final dataset in CSV format with approximately 1100 dataset.

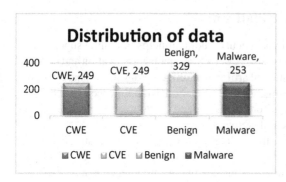

Finally, extracted attribute is labelled as- 1 for the sentiment related to the vulnerability, weakness or malware and 0 for the sentiment related to the benign posts in order to prepare the preprocessed dataset for implementation of ML classifier.

5.3 Feature Extraction and Language Processing

Collected information is in text format which required conversion to the suitable data format for the acceptance of ML Algorithm. Natural language processing approach is employed on the raw dataset such as remove duplicate word, punctuation

Keywords	Category
denialofservice, exploitation, Out-of-bounds, unauthenticated, memory corruption, privilege, destroywindow , Uncontrolled, vulnerability, firmware,	Threat
ReadFile, Sleep, GetSystemDirectoryW, HeapFree, CreateDirectoryW, CopyFileW, FindClose	Non-threat

and stop words to extract the clean text words. Thereafter, clean text is tokenized to form the lemmas and converted text to matrix of token counts using Bag of Words, count vectorization technique to extract the potential keywords related to the threat and non-threat as tabulated here.

5.4 Machine Learning Classifier

Several algorithms are there for natural language processing and text analysis; deep learning classifiers such as CNN, RNN are suitable for text analysis. In this experiment we have adopted Naïve-Bayes classifier for extracting high level threat intelligence from the dataset, considering 70% data for training dataset and 30% data for test dataset. Naïve Bayes algorithm is used for classification problem specially for text classification. In this model one feature is independent of existence of another feature i.e. each feature contributes to the prediction without having correlation. Text vector is the data feed for this model to train the model, followed by testing the model to evaluate the performance of the model and finally, predict true events (malware or threat) for unknown data.

5.5 Performance of the Proposed Model

We have evaluated different performance metrics such as accuracy, precision and f1-score of the model against the training as well as test dataset using Naïve Bayes classifier and accuracy of the model reflects as 98.2% and 96.6% for the training dataset and test dataset respectively as furnished below

- Accuracy of the model for training dataset

```
              precision    recall  f1-score

           0       1.00      0.94      0.97
           1       0.98      1.00      0.99

    accuracy                           0.98
   macro avg       0.99      0.97      0.98
weighted avg       0.98      0.98      0.98

Confusion Matrix:
[[210  13]
 [  0 535]]
Accuracy NB Train Dataset:
0.9828496042216359
```

- Accuracy of the model for test dataset

```
              precision    recall  f1-score

           0       1.00      0.90      0.95
           1       0.95      1.00      0.98

    accuracy                           0.97
   macro avg       0.98      0.95      0.96
weighted avg       0.97      0.97      0.97

Confusion Matrix:
[[ 97  11]
 [  0 217]]
Accuracy NB Test Dataset:
0.9661538461538461
```

6 Future Scope of the Proposed Model

Although, the proposed model illustrated in the earlier section is based on the Naïve Bayes classifier, an identical experiment may be carried out in future by employing recurrent neural network (RNN) of deep learning methodology in order to measure the prediction accuracy level of the alternately developed model and subsequently a comparison may be drawn on the different evaluation metrics. Moreover, Scope of this model can be extended to design an automated framework that will interact the underlying standards dictionary in sustainable fashion to retrain the model in continuous mode at the same time integrate the intelligence with the signature based security mechanism seamlessly to arrest the zero-day vulnerability of security architecture.

7 Conclusion

Rapid evolving of security realm in cyberspace compelled IoC to change its nature significantly. In this research we have identified several issues, challenges and opportunities of threat intelligence and through rigorous survey it has emerged that, cyber threat intelligence platform is still at its infant stage and profound scope still exists to be uncovered. However, threat intelligence is much more organized nowadays with due support of structured standards such as STIX, TAXII and more others. Perhaps, CTI demands more inputs to develop a systematic and streamlined ontology within the cyber threat intelligence.

Integration of artificial intelligence, machine learning with cyber threat intelligence assists to deceive the cyber threat automated and accurately with less computational time. Here we have developed a machine leaning based model implementing Naive Bayes classifier to extract the potential threat intelligence from structured data source and predict the threat with more than 96% of accuracy level.

References

1. Ussath, M., et al.: Pushing the limits of cyber threat intelligence: extending STIX. Springer Conference Paper Information Technology New Generations, pp. 213–225 (2016)
2. Ghazi, Y., et al.: A supervised machine learning based approach for automatically extracting high-level threat intelligence from unstructured sources. IEEE-2018 International Conference on Frontiers of Information Technology (FIT), pp. 129–134 (2018)
3. Kim, I., et al.: Cyber threat detection based on artificial neural networks using event profiles IEEE Access, 7, 165607–165626 (2019)
4. Buczak, A.L., Guven, E.: A survey of data mining and machine learning methods for cyber security intrusion detection. IEEE Commun. Surv. Tutor. 18(2), 1153–1176 (2015)
5. Liu, H., Lang, B.: Machine Learning and Deep Learning Methods for Intrusion Detection Systems: A Survey. MDPI (2019)
6. Raad Abbas, A., et al.: Detection of phishing websites using machine learning. Springer Nature Singapore Pte Ltd. 2020, Lecture Notes, vol 1989, pp. 1307–1314 (2018)
7. Bhanu Prakash, B., et al.: An integrated approach to network intrusion detection and prevention using KNN. Springer Nature Singapore Pte Ltd. 2020, Lecture Notes Vol-89, pp. 43–51 (2020)

Machine Learning Based Android Vulnerability Detection: A Roadmap

Shivi Garg[1,2] and Niyati Baliyan[2(✉)]

[1] Faculty of Computer Engineering, J.C. Bose University of Science and Technology, YMCA, Faridabad, India
`shivi1989@gmail.com`
[2] Information Technology Department, Indira Gandhi Delhi Technical University for Women, Delhi, India
`niyatibaliyan@igdtuw.ac.in`

Abstract. Cyber-security risk is increasing at an alarming rate due to global connectivity. It is important to protect sensitive information and maintain privacy. Machine learning algorithms have shown their superiority and expertise in detecting as well as predicting cyber-threats, as compared to the conventional methods. The paper discusses the role of such algorithms in cyber-security, particularly in Android mobile operating system. This statistical analysis identifies different vulnerabilities affecting Android and trend of these vulnerabilities between 2009–2019. Trend analysis can help in assessing the impact of each vulnerability. There are major research gaps in the existing work and hence the paper presents concrete suggestion for improvement.

Keywords: Android · Cyber-security · Machine learning · Malware · Vulnerability

1 Introduction

Cyber-security [1] is a practice that has an aggregation of different technologies and methods that are designed to protect data, programs, systems and networks from attacks, damages or any unauthorized access. Machine Learning (ML) approaches have proven to be efficient in various areas of cyber-security. ML is critical in today's day and age as it can help analyze voluminous data; more hardware and sophisticated algorithms are readily available and evolving every day [2]. There are three dimensions in which ML can be applied. These dimensions are - why, what and how.

The first-dimension answers *Why?* i.e. the reasons to perform a cyber-security task. According to Gartner model, the reasons to perform cyber-security tasks are divided into five categories - Predict, Prevent, Detect, Response, and Monitor [3].

The second-dimension answers *What?* i.e. at what technical level, issues are monitored. There are different layers listed in this dimension, namely, network, endpoint, application, user, and process.

The third-dimension answers *How?* to check security mechanisms. It can be historical, at rest, or in transit in real time. Table 1 summarizes this information.

© Springer Nature Switzerland AG 2020
S. Kanhere et al. (Eds.): ICISS 2020, LNCS 12553, pp. 87–93, 2020.
https://doi.org/10.1007/978-3-030-65610-2_6

Table 1. ML dimensions in cyber-security areas.

Protection Layer (What?)	Task (Why?)	Role of ML (How?)
Network (SCADA systems, Ethernet, Virtual networks)	Prediction & Detection	Prediction of network packet parameters, Detection of varied network attacks
Endpoint (IoT device, Mobile, Server)	Prediction & Detection	Prediction of the next system call, Categorizing programs into malware, spyware, adware, etc.
Application security	Detection & Prevention	Anomaly detection in HTTP requests, Detection of known attacks
User behavior	Detection, Prevention, Monitoring	Anomaly detection in User actions, Peer-group analysis based on different users
Process behavior	Prediction & Detection	Prediction of the next user action, Detection of known frauds

ML is an intersection of data science, data mining and classical programming [4] as shown in Fig. 1. ML exemplifies principles of data mining, but is also capable of self-learning and making automatic correlations that it applies to new algorithms. ML models are broadly categorized into Shallow (conventional) Learning (SL) and Deep Learning (DL) models. SL is a manual learning process that requires domain knowledge of the data described by pre-defined features, whereas DL [5] is a subclass of ML where neural networks comprising hidden layer(s) (each comprising perceptron(s)) are used progressively to extract features from the raw data. Different approaches are used in SL and DL to solve real-world problems e.g., Supervised, Unsupervised, Reinforcement learning. Few of the problems where ML can prove to be efficient are categorized as - regression (prediction), classification, clustering, and dimensionality reduction. Some of the examples of corresponding algorithms for each problem are shown in Fig. 2.

These days there is an extensive need of cyber-security as the number of software vulnerabilities is increasing rapidly. Software vulnerability can be defined as a weakness in the system procedures, information systems or policy that allows attackers to exploit information security. In this paper, we focus on Android operating system (OS) and its vulnerabilities. The reason for choosing Android is that it was the most vulnerable OS of the year 2016 [6]. Android is a complex open network of different collaborating companies. Android is customized by many hardware and network providers to meet their requirements. This makes Android more vulnerable as compared to other mobile OS. Different vulnerabilities present in Android are - Denial-of-Service (DoS), Code Execution, Overflow, Memory Corruption, Directory Traversal, Bypass something, Gain Information, and Gain Privileges.

The paper is organized as follows - Sect. 2 discusses the related work in this area. Section 3 describes the data extraction methodology. Section 4 presents the trends of

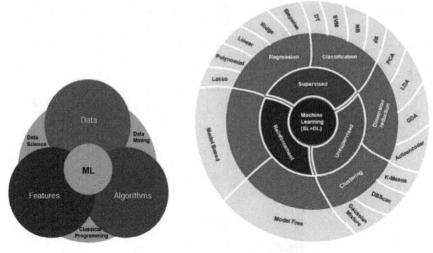

Fig. 1. Venn Diagram for ML/DL terminology

Fig. 2. Different approaches in ML

vulnerabilities in Android between 2016-2019. Section 5 discusses general insights and future directions. Finally, Sect. 6 concludes the paper.

2 Related Work

The section provides detailed literature review basis the role of ML in Android security. Tchakounté and Hayata [7] used supervised ML to detect Android malware. They used permissions as a feature to detect malicious behavior. Hussain et al. [8] presented a conceptual framework for improving the privacy of the users and to secure medical data related to Android Mobile Health applications (mHealth). Liang et al. [9] proposed an end to end DL model for Android malware detection using raw system call sequences and achieved an accuracy of 93.16%. Ganesh et al. [10] presented a CNN based malware detection solution using permissions. This solution detected malware with an accuracy of 93%. Garg and Baliyan [11] proposed a novel parallel classifier scheme for detection of vulnerabilities in Android with an accuracy of 98.27%. Details on data collection and various preprocessing steps are discussed in [12].

3 Data Extraction Methodology

CVE details [13] is chosen as the main source of data for analysis. CVE details provides vulnerability statistics that can be filtered on products, versions, and vendors. CVE vulnerability data are primarily taken from National Vulnerability Database (NVD) xml feeds provided by National Institute of Standards and Technology (NIST). Additional data from several sources, such as exploits from www.exploit-db.com, vendor statements and additional vendor supplied data.

Android vulnerabilities are extracted using three phases as shown in Fig. 3.

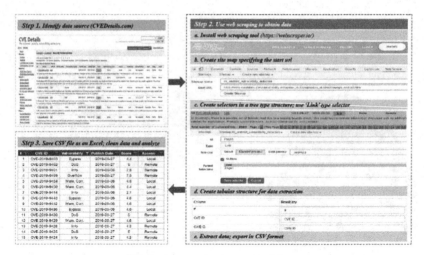

Fig. 3. Data extraction methodology

- **Step 1** - 563 vulnerabilities are listed in the database between 2009–2019.
- **Step 2** - Web-based scraper tool Web Scraper 0.4.0 [14] is used to extract data from CVE details portal. The process of web scraping starts with the creation of sitemap, which is a start URL. After this, the data is selected as a tree type structure and 'Link' selector is specified. Post this, a tabular structure is specified for data extraction and scraping is started. The scraped data is then exported as a CSV file.
- **Step 3** - Scarped data is saved as an excel file and cleaned up for further analysis.

4   Android Vulnerability Trend

Android vulnerabilities trends are shown between the year 2009–2019 [13] in Fig. 4. We see a continuous increase in the number of vulnerabilities between 2009–2017 post which there is a steep decline between 2017–2019. In this study, we primarily focus on the vulnerability trend between 2016–2019 which has a total of 2,395 vulnerabilities. Table 2 shows that most vulnerabilities have reduced between 2016-2019.

Vulnerability assessment is carried out on mean impact scores of vulnerabilities (μ) and number of instances (N) of occurrence as shown in Table 3. Number of instances depict the spread/volume while impact score depicts the severity of each vulnerability. The total score hence captures a cumulative effect of both 'volume' and 'impact'. The Total impact (I) is calculated as follows:

$$Total\ score\ of\ each\ vulnerability\ (TS) = \mu \times N \tag{1}$$

$$Total\ Impact\ (I)\ of\ each\ vulnerability = \frac{TS}{\sum TS} \times 100 \tag{2}$$

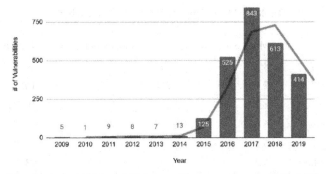

Fig. 4. Android Vulnerabilities trend between the year 2009–2019

Table 2. Vulnerability Trends from 2016–2019.

Vulnerability	Share 2016	Share 2019	Share (2016–2019)	% change (2016–2019)	Remarks
Code Execution	14%	21%	19%	8 pp ↑	libstagefright file in Media server
Overflow	18%	8%	18%	9 pp ↓	Improved input validation
Gain Privileges	48%	0%	12%	48 pp ↓	Better encryption mechanisms
Gain Information	19%	4%	12%	15 pp ↓	Regular software updates
DoS	20%	8%	11%	12 pp ↓	Improved validation & checks
Bypass something	9%	7%	5%	2 pp ↓	Improved security policies
Memory Corruption	7%	5%	4%	2 pp ↓	Improved memory management

5   Discussions and Future Directions

Existing ML approaches are effective; however, single ML approach does not fit every situation as stated by "No Free Lunch" theorem [15].

ML models can achieve higher detection rates if we ensure and follow simple thumb rules. First, ML models need to be trained using a rich dataset of malicious/benign apps, obtained from a central open source repository like AMD [16]. Second, all key features need to be extracted while maintaining minimum dimensions in the data to improve the classification time without compromising on performance.

ML models besides helpful in detecting Android vulnerabilities, can also be leveraged to analyze Android malware, to map vulnerabilities to malware and to classify malware.

Table 3. Mean impact score of each vulnerability.

Vulnerability	Mean Score (μ)	Vulnerability Count (N)	Total Impact (I)
Code Execution	8.3	310	14.7%
Overflow	7.1	256	10.3%
Gain Privileges	8.7	215	10.6%
Gain Information	4.6	259	6.8%
DoS	6.2	191	6.7%
Bypass Something	5.8	97	3.2%
Memory Corruption	6.4	20	0.73%

6   Conclusion

The paper presents insights on the role of ML in handling cyber-threats. The focus is on Android OS since it is highly vulnerable to attacks. First part of the paper presents a comprehensive study on different ML techniques while the second part details out various vulnerabilities, their trends between 2009–2019, and their overall impact, which helps in segregating the most severe vulnerabilities that researchers can prioritize as these have higher spread as well as higher mean impact. An in-depth analysis of vulnerabilities pointed out in this paper is both necessary and sufficient for researchers in order to resolve these vulnerabilities because they are the most prevalent and severe vulnerabilities.

References

1. von Solms, B., von Solms, R.: Cybersecurity and information security–what goes where? Inform. Comput. Secur. **26**(1), 2–9 (2018)
2. Narayanan, A., Chandramohan, M., Chen, L., Liu, Y.: A multi-view context-aware approach to Android malware detection and malicious code localization. Empirical Softw. Eng. **23**(3), 1222–1274 (2017). https://doi.org/10.1007/s10664-017-9539-8
3. Carpenter, P.: Using the Predict, Prevent, Detect, Respond Framework to Communicate Your Security Program Strategy (2016). https://www.gartner.com/
4. Polyakov, A.: Machine Learning for Cybersecurity (2020). https://towardsdatascience.com/machine-learning-for-cybersecurity-101-7822b802790b/
5. Alzaylaee, M.K., Yerima, S.Y., Sezer, S.: DL-Droid: deep learning based android malware detection using real devices". Comput. Secur. **89**, 101663 (2020)
6. Garg, S., Singh, R.K., Mohapatra, A.K.: Analysis of software vulnerability classification based on different technical parameters. Inform. Secur. J. Glob. Perspect. **28**, 1–19 (2019)
7. Tchakounté, F., Hayata, F.: Supervised learning based detection of malware on android. In: 2017 Mobile Security and Privacy, pp. 101–154 (2017)
8. Hussain, M., Zaidan, A.A., Zidan, B., Iqbal, S., Ahmed, M.M., Albahri, O.S., Albahri, A.S.: Conceptual framework for the security of mobile health applications on android platform. Telematics Inform. **35**(5), 1335–1354 (2018)
9. Liang, H., Song, Y., Xiao, D.: An end-To-end model for Android malware detection. In: 2017 IEEE International Conference on Intelligence and Security Informatics (ISI), pp. 140–142 (2017)

10. Ganesh, M., Pednekar, P., Prabhuswamy, P., Nair, D.S., Park, Y., Jeon, H.: CNN-based android malware detection. In: 2017 International Conference on Software Security and Assurance (ICSSA), pp. 60–65 (2017)
11. Garg, S., Baliyan, N.: A novel parallel classifier scheme for vulnerability detection in android. Comput. Electr. Eng. **77**, 12–26 (2019)
12. Garg, S., Baliyan, N.: Data on vulnerability detection in android. Data Brief **22**, 1081–1087 (2019)
13. CVE details, Jan 2020. https://www.cvedetails.com/
14. Web Scraper. Making web data extraction easy and accessible for everyone, Jan 2020. https://webscraper.io/
15. Ryan, S., Corizzo, R., Kiringa, I., Japkowicz, N.: Deep learning versus conventional learning in data streams with concept drifts. In: 18th IEEE International Conference On Machine Learning And Applications (ICMLA), pp. 1306–1313 (2019)
16. Wei, F., Li, Y., Roy, S., Ou, X., Zhou, W.: Deep ground truth analysis of current android malware. In: Polychronakis, M., Meier, M. (eds.) DIMVA 2017. LNCS, vol. 10327, pp. 252–276. Springer, Cham (2017). https://doi.org/10.1007/978-3-319-60876-1_12

Privacy and Web Security

Revelio: A Lightweight Captcha Solver Using a Dictionary Based Approach

Abhijeet Chougule$^{(\boxtimes)}$, Harshal Tupsamudre, and Sachin Lodha

TCS Research, Pune, India
{abhijeet.chougule,harshal.tupsamudre,sachin.lodha}@tcs.com

Abstract. Captcha is an important security measure used by many websites to defend against malicious bot programs. However, with the advancement in the field of computer vision, seemingly complex Captcha schemes have been broken. Although Captcha solving techniques have improved significantly, we observed that many major banking and government websites are still relying on a relatively simple class of text Captchas to counter bot attacks. In this paper, we demonstrate that Captcha schemes deployed on State Bank of India (SBI), Axis bank and Indian Railways (IRCTC) websites can be easily broken using a repertoire of standard image processing techniques. We develop a Captcha solver tool called *Revelio* which is lightweight, automatic, efficient, and requires minimal labeled data and works in real-time. We evaluate the performance of our tool with the state-of-the-art CNN model on diverse Captcha schemes from 14 major Indian websites. The proposed solver achieves at least 90% accuracy on 10/14 Captcha schemes. Further, we found that for the targeted class of Captcha schemes and a given amount of labeled data, our solver outperforms the CNN based solver.

Keywords: Captcha · Image processing · Bot attacks · Algorithms

1 Introduction

CAPTCHA is an acronym for Completely Automated Public Turing test to tell Computer and Humans Apart [18]. As the name suggests, Captcha is a challenge response test that allows websites to distinguish humans from bots. Such tests are common on web pages containing account signup forms, signin forms and feedback forms. The purpose of Captcha varies from stopping malicious bots from creating fake accounts to preventing the launch of credential stuffing attacks to countering denial-of-service attacks and averting spam. Captchas are available in different modalities including text [23], image [29], audio [1] and video [33]. Among all, text Captchas are very popular and widely used. Typically, a text Captcha is an image consisting of a distorted sequence of alphanumeric characters, and the user has to recognize the characters within the image and enter them in the exact given sequence in the input textbox. The usage of different characteristics such as font variations, noisy background, occluding lines, collapsed and wavy letters is supposed to make the Captcha challenge harder for

© Springer Nature Switzerland AG 2020
S. Kanhere et al. (Eds.): ICISS 2020, LNCS 12553, pp. 97–116, 2020.
https://doi.org/10.1007/978-3-030-65610-2_7

bots, while it is expected that humans can still identify the distorted characters with relative ease [23].

With the advancement in Computer Vision in the last decade, the ability of Captcha solver techniques has improved significantly. As a consequence, seemingly complex text Captchas have been broken. Many solvers proposed in the literature utilize machine learning [23], reinforcement learning [21] and deep learning techniques [39] to break text Captchas containing different characteristics such as text distortion, noisy background, text collapsing, rotations, occluding lines etc. However, we observed that major Indian organizations are still relying on simple Captcha schemes to defend their websites against bot attacks. Figure 1 depicts the Captcha schemes present on some of the major Indian banking websites (SBI, Axis bank, Allahabad bank), government websites (Vahan, Service Plus[1], SBI Collect[2]) and online ticket booking websites (IRCTC, MSRTC, Vistara). All illustrated Captchas use either plain or uniform background with constant font color, size and style, and have at most a single occluding line passing over the text. They lack features such as random background noise, collapsed letters and font variations that contributes to the hardness of Captcha. In this paper, we demonstrate that such Captcha schemes can be easily broken using simple image processing techniques on a standard configuration machine. The use of deep learning algorithms to break these Captcha schemes would be an overkill as they require a large amount of labeled data and high computational hardware.

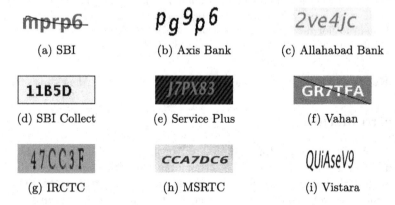

(a) SBI   (b) Axis Bank   (c) Allahabad Bank

(d) SBI Collect   (e) Service Plus   (f) Vahan

(g) IRCTC   (h) MSRTC   (i) Vistara

Fig. 1. Captchas used on major Indian banking, government and online booking websites.

With the advent of Digital India revolution, the number of internet users has grown from 239 million in 2014 to 560 million in 2018, and it is expected

---

[1] Service Plus Captchas are used on different government websites including CM Relief Fund websites of Chhattisgarh and Karnataka.

[2] SBI Collect Captchas are used on various government websites including CM Relief Fund websites of Assam, Gujarat, Haryana, Goa and Tripura.

to grow to 840 million by 2023 [30]. Further, Digital India have had a huge impact on government sectors including financial, judicial and transport [38]. As per data collected by SimilarWeb [16], a website providing web analytics services, in July 2020, SBI online banking website had over 64.27 million visitors whereas IRCTC railway ticket booking website had over 8.25 million visitors. According to a recent report [36], nearly a quarter of all internet traffic is generated by malicious bots which is detrimental to the online businesses. Further, financial and government services are the most targeted sectors. Therefore, it is important that large-scale organizations take the necessary steps to protect their digital infrastructure. Captcha is an important security measure to guard against malicious bot programs. However, major banking organizations (e.g., SBI) and government organizations (e.g., IRCTC) are using simple text Captcha schemes to protect their websites (Fig. 1). One primary reason for using simple Captcha schemes could be the requirement to serve users with diverse demographics and abilities. This is a classic usability vs security trade-off. Other potential factors could be the ease of development, faster deployment, assumption of unrealistic threat model and lack of security awareness.

In this paper, we highlight the weaknesses of Captcha schemes deployed on major Indian websites. Specifically, our contributions are as follows:

- We propose a Captcha solver called *Revelio* which is lightweight, automatic, efficient, and requires less amount of labeled data and consumes relatively less computational resources. Our solver is lightweight as it has only two stages, Captcha training and Captcha solving, and both these stages rely only on image processing techniques. It is efficient since it solves Captchas using a dictionary of characters created during the training phase. Further, it requires at most 100 labeled Captcha images in the training phase, hence the proposed system is cost effective in terms of human effort required to gather and label the Captchas. Apart from manually labeling the 100 Captchas, the rest of the system is fully automatic.
- We compare the performance of our solver with the state-of-the-art CNN based Captcha solver. We evaluate both solvers on diverse Captcha schemes used on 14 major Indian websites which includes banking websites, government websites and online booking websites. Our results show that for the targeted class of Captchas, the proposed Captcha solver is not only more accurate but also consumes less computational resources (time and memory) than the CNN based solver.
- Based on our evaluation, we provide several recommendations for Captcha designers, and discuss possible future directions for producing more robust yet usable Captcha schemes.

The organization of this paper is as follows. First, we describe the characteristics of Captchas used on major Indian websites. Then, we give a detailed explanation of the proposed Captcha solver *Revelio* which exploits these observed characteristics. Subsequently, we describe the experimental setup and provide comparative results of our image processing based solver and the state-of-the-art CNN based solver. Later, we give a brief overview of different Captcha schemes and Captcha solving techniques proposed in the literature. Finally, we conclude the paper.

2   Automatic Captcha Solver

In this section, we give a detailed description of our Captcha solver *Revelio*. We begin by describing the class of Captchas that is targeted by our proposed system.

2.1   Captcha Characteristics

Table 1 shows the organization name, the sample Captcha image used on the organization's website along with its characteristics. Broadly, the characteristics of the Captchas are as follows:

- Plain/Uniform background: Captchas either have no background or uniform color background. For instance, Captchas deployed on Allahabad bank website have pale blue background whereas Captchas on Axis bank website have no background at all.
- Fixed length: Captchas are of fixed length. For instance, Captchas on Karnataka bank have 6 digits, Captchas on SBI have 5 alphanumeric characters (lowercase + digits) and Captchas from Service Plus have 6 alphanumeric characters (uppercase + digits).
- Uniform font: All letters within a given Captcha have same font color, size and style. For instance, all characters in Service Plus Captcha are of green color. However, we note that the text color may change from one Captcha image to another.
- Occluding Line(s): There is a single (possibly multiple lines) passing through characters within the Captcha. For instance, SBI Captchas have a single line passing over the Captcha text.
- Simple Border: Captchas are surrounded with a border. For instance, SBI Collect Captchas have a black border.
- Segmentable Letters: There is a gap between every two letters within a Captcha. Such a gap is observed in all Captcha schemes depicted in the table.

We show that Captchas with aforementioned characteristics can be solved in real-time merely using standard image processing algorithms with a high accuracy. Our proposed tool *Revelio* can solve Captchas of fixed length, having uniform background, constant font colors, simple border and occluding line(s). The working of *Revelio* is depicted in Fig. 2. The tool has two parts, namely *Captcha training* and *Captcha solving*. In the training phase, all labeled Captcha images are preprocessed, segmented and a character dictionary is created. In the solving phase, the Captcha image is processed and segmented into individual characters as before. To infer the Captcha label, each segmented character is matched against characters in the dictionary created during the training phase.

Table 1. List of Captchas targeted by the proposed Captcha Solver *Revelio*.

Organization Name	Captcha Example	Captcha Characteristics
Allahabad Bank [6]	2ve4jc	plain background, fixed length, constant font
Karnataka Bank [10]	776207	plain background, fixed length, constant font
Axis Bank [7]	Pg9p6	no background, fixed length, constant font
SBI [12]	mprp6	no background, occluding line, fixed length, constant font
Fast Tag HDFC [8]	GvasPf	plain background, occluding lines, fixed length, constant font
Maharashtra CM Relief Fund [2]	1soqW	plain background, gradient text, fixed length, constant font
Andhra Pradesh CM Relief Fund [3]	11834	background with lines, fixed length, constant font
Bihar CM Relief Fund [4]	hco5os	noisy background, fixed length, constant font
Service Plus [13]	l7PX83	background with lines, fixed length, constant font
SBI Collect [15]	11B5D	plain background, fixed length, constant font
Vahan [17]	GR7TFA	plain background, occluding line, fixed length, constant font
Vistara [14]	QUiAseV9	no background, fixed length, constant font
MSRTC [11]	CCA7DC6	plain background, fixed length, constant font
IRCTC [9]	47CC3F	plain background, fixed length, constant font

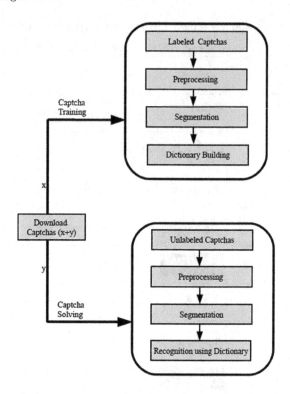

Fig. 2. The working of proposed automatic Captcha solver *Revelio.*

2.2 Captcha Training

Algorithm 1 shows the Python pseudocode for Captcha training. In the training phase (lines 3–20), Captcha images are manually labeled and subsequently preprocessed to remove background noise, occluding lines and border. Then, the resulting image is segmented into individual characters. Finally, features of each segmented character is extracted and stored in a dictionary.

We need a set of labeled Captcha examples for training *Revelio*. For this, we visit the target website and download $x + y$ Captchas. We manually label x Captcha images and use Algorithm 1 to build a dictionary containing a character as key and its extracted feature as value. We use y Captchas for testing the prediction accuracy of solver. We denote the training set by $T = \{(I_1, L_1), (I_2, L_2), \ldots (I_x, L_x)\}$ where I is the Captcha image and L is its label. The training phases consists of four steps, labeling, preprocessing, segmentation and building dictionary. The result of the training phase is a dictionary D of m characters used for constructing Captchas and their features. Now, we explain each step in more detail.

Number of Labeled Captchas: For the training phase, we require labeled Captcha examples. We determine the number of labeled examples x required for creating the dictionary. Since there is no variation in the font of letters, we need to extract each unique character from the Captcha image, calculate its feature value and store it in a dictionary. Let γ represents the alphabet set from which the Captcha is created. Let the number of characters in γ be m. Thus, the probability of choosing a specific character uniformly at random for constructing a Captcha is $p = \frac{1}{m}$. The probability that a specific character is not chosen is then:

$$\tilde{p} = 1 - p = 1 - 1/m \tag{1}$$

Consider x Captcha images each of fixed length n. Hence, the total number of characters in x images is:

$$\sum_{i=1}^{x} |L_i| = x \cdot n \tag{2}$$

The probability that a specific character is not present among $x \cdot n$ characters is:

$$\prod_{j=1}^{x \cdot n} \tilde{p} = (\tilde{p})^{x \cdot n} = (1 - 1/m)^{x \cdot n} \approx e^{-x \cdot n/m} \tag{3}$$

Let $e^{-x \cdot n/m} \leq \epsilon = 10^{-5}$. Therefore, the minimum number of labeled examples x required to train $Revelio$ can be computed as follows:

$$x \approx m \cdot ln(1/\epsilon)/n = m \cdot ln(10^5)/n \approx m \cdot 11.51/n \tag{4}$$

Typically, the alphabet set γ typically consists of 26 lowercase letters (a-z) and 10 digits (0–9), and the Captcha length is 5. Therefore, we have $|\gamma| = m = 36$ and $n = 5$. Hence, the required number of Captcha examples x for $\epsilon = 10^{-5}$ is:

$$x \approx 36 \cdot 11.51/5 \approx 83 \tag{5}$$

Table 2 shows the minimum number of labeled examples x required for $\epsilon = 10^{-5}$, and different combinations of alphabet set γ and Captcha length n. As we have to label around 100 Captchas in most of the cases, the training phase of $Revelio$ requires minimum human effort and time.

Preprocessing of Captcha Image: In the second step of the training phase, we preprocess the Captcha image to remove the background noise (lines 22–33). For this, we use various functions from the OpenCV library. The Captcha image I is read using $cv2.imread()$ function. By default the image is read in BGR mode. For simplicity, we convert BGR image to grayscale image using $cv2.cvtColor()$ function (line 25). The resulting grayscale image is then converted into pure black and white image using a process known as binary thresholding. In binary thresholding, a threshold value is chosen such that gray pixels below threshold value is converted to black while gray value above threshold is converted to white. After applying thresholding all background noise is removed and we get Captcha text on clear background.

Table 2. The minimum number of labeled examples x required for different alphabet set γ and Captcha length n so that the probability that a specific character is not present in the labeled dataset is $\epsilon = 10^{-5}$.

Alphabet γ	$|\gamma| = m$	n	x
{0–9}	10	5	24
{0–9}	10	6	20
{0–9}	10	7	17
{a-z}	26	5	60
{a-z}	26	6	50
{a-z}	26	7	43
{a-z, 0–9}	36	5	83
{a-z, 0–9}	36	6	70
{a-z, 0–9}	36	7	60
{a-z, A-Z}	52	5	120
{a-z, A-Z}	52	6	100
{a-z, A-Z}	52	7	86
{a-z, A-Z, 0–9}	62	5	143
{a-z, A-Z, 0–9}	62	6	119
{a-z, A-Z, 0–9}	62	7	102

We find the threshold value automatically using Otsu's binarization technique [35]. Otsu's binarization technique is a global thresholding technique that works on a bimodal image i.e. image whose histogram has two peaks. For such an image, Otsu binarization chooses a value in the middle of those peaks as a threshold value. Most of the Captchas listed in Table 1 have only two distinct colors, one used for background and the other used for Captcha characters. Hence, the targeted Captcha images are bimodal and we can use Otsu's thresholding technique to automatically calculate a threshold value from the image histogram. To apply Otsu's binarization on Captcha image, we use *cv2.threshold*() function with an extra flag cv2.THRESH_OTSU (line 26).

After thresholding, we make sure that background is black color and foreground (Captcha text) is white color. To achieve this, we convert our thresholded image to an array (line 27) and we count the number of black and white pixels using *unique*() function in the Numpy library (line 28). If the number of white pixels is greater than the number of black pixels, we use *cv2.bitwise_not*() function which converts all white pixels to black and black pixels to white (lines 29–31). As background occupies more area compared to foreground, the condition in line 29 is true only if background has white color after applying Otsu thresholding. Finally, the preprocessed image P is returned (line 32).

Algorithm 1. Captcha Training

1: *import cv2*
2: *import numpy as np*
3: **procedure** $TrainCaptcha$
4: **Input:** A set $T = \{(I_1, L_1), (I_2, L_2), \ldots (I_x, L_x)\}$ of x labeled Captchas where I_j is a Captcha image and L_j is its label containing n characters
5: **Output:** A dictionary $D = \{c_1 : f_1, c_2 : f_2, \ldots, c_m : f_m\}$ of m characters where f_k is HOG feature extracted from image corresponding to character c_k
6:     $D = \{\}$
7:     $n = |L|$
8:     $hog = cv2.HOGDescriptor()$
9:     **for** $(I, L) \in T$ **do**
10:         $P = PreprocessCaptcha(I)$
11:         $S = SegmentCaptcha(P, n)$
12:         **for** $i = 0$ to $n - 1$ **do**
13:             $s = S[i]$
14:             $c = L[i]$
15:             **if** $c \notin D$ **then**
16:                 $D[c] = hog.compute(s)$
17:             **end if**
18:         **end for**
19:     **end for**
20: **end procedure**
21:
22: **procedure** $PreprocessCaptcha$
23: **Input:** Captcha image I
24: **Output:** Preprocessed image P
25:     $I = cv2.cvtColor(I, cv2.COLOR\_BGR2GRAY)$
26:     $t, P = cv2.threshold(I, 0, 255, cv2.THRESH\_OTSU)$
27:     $A = np.array(P)$
28:     $unique, counts = np.unique(A, return\_counts = True)$
29:     **if** $counts[BLACK=0] < counts[WHITE=1]$ **then**
30:         $P = cv2.bitwise\_not(P)$
31:     **end if**
32:     **return** P
33: **end procedure**
34:
35: **procedure** $SegmentCaptcha$
36: **Input:** Preprocessed Captcha P and the number of characters n in P
37: **Output:** Segmented letters S in the preprocessed Captcha P
38:     $S = []$
39:     $contours = cv2.findContours(P, cv2.RETR\_EXTERNAL, cv2.CHAIN\_APPROX\_SIMPLE)$
40:     **if** $len(contours) == 1$ **then**
41:         **if** $cv2.contourArea(contours) > 0.9 \cdot area(P)$ **then**
42:             $P = cv2.drawContours(P, contours, BLACK = 0)$
43:         **end if**
44:         $P = cv2.erode(P, kernel = np.ones((5, 5)))$
45:         $P = cv2.dilate(P, kernel = np.ones((2, 2)))$
46:         $contours = cv2.findContours(P, cv2.RETR\_EXTERNAL, cv2.CHAIN\_APPROX\_SIMPLE)$
47:     **end if**
48:     $contours = SortContours(contours, 'area', 'desc')[0:n]$
49:     $contours = SortContours(contours, 'leftToRight', 'asc')$
50:     **for** $i = 0$ to $n - 1$ **do**
51:         $(x, y, w, h) = cv2.boundingRect(contours[i])$
52:         $segment = P[y : y + h, x : x + w]$
53:         $S[i] = cv2.blur(segment, kernel = np.ones((3, 3)))$
54:     **end for**
55:     **return** S
56: **end procedure**

Segmentation of Captcha Characters: The third step of the training phase is segmentation (lines 35–56). We segment characters within the preprocessed image P by finding contours using $findContour()$ function. The contours are obtained simply by joining all continuous points along the boundary with same color intensity. The contours are a useful tool for shape analysis and object

---

Algorithm 2. Captcha Solving

1: **procedure** $SolveCaptcha$
2: **Input:** A Captcha image I, n the number of characters in I, dictionary D containing character and HOG feature extracted during Captcha training
3: **Output:** Solution L for the Captcha image I
4:     $L = ''$
5:     $P = PreprocessCaptcha(I)$
6:     $S = SegmentCaptcha(P, n)$
7:     $hog = cv2.HOGDescriptor()$
8:     **for** $i = 0$ to $n - 1$ **do**
9:         $s = S[i]$
10:         $f = hog.compute(s)$
11:         $min = \infty$
12:         $l = ''$
13:         **for** $c \in D$ **do**
14:             $dist = np.linalg.norm(f - D[c])$
15:             **if** $dist < min$ **then**
16:                 $min = dist$
17:                 $l = c$
18:             **end if**
19:         **end for**
20:         $L+ = l$
21:     **end for**
22:     **return** L
23: **end procedure**

---

detection and recognition. The accuracy is better if the image is binary. Note that, we have already converted the original Captcha image into black and white image, where letters are white and background is black. Each individual contour is a numpy array of (x, y) coordinates of boundary points of the object. There are three arguments in $cv2.findContours()$ function, first one is source image, second is contour retrieval mode and third is contour approximation method. We use cv2.RETR_EXTERNAL which retrieves all boundary points of an object and cv2.CHAIN_APPROX_SIMPLE which stores only the relevant boundary points of the object, thereby saving memory.

If the number of contours is one, then we determine if the Captcha contains a border. We calculate the area of the retrieved contour and compare it with the area of the image (lines 41–43). If the areas are similar, we determine that there is a border. To remove border, we use $cv2.drawContours()$ function (line 42) which simply makes the border color same as the background color i.e., black. Subsequently, we determine whether the Captcha contains occluding line(s) passing through the text. To remove line(s), we first performs erosion on the image using $cv2.erode()$ method followed by dilation using $cv2.dilate()$ (lines 44–45). Erosion and dilation are morphological operations and are performed on binary images. They need two inputs, our original image and structuring element or kernel which decides the nature of operation. The basic idea of erosion is just like soil erosion, it erodes away the boundaries of foreground object. The kernel slides through the image (as in 2D convolution) and a pixel in the original image is 1 only if all the pixels under the kernel is 1, otherwise it is eroded (made to zero). We use erosion to remove line from the Captcha. Dilation is just opposite of erosion. Here, a pixel element is set as 1 if atleast one pixel under the kernel is 1. So it increases the white region (Captcha characters) in the image. For erosion, we use 5×5 kernel and for dilation we use 2×2 kernel.

Once the line is removed we perform the contour operation again. This time we get a separate contour for each character (line 46) as there is a gap between every two characters within targeted Captchas. We sort the contours in descending order of area and retain only first n contours, where n is the length of Captcha which is fixed for a given Captcha scheme (line 48). This way, we can get rid of small noisy (bad) contours (if any). Then, we sort the retained contours from left to right by x-coordinate (line 49). We draw a bounding box surrounding each contour (lines 50–54), store them in the list and return the list to the calling function (line 55). We apply $cv2.blur()$ function for smoothing the edges of our contour image. The smoothing is achieved by convolving the contours with the 3×3 kernel filter. It slides the kernel over the image, computes the average of pixels under the kernel filter area and replaces the central pixel with the average.

Figure 3 shows the result of preprocessing and segmentation on Captchas from SBI, SBI Collect, Allahabad bank and Andhra CM Relief Fund websites.

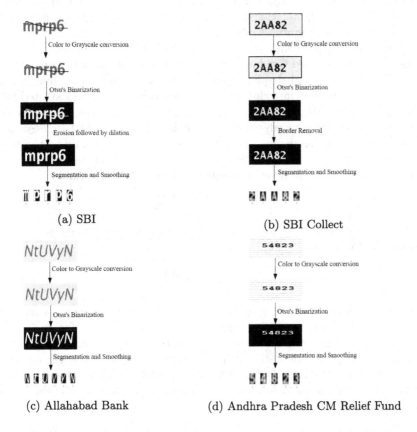

(a) SBI

(b) SBI Collect

(c) Allahabad Bank

(d) Andhra Pradesh CM Relief Fund

Fig. 3. The result of training phase on four different websites.

Building Dictionary of Captcha Characters: The fourth and final step of the training phase is building dictionary of unique characters used in the Captcha (lines 12–19). As we have the contours of each segmented character and we know the label of Captcha L, we can map each contour to a character in the label L. We then extract features from each character image and store it in a dictionary D. Since there are no font variations, we need to extract features for each character only once. We explore the following two techniques for feature extraction:

1. Image hash: Image hashes are typically used to determine whether two images look nearly identical. There are multiple ways of computing image hashes. We consider average Hash (ahash), perceptive hash (phash) and difference hash (dhash) algorithms. The ahash algorithm converts the image into a grayscale 8×8 image and sets the 64 bits in the hash based on whether the pixel's value is greater than the average color for the image. The dhash algorithm is similar to aHash but it uses a discrete cosine transform (DCT) and compares pixels based on frequencies rather than color values. The dhash algorithm works on the difference between adjacent pixels. Each bit is simply set based on whether the left pixel is brighter than the right pixel. The hash values represent the relative change in brightness intensity. Thus, aHash focuses on average values, pHash evaluates frequency patterns and dHash tracks gradients.
2. Histogram of Oriented Gradient (HOG): HOG descriptors are mainly used to describe the structural shape and appearance of an object in an image. HOG descriptors were first introduced in [31] and have been demonstrated to be effective in detecting objects in static images [25]. As HOG captures local intensity gradients and edge directions, it is also used as texture descriptor. The first step in retrieving the HOG descriptor is to compute the image gradient in both the x and y direction. Once the gradient image is obtained, the magnitude of each pixel is calculated using following formula:

$$|G| = \sqrt{Gx^2 + Gy^2} \tag{6}$$

The orientation of the gradient for each pixel in the input image is computed using the following formula:

$$\theta = arctan(\frac{Gy}{Gx}) \tag{7}$$

After obtaining gradient magnitude and orientation representations, the image is divided into small connected regions called cells. For each cell in the image, a histogram of oriented gradients is constructed using gradient magnitude $|G|$ and orientation θ. The histogram of each cell is then concatenated to form the final feature vector. Algorithm 1 shows how to extract HOG descriptor from each segmented character using $cv2.HOGDescriptor()$ function of the OpenCV library.

Now that, the character dictionary is created, we can be use it for the Captcha recognition task.

2.3 Captcha Solving

Once we have built the character dictionary, we can use it to break Captchas. Algorithm 2 shows the pseudocode for Captcha solving. First, we apply the same set of operations on the test Captcha image that were used during the training phase. The test image is preprocessed and converted into grayscale which is then converted into binary image using Otsu's thresholding. This will remove background noise from the captcha image. Subsequently, we find contours and segment the preprocessed image into n unlabeled contours, where n is the length of the Captcha. Now, we need to recognize character within each contour. Our dictionary consists of characters observed during the training phase along with their features.

Recognition of Captcha: To recognize the Captcha we need to recognize the characters within individual contours. Based on the technique used for creating character dictionary during the training phase, there are two cases:

1. Image Hash: If the dictionary consists of image hash for each character, then we apply the same hash function on each of the n segmented characters. We compare two image hashes using Hamming distance, which measures the number of bits in two hashes that are different. The Hamming distance of zero implies that the two hashes are identical (since there are no differing bits) and that the two images are identical/perceptually similar. We label each segmented image with a character which has least Hamming distance value among all characters in the dictionary. By combining the labels of each individual contour image, we get the solution L for the Captcha image.
2. Histogram of Oriented Gradient (HOG): If the dictionary contains HOG feature for each character, then we compute the HOG features of all n contours. To recognize the character within a contour, we compute the Euclidean distance between its HOG feature and HOG feature of each character in the dictionary. To perform this operation, we use $np.linalg.norm()$ function from the Numpy library. We label the contour image with a character which has least Euclidean distance value among all characters in the dictionary. In this way, we label each contour image with a character such that their HOG features have a minimum Euclidean distance. By combining the labels of each individual contour image, we get the solution L for the Captcha image. The pseudocode described in Algorithm 2 assumes that the dictionary contains HOG features.

3 Experiments

Now we evaluate the performance of *Revelio* with the state-of-the-art CNN based solver [32] on 14 Captcha schemes depicted in Table 1. For each website, we employ 100 labeled Captcha images for training and 100 distinct images for testing. We measure the solver's performance using accuracy which is calculated as follows:

$$Accuracy = \frac{Number\ of\ test\ Captchas\ solved\ correctly}{Total\ number\ of\ test\ Captchas} \quad (8)$$

We also report the training time and the average time required to solve a Captcha. We conduct all experiments on a standard configuration machine with Intel(R) core(TM) i7-4600U CPU @ 2.10 GHz and 8GB RAM. We implemented *Revelio* using Python (v3.7). To perform image processing tasks, we used the OpenCV library for Python.

3.1   CNN Based Approach

For comparative purpose, we used recently proposed Convolutional Neural Network (CNN) based Captcha Solver [32]. Its source code is available on Github [5]. The CNN architecture consists of an input convolutional layer followed by two convolution-max pooling pair followed by a dense layer with 512 neurons with 30% dropout. All convolutional layers employ ReLu activation function and 5×5 kernel while max-pooling layer uses 2×2 window. The authors of [32] trained CNN model using 500,000 labeled Captcha images, and obtained 98.94% accuracy on numeric Captchas and 98.31% accuracy on alphanumeric ones. The CNN model requires the number of Captcha letters and image size (height and width) as its input. Before running the code, we set the input for each Captcha scheme appropriately. The hyperparameters required for training CNN were used as suggested in [32].

3.2   Results

Table 3 shows the accuracy of *Revelio* and the CNN based Captcha solver [32]. The accuracy of CNN based Captcha in each case is 0%. One primary reason for low performance of the CNN based solver is the lack of adequate training data (we trained CNN on only 100 labeled examples). Even, the training accuracy of CNN based solver for each of the targeted Captcha schemes never exceeded 5%. We also tried with the reduced number of convolutional layers, but without any success. Among four different features considered for training *Revelio*, HOG feature performed better in all cases. It broke 10 out of 14 Captcha schemes with at least 90% accuracy. As features are extracted from binary images consisting of white character segments and black background, there are no frequency patterns (phash) or gradients (dhash) to exploit. Hence, ahash outperformed both phash and dhash. For a given Captcha scheme, the average time required to train a CNN was around 600s whereas *Revelio* built the character dictionary within 25s (for all four features). The time required to solve the Captcha using *Revelio* was also small 0.3s (for all four features).

The accuracy of *Revelio* for four Captcha schemes is below 90%. The reasons for low accuracy rates are as follows.

– Our approach assumes that there is a clear gap between the characters of the Captcha. However, few HDFC Fast Tag Captchas contained collapsed characters as shown in Fig. 4a. Hence, predicted Captcha label is incorrect. As shown in the figure, only collapsed part is recognized incorrectly but the rest of the characters in the Captcha are recognized correctly.

Table 3. The accuracy of *Revelio* and CNN on 14 different Captcha schemes when trained on 100 labeled Captcha images. It shows the accuracy of *Revelio* for four different feature extraction techniques, HOG, ahash, dhash and phash.

Organization Name	HOG	ahash	dhash	phash	CNN
Allahabad Bank	**93%**	77%	56%	49%	0%
Karnataka Bank	**96%**	96%	96%	96%	0%
Axis Bank	**90%**	87%	85%	85%	0%
SBI	**60%**	59%	43%	35%	0%
Fast Tag HDFC	**71%**	53%	40%	41%	0%
Maharashtra CM Relief Fund	**100%**	100%	93%	93%	0%
Andhra Pradesh CM Relief Fund	**100%**	89%	71%	83%	0%
Bihar CM Relief Fund	**72%**	58%	32%	30%	0%
Service Plus	**97%**	93%	79%	69%	0%
SBI Collect	**100%**	100%	85%	80%	0%
Vahan	**100%**	94%	84%	32%	0%
Vistara	**96%**	80%	75%	76%	0%
MSRTC	**100%**	100%	100%	74%	0%
IRCTC	**68%**	36%	0%	0%	0%

- Another reason for the reduced accuracy is the inability of dictionary based approach to distinguish between confusing characters (e.g., o vs. O, l vs. I, 1 vs. l) present in the Captcha. The mislabeled Bihar CM Relief fund Captcha is shown in Fig. 4b. Here, the letter o is recognized as digit 0. However, we hypothesize that such character pairs would also cause confusion among humans.
- Further, the removal of occluding line(s) results in the removal of part of character that sometimes leads to mislabeling of the Captcha. For instance, in SBI Captcha of Fig. 4c, a line passing throught letter k causes it to be incorrectly recognized as letter r.
- Our approach assumes that there are no font variations. However, there are few font variations in some of the Captcha schemes which leads to relatively lower accuracy. If the number of font variations is small, then the accuracy can be improved by storing all character variations and their features in the dictionary.

Note that, not all characters in the Captcha images are recognized incorrectly. For instance, the Captchas shown in Fig. 4a is predicted as GmZls (true label is GmeZls), that in Fig. 4b is predicted as VF00R9 (true label is VF0oR9) and that in Fig. 4c is predicted as pr7bp (true label is pk7bp).

112 A. Chougule et al.

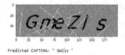

(a) Collapsed characters (b) Character confusion (c) Occluding line

Fig. 4. Mislabeled Captchas from HDFC Fast Tag (collapsed characters), Bihar CM Relied Fund (character confusion) and SBI Netbanking (occluding line) websites.

3.3 Design Recommendations

From the results, it is clear that simple Captcha schemes can be easily broken using *Revelio* with high accuracy. To make Captcha schemes more robust, we provide the following recommendations.

- Variable font style and size: Font variations such as different style, size and colors can reduce the learnability of the solvers without affecting usability. Using complex background is considered insecure, hence it should be used as the second line of defence [23].
- Collapsing: The use of collapsed (overlapped) letters makes it difficult to segment the Captcha letters. The more the overlapping of characters, more is the robustness of Captcha [27].
- Warping: Warping is the process of manipulating image such that any shape present in the image gets distorted. In global warping, transformation is performed on whole Captcha string while in local warping, transformation is performed on individual characters. Both global and local warping enhances the security of the Captcha but too much warping decreases the usability [27].
- Character Orientation: Different orientation of Captcha characters in an image can be used to enhance the security of Captcha [19].
- Randomizing Captcha length: The fixed length Captchas enables the attacker to find segmentation coordinates easily [26]. Hence, the Captcha length should be randomized.
- Distortion: The use of distorted alphanumeric character strings that include one or more glyphs, pictures or symbols foreign to a target audience is considered as secure [26]. Adding local or global distortion to the characters can make Captcha stronger but it can have severe impact on usability [24].
- Adding adversarial noise: The addition of small carefully chosen perturbation called adversarial noise to the source image can make the Captcha resistant to deep learning based attacks without impacting usability [34].

4 Related Work

Captcha is an important security measure to defend against malicious bot programs. Various types of Captchas have been proposed in the past including text Captchas, image Captchas, audio Captchas and video Captchas. In Image Captcha, multiple images are arranged in a rectangular grid and the user is asked to select the images matching the given textual or image description [28,29]. Audio Captchas are composed of a sequence of characters layered on top of noise and provide accessible alternative to visually impaired people. In Video Captcha, moving letters are presented to the user in form of video [33]. However, text based Captchas remain the popular choice on the internet due to various factors such as ease of construction and user friendliness.

With the advancement in the field of Artificial Intelligence, all form of Captchas have shown to be broken [20,22,37]. Sivakorn et al. [37] designed a novel deep learning based attack which solved 70.78% of the Google image reCaptcha challenges and 83.5% of the Facebook image challenges. Bursztein et al. [22] solved 75% of eBay audio Captchas using an open-source speech recognition system Sphinx. NuCaptcha, a type of video Captcha, was also broken with 90% accuracy [20].

Various generic solvers have been proposed to solve text Captchas in recent years. Bursztein et al. [23] proposed a machine learning based tool (SVM), Decaptcha, and successfully attacked 13 out of 15 real Captcha schemes from popular websites. The tool employed 11,000 Captcha examples from each website which were labeled using Amazon's crowdsourcing-service Mechanical Turk. Later, Bursztein et al. [21] proposed a novel approach to solve Captchas in a single step that uses machine learning and reinforcement learning to attack the segmentation and the recognition problems simultaneously. They were able to solve 8 real-world captcha schemes with high enough accuracy again using 11,000 labeled examples from each targeted website.

Gao et al. [27] proposed an attack based on Log-Gabor filters and KNN, and demonstrated that it can break a wide range of text Captchas with distinct design features, including those deployed by Google, Microsoft, Yahoo! and Amazon. The tool employed only 500 Captcha examples for training, however the average speed of solving a Captcha was around 15 s on a standard desktop computer. The problem with the previous approaches is that they requires a large number of labeled images to achieve high accuracy. Recently, Ye et al. [39] attempted to address the problem of data availability by using GANs. However, the computational resources required to train such networks is very high.

5   Conclusion

In this paper, we proposed a lightweight image processing based Captcha solver called *Revelio*. The working of *Revelio* is simple and involves two phases, Captcha training and Captcha solving. During the training phase, all labeled Captcha images are preprocessed, segmented and a character dictionary is created. In the solving phase, the Captcha image is processed and segmented into individual characters as before. To infer the Captcha label, each segmented character is matched against characters in the dictionary created during the training phase. We demonstrated that *Revelio* can break Captchas deployed on 14 major Indian websites in real-time (0.3s) with a greater accuracy, using only 100 labeled Captcha images. We explored four different feature extraction techniques, namely average hash, difference hash, perpetual hash and histogram of oriented gradient (HOG). We found that HOG features performed better than image hashes. We also gave several recommendations for Captcha designers to create more robust Captcha schemes. In future, we aim to extend the capability of *Revelio* to break more complex Captchas. Further, we plan to conduct a user study to determine the usability of Captchas with recommended characteristics.

References

1. BotDetect Audio CAPTCHA Samples. https://captcha.com/audio-captcha-examples.html. Accessed 8 Aug 2020
2. CM Relief Fund. https://cmrf.maharashtra.gov.in/CMRFCitizen/showdonform.action. Accessed 8 Aug 2020
3. CM Relief Fund. https://apcmrf.ap.gov.in. Accessed 8 Aug 2020
4. CM Relief Fund. www.cmrf.bih.nic.in/users/quickdonate.aspx. Accessed 8 Aug 2020
5. Deep-CAPTCHA. https://github.com/DrMahdiRezaei/Deep-CAPTCHA. Accessed 8 Aug 2020
6. Login to Allahabad Netbanking. https://www.allbankonline.in/jsp/startnew.jsp. Accessed 8 Aug 2020
7. Login to Axis. https://retail.axisbank.co.in. Accessed 8 Aug 2020
8. Login to Fast tag HDFC. https://fastag.hdfcbank.com/RetailRoadUserLogin/Index. Accessed 8 Aug 2020
9. Login to IRCTC. https://www.irctc.co.in/nget/train-search. Accessed 8 Aug 2020
10. Login to Karnataka Bank. https://moneyclick.karnatakabank.co.in/BankAwayRetail/AuthenticationController?FORMSGROUP_ID_=AuthenticationFG&_START_TRAN_FLAG_=Y&_EVENT_ID_=LOAD&ACTION.LOAD=Y&_CALL_MODE_=52&AuthenticationFG.LOGIN_FLAG=1&BANK_ID=KBL. Accessed 8 Aug 2020
11. Login to MSRTC. https://public.msrtcors.com/ticket_booking/index.php. Accessed 8 Aug 2020
12. Login to OnlineSBI. https://retail.onlinesbi.com/retail/login.htm. Accessed 8 Aug 2020
13. Login to Service Plus. https://serviceonline.gov.in/. Accessed 8 Aug 2020
14. Registration on Vistara. https://www.airvistara.com/in/en/club-vistara/register. Accessed 8 Aug 2020
15. SBI Collect Payment. https://www.onlinesbi.com/sbicollect/payment/showpaymentdetails.htm. Accessed 8 Aug 2020
16. SimilarWeb. https://www.similarweb.com/. Accessed 8 Aug 2020
17. VAHAN search. https://vahan.nic.in/nrservices/faces/user/searchstatus.xhtml. Accessed 8 Aug 2020
18. von Ahn, L., Blum, M., Langford, J.: Telling humans and computers apart automatically. Commun. ACM **47**(2), 56–60 (2004). https://doi.org/10.1145/966389.966390
19. Brodić, D., Amelio, A.: Captcha programming. In: The CAPTCHA: Perspectives and Challenges, pp. 55–76. Springer (2020)
20. Bursztein, E.: How we broke the nucaptcha video scheme and what we propose to fix it. https://elie.net/blog/security/how-we-broke-the-nucaptcha-video-scheme-and-what-we-propose-to-fix-it. Accessed 08 Aug 2020

21. Bursztein, E., Aigrain, J., Moscicki, A., Mitchell, J.C.: The end is nigh: generic solving of text-based CAPTCHAs. In: 8th USENIX Workshop on Offensive Technologies (WOOT 2014). USENIX Association, San Diego, CA (2014). https://www.usenix.org/conference/woot14/workshop-program/presentation/bursztein
22. Bursztein, E., Bethard, S.: Decaptcha: breaking 75% of EBay audio CAPTCHAs. In: Proceedings of the 3rd USENIX Conference on Offensive Technologies (WOOT 2009). p. 8. USENIX Association, USA (2009)
23. Bursztein, E., Martin, M., Mitchell, J.: Text-based CAPTCHA strengths and weaknesses. In: Proceedings of the 18th ACM Conference on Computer and Communications Security (CCS 2011), pp. 125–138. Association for Computing Machinery, New York, NY, USA (2011). https://doi.org/10.1145/2046707.2046724
24. Chow, Y.-W., Susilo, W., Thorncharoensri, P.: CAPTCHA design and security issues. In: Li, K.-C., Chen, X., Susilo, W. (eds.) Advances in Cyber Security: Principles, Techniques, and Applications, pp. 69–92. Springer, Singapore (2019). https://doi.org/10.1007/978-981-13-1483-4_4
25. Dalal, N., Triggs, B.: Histograms of oriented gradients for human detection. In: 2005 IEEE Computer Society Conference on Computer Vision and Pattern Recognition (CVPR 2005), vol. 1. pp. 886–893 (2005)
26. Foote, E.M.: More secure image-based "CAPTCHA" technique, US Patent 9,075,983 (2015)
27. Gao, H., et al.: A simple generic attack on text Captchas. In: 23rd Annual Network and Distributed System Security Symposium, NDSS 2016, San Diego, California, USA, February 21–24, 2016. The Internet Society (2016). http://wp.internetsociety.org/ndss/wp-content/uploads/sites/25/2017/09/simple-generic-attack-text-captchas.pdf
28. Google: reCAPTCHA protects your website from fraud and abuse. https://www.google.com/recaptcha/about/. Accessed 8 August 2020
29. hCaptcha: Stop more bots. Start protecting user privacy. https://www.hcaptcha.com/. Accessed 8 Aug 2020
30. Institute, M.G.: Digital India: technology to transform a connected nation, https://www.mckinsey.com/business-functions/mckinsey-digital/our-insights/digital-india-technology-to-transform-a-connected-nation. Accessed 8 Aug 2020
31. McConnell, R.K.: Method of and apparatus for pattern recognition (1986)
32. Nouri, Z., Rezaei, M.: Deep-CAPTCHA: a deep learning based CAPTCHA solver for vulnerability assessment. Available at SSRN 3633354 (2020)
33. NuCaptcha: How Much Is User Abandonment Costing Your Company?. https://www.nucaptcha.com. Accessed 8 Aug 2020
34. Osadchy, M., Hernandez-Castro, J., Gibson, S., Dunkelman, O., Pérez-Cabo, D.: No bot expects the deepcaptcha! introducing immutable adversarial examples, with applications to captcha generation. IEEE Trans. Inf. Forensics Secur. 12(11), 2640–2653 (2017)
35. Otsu, N.: A threshold selection method from gray-level histograms. IEEE Trans. Syst. Man Cybern. 9(1), 62–66 (1979)
36. Roberts, E.: Bad Bot Report 2020: Bad Bots Strike Back. https://www.imperva.com/blog/bad-bot-report-2020-bad-bots-strike-back/. Accessed 8 Aug 2020
37. Sivakorn, S., Polakis, I., Keromytis, A.D.: I am Robot: (Deep) learning to break semantic image CAPTCHAs. In: 2016 IEEE European Symposium on Security and Privacy (EuroS P), pp. 388–403 (2016)

38. Verma, N., Dawar, S.: Digital transformation in the indian government. Commun. ACM **62**(11), 50–53 (2019). https://doi.org/10.1145/3349629
39. Ye, G., et al.: Yet another text Captcha solver: a generative adversarial network based approach. In: Proceedings of the 2018 ACM SIGSAC Conference on Computer and Communications Security (CCS 2018), pp. 332–348. Association for Computing Machinery, New York, NY, USA (2018). https://doi.org/10.1145/3243734.3243754

Privacy-Preserving Friend Recommendation in an Integrated Social Environment

Nitish M. Uplavikar[1(✉)], Jaideep Vaidya[2], Dan Lin[1], and Wei Jiang[1]

[1] University of Missouri, Columbia, MO 65201, USA
nmu455@mail.missouri.edu, {lindan,wjiang}@missouri.edu
[2] Rutgers University, Newark, NJ 07102, USA
jsvaidya@business.rutgers.edu

Abstract. Ubiquitous Online Social Networks (OSN)s play a vital role in information creation, propagation and consumption. Given the recent multiplicity of OSNs with specially accumulated knowledge, integration partnerships are formed (without regard to privacy) to provide an enriched, integrated and personalized social experience. However, given the increasing privacy concerns and threats, it is important to develop methods that can provide collaborative capabilities while preserving user privacy. In this work, we focus on friend recommendation systems (FRS) for such partnered OSNs. We identify the various ways through which privacy leaks can occur, and propose a comprehensive solution that integrates both Differential Privacy and Secure Multi-Party Computation to provide a holistic privacy guarantee. We analyze the security of the proposed approach and evaluate the proposed solution with real data in terms of both utility and computational complexity.

Keywords: Friend recommendation · Differential privacy · Secure multiparty computation · OSNs

1 Introduction

Online Social Networks (OSNs) are ubiquitous today, and have gone far beyond their original intent and impacted human life across multiple spheres such as enabling knowledge creation [4], sociopolitical movements [14], health management [1,16], etc. Following the original OSNs that enable users to connect with old or new friends/acquaintances, there are other emerging and more specialized OSNs that cater to certain demand or enable specific services for the users, such as, Spotify (Music), Instagram (Photos), Fitbit (Fitness), and so on.

Depending on the function and the type of an OSN, personalised recommendations can be made to its users regarding new friends, groups, events, goods for purchase, etc. OSNs use friend recommender systems (FRS) to increase their user base and enrich online user interaction. In order to provide more accurate recommendations, the existing FRS also leverages information from other OSNs

© Springer Nature Switzerland AG 2020
S. Kanhere et al. (Eds.): ICISS 2020, LNCS 12553, pp. 117–136, 2020.
https://doi.org/10.1007/978-3-030-65610-2_8

by forming integration partners (IP) [22]. However, these partnerships have led to many security and privacy issues. For example, Facebook's (FB) partners namely Microsoft's Bing can see virtually all FB users' friends without consent, and Netflix and Spotify were able to read FB user's private messages [6,28].

Consider the example of Spotify which allows its users to connect or create an account using the individual's Facebook account. The users can listen to songs and create their own contents, they can also follow their friends' collection or some artist. As a result, a small network can be formed by Spotify users. However, Spotify cannot boast of a rich, stable and robust network that Facebook has of its users, that is created over a duration of almost a decade. Reaching that stage of network structure would take some time and not allow Spotify the ability to provide more accurate recommendations, of either users or songs, to its users. One solution to this problem is that Spotify can, in collaboration with Facebook, provide diverse yet relevant recommendations to its users. Here, Spotify (the client) and Facebook (the server) would be in an integration partnership with the server providing recommendation services, based on its social network data, to the client. While this has benefits, there are numerous privacy/security risks:

1. *Leaking the server's social network data to the client*: The client can recreate the server's owned network to a certain extent by repeatedly running queries for the same users. Using a mutual friends based FRS, the client can repeatedly execute such type of query to infer one friendship at a time. Eventually, the client may be able to construct the original graph or sub-graph of friendship that is owned by the server.
2. *Leaking client's user information*: The server knows which users in its network are subscribing to the services provided by the client. Users subscribing to client's services might want to keep this membership information private from the server. On the other hand, the client may want to keep its users' information private.
3. *Leaking client's network data to the server*: The server can recreate the network on the client by analyzing the recommendation scores and patterns of users queried. It can assume that the user always picks the top one or two recommended users and create a sub-graph of the possible friendship graph for a user that would be created on the client.

1.1 Problem Definition

In this paper, we propose privacy-preserving friend recommendation (PPFR) protocols in the aforementioned integration partnership environment to protect the private network data at both the server S and the client C. In practice, the server in our application domain is a well-established social network like Facebook, and the client is a specialized social network who wants to provide friend recommendations to its own users based on the social network data from the server. The network datasets are modeled as graphs and denoted by G_S and G_C at the server and the client respectively.

Without any security guarantee, a mutual friend based FR generally works as follows: given a user u at the client C, C selects a set of users $\{v_1,\ldots,v_m\}$ who may potentially become friends with u. C issues a query in the form of m pairs of user-ids, $(u,v_1),\ldots,(u,v_m)$, to the server S. For each pair (u,v_i), S performs the necessary computation to obtain the mutual friends count $s_i \leftarrow m_{G_S}(u,v_i)$ which will be sent to C. The client can then make use of the scores to recommend some users (e.g., top k or above a predefined threshold) in $v_1,\ldots,v_m$ to u. Thus, the FR functionality is defined as follows between a server S and a client C:

$$\mathrm{FR}(\langle S,G_S\rangle,\langle C,(u,v_1),\ldots,(u,v_m)\rangle) \rightarrow \langle C,s_1,\ldots,s_m\rangle \qquad (1)$$

1.2   Problem Relevance

The problem addressed in this paper does commonly occur in the real world. Specifically, [6] and [28] highlight the privacy issues that can occur amongst existing integration partners. Here, we provide a privacy-preserving solution that can serve as an alternative to the existing non-private solutions among the OSNs.

The solution is targeted for instances where the Memorandum of Understanding (MOU) agreement cannot guarantee exact private or sensitive data or in situations where the user is not fully willing to agree to the OSN's End User License Agreement (EULA), which might offer a weak privacy-guarantee. Generally, the user is forced to agree to the EULA by the need to use the service and has very little to say in the matter. In this case, this PPFR system can provide an alternative privacy-preserving solution for the service.

This solution gives the OSNs the ability to provide multiple options to users, and thereby empowering the user, in terms of how their data could be handled i.e. either in a non-private way or in a Differentially Private way.

1.3   Adversary Model and Protocol Overview

We assume the server and the client are semi-honest [12]. That is, the participants follow the prescribed steps of the protocol, and then try to learn additional information. In addition, we assume the parties are computationally bounded. For a privacy-preserving friend recommendation (PPFR) protocol in the integration partnership environment, the following information needs to be protected.

- G_S: The server's network data that needs to be protected from the client. Since information regarding G_S can be inferred from the mutual friends counts, this implies that $s_1,\ldots,s_m$ should be protected.
- G_C: Information regarding the client's network data should not be disclosed to the server. This implies that the server should not know the user ids, e.g., $(u,v_1),\ldots,(u,v_m)$ used in the recommendation.

In order to prevent the server from knowing $(u,v_1),\ldots,(u,v_m)$ and simultaneously derives $s_1,\ldots,s_m$, one natural choice is to adopt Secure Multiparty Computation (SMC) techniques [12] to implement the FR functionality given in

Eq. 1. However, SMC alone is not sufficient. As discussed previously, the similarity scores can leak information regarding the server's network data G_S.

Let u be the user for which party C performs friend recommendation over a set of recommendation candidates v_j, such that, $1 \leq j \leq m$. In this case, the query tuples would be $\langle u, v_j \rangle$. To select candidate user id v_j for running queries along a fixed user u, candidate pool for v_j can be narrowed down depending upon the users' information at C e.g. affiliation, contact lists etc. [20].

An approach to address this issue could involve party S sharing the network homophily parameters with party C and C then computing the similarity scores. However, there are limitations within this architectural approach. Firstly, in the sharing of parameters approach the recommender system may not be able to leverage real-time nature of database present at S and in order to do achieve this at a lesser extent, parameters need to be periodically shared with C. Such updates may also leak some information about latest database changes. Additionally, quantifying the interval period may be subjective, complex and may further require domain expert involvement to guarantee privacy and utility.

What if we modify the FR functionality? Instead of returning the similarity scores, the server can return (1) the top k most similar users where $1 \leq k \leq m$, or (2) all the users whose similarity scores are above a given threshold. While both options seemingly leak less information about G_S, it is hard to actually quantify the exact degree of information leakage. Instead, we adopt Differential Privacy (DP) [3,18,29] as a formal and quantifiable model to control information leakage from the similarity scores. Specially, only differentially private similarity scores are returned to the client. In summary, the key novelty of our proposed PPFR protocol is to intelligently combine two dominant privacy-preserving technologies to prevent information leakage during the friend recommendation process.

The aim of the proposed protocol involves privacy-preserving computation of mutual friend count for friend recommendation purposes in an integrated environment. Using other friendship recommendation criteria, apart from using number of mutual friends as addressed here, is out of the scope of this paper. However, since the protocol relies on privacy-preserving set intersection computation, any other criteria that involves set intersection computation can be supported by this work e.g. recommendation based on similar interests, groups, locations etc.

2   Preliminaries

Here we will discuss mutual friends based friend recommendation (FR). Additionally, we present an overview of differential privacy (DP) [10], and the way it is applied to graph problems to enhance the privacy in relevance to our work.

2.1   Friend Recommendation Based on Mutual Friends

The topic of FR is widely addressed [2,25]. One of the most common features in a social network to use for FR is related to the number of common/mutual friends between two users. This feature assumes that two people are more likely to be *friends* if they have some common friends amongst themselves. The similarity score using mutual friends can be computed based on set intersection. Given two users u and v, let l_u and l_v denote the friend lists of u and v respectively. Then, the similarity of u and v is computed as:

$$\text{Similarity}(u, v) = |l_u \cap l_v| \tag{2}$$

2.2 Differential Privacy (DP)

Differential Privacy (DP) [10] is a privacy model that provides a formal mathematical bound on the increase in privacy risk to any person due to the use of their data in a given computation. An algorithm can be considered to be differentially private if for all possible outputs, the likelihood of getting any output does not significantly vary based on the inclusion or exclusion of any single person's data. The formal definition is as follows:

For $\epsilon > 0$, a mechanism (viz algorithm) $T(\cdot)$ with domain G is ϵ-differentially private if for every $x, y \in G$ such that $\|x - y\|_1 \leq 1$ and every $\Lambda \subseteq \text{Range}(T)$,

$$Pr\left[T(x) \in \Lambda\right] \leq e^{\epsilon} Pr\left[T(y) \in \Lambda\right]$$

While there are many general ways to achieve Differential Privacy, here we consider the simple Laplace Mechanism [9] which adds suitably scaled noise to the output. Specifically, the global sensitivity S_m of the function m is computed as the maximum change in the output for any two neighboring inputs, and Laplace noise proportional to S_m/ϵ is added to the output.

3 The Proposed Protocol

In this section, we discuss the details of our proposed PPFR protocol. Under Secure Multiparty Computation (SMC), there are several ways to implement a secure protocol, e.g., additive homomorphic encryption (HEnc), secret sharing (SS), oblivious transfer (OT), garble circuits (GC), and fully homomorphic encryption (FHE). Approaches based on OT, GC and FHE requires the FR functionality being represented as a Boolean or an arithmetic circuit. When the dataset at the server is very large, the size of the circuit can become intractable. In addition, the social network data G_S keep changing all the time, the circuit has to be reconstructed every time a change is made to G_S. SS based approach requires at least three independent parties. HEnc provides a good balance among these factors. As a result, the proposed protocol utilizes an HEnc scheme, such as Paillier [21]. More importantly, our protocol design provides a novel way to securely compute the similarity score based on mutual friends which can be implemented with any specific aforementioned SMC approach.

3.1 Protocol Initialization

The algorithm and sub-algorithms are dependent upon an encryption system (HEnc) which exhibits homomorphic additive properties. We use the Paillier Cryptosystem [21] for this purpose, with pu being the public key and pr, the private key, known by the client only. Under DF, ϵ guarantees an upper bound on the difference of the output distributions from any two input datasets that differ by a single record. The lower the value of ϵ, the more similar the two distributions would be and the more similar the two distributions are, the more difficult it would be to predict which dataset out of the two was the actual input. The parties running the PPFR protocol should agree upon this value prior to the execution. From ϵ, we can derive λ, the scaling parameter of Laplace distribution from which the noise will be generated. Note that the global sensitivity of the similarity is 1 since at most the number of common users can increase (or decrease) by 1. Therefore λ set to $1/\epsilon$ is sufficient to ensure ϵ-differential privacy.

3.2 The Main Protocol

The key steps of the proposed PPFR protocol are given in Algorithm 1. The private input from the server is its network data G_S, represented as an adjacency list L: user u_i's friend list is denoted by L_i. The private input from the client is a pair of users (u_a, u_b), and the protocol returns a similarity score between the two users based on G_S. To achieve the functionality given in Eq. 1, the protocol can be run in parallel with each of m user pairs: $(u, v_1), \ldots, (u, v_m)$, and m similarity scores are returned to the client at the end. We assume that there is a mapping from a user id to a value in $\mathbb{Z}_N^*$. All notations in Algorithm 1 that represent users are in $\mathbb{Z}_N^*$. Step-by-step explanations of the protocol are given below, and the index i is in $\{1, \ldots, n\}$ where n is the number of users at the server.

- Step 1: The client encrypts the users ids. Instead of u_a and u_b, the client encrypts $-u_a$ and $-u_b$ which is equivalent to $N - u_a$ and $N - u_b$. At the end of the step, the encrypted inverses of the user ids, $E_{pu}(-u_a)$ and $E_{pu}(-u_b)$, are sent to the server.
- Step 2: Γ_i is an encryption of user id u_i, and $\hat{\Gamma}_i$ is a random permutation of Γ_i to hide the relative positions of u_a and u_b in G_S. In practice, it seems this permutation is not necessary; however, it is needed to formally prove the security of the protocol. η_i is equal to 0 if $u_i = u_a$ in the permuted user list; otherwise, it is a random value chosen from $\mathbb{Z}_N^*$. Note that the server cannot determine which user is u_a as the ciphertext $E_{pu}(\eta_i)$ is derived using a probabilistic encryption algorithm with homomorphic additive properties, e.g. the Paillier Cryptosystem [21], even for $\eta_i = 0$. θ_i is defined similarly, except that it is equal to 0 if $u_i = u_b$. Since the computations are performed based on the encrypted u_a and u_b, the server does not know which u_i corresponds to u_a or u_b. In other words, the server does not know the similarity score is computed for which two users.
- Step 3: The client decrypts $E_{pu}(\eta_i)$ and $E_{pu}(\theta_i)$, and construct n encrypted values, each of which is denoted by $E_{pu}(k_i)$, where k_i is equal to 1 if either η_i

or θ_i is 0. Alternatively, we can interpret that k_i is equal to 1 if either $u_a = u_i$ or $u_b = u_i$. This implies that there are only two k_is equal to 1, and the rest of k_i values are 0s.

- Step 4: For each friend list L_i, the server computes $E_{pu}(\omega_i)$: each user u_j in L_i is replaced with $E_{pu}(k_j)$ or the jth encrypted value received from the client. Then these encrypted values are multiplied together to get $E_{pu}(\omega_i)$. Based on the k_j values, ω_i can only have three distinct values:
  - $\omega_i = 0$: indicating that u_i is not a friend of u_a or u_b.
  - $\omega_i = 1$: indicating that u_i is a friend of u_a or u_b, but not both.
  - $\omega_i = 2$: indicating that u_i is a friend of both u_a and u_b.

Suppose that we can derive a value ω_i' such that $\omega_i' = 0$ if $\omega_i = 1$ or $\omega_i = 0$, and $\omega_i' = 1$ if $\omega_i = 2$. Then $\sum_{i=1}^{m} \omega_i'$ is the mutual friend count of u_a and u_b. To derive ω_i', we use the following equation:

$$\omega_i' = \frac{\omega_i(\omega_i - 1)}{2} \tag{3}$$

The goal of Steps 5 and 6 is to derive $E_{pu}(\omega_i')$ from $E(\omega_i)$. Since ω_i can leak information about G_S, the server randomizes it, by adding a random value, to produce $E_{pu}(\omega_i + r_i)$.

- Step 5: Decrypting $E_{pu}(\omega_i + r_i)$, the client obtains $\omega_i + r_i$. Then the client computes $(\omega_i + r_i)(\omega_i - 1 + r_i)$, and sends the encrypted result to the server.
- Step 6: Since the server knows r_i and $E_{pu}(\omega_i)$, the server can obtain

$$E_{pu}(-2r_i\omega_i + r_i - r_i^2)$$

Multiplying it with $E_{pu}((\omega_i + r_i)(\omega_i - 1 + r_i))$, the server obtains $E_{pu}(\omega_i(\omega_i - 1))$. Because h is the multiplicative inverse of 2 in $\mathbb{Z}_N^*$, the sub-step (c) produces the encryption of ω_i'. Based on how ω_i' is derived, we know that ρ is the mutual friend count. The sub-step (f) randomizes the actual score by adding a noise generated from a Laplace distribution.
- Step 7: The client decrypts the encrypted score to get the differentially private similarity score for u_a and u_b.

3.3   Security Analysis

The security of PPFR can be proved using the simulation method in [12]. First, we need to build a simulator based on the private input and output for each party. Since the computations between the two parties are asymmetric, the simulators are different for the individual parties. Let Π_S and Π_C denote the real execution images for the server and the client respectively. Similarly, $\Pi_{\widetilde{S}}$ and $\Pi_{\widetilde{C}}$ denote the simulated execution images. Next, we show how to construct a simulator Simulator-S to produce $\Pi_{\widetilde{S}}$.

Simulator-S. For a two-party distributed protocol, private information can be disclosed from the messages exchanged during the execution of the protocol. The server receives messages from the client at Steps 2, 4 and 6 of the PPRF protocol. Thus, the real execution image Π_S consists of the following information $(1 \leq i \leq n)$:

Algorithm 1. PPFR($\langle$Server, $G_S\rangle$, $\langle$Client, $u_a, u_b\rangle$) $\rightarrow$ $\langle$Client, $s\rangle$

Require: $h \leftarrow 2^{-1} \mod N$, and the index i varies from 1 to n where n denotes the number of users at the server

1: Client:
   (a) Compute $E_{pu}(-u_a)$ and $E_{pu}(-u_b)$
   (b) Send both to the server
2: Server:
   (a) Receive $E_{pu}(-u_a)$ and $E_{pu}(-u_b)$ from the client
   (b) Compute $\Gamma_i \leftarrow E_{pu}(u_i)$
   (c) $\hat{\Gamma}_i \leftarrow \pi(\Gamma_i)$, where π is a random permutation
   (d) $E_{pu}(\eta_i) \leftarrow \left[\hat{\Gamma}_i \cdot E_{pu}(-u_a)\right]^{r_i}$, where $r_i \in_R \mathbb{Z}_N^*$
   (e) $E_{pu}(\theta_i) \leftarrow \left[\hat{\Gamma}_i \cdot E_{pu}(-u_b)\right]^{r_i'}$, where $r_i' \in_R \mathbb{Z}_N^*$
   (f) Send $E_{pu}(\eta_i)$ and $E_{pu}(\theta_i)$ to the client
3: Client:
   (a) Receive $E_{pu}(\eta_i)$ and $E_{pu}(\theta_i)$ from the server
   (b) Decrypt $E_{pu}(\eta_i)$ and $E_{pu}(\theta_i)$ to obtain η_i and θ_i
   (c) Compute $E_{pu}(k_i)$, such that,

$$k_i \leftarrow \begin{cases} 1 & \text{if } \eta_i = 0 \text{ or } \theta_i = 0 \\ 0 & \text{otherwise} \end{cases}$$

   (d) Send $E_{pu}(k_i)$ to the server
4: Server:
   (a) Receive $E_{pu}(k_i)$ from the client
   (b) $E_{pu}(\omega_i) \leftarrow \prod_{u_j \in L_i} E_{pu}(k_j)$
   (c) $E_{pu}(\omega_i + r_i) \leftarrow E_{pu}(\omega_i) \times E_{pu}(r_i)$, where $r_i \in_R \mathbb{Z}_N$
   (d) Send $E_{pu}(\omega_i + r_i)$ to the client
5: Client:
   (a) Receive $E_{pu}(\omega_i + r_i)$ from the server
   (b) $\omega_i + r_i \leftarrow D_{pr}(E_{pu}(\omega_i + r_i))$
   (c) Compute $E_{pu}((\omega_i + r_i)(\omega_i - 1 + r_i))$ and send them to the server
6: Server:
   (a) Receive $E_{pu}((\omega_i + r_i)(\omega_i - 1 + r_i))$ from the client
   (b) $E_{pu}(\omega_i(\omega_i - 1)) \leftarrow E_{pu}((\omega_i + r_i)(\omega_i - 1 + r_i)) \times E_{pu}(-2r_i\omega_i + r_i - r_i^2)$
   (c) $E_{pu}(\omega_i') \leftarrow [E_{pu}(\omega_i(\omega_i - 1))]^h$
   (d) $E_{pu}(\rho) \leftarrow \prod_{i=1}^n E_{pu}(\omega_i')$
   (e) Compute noise $\delta' \leftarrow \lceil \delta \rceil$, where $\delta \sim_R$ Laplace$(0, \lambda)$
   (f) $E_{pu}(s) \leftarrow E_{pu}(\rho) \times E_{pu}(\delta')$
   (g) Send $E_{pu}(s)$ to the client
7: Client:
   (a) Receive $E_{pu}(s)$ from the server
   (b) $s \leftarrow D_{pr}(E_{pu}(s))$

Algorithm 2. Simulator-$S(pu)$

Require: pu is the public key of Paillier
  1: Generate four randoms r_1, r_2, r_3 and r_4 from Z_N
  2: Return $E_{pu}(r_1)$, $E_{pu}(r_2)$, $E_{pu}(r_3)$ and $E_{pu}(r_4)$

- $E_{pu}(-u_a)$, $E_{pu}(-u_b)$, $E_{pu}(k_i)$ and $E_{pu}((\omega_i + r_i)(\omega_i - 1 + r_i))$

The key steps of Simulator-S are given in Algorithm 2, and the simulated execution image $\Pi_{\widetilde{S}}$ consists of

- $E_{pu}(r_1)$, $E_{pu}(r_2)$, $E_{pu}(r_3)$ and $E_{pu}(r_4)$

where each encrypted value corresponds to the value from the real execution.

Claim 1. $\Pi_{\widetilde{S}}$ is computationally indistinguishable from Π_S.

Proof. Suppose the claim is not true, then this implies that one of the $E_{pu}(r_i)$ values is computationally distinguishable from the corresponding value of the real execution image. Without loss of generality, assume $E_{pu}(r_1)$ is computationally distinguishable from $E_{pu}(u_a)$. However, this contradicts the fact that the Paillier encryption scheme is semantically secure or computationally indistinguishable [21]. Therefore, $\Pi_{\widetilde{S}}$ must be computationally indistinguishable from Π_S.

The above claim demonstrates that fact that any information that the server learned during the execution of PPFR can be derived by what the server already knows. Thus, from the client's perspective, the protocol is computationally secure. Next we need to prove the protocol is secure from the server's perspective by building a simulator to simulate the client's execution image.

Algorithm 3. Simulator-$C(pr, s)$

Require: pr is the private key of Paillier, s is the output from PPRF
  1: For $1 \leq j \leq n$, randomly generate r_{1j}, r_{2j}, and r_{3j} from Z_N
  2: For $1 \leq j \leq n$, compute $E_{pu}(r_{1j})$, $E_{pu}(r_{2j})$ and $E_{pu}(r_{3j})$
  3: Let η' and θ' be random permutations of a sequence of n values, such that only one of them is 0 and the rest are randomly generated from $\mathbb{Z}_N^*$
  4: Return the following ($1 \leq j \leq n$)
    - $X' \sim \langle E_{pu}(r_{1j}), E_{pu}(r_{2j}), \eta', \theta' \rangle$
    - $Y' \sim \langle E_{pu}(r_{3j}), r_{3j} \rangle$
    - $Z' \sim \langle E_{pu}(s), s \rangle$

Simulator-C. The client receives messages from the server at Steps 3, 5 and 7 of the PPRF protocol. Thus, the real execution image Π_C consists of the following:

- $X \sim \langle E_{pu}(\eta_1), \dots, E_{pu}(\eta_n), E_{pu}(\theta_1), \dots, E_{pu}(\theta_n), \eta \equiv \eta_1 \cdots \eta_n, \theta \equiv \theta_1 \cdots \theta_n \rangle$
- $Y \sim \langle E_{pu}(\omega_1 + r_1), \dots, E_{pu}(\omega_n + r_n), \omega_i + r_i, \dots, \omega_n + r_n \rangle$

$- \ Z \sim \langle E_{pu}(s), s \rangle$

where X, Y and Z denote the random variables related to the corresponding pair of values. For each pair, the first component is the message received, and the second component is the value derived from the first component. The simulator needs to simulate these messages and the information derived from them. Algorithm 3 provides the key steps for Simulator-C.

Claim 2. $\Pi_{\widetilde{C}}$ is computationally indistinguishable from Π_C.

Proof. This proof is very similar to that of the previous claim. We omit some of the technical details. However, we want to emphasize that η' is indistinguishable from η due to the fact that the user list is randomly permuted at Step 2(c) of Algorithm 1.

The above claim demonstrates that fact that any information that the client learned during the execution of the PPFR protocol can be derived by its private input and output. Thus, from the server's perspective, the protocol is computationally secure. Combining both, we prove the security of PPFR. Since appropriately scaled Laplacian noise is added to the output, differential privacy is achieved as well.

3.4 Complexity Analysis

In order to theoretically measure the computation complexity of PPFR, our analyses are based on the number of the most expensive operations used in the protocol which happen to be the encryption E and decryption D operations, as well as the exponentiation of a ciphertext. We use the Paillier cryptosystem where the costs of E and D are approximately similar. We represent both costs as e, use x to represent the cost of obtaining the exponentiation of a ciphertext, and use p to represent the cost of multiplying two ciphertexts. Let t be the number of bits required for representing the ciphertext. n is the number of users present in server's OSN graph. The overall protocol complexity is derived for both the parties (the client and server), and provided in Table 1, where O and T_x represent the computation and communication complexity, respectively.

4 Experimental Results

In this section, we provide a detailed empirical analysis, both qualitative and quantitative, of the performance of the various algorithms proposed.

4.1 Experimental Setup

Dataset: Given privacy concerns, real world OSN data is difficult to gather for this purpose. Two potential alternatives are to use simulated datasets or real world data from other domains. We use the real-world DBLP computer science

Table 1. Computation and communication complexity of the PPFR algorithm

Step	Server O	Server T_x	Client O	Client T_x
1			$2e$	$2t$
2	$ne + 2nx + 2np$	$2nt$		
3			$3ne$	nt
4	$(n^2 - 2m)e + ne + np$	nt		
5			$2ne$	nt
6	$(n+1)e + (2n+1)p + x$	t		
7			e	
Total	$(n^2 + 3n - 2m + 1)e +$ $(2n+1)x + (5n+1)p$	$(3n+1)t$	$(5n+3)e$	$2(n+1)t$

bibliography dataset (Aug. 2018) [5] to test our system. Note that DBLP can be considered as an OSN for co-authorship. This dataset helps us in gaining a good idea about the performance and utility of our protocol applied on real-world relationships. We believe that this is preferable to using simulated OSN datasets since then the results would also depend on the quality of the simulation, which might be difficult to ascertain.

The original DBLP dataset contains 6420665 bibliographic records. The dataset is preprocessed as follows:

From the dataset we extract 2185132 authors, which are represented as nodes. We extract their corresponding collaborator list. This gives us 9507042 edges that represent each collaboration relationship. All the publication records within DBLP database are parsed. As they are parsed, new authors are identified by their full names and their collaborators are noted to form an OSN graph G. Vertices and edges in G represent authors and their collaboration relationships, respectively. One issue with the DBLP dataset is that author names are used to identify authors, and therefore, common names would be associated with all the papers attributed for that particular name and consequently all the collaborators for those papers as well e.g. a commonly occurring name had 2575 collaborators. Since the recommendation functionality is based on the collaborator (or friend) count, we removed outliers (i.e., authors with collaborator count that is more than three standard deviations above the mean). Non-removal of these outliers can significantly impact the performance and the recommendation utility of the algorithm. After this we still have 2156785 authors, but the maximum number of collaborators is reduced to 73.

Machine Hardware Details: The machines used for both S and C have the following specifications:

- Processor: 64-bit Intel® Xeon® CPU E2186G @ 3.80 GHz 12CPU(s)
- Memory: 62 GiB DIMM DDR4 2666 MHz (0.4 ns)
- Hard disk: 1024 GB PC400 NVMe SK hynix

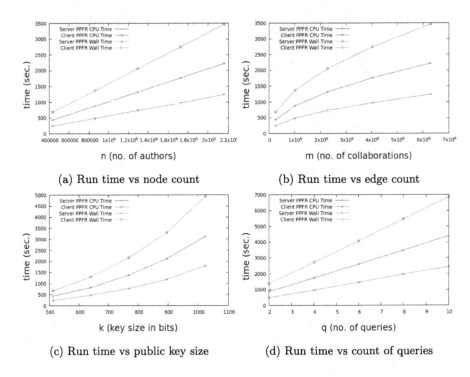

(a) Run time vs node count   (b) Run time vs edge count

(c) Run time vs public key size   (d) Run time vs count of queries

Fig. 1. Performance of the PPFR algorithm

Programming Languages and Libraries: The entire implementation is in C. The GNU GMP [27] library was used for efficiently computing the cryptographic primitives required for the algorithms. The public key encryption scheme, used in the algorithms, was based on the Pailler Cryptosystem [21] for the cryptosystem's additive homomorphic properties.

4.2   Empirical Analysis

In this section, we report on the performance of the algorithm with the strongest privacy guarantee viz. the optimum PPFR algorithm, by varying different parameters such as the dataset size, the key size, and the count of queries.

Performance Evaluation: Performance is measured using the CPU time and wall time or the wall clock time. CPU time indicates the amount of time spent by CPU to run program instructions. Wall clock time is the amount of actual time required or elapsed to run the operation. It may include time for system operations at OS level too. First, we vary the user count (n).

As seen in Fig. 1a, the query response time linearly increases with the number of users in the database. A single query run for 20%, i.e. roughly 0.4 million, of the total DBLP authors takes under 685 s to complete. Typically, the size of the dataset considered by any OSN to run queries over would be lesser, by orders of magnitude than the 0.2 million users here, for any normal user. It is to be noted that certain online social services (C) restrictively operate for a given region, or a set of users only. Based on this background information, the data owner (S) can always consider a subset of its graph G_S to run queries. Access to this background information does not harm our privacy guarantee of maintaining relationships or friends private nor leak users ids in G_M nor leak potential new friendships formed in G_M by way of this application. In general, as compared to the non-privacy-preserving solutions, privacy-preserving solutions are computationally more expensive and trade off performance for enhanced privacy and security.

Next, we vary the edge count (m). The results are shown in Fig. 1b, and are similar to the case of varying author (node) count.

Note however, that Fig. 1b was generated by regulating the node percentage. Therefore, it involves a combined effect of edge count and node count variation on times reported, i.e. it is not purely independent of the number of authors n.

Additionally, the protocol is highly parallelizable and thus could be scaled up, within cloud environments, in order to reduce the query processing time further.

Figure 1c shows the time taken by S and C when the keysize is varied. As expect, the time for execution increases exponentially with respect to the key size. Typically, the key size used is 1024. 20% of the nodes were considered in order to obtain this result. Figures 1a, b and c represent the algorithm's performance for a single query.

Wall clock time plots are provided to give an idea about the actual time required for the computation. The wall clock plots appear to be overlapping for S and C because the timer is started when client submits the query and stopped once it obtains the score. Server's wall clock time starts just when it receives the query and stops as soon as it delivers the encrypted DP score to client. Here, client requires a single decryption once it receives the DP score to obtain the result. Hence they appear to be the same but the difference is minuscule.

Finally, we vary the count of queries(q) and obtain the total CPU time and the Wall clock time. As can be seen from the Fig. 1d, the times are linear in q.

Utility Evaluation: We plot Spearman's corrected ρ [8], Kendall's τ, τ_b [23] as well as the precision, recall and f-measure statistics [26] of the top-k recommended users in order to measure the utility of the proposed approach. ρ measures the magnitude and direction of the monotonic relationship amongst the variables while τ (τ_b) measures the difference in probabilities of data being in the same order and in different order [23]. We measured both Kendall's τ and Kendall's τ_b, since τ_b accounts for ties that can occur, especially, in ranked lists for non-DP scores. Although the number of ties depends on the underlying

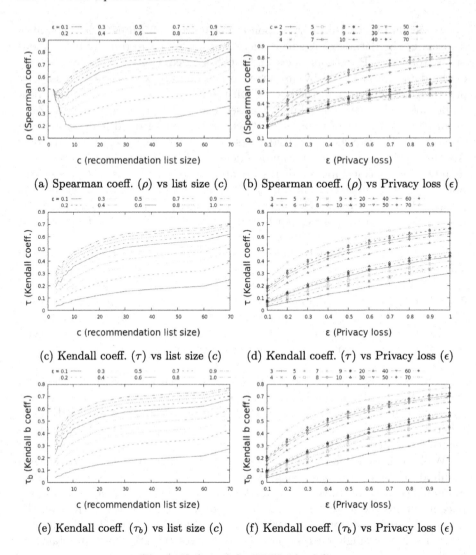

Fig. 2. Utility of the PPFR algorithm

DBLP dataset, in this case, measuring τ and τ_b provides some information about the underlying dataset while highlighting the need for using pre-processing techniques that can reduce the ties and improve the overall utility of the system or vice-versa.

The utility coefficients are computed over the ranked list of size c before and after perturbation. These coefficients are averaged over 10000 times with a list generated each time for a randomly selected author. Please note that for $c = 70$ there were less number of authors to choose from as compared to other list sizes.

Figures 2a, c, and e measure the utility when the list size (c) is varied. From Fig. 2a, we can see how PPFR's ρ initially decreases as the list size increases (until $c = 10$) and then subsequently rises along with c. This is uniquely captured just by the Spearman coefficient and not by τ or τ_b. The reason for this behaviour might be that for a given ϵ and sensitivity S ($S = 1$ for edge DP), for any list score, the differences in ranks before and after perturbation might be bounded to some extent while the n, i.e. c in this case, is incremented. Figures 2b, d, and f measure the utility for different values of the privacy parameter ϵ. As expected, the utility of PPFR increases as ϵ is increased. The utility also increases as the list size is increased. For $\epsilon = 1$ and $c = 70$, $\max(\rho) = 0.888$ while for $\epsilon = 0.1$ and $c = 10$, $\min(\rho) = 0.192$. From Fig. 2f, it can be seen that low c values with high ϵ perform better than high c value and low ϵ values. e.g. $\tau_b = 0.337$ at $c = 3$, $\epsilon = 0.9$ while $\tau_b = 0.274$ at $c = 70$, $\epsilon = 0.1$. Figures 2 and 3 provide an understanding for the server and client OSNs about setting the value of privacy loss parameter ϵ and the corresponding utility obtained.

Unlike Spearman's, Kendall's coefficients do not reach their lowest values closer to $c = 10$, see Figures 2c, e, however, they do show mild fluctuations around it indicating greater uncertainty. In general, $\tau_b \geq \tau$ against both c and privacy loss parameter ϵ, which can be seen from Figures 2c–f

We also measure precision, recall and the f-measure statistic for top-k ranks within a list of size c. Due to space restrictions we only report results for $k = 5$ and $k = 10$. From Fig. 3, it can be seen that the observed precision is generally higher than the recall. This effect is due to the multiple rank ties found in scores before DP perturbation.

Figures 3 and 4 show the relation of precision, recall and f-measure with c. For both top-5 and top-10, as c rises, all the three metrics decrease and the relationship increasingly represents a decreasing logarithmic relation. It can be seen that top-10 performs better as compared to top-5 for the f-measure statistic.

Furthermore utility increases with rise in ϵ, except for $c = 5$ and $c = 10$ where it is constant at 1. It can be seen that for lower values of c, the precision, recall and f-measure increase in an approximately linear way.

Figure 4 shows the relation of utility with respect to k. In this figure we plot precision, recall and f-measure by varying list sizes (c) for $\epsilon = 0.1$. As expected, the utility for a fixed k decreases as c is incremented. It is seen that by incrementing k, the utility score initially decreases but then rises depending significantly on the other parameters. This information is useful if top-k has to be applied on some sub-graph only as depending on the sub-graph size (c) selected, system utility may get unintentionally modified.

5   Related Work

As specified earlier, Differential Privacy guarantees an individual's privacy while enabling the analysis of the differentially private data. In this section, we consider other similar works in the areas of differential privacy (DP), multi-party computing (MPC) and online social networks (OSN).

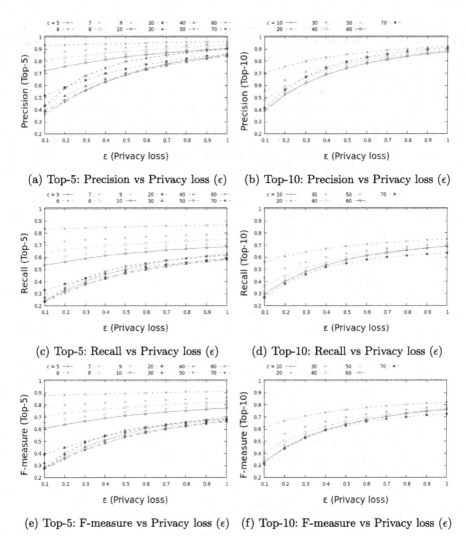

(a) Top-5: Precision vs Privacy loss (ϵ)   (b) Top-10: Precision vs Privacy loss (ϵ)

(c) Top-5: Recall vs Privacy loss (ϵ)   (d) Top-10: Recall vs Privacy loss (ϵ)

(e) Top-5: F-measure vs Privacy loss (ϵ)   (f) Top-10: F-measure vs Privacy loss (ϵ)

Fig. 3. Utility of the PPFR algorithm

Due to the promise of providing user-level privacy, DP has been widely used in Online Social Networks. Primarily, within OSNs, DP is used for publishing the network data in the form of histograms [7,11,15,30,32]. Our work does not use DP for publishing purposes but to enable interactive cross-OSN collaboration for recommendation purposes. The aforementioned DP histogram publication solutions cannot capture large-scale and frequent changes within the network that could be possible in our method.

Apart from using DP for publishing network histograms, considerable amount of work focusses on publishing non-histogram data which prevents node re-

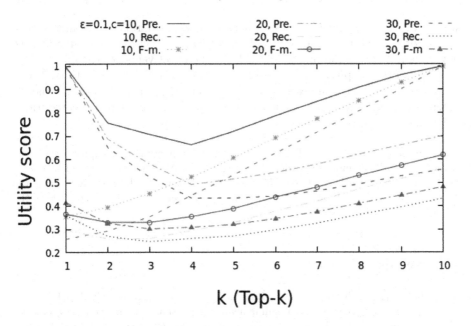

Fig. 4. Precision, Recall, F-measure vs k for the algorithm PPFR

identification or edge disclosure. Generally, these techniques are termed as *node-DP* [7] and *edge-DP* [19], respectively. Node-DP protects the presence of a user within the dataset, whereas edge-DP protects the presence of a relationship. In Friend-Rec-P^2, we are protecting existing friendships while recommending friends. *k-edge* privacy is a general form of *node-DP* ($k \leftarrow (n-1)$) and *edge-DP* ($k \leftarrow 1$) for n nodes. [13] propose a trust-based friend recommendation system in OSNs using multi-hop trust chain based on user attributes. Their approach uses kNN for co-ordinate matching and creating a trust network. [17] computes recommender results by aggregating multi-hop trust chain utilities in a privacy-preserving way. Trust-based networks are difficult to quantify and track with time. [24] provide two algorithms based on additive homomorphic encryption scheme and anonymous message routing. The solution maintains the users' friend list private, which is similar to our approach, however, their friend recommendation is accurate and may leak more information than required. All the solutions are developed for a single OSN as against our solution for two integration partner OSNs. Other private friend recommendation techniques involve using anonymization techniques e.g. [31] propose segmentation tree approach over hypergraph model of graph.

6   Conclusion

In this work, we present an approach that enables online social networks to form integration partnerships to provide friend recommendation services in a privacy-preserving manner. Our approach combines secure multiparty computation as well as differential privacy to give a holistic privacy guarantee. We analyze the complexity of the proposed approach as well as its security. A comprehensive experimental evaluation on real data shows the effectiveness of the approach in terms of both computation and communication cost, as well as utility. While our current solution assumes semi-honest adversaries, in the future, we plan to extend our work to the fully malicious model, as well as more complicated friend recommendation approaches.

Acknowledgments. Research reported in this publication was supported by the National Science Foundation under awards CNS-1564034 and the National Institutes of Health under awards R01GM118574 and R35GM134927. The content is solely the responsibility of the authors and does not necessarily represent the official views of the agencies funding the research.

References

1. Balatsoukas, P., Kennedy, C.M., Buchan, I., Powell, J., Ainsworth, J.: The role of social network technologies in online health promotion: a narrative review of theoretical and empirical factors influencing intervention effectiveness. J. Med. Internet Res. **17**(6), e141 (2015)
2. Bao, J., Zheng, Yu., Wilkie, D., Mokbel, M.: Recommendations in location-based social networks: a survey. GeoInformatica **19**(3), 525–565 (2015). https://doi.org/10.1007/s10707-014-0220-8
3. Beimel, A., Nissim, K., Omri, E.: Distributed private data analysis: simultaneously solving how and what. In: Wagner, D. (ed.) CRYPTO 2008. LNCS, vol. 5157, pp. 451–468. Springer, Heidelberg (2008). https://doi.org/10.1007/978-3-540-85174-5_25
4. Chiu, C.-M., Hsu, M.-H., Wang, E.T.G.: Understanding knowledge sharing in virtual communities: an integration of social capital and social cognitive theories. Decis. Support Syst. **42**(3), 1872–1888 (2006)
5. Schloss Dagstuhl: dblp: computer science bibliography (2018). https://dblp.uni-trier.de/
6. Dance, G.J.X., LaForgia, M., Confessore, N.: As Facebook raised a privacy wall, it carved an opening for tech giants. The New York Times (2018)
7. Day, W.-Y., Li, N., Lyu, M.: Publishing graph degree distribution with node differential privacy. In: Proceedings of the 2016 International Conference on Management of Data, SIGMOD 2016, pp. 123–138. Association for Computing Machinery, New York (2016)
8. Dodge, Y.: Spearman rank correlation coefficient. The Concise Encyclopedia of Statistics, pp. 502–505. Springer, New York (2008). https://doi.org/10.1007/978-0-387-32833-1_379
9. Dwork, C., McSherry, F., Nissim, K., Smith, A.: Calibrating noise to sensitivity in private data analysis. In: Halevi, S., Rabin, T. (eds.) TCC 2006. LNCS, vol. 3876, pp. 265–284. Springer, Heidelberg (2006). https://doi.org/10.1007/11681878_14
10. Dwork, C., Roth, A.: The algorithmic foundations of differential privacy. Found. Trends Theor. Comput. Sci. **9**(3–4), 211–407 (2014)

11. Ghane, S., Kulik, L., Ramamohanarao, K.: Publishing spatial histograms under differential privacy. In: Proceedings of the 30th International Conference on Scientific and Statistical Database Management, SSDBM 2018. Association for Computing Machinery, New York (2018)
12. Goldreich, O.: Foundations of Cryptography: Volume 2, Basic Applications. Cambridge University Press, New York (2009)
13. Guo, L., Zhang, C., Fang, Y.: A trust-based privacy-preserving friend recommendation scheme for online social networks. IEEE Trans. Dependable Secure Comput. **12**(4), 413–427 (2015)
14. Jost, J.T., et al.: How social media facilitates political protest: information, motivation, and social networks. Polit. Psychol. **39**(S1), 85–118 (2018)
15. Kuo, Y.-H., Chiu, C.-C., Kifer, D., Hay, M., Machanavajjhala, A.: Differentially private hierarchical count-of-counts histograms. Proc. VLDB Endow. **11**(11), 1509–1521 (2018)
16. Laranjo, L., et al.: The influence of social networking sites on health behavior change: a systematic review and meta-analysis. J. Am. Med. Inform. Assoc. **22**(1), 243–256 (2015)
17. Ma, X., Ma, J., Li, H., Jiang, Q., Gao, S.: Armor: a trust-based privacy-preserving framework for decentralized friend recommendation in online social networks. Future Gener. Comput. Syst. **79**, 82–94 (2018)
18. Mardziel, P., Hicks, M., Katz, J., Srivatsa, M.: Knowledge-oriented secure multiparty computation. In: Proceedings of the 7th Workshop on Programming Languages and Analysis for Security, pp. 1–12 (2012)
19. Mülle, Y., Clifton, C., Böhm, K.: Privacy-integrated graph clustering through differential privacy. CEUR Workshop Proc. **1330**, 247–254 (2015)
20. Ning, X., Desrosiers, C., Karypis, G.: A comprehensive survey of neighborhood-based recommendation methods. In: Ricci, F., Rokach, L., Shapira, B. (eds.) Recommender Systems Handbook, pp. 37–76. Springer, Boston, MA (2015). https://doi.org/10.1007/978-1-4899-7637-6_2
21. Paillier, P.: Public-key cryptosystems based on composite degree residuosity classes. In: Stern, J. (ed.) EUROCRYPT 1999. LNCS, vol. 1592, pp. 223–238. Springer, Heidelberg (1999). https://doi.org/10.1007/3-540-48910-X_16
22. Papamiltiadis, K.: Let's clear up a few things about Facebook's partners (2018). https://about.fb.com/news/2018/12/facebooks-partners/
23. Puka, L.: Kendall's tau. In: Lovric, M. (ed.) International Encyclopedia of Statistical Science, pp. 713–715. Springer, Berlin (2011). https://doi.org/10.1007/978-3-642-04898-2_324
24. Samanthula, B.K., Cen, L., Jiang, W., Si, L.: Privacy-preserving and efficient friend recommendation in online social networks. Trans. Data Priv. **8**(2), 141–171 (2015)
25. Tang, J., Chang, Y., Liu, H.: Mining social media with social theories: a survey. SIGKDD Explor. Newsl. **15**(2), 20–29 (2014)
26. Ting, K.M.: Precision and recall. In: Sammut, C., Webb, G.I. (eds.) Encyclopedia of Machine Learning, p. 781. Springer, Boston (2010). https://doi.org/10.1007/978-0-387-30164-8_652
27. Gnu multiple precision arithmetic library (2020). https://gmplib.org/
28. Valentino-DeVries, J.: 5 ways Facebook shared your data. The New York Times (2018)
29. Wu, G., He, Y., Wu, J., Xia, X.: Inherit differential privacy in distributed setting: multiparty randomized function computation. CoRR, abs/1604.03001 (2016)

30. Xu, J., Zhang, Z., Xiao, X., Yang, Y., Yu, G.: Differentially private histogram publication. In: Proceedings of the 2012 IEEE 28th International Conference on Data Engineering, pp. 32–43 (2012)
31. Zhang, S., Li, X., Liu, H., Lin, Y., Sangaiah, A.K.: A privacy-preserving friend recommendation scheme in online social networks. Sustain. Cities Soc. **38**, 275–285 (2018)
32. Zhang, X., Chen, R., Xu, J., Meng, X., Yingtao, X.: Towards accurate histogram publication under differential privacy. In: Towards Accurate Histogram Publication Under Differential Privacy, pp. 587–595. SDM (2014)

A Toolkit for Security Awareness Training Against Targeted Phishing

Simone Pirocca[1], Luca Allodi[2], and Nicola Zannone[2(✉)] ⓘ

[1] University of Trento, Trento, Italy
simone.pirocca@studenti.unitn.it
[2] Eindhoven University of Technology, Eindhoven, The Netherlands
{l.allodi,n.zannone}@tue.nl

Abstract. The attack landscape is evolving, and attackers are employing new techniques to launch increasingly targeted and sophisticated social engineering attacks that exploit human vulnerabilities. Many organizations provide their employees with security awareness training to counter and mitigate such threats. However, recent studies have shown that current embedded phishing training programs and tools are often ineffective or incapable of addressing modern, tailored social engineering attacks. This paper presents a toolkit for the deployment of sophisticated, tailored phishing campaigns at scale (e.g., to deploy specific training within an organization). We enable the use of highly customizable phishing email templates that can be instantiated with a large range of information about the specific target and a semi-automated process for the selection of the phishing domain name. We demonstrate our tool by showing how tailored phishing campaigns proposed in previous studies can be enhanced to increase the credibility of the phishing email, effectively addressing the very limitations identified in those studies.

1 Introduction

As technical defences against software-based attacks (e.g., vulnerability exploitation) become more and more sophisticated, cyber-attacks exploiting system vulnerabilities become increasingly prohibitive for attackers to engineer. As a consequence, cyber-attackers are shifting their target from the system to the human operating it. To this end, they are developing a new set of attack capabilities to collect and exploit socio-technical information on their victims and their systems. The collection of open source intelligence (OSINT) on the victims (e.g., available through their social media feeds), mixed with the availability of sophisticated phishing kits and attack infrastructures available in the underground, open an entirely new threat landscape where attackers can systematically deliver highly targeted attacks against an arbitrary, attacker-chosen set of victims worldwide [12]. For example, recent user-impersonation services[1] providing full user profiles

---

[1] Security experts at Kaspersky Lab over 60,000 stolen profiles are offered for sale on an invitation-based private marketplace. https://securityaffairs.co/wordpress/83630/deep-web/genesis-store-fingerprints.html.

© Springer Nature Switzerland AG 2020
S. Kanhere et al. (Eds.): ICISS 2020, LNCS 12553, pp. 137–159, 2020.
https://doi.org/10.1007/978-3-030-65610-2_9

(spanning multiple online personas of the victim) allow attackers to collect both OSINT as well as private information on their targets. This information can be exploited by the attacker, jointly with phishing and malware services available in the underground, to engineer and deliver highly targeted social engineering attacks against their victims.

By contrast, organizations' defensive toolset struggles to keep the pace with new threat landscacpes [5]. Well-engineered social engineering attacks often bypass automated protection systems such as spam/phishing filters [16], making 'rule-based' detection strategies ineffective or, at worst, counter-productive [13]. 'Rule-based' detection strategies rely on the 'usual suspects' indicators, such as url domains, certificates, sender addresses, misspelling in a phishing email, etc. On the other hand, sophisticated, well-targeted social engineering attacks relying on accurate information about the victim and their environment can easily evade these simple detection rules (e.g., by tuning the pretext to create an arbitrary *shared experience* with their victim, as was done in the attacks studied in [16]). 'Mindful' training (i.e. context-aware detection) strategies has been proposed to mitigate this problem [13]; however, the issue remains: how to efficiently and effectively provide *realistic* and *scalable* targeted social engineering training to a large number of users?

In this work, we present a novel framework to support and automate the execution of targeted phishing campaigns at scale. In particular, we present a toolkit, extending state-of-the-art phishing simulation solutions, that provides a twofold contribution to the problem of targeted phishing training campaigns: *email personalization* and *domain selection*. The former requires a solution that can seamlessly and automatically integrate available information on a victim in the phishing email, with a semantically consistent fallback scenario for cases where that information is not available. The latter requires the (semi)automated selection of available domains from which to send the attack, to avoid specific technical protections (e.g., DMARC [15]) while maintaining the credibility of the selected domain. These two capabilities closely mimic the operations an attacker would have to go through when preparing and launching a targeted attack. To showcase the potential of our framework, we demonstrate its application to address the limitations identified in a previous study on targeted phishing [18] concerning the lack of specificity to the target profiles in their experiment design.

The remainder of the paper is structured as follows. The next section provides background on targeted phishing attacks and security awareness training. Section 3 presents our framework along with its implementation. Section 4 presents a demonstration of the framework through a case study. Finally, Sect. 5 concludes the paper and provides directions for future work.

2   Background and Related Work

2.1   Security Awareness Training

To counter the high risk of losses caused by Social Engineering (SE) attacks, organizations worldwide are investing significant effort in effective countermeasures [21]. The NIST Cybersecurity Framework identifies three different classes of countermeasures: *protection*, *detection* and *response* [17]. Protection encompasses activities related to the prevention of an attack, including training and awareness.

Response comprises actions aimed at containing and mitigating the impact of an attack. Network monitoring tools are used for detection, as well as software for identifying illegitimate websites and email filtering [9]. Even though these elements can help reducing the impact or the likelihood of a phishing attack, protection remains the crucial aspect: many yet-to-be seen attacks, especially well-engineered ones, pass the detection filters [5]; furthermore, the velocity at which well-engineering attacks achieve their objectives make it hard to devise effective response actions [5,8].

To boost their attack prevention capabilities, companies often deliver security awareness training programs to their employees. Recent research has shown that specific training techniques (e.g., embedded training [21]) are particularly effective at decreasing the likelihood of success of an SE attack. These trainings focus on delivering awareness messages *after* the employee has clicked on a 'malicious' link (part of a phishing campaign). On the other hand, the duration of these effects has been questioned in the literature, with some studies showing that after only a few weeks from the training phishing susceptibility returned to pre-training levels [6]. Several studies evaluated the effectiveness of training techniques and the relative predisposition of (potential) victims in falling for an attack [13,14,23]. A set of techniques ranging from tuning the training outcome between a 'gain' or a 'loss' [9], to shifting the training paradigm from rule-based to a *mindfulness* approach [13] has been proposed and tested in field experiments. The applicability of training techniques to different scenarios remains however an open issue, particularly for more 'targeted' attacks where the pretext employed by the attacker closely matches what the victim would expect from a legitimate communication. For example, Jensen et al. [13] employ 'customized' emails that include the name of the organization (a university) that employs the victim. Similarly, Oliveira et al. [18] employ a set of attacks targeted at victim demographics (e.g., age). On the other hand, Burda et al. [8] showed that the effectiveness of different attack techniques can vary greatly across application domains (e.g., university vs. industry) and that the way in which the attack is conveyed to the victim may backfire against specific targets. Training techniques have not yet been extensively tested across domains and as targeting specific *types* of victims, a problem already underlined in the literature [14]. This is partially due to the lack of a formal understanding of the mental models operated by the victims [7,22], and partially to the lack of an operative infrastructure capable of scaling realistic simulations to victims in multiple domains, and of different characteristics [24], simultaneously.

2.2 Targeted Phishing

The necessity of a scalable approach to *targeted* phishing simulations is of particular relevance as social engineering attacks 'in the wild' are becoming more and more sophisticated and targeted. More generally, (targeted) SE attacks are becoming a major threats for organizations. These attacks target the human operating the system rather than the system itself by exploiting human emotions and cognitive biases, and are aided by the vast amount of *open source intelligence* (OSINT) available to attackers regarding victim's preferences, activ-

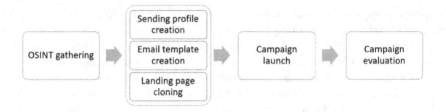

Fig. 1. Targeted phishing campaign flow

ities, working environment, etc. Furthermore, an SE attack can take different forms based on the medium exploited for communication.

Whereas 'regular' phishing has been the subject of numerous studies, more targeted scenarios are becoming the focus of current research as new threat scenarios become possibles for attackers to generate [5,18]. Targeted phishing denotes a phishing attack in which, rather than sending thousands of emails to generic victims (as in the case of generic phishing), the attack targets a niche of targets by sending more contextualized and customized email, which increases the level of credibility and, thus, success of the attack.

Differently from 'regular' phishing, targeted phishing attacks typically consist of multiple stages [5]. Initially, the attacker establishes the final objective (e.g., stealing credentials, taking control of victims' machine) and the targeted victim(s). The target can be a single person, a group of people with something in common, or an entire organization. An OSINT (Open Source INTelligence) gathering phase is often performed by the attacker to retrieve contextual information about the victims, like their hobbies, family, work or holidays details. This information can be used to create a pretext, i.e. the scenario that the attacker would use to get the victims to accept the phishing email [10].

On the other hand, similar circumstances are rarely reproduced in simulation and training settings, generally due to limitations in the adopted simulation infrastructure [18, Limitations of the Study Design, p. 6420] and the lack of a clear framework [5]. Following [5], Fig. 1 provides an overview of the phases of a targeted phishing training campaign:

OSINT Gathering: A crucial phase of targeted phishing is the gathering of information about the victims. This information is used to create believable artifacts that lure the victims in performing the desired action. To this end, the gathered information should be stored in a structured way so that it can be used to the customization of the artifacts and, in particular, the phishing email.

Sending Profile Creation: The sender of the phishing emails has a significant impact on the success of an awareness campaign [24]. If the campaign is done internally to the company or if access to the domain and to an email account of the tested company is available, its domain name can be used directly. Otherwise, we should find out an email address similar to the original one, so we can try to trick targets in thinking that the email is sent by a reliable sender. We describe how to create the sending profile in Sect. 3.2.

Table 1. Tool comparison: ● means "full support", ◐ "partially support", ○ "no support".

Tool	GUI	OSINT	Domain selection	Landing page	Email customization	Event capture	Evaluation
Gophish	●	○	○	●	◐	●	●
King Phisher	●	○	○	●	◐	●	●
SPToolkit	●	○	○	○	◐	◐	●
Phishing Frenzy	●	○	○	●	○	◐	◐
SET	○	○	○	◐	○	○	○
SPF	○	○	○	◐	○	○	○
Spear Phisher	○	○	○	○	○	○	○
Our solution	●	○	●	●	●	●	●

Email Template Creation: Targeted phishing is typically characterized by a high level of sophistication. Such sophistication can be achieved, for instance, by exploiting the information gathered in the OSINT phase to create tailored phishing emails, as the vector artifact of the campaign. However, creating a phishing email for each target is time consuming. Therefore, it would be desirable to create email templates that can be instantiated based on the target's characteristics. In particular, the template should not only allow referring to the target's information but it should also allow inserting a portion of text depending on the target's characteristics.

Landing Page Cloning: Depending on the purpose of the campaign, a landing page where the victim should provide the desired information (i.e., their *credentials*) should be created. We should be able to clone the selected page just inserting its URL, and modify it based on the needs.

Campaign Launch: Once all artifacts have been created, the campaign can be executed. For each victim, a phishing email should be generated from the selected email template by instantiating the template based on the information on that victim. The generated emails are then sent to the corresponding victim.

Campaign Evaluation: To assess the security awareness level of the organization, it should be possible to visualize the results of the campaign, including, how many targets opened the email, how many clicked the link, how many submitted their credentials and how many reported the email as suspicious.

2.3   Existing Tooling for (targeted) Phishing Simulations

Numerous tools for phishing simulations are currently available; to maximize the relevance of this review to organizations of any size and operating in any domain, here we focus on free and open source tools that are popularly used for training activities. To sufficiently support training for *targeted* phishing scenarios, these tools should provide coverage for each of the attack phases outlined in

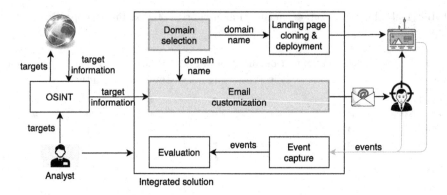

Fig. 2. Overview of our solution. Green boxes represent our contribution. (Color figure online)

Fig. 1. Table 1 provides an overview of the coverage of the different attack phases supported by current tools, as well as of the features of the tool (e.g., GUI).

Since the tool can be used also by non-technical people, it should have a user-friendly interface; only the first four tools offer a **GUI**, particularly well designed and modern for the first two ones. Two important aspects in a targeted campaign are the embedding of **OSINT** gathering and the **selection of the domain** for the sending profile and fake landing page, which are not offered by any tool. To increase the credibility of the email, the tool should also be able to clone the original **landing page** automatically, letting user modifying it if needed; Gophish, King Phisher and SPToolkit allow this, while SET and SPF just clone the entire website, without the chance to change the text. The most important feature is the possibility to **customize the phishing email** based on different information about each target; with the first three tools we can import or use an email template and modifying it, but we can refer to only a few basic parameters to create different emails. Another important aspect for the training point of view is the variety of **event captured** by the tool, after launching the campaign; the first four tools show when the email is sent and opened by the victim, as well as whether he clicked the link or submitted data through the fake landing page. Additionally, the first two tools offers the possibility, respectively, to report the email as suspicious and to see if the target has completed the training, after having been phished. Finally, an **evaluation** of the results of the campaign should be available in form of graphs and tables to see the trend. This is supported by the first three tools, and in a simpler way by Phishing Frenzy.

2.4   Discussion

Many companies tend to base their awareness training about classic phishing attacks, which actually are less effective than some years ago. Still, a number of experiments show that it is much harder to train users not to fall in the trap when they are victim of a targeted attack, due to a higher level of credibility of the email [5,8,9]. Moreover, nowadays several advanced attacks start with a targeted phishing rather than a generic one. In general, existing countermeasures are less effective when applied to targeted attacks, as they are not able to handle the human sphere [5]. For these reasons, companies should increase the level of protection against SE attacks, defending also from targeted phishing, without using their tools just for classic phishing protection and detection.

On the other hand, as we saw in the previous section, the most significant lack of existing tools for campaign simulations is about the OSINT phase and the customization of the email template, which is fundamental to design an ad hoc email for each target (using specific information or conditions) using the same baseline. Our contribution aims to fill this gap, creating a new infrastructure that can be used as training tool for targeted phishing awareness.

3 Proposed Framework and Implementation

To address this gap, we propose a novel framework to semi-automatically integrate victim's information into an operational setup for the delivery of targeted phishing emails at scale. The goal of the proposed framework is to integrate state-of-the-art solutions already available with the functionalities needed to provide targeted attack simulations that can be used for training and awareness procedures in an organization. An overview of the proposed solution is shown in Fig. 2. The blocks indicate different functionalities required for a targeted phishing campaign, as presented in Table 1 and discussed in Sect. 2.3. Our contribution is marked in the figure by the green boxes representing the *Email customization* and *Domain selection* functionalities.

Email Customization: Our solution enables the design of fully flexible email templates that can be instantiated with available (OSINT) information on the recipient. The setup allows the definition of a *default* condition that triggers when no value specific to a subject's variable is found. To implement this, we propose a novel grammar that can be used to program email templates to integrate arbitrary victim information into the email.

Domain Selection: Further, our solution enables the identification of *realistic* domains resembling the one associated with the pretext of the attack; the tools automatically identifies domains that can be registered and used for the delivery of the attack, fully mimicking the conditions in which the attacker would find themselves at attack design time. Our solution further evaluates the presence of DMARC records (including the default policy for mismatching domains) of the spoofed domain (e.g., in the From: address), to provide the operator with direct information on the actionability of an attack employing spoofing.

Implementation Environment. To implement the proposed solution we rely on Gophish [2], one of the most popular and widely used open-source frameworks to test organizations' security awareness and exposure to phishing. Gophish offers a server-client architecture that relies on a database to store victim and campaign information. Although Gophish provides the main functionalities to perform a phishing campaign (cf. Table 1), it is not well suited for tailored phishing. For example, the victim information that can be used for email customization is rather basic (i.e., `first name`, `last name`, `email` and `position`) and is not sufficient to test security awareness against well-engineered targeted phishing attacks. To this end, we modified Gophish to augment its capabilities for email customization by allowing the use of arbitrary target information and we created a bash script to support the selection of a domain to be used as email sender and to host the landing page.

3.1   Email Customization

To test the resilience of an organization against realistic attacks, a security awareness campaign should be customized with respect to each victim, thus reflecting the sophistication of modern, tailored social engineering attacks. To this end, we need methods that enable to perform a security awareness campaign at scale, while tailoring the email per each victim. In this section, we present our approach to define highly customizable email template.

The basic form of email customization is the use of the victim's information gathered, for instance, during the OSINT phase. In particular, the email template should allow the use of placeholders, hereafter called *target fields*, that represent the type of information that should be used to generate the email for a specific target (e.g., `username`, `role`).

In certain case, it may also be desirable to append some predefined text to a target's email only if the target meets some conditions or has certain characteristics. An example is the customization of the e-mail salutation. In certain context, it can be undesirable to address professors and students in the same way, even though the body of the email is the same. Therefore, one might want to customize the tone and greeting based on the role of the target. To this end, we introduce the notion of *variable*. A variable is a placeholder that is associated to a number of conditional assignments, where each assignment consists of a *value* and a *condition*. The value represents the string to be used in the instantiation of the variable and the condition is a Boolean expression specifying in which cases that string should be used.[2] Conditions are defined using the following grammar:

```
<condition> := <field> <operator> <value> | <condition> and <condition> |
               <condition> or <condition>
<operator>  := "==" | "!="
```

Conditions consist of (in)equality statements used to check whether the field `<field>` for the target does (not) match a given value `<value>`. More complex conditions can be constructed using the **and** and **or** operators. A condition is met by a target if it evaluates to *true*. Any malformed condition is evaluated to *false*.

---

[2] If more than one condition is satisfied by the victim, the variable is instantiated with the value associated to the first condition met by the victim.

Table 2. Example of conditions and related value for variable `greeting`

Condition	Value
`role` == *"Professor"*	*Dear*
`role` == *"Student"*	*Hi*
`role` != `Null` and (`country` == *"DE"* or `country` == *"NL"*)	*Hallo*

Table 2 shows the definition of variable `greeting` for the customization of the salutation in the mail. The first condition assigns the string *"Dear"* to variable `greeting` if the role of the victim is *Professor* and the string *"Hi"* if her role is *Student*. The last condition assigns assigns the string *"Hallo"* to variable `greeting` if the role of the victim is undefined (`Null`) and his country is Germany (*DE*) or the Netherlands (*NL*).

Target fields, variables and conditions are used to create customizable email templates. Figure 3 shows an example of email template along with a possible instantiation. Customizable information is added through *references* in the form of variables (e.g., `greeting`) and target fields (e.g., `username`). References are specified in the email template using *blocks*, whose syntax is provided below.

```
<block>       := {<ref>} | <cond-block>
<ref>         := %<field>% | %<variable>% | "%%"
<cond-block>  := { if(<ref>) then {<statement>} else {<statement>} }
<statement>   := <element>* | <cond-block>
<element>     := <text> | <ref>
```

A block `<block>` can be a reference `<ref>` or a conditional block `<cond-block>`. A reference `<ref>` is a field or a variable name, represented by `<field>` or a `<variable>` respectively. In some cases, the value of a field or a variable, however, might not be known for a certain target. If such a value is referenced in the email template, it might result in a malformed email, potentially raising suspicion on the target. Conditional blocks can be used to deal with these situations. A conditional block `<cond-block>` has the form of a *if-then-else* statement. Intuitively, if the value of the reference in the `if` statement is available for the target, then the `then` statement is evaluated and instantiated in the email; otherwise the `else` statement is evaluated and instantiated.

The `then` and `else` statements consist of an arbitrary sequence of predefined text (`<text>`) and references or of a nested conditional block, thus allowing a fine-grained tuning of the email template. An example of nested conditional block is the block `if(%greeting%) then {...} else {...}` in Fig. 3a, which is evaluated only if the value of field `birthdate` is not available for the target. It is worth noting that keywords `then` and `else` can be omitted in a conditional block, as shown for block `if(%phone%) {...} {...}` in Fig. 3a. Also, shortcut `%%` can be used to refer to the last evaluated variable. For instance, `%%` in the salutation of the email returns the value of variable `greeting` if there exists a value of such a variable for the target; otherwise, the default salutation *Hello* is used when instantiating the template.

```
{if(%greeting%) then {%%} else {Hello}} {%username%},
we send you this email because you registered on our website on date
{%date%}. {if(%phone%) {Is your phone number %phone%} {Is your address
%address%}}? Please click the link below if the following information about
you is correct:
{if(%birthdate%) then
    {The birthdate is %%.}
    else
    { {if(%country%) then
        {Your home country is %country%.}
        else
        {No information about you.}
    } }
}
...
```

(a) Email template

```
Dear John67,
we send you this email because you registered on our website on date
12/12/2019. Is your phone number 1234567890? Please click the link below
if the following information about you is correct:
Your home country is Netherlands.
...
```

(b) Template instantiation

Fig. 3. Email template and its instantiation

It is worth noting that variables along with conditions provide features similar to conditional blocks. In fact, the same set of conditions linked to a certain variable can be also implemented using a series of nested blocks. The choice to introduce variables is twofold. The first reason is that defining conditions as part of a variable allows a more compact and readable template, since long conditions can be included by only inserting a reference to that variable in the text. The second reason is to enable the reusability of customizable text: the same conditions, if defined through a variable, can be used multiple times in the same template or in different templates.

Implementation: We extended Gophish to support the specification of highly customizable email templates as described above and their instantiation with targets' information. To this end, we changed the front-end and back-end and created additional tables in the database to store target information. In the database, we added two tables to expand the type of target information that can be stored: fields and target fields. The first table represents a conceptual extension of table targets already existing in Gophish. We decided to not directly modify the original table of Gophish because the approach adopted by Gophish requires to specify all target fields of interests, which may vary from campaign to campaign. Instead, we adopted a more flexible and extensible approach in which table fields stores the target fields of interest and table target fields is used to link a field to the corresponding value for a specific target. We also added tables variables and conditions to store variables and conditions respectively. These tables follows the same logic underlying tables fields and target fields.

(a) Fields & Values   (b) Variables & Conditions

Fig. 4. Configuration of victim information and variables in our Gophish extension

We have also extended the GUI of Gophish to add and configure victim information and variables. Our extension of Gophish provides two new sections in the navbar, called *Fields & Values* and *Variables & Conditions* (Figs. 4a and b). The first section is used to insert, modify and delete target fields. Moreover, it allows inserting and editing the values of target fields for each target. The *Variables & Conditions* section allows the user to create and edit variables along with the associated conditions. To facilitate the insertion of target information, we developed a CSV analyzer that allows automatically inserting the targets along with their target fields and corresponding values at once into the database.

Figure 5 shows the campaign preparation and launch process supported by our extension of Gophish. In the preparation phase, targets' information and the email template are provided to the server, which store them in the database. Whenever a campaign is launched, the back-end generates and sends the phishing emails to the selected targets. To this end, the back-end retrieves the email template configured for the campaign along with the relative references and, for each target, prepares an email instance by setting all required parameters like destination email address, subject, attachments, etc. Moreover, for every target, the template is parsed to instantiate the references. For each reference, the back-end determines whether the reference is a target field (and, therefore, retrieves the value for the target from the database) or a variable (and, therefore, retrieves the associated conditions and determine which one applies to the target). References are replaced with the corresponding portion of text, generating the body of the email for the current target. Once the emails for all targets have been generated, the back-end sends them, each to the corresponding destination email address.

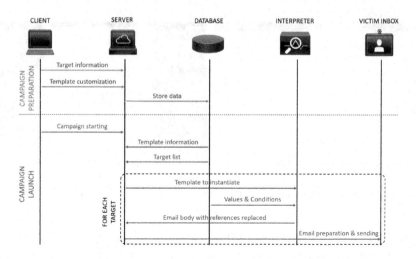

Fig. 5. Campaign preparation and launch process. Target information is stored in the database along with the email template and variables. For each target, this information is retrieved to instantiate the template by replacing the references, before sending the email.

3.2 Domain Selection

To increase the credibility of a phishing attack, it is also important that the email address from which the email is sent and the phishing website look legit and authentic to the victim, e.g. the domain name is aligned with the pretext [20]. To this end, an attacker might have to impersonate a legitimate domain or service. However, domain spoofing is not always possible as many companies and email providers have started employing sophisticated countermeasures, especially to guarantee the authentication of the email sender [11]. This is typically achieved through different protocols. Among them, the most important is DMARC [15], a mechanism for policy distribution that enables handling messages that fail authentication checks. DMARC allows an organization to publish a policy defining its email authentication practices and provides instructions to the receiving mail server on how the policy should be enforced in case the security checks fail. The policy can be set to *none* (to consider the email anyway), *quarantine* (to accept it but move it, e.g., in the spam folder) or *reject* (to discard completely the email, avoiding the end-user sees it). The choice of the domain name, thus, depends on the ability of an attacker to spoof the desired domain. Next, we present our approach to automatize the choice of the sender email address along with the underling mental process (Fig. 6).

First, we check if the domain owner has configured the DMARC record for its email server. If the DMARC record is present and the policy is set to *none*, we can directly configure the `From:` field of the email header using an email address from that domain, since with high probability the receiver will ignore any failure of the authentication test. Otherwise, if the DMARC record is not present (or its policy is set to *quarantine* or *reject*), we have to find an alternative domain resembling the name of the target domain.

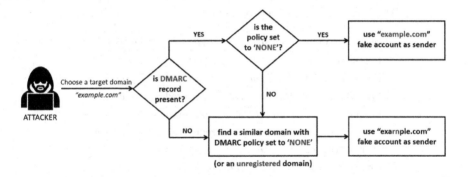

Fig. 6. Mental process to automatize the choice of the sender email address

Potential domain names can be generated using a wide range of existing domain fuzzing algorithms to create fake URLs resembling the original one, based on the several types of modifications [4,19], like adding, replacing and removing characters, typosquatting, etc. For example, domain names `grnail.com` or `gmail.com` can be used to deceive a victim to believe the email came from a `gmail.com` account. The resulting domain names should be checked to determine if they correspond to registered domains, in which case the presence of the DMARC record along with the associated policy should be verified (see above), or if they correspond to unregistered domains. In the latter case the domain can be used both as sender email address and to host the landing page.

Implementation: We created a bash script to support the selection of the phishing domain name and sending profile. The script takes the target domain name as input and checks the DMARC record of that domain. The check is done by querying the DNS using `nslookup` [3], a command-line tool used to obtain domain name or IP address mapping, or other DNS records.

Domain names resembling the target domain are generated using `dnstwist` [1]. `dnstwist` is an open source tool developed to find similar-looking domains that adversaries can use to attack a target, exploiting domain fuzzing algorithms. The user can decide to display *all* domains, *only registered* domains or *only unregistered* domains along with their DMARC record (if any). To this end, for each domain name, the script checks if the domain name is registered, the presence of its DMARC record and, if possible, the associated policy (as described above for the target domain).

We tested our script using `linkedin.com` as the target domain. This domain has a DMARC record with policy set to *reject*. Therefore, the script retrieves plausible domains that can be used as the email sender as it cannot be spoofed. Table 3 shows an excerpt of the domain names returned by `dnstwist` along with the type of modification and DMARC record (if any). Among them, `linkedlm.com` appears to be the most suitable domain to be spoofed as its DMARC record is set to *none*.

Table 3. Analysis of domain names resembling `linkedin.com`

Domain name	Modification	Type	DMARC
`linkedin.com`	–	registered	*reject*
`linkedinc.com`	*Addition*	registered	*reject*
`lynkedin.com`	*Bitsquatting*	registered	*reject*
`linkedlm.com`	*Homoglyph*	registered	*none*
`l-inkedin.com`	*Hyphenation*	registered	*quarantine*
`linkledin.com`	*Insertion*	registered	–
`lonkedin.com`	*Replacement*	registered	*reject*
`lenkedin.com`	*Vowel-swap*	registered	*reject*
`linkdin.com`	*Omission*	unregistered	–
`llinkedin.com`	*Repetition*	unregistered	–
`linked.in.com`	*Subdomain*	unregistered	–
`linkeidn.com`	*Transposition*	unregistered	–

4   A Case Study Application to Oliveira et al.

Even if OSINT information about the victims is available, the execution of a
targeted security awareness campaign requires automatizing the instantiation
of the phishing email template with such information for a large number of
subjects. To show how this problem can be tacked, in this section, we illustrate
an application of our framework for email customization (cf. Sect. 3.1) by giving a
concrete example of how it can be used to improve the credibility of the phishing
emails employed by Oliveira et al. [18] in their study on the susceptibility to spear
phishing. We chose this study because it provides a well-designed experiment
focusing on spear phishing.

4.1   Scenario Limitation of Previous Studies and Research Gap

Oliveira et al. [18] conducted a field experiment to study how different principles of influences (also called *weapons of influence*) and life domains affect the
susceptibility to spear phishing emails, operationalized as the clicking on the
link provided in the phishing emails. Their research questions focus on which
weapons and life domains are more effective, and how the susceptibility varies
with respect to age and gender. To address these questions, Oliveira and col-
leagues designed an experiment involving 158 Internet users recruited from the
North Central Florida area. Every participant received 21 spear phishing emails
over the course of the study, each email exploiting a different weapon and 'life
domain'. To increase email credibility, the authors also included information
(e.g., events, context) related to the targeted geographic area (e.g., city, country). Participants were partitioned in four groups, each participant in a group
receiving the same 21 emails; a total of 84 spear phishing emails were used for
the experiment.

> Would you like to put an end to animal abuse? 3 out of 10 domestic animals in the
> US are currently abused by their owners. That is why we started our non-profit
> organization, PetLove, to lobby for additional support for shelters that take in
> abused pets. Help us end this unfair treatment of our beloved pets. Last year we
> were able to collect just over 15,000 signatures, and this year we look forward to
> collecting more. Make your mark by signing the petition to help these animals have
> the future they deserve. Please click the link below to sign digitally! <link>

(a) Original template

> Would you like to put an end to {%abuse-type%}? {%statistics%} in
> {if(%country%){%%}{the US}}. That is why we started our non-profit organization,
> {%org-name%}, to lobby for additional support for {%abuse-claim%}. Help us
> end {%abuse-sbj%}. Last year we were able to collect just over {%sig-number%}
> signatures, and this year we look forward to collecting more. Make your mark
> by signing the petition to {%petition%}. Please click the link below to sign
> digitally! <link>

(b) Enhanced template

> Would you like to put an end to **climate change**? **Damages caused by climate change
> are increasing significantly over the past years** in **Germany**. That is why we
> started our non-profit organization, **WorldLove**, to lobby for additional support
> for **research in new technologies with low environmental impact**. Help us end
> **the age of fossil fuels**. Last year we were able to collect just over **20,000**
> signatures, and this year we look forward to collecting more. Make your mark by
> signing the petition to **increase national funding for green technology projects**.
> Please click the link below to sign digitally! <link>

(c) Template instantiation

Fig. 7. Commitment and Ideological template and our modifications

Whereas the study is very well designed and executed, it also acknowledges a number of limitations that might have impacted the experimental findings, especially related to the credibility of the emails [18, 'Limitations of the Study Design', p. 6420]:

> "[...] our emails controlled for a variety of confounding factors that could
> have influenced attack effectiveness [...] such as bad grammar and spelling,
> established on line domains, and lack of specificity to the victim's inter-
> ests."

Our case study application showcases how the lack of specificity to user profiles could have been effectively tackled by our toolkit. In particular, we show how our solution can be used to generate several email variants from the same email template, each variant specifically targeting a certain victim based her characteristics.

4.2 Improved Experiment Design

To analyse the benefits that our tool could have provided to their experiment design, we present as an example three of the seven original emails reported in [18], namely Commitment and Ideological, Liking and Security and Reciprocation and Social, and modified them to exploit the available (OSINT) information on the targets.

Next, we describe in detail the modifications to the Commitment and Ideological template, exploring how target fields and variables can be used to exploit a large range of target information for the automatic generation of

Table 4. Target fields in the `Commitment and Ideological` template

Target field	Description
`interest`	The interests of the target based, for instance, on what he posted on social networks
`country`	The country where the target lives

phishing emails tailored to each target. For each variable, the last condition represent the *default* value, so that if target information is not available, the instantiated email is the same as the original template presented in [18]. The other two templates are presented and discussed in the Appendix.

`Commitment and Ideological`: The `Commitment and Ideological` template proposed in [18] refers to a particular fact of interest, namely animal abuse, where a given non-profit organization asks the target to commit with a signature (Fig. 7a). We enhanced it by allowing the attacker/analyst to select the pretext automatically based on the specific interests of the target (Fig. 7b), throughout the variables `abuse-type`, `abuse-claim` and `abuse-sbj` (Table 5).

This allows the analyst to automatically generate well-tailored emails that directly connect to the victim's *personal interests* and preferences, as opposed to having to rely to a generalistic pretext that will resonate differently with different victims (therefore *not* mimicking the capabilities of a real attacker). The name of the organization (`org-name`), the number of signatures collected (`sig-number`) and additional facts on the topic (`statistics`) are instantiated based on the specific pretext, thus maintaining consistency throughout the email. These modifications are based on target field `interest`, which can be retrieved in the OSINT phase by observing, for instance, the posts that the victim has published on social networks (for example, on animal rights or environmental issues, cf. Tables 4 and 5). Target field `country`, if the field is available for the target, is instantiated to the country of the victim, thus helping relate the pretext to the target. The use of this field allows the analyst/attacker to personalize the attack to victims from different countries (e.g., for a large organization with departments spanning several countries) without the need to create a new email template for each country, which on the other hand would have been the case in the original experiment design of Oliveira. It is worth noting that if target information (`interest` and `country`) is not available, the generated email is the same as the template proposed in [18] (*default* options in Table 5). This assures that, even if there is no available information relevant to that pretext for a victim, the delivered email is still consistent and meaningful. Alternatively, this setup could be used to create *control conditions* in an experiment for the participants that receive no treatment.

4.3   Discussion

The final email can vary based on the different values of just one target field (that may influence all the other variables), like for templates `Commitment and`

Table 5. Variables & Conditions for the `Commitment and Ideological` template

Variable	Condition	Value
`abuse-type`	interest == "vaccines"	disinformation about vaccines
	interest == "climate"	climate change
	true (default)	animal abuse
`statistics`	interest == "vaccines"	Autism in children has been proved to be not related to the use of vaccines as claimed by no-vax people
	interest == "climate"	Damages caused by climate change are increasing significantly over the past years
	true (default)	3 out of 10 domestic animals in the US are currently abused by their owners
`org-name`	interest == "vaccines"	VaxInfo
	abuse == "climate"	WorldLove
	true (default)	PetLove
`abuse-claim`	interest == "vaccines"	disseminating scientific information about vaccines
	interest == "climate"	research in new technologies with low environmental impact
	true (default)	shelters that take in abused pets
`abuse-sbj`	interest == "vaccines"	this disinformation about vaccines
	interest == "climate"	the age of fossil fuels
	true (default)	this unfair treatment of our beloved pets
`sig-number`	interest == "vaccines"	10,000
	interest == "climate"	20,000
	true (default)	15,000
`petition`	interest == "vaccines"	support the dissemination of scientific information about vaccines
	interest == "climate"	increase national funding for green technology projects
	true (default)	help these animals have the future they deserve

`Ideological` (Fig. 7) and `Reciprocation and Social` (Fig. 9). Even in these cases, we decided to use a generic template instead of preparing three different versions; this is for two main reasons. One is the fact that in every template there is always at least one reference to a target field, which could take on any value based on the information of each target; therefore, we have to keep the template abstract. The second is that, in a campaign, it is much easier for the social engineer to prepare just one template that enhances the right scenario automatically, instead of finding a way to understand which is the best version to send to each single target.

Another important benefit that our tool could enable in such an experiment design is in the way life domains are chosen. In the original paper by Oliveira et al., indeed, only six life domains have been considered, and linked manually to different weapons to create completely different scenarios. By contrast, in an alternative design implementing our solution the experimenter could have created seven templates only, one for each principle of influence; based on the available target information, each template could then be automatically enriched with the assigned 'life domain' for that victim. This enrichment would be on a target-base, and implemented through variables and conditions.

The scalability enabled by the presented solution allows analysts and trainers to design and implement highly-targeted social engineering attacks that can employ state-of-the-art attack techniques against users at large. Whereas the attacker will strike by targeting a handful of employees only, the organization must prepare *all* (or most) of its employees to the possibility of receiving a targeted attack. The presented toolkit significantly decreases the competitive *disadvantage* that organizations have in this setting, by allowing them to effectively *mimic* what an attacker would have to do for their specific targets, without having to manually engineering an attack for each employee in the campaign. Further, the collection of OSINT information has limited ethical constraints, and the same information can be re-used across multiple campaigns to enable completely new, yet still highly-targeted, phishing training campaigns.

5   Conclusion

In this paper, we presented a toolkit to support organizations in offering their employees security awareness training against tailored phishing attacks. Our toolkit is built on top of Gophish, a widely used open-source framework to test organizations' security awareness and exposure to phishing, and extends such framework to enable the specification and instantiation of highly customizable phishing email templates along with a procedure for the selection of the phishing domain. We have demonstrated the toolkit by showing how it can be used to address the limitations in the experiment design presented in [18]. We plan to use the toolkit to conduct field experiments to test the effectiveness of tailored phishing. We also plan to extend the toolkit to support the OSINT phase, thus providing the complete pipeline for the execution of tailored phishing campaigns.

A   Phishing Email Templates

A.1   Liking and Security Template

The Liking and Security template aims to exploit the liking principle by letting the target believe that the email sender is someone like the victim. Figure 8a presents the template proposed by Olivera et al. [18] for their experiment and

My name is Dan. I don't know if I ever formally introduced myself to you, but I am
your neighbor from down the street. I'm glad to finally be in touch with you! I am
writing to ask you if you have seen any suspicious activity. I know there have been
some issues of security breaches around town of people breaking into homes or cars
in the past, and I just wanted to make sure everyone stays safe in our neighborhood.
If you're interested, I made a blog with tips on how to keep your home and family
safe that you can visit at <link> Please let me know if you have any questions or
want to get together some time; I love spending time with my fellow neighbors.

(a) Original template

My name is {%fake-name%}. I don't know if I ever formally introduced myself to
you, but I am your {if(%american-spelling%){neighbor}{neighbour}} from down the
street{if(%neighbourhood%){ in %%}{}}. I'm glad to finally be in touch with you!
I am writing to ask you if you have seen any suspicious activity. I know there
have been some issues of security breaches around town of people breaking into
{%break-into%} in the past {%incident-event%}, and I just wanted to make sure
everyone stays safe in {if(%neighbourhood%) {%%}{ {if(%american-spelling%){our
neighborhood}{our neighbourhood}}}}. If you're interested, I made a blog with
tips on how to keep your home and family safe that you can visit at <link>. Please
let me know if you have any questions or want to get together some time; I love
spending time with my fellow neighbors.

(b) Enhanced template

Fig. 8. Liking and Security template and our modification

Table 6. Target fields in the Liking and Security template

Target field	Description
gender	The gender of the target
american-spelling	Based on if the country of the victim is USA, easy to know. If yes, that field should be set to true, the conditional block of the template understands whether to use American spelling or British English
neighbourhood	The neighbourhood of the target
owns	What the target owns (a car, a shop, etc.). This field can be derived, for instance, by observing the photos posted on the social networks by the target

Fig. 8b shows how the template can be enhanced to exploit target information.
In particular, we have enhanced the template in [18] to strengthen the liking
weapon and to avoid possible mismatches between the spelling used in the email
and the one typically used by the target, which may raise suspicion in the target.

To emulate the spelling typically used by the victim, we use target field
american-spelling to determine, for instance, from the country of the target
and from previous communications that the target had, whether he usually communicates in American English or not, and, based on this field, customize the
email using the proper spelling (e.g., *neighbor* vs. *neighbour*). We also use vari-

Table 7. Variables & Conditions for the Liking and Security template

Variable	Condition	Value
fake-name	gender == "male"	Dan
	gender == "female"	Lucy
	true (default)	Mel
break-into	owns == "shop"	shops
	owns == "car"	cars
	true (default)	homes or cars
incident-event	owns == "shop"	(for example, when three people destroyed the entire grocery last year in our street)
	owns == "car"	(for example, many years ago 10 cars were stolen in our street)
	true (default)	*(empty text)*

able fake-name to choose a name for the email sender that reflects the gender of the target, as it has been shown that people are more inclined to respond to persons of the same gender [6]. If the gender of the victim is unknown, a gender-neutral name is used for the sender (*default* option in Table 7). Other target fields (Table 6) and variables (Table 7) are used to customize the email based on information about the target. For instance, variable break-into and incident-event are used to customize the pretext based on the target field own.

A.2   Reciprocation and Social Template

The Reciprocation and Social template aims to trigger a reciprocation feeling in the target by promising to donate a given amount of money to promote a particular product. Figure 9a presents the template proposed by Olivera et al. [18] for their experiment and Fig. 9b shows how the template can be enhanced to exploit target information. As for the Commitment and Ideological template (Fig. 7), the pretext and relative variables (see Table 9) are instantiated based on the interest (see Table 8) of the target (which objects he is interested in), so that he is more inclined to click the link in order to know more details. In particular, award is the amount of money donated to the target, obj-bought is what he can buy with that donation, donated-by is the organization who provided the award, org-claim is the purpose of the organization and award-application describes the shops where the target can use the donation, based on the product promoted. This way, the email template is instantiated automatically based on the value of target field interest. Additional target information (address, email, region in Table 8) are used to increase the credibility of the generated phishing email.

Congratulations, you have won $20 dollars towards your next purchase of edible
goods. This money has been donated by APPLES Co., a non profit organization founded
to promote the purchase of organic foods. These $20 will be applicable in any local
grocery supermarket. You will receive it in the form a gift card that will be sent
to your mailing address. In the meantime, please click the link below to vote for
APPLES Co. as the top 10 non-profit of the year in our region! <link>

(a) Original template

Congratulations, you have won {%award%} dollars towards your next purchase of
{%obj-bought%}. This money has been donated by {%donated-by%}, a non profit
organization founded to promote the purchase of {%org-claim%}. These {%award%} will
be applicable in {%award-application%}. You will receive it in the form a gift card
that will be sent to {if(%address%){%%}{%email%}}. In the meantime, please click
the link below to vote for {%donated-by%} as the top 10 non-profit of the year in
{%region%}! <link>

(b) Enhanced Template

Fig. 9. Template Reciprocation and Social and our modification

Table 8. Target fields in the Reciprocation and Social template

Target field	Description
interest	The interests of the target, based on what he/she published in social networks
address	The address where the target lives
email	E-mail address of the target
region	The region (state, province, etc.) where the target lives

Table 9. Variables & Conditions for the Reciprocation and Social template

Variable	Condition	Value
award	interest == "smartphone"	$40
	interest == "cycling"	$50
	true (default)	$20
obj-bought	interest == "smartphone"	Wiko smartphone
	interest == "cycling"	electric bicycle
	true (default)	edible goods
donated-by	interest == "smartphone"	EUTech
	interest == "cycling"	EcoLife
	true (default)	APPLES Co.
org-claim	interest == "smartphone"	european technologies
	interest == "cycling"	eco-friendly vehicles
	true (default)	organic food
award-application	interest == "smartphone"	any electronics store
	interest == "cycling"	any local shop
	true (default)	any local grocery supermarket

References

1. dnstwist. https://github.com/elceef/dnstwist. Accessed 13 July 2020
2. Gophish - Open-Source Phishing Framework. https://getgophish.com. Accessed 13 July 2020
3. nslookup(1) - Linux man page. https://linux.die.net/man/1/nslookup. Accessed 13 July 2020
4. Agten, P., Joosen, W., Piessens, F., Nikiforakis, N.: Seven months' worth of mistakes: a longitudinal study of typosquatting abuse. In: Network and Distributed System Security Symposium. Internet Society (2015)
5. Allodi, L., Chotza, T., Panina, E., Zannone, N.: The need for new anti-phishing measures against spear-phishing attacks. IEEE Secur. Priv. **18**(2), 23–34 (2020)
6. Bullee, J.-W.: Experimental social engineering: investigation and prevention. Ph.D. thesis, University of Twente (2017)
7. Burda, P., Allodi, L., Zannone, N.: Don't forget the human: a crowdsourced approach to automate response and containment against spear phishing attacks. In: Proceedings of Workshop on Attackers and Cyber-Crime Operations. IEEE (2020)
8. Burda, P., Chotza, T., Allodi, L., Zannone, N.: Testing the effectiveness of tailored phishing techniques in industry and academia: a field experiment. In: International Conference on Availability, Reliability and Security. ACM (2020)
9. Burns, A., Johnson, M., Caputo, D.: Spear phishing in a barrel: insights from a targeted phishing campaign. J. Organ. Comput. Electron. Commer. **29**, 24–39 (2019)
10. Hadnagy, C.: Social Engineering: The Science of Human Hacking. Wiley, Hoboken (2018)
11. Hu, H., Wang, G.: End-to-end measurements of email spoofing attacks. In: USENIX Security Symposium, pp. 1095–1112. USENIX Association (2018)
12. Jagatic, T.N., Johnson, N.A., Jakobsson, M., Menczer, F.: Social phishing. Commun. ACM **50**(10), 94–100 (2007)
13. Jensen, M., Dinger, M., Wright, R., Thatcher, J.: Training to mitigate phishing attacks using mindfulness techniques. J. Manage. Inf. Syst. **34**(2), 597–626 (2017)
14. Karumbaiah, S., Wright, R.T., Durcikova, A., Jensen, M.L.: Phishing training: a preliminary look at the effects of different types of training. In: Proceedings of the 11th Pre-ICIS Workshop on Information Security and Privacy, pp. 1–10 (2016)
15. Kucherawy, M., Zwicky, E.: Domain-based Message Authentication, Reporting, and Conformance (DMARC). RFC 7489, IETF (2015)
16. Le Blond, S., Uritesc, A., Gilbert, C., Chua, Z.L., Saxena, P., Kirda, E.: A look at targeted attacks through the lense of an {NGO}. In: 23rd {USENIX} Security Symposium, {USENIX} Security 14, pp. 543–558 (2014)
17. National Institute of Standards and Technology. Framework for improving critical infrastructure cybersecurity. Technical report (2018)
18. Oliveira, D., et al.: Dissecting spear phishing emails for older vs young adults: on the interplay of weapons of influence and life domains in predicting susceptibility to phishing. In: Conference on Human Factors in Computing Systems, pp. 6412–6424. ACM (2017)
19. Szurdi, J., Kocso, B., Cseh, G., Spring, J., Felegyhazi, M., Kanich, C.: The long "taile" of typosquatting domain names. In: USENIX Security Symposium, pp. 191–206. USENIX Association (2014)
20. Tsow, A., Jakobsson, M.: Deceit and Deception: A Large User Study of Phishing. Technical report TR649, Indiana University (2007)

21. Wash, R., Cooper, M.M.: Who provides phishing training? Facts, stories, and people like me. In: Conference on Human Factors in Computing Systems, pp. 1–12. ACM (2018)
22. Wash, R., Rader, E.: Influencing mental models of security: a research agenda. In: Proceedings of New Security Paradigms Workshop, pp. 57–66 (2011)
23. Wright, R.T., Jensen, M.L., Thatcher, J.B., Dinger, M., Marett, K.: Research note-influence techniques in phishing attacks: an examination of vulnerability and resistance. Inf. Syst. Res. **25**(2), 385–400 (2014)
24. Wright, R.T., Marett, K.: The influence of experiential and dispositional factors in phishing: an empirical investigation of the deceived. J. Manage. Inf. Syst. **27**(1), 273–303 (2010)

Forensic Source Identification of OSN Compressed Images

Sobhan Mondal[✉], Deependra Pushkar, Mrinali Kumari, and Ruchira Naskar

Department of Information Technology, Indian Institute of Engineering Science
and Technology, Shibpur 711103, India
sobhaniiest@gmail.com, deependrap.dakshana16@gmail.com,
mrinalikumari26@gmail.com, ruchira.naskar@gmail.com

Abstract. Source camera identification is used in legal applications
involving cybercrime, terrorism, pornography, etc. It is a digital forensic
way to map the image to its authentic source. In today's digital era online
social networks have become a great source of image transmission as well
as mapping of the OSNs images to its source device has become difficult
due to its implicit compression technique and altering of metadata. In
this paper, we propose a deep learning model for SCI, on images downloaded from Facebook, and Whatsapp. We adapt the ResNet50 network
and add our own layer head to fine-tune the model for the classification
of source cameras of OSNs compressed images. It can be seen by observing the experimental results that the proposed technique addresses the
results efficiently for images downloaded from OSNs.

Keywords: Deep learning · Online social networks (OSNs) ·
ResNet50 · Source camera identification (SCI) · Transfer learning

1 Introduction

Source camera identification is a digital forensic problem of mapping images to
their source devices. In today's digital era almost everybody uses social networks
such as Facebook, Whatsapp, etc. to share images. Each such OSN uses an
inherent compressor to compress the images before upload, hence reducing their
quality and eliminating their metadata. Generally, mapping of images to their
sources, are hindered due to such compressions in OSNs (see Fig. 1).

For source camera identification, many approaches have been proposed in the
past. The pioneering among those being the fingerprint-based source identification techniques proposed by Lukas et al. [2], Chen et al. [7], Zeng et al. [8]. However, due to the recent advancements in counter forensics [3,4], the fingerprint-
based source identification methods have become highly vulnerable, especially
to source anonymization attacks on digital images. The other class of source
identification techniques is feature-based, which include the methods proposed
by Kharrazi et al. [1], and Sameer et al. [9] to mention a few. Such techniques are
comparatively much more robust towards present-day counter-forensic attacks.

© Springer Nature Switzerland AG 2020
S. Kanhere et al. (Eds.): ICISS 2020, LNCS 12553, pp. 160–166, 2020.
https://doi.org/10.1007/978-3-030-65610-2_10

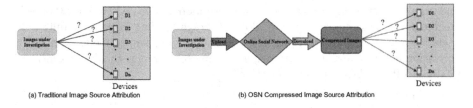

(a) Traditional Image Source Attribution   (b) OSN Compressed Image Source Attribution

Fig. 1. Image source attribution

In this paper, we propose a deep learning CNN model for image source mapping. The proposed model achieves an average accuracy of over 97%. The results have been compared with the state-of-the-art.

Rest of the paper is organized as follows. In Sect. 2, we present the proposed deep learning network. In Sect. 3, we present our experimental set-up, performance evaluation results and related discussions. In Sect. 4, we conclude the work with future research directions.

2   Proposed Deep Learning Model for Source Camera Identification of OSN Compressed Images

In this work, we propose a deep learning based classification model to identify the source device of the OSN compressed images. We train the model using the images of the Vision dataset [5]. In order to improve the performance and due to comparatively less number of images per device, transfer learning is used in the proposed deep learning model. We have used the pre-trained model of ResNet50 [6] and then fine-tuned to perform source identification.

Transfer learning is a machine learning technique where the knowledge gained from solving a task is reused to solve another related task. To fine-tune the model, the last predicting layer of the pre-trained model is altered with the new predicting layers specific to the target data. Initial lower layers of the network learn very generic features from the pre-trained model and the weights of these layers are made frozen and not updated during training whereas the higher layers are used to learn task-specific features and trained.

2.1   Network Architecture

Here, we adapt the ResNet50 [6] network for the classification of source cameras of OSNs compressed images. Unlike traditional sequential network architectures, ResNet is built out something called residual block - skip connections which allows to take the activation from one layer and suddenly feed to another layer even much deeper in the neural network. ResNet [6] is a form of "exotic architecture" with micro-architecture modules also known as "network-in-network architecture". These micro architectures collectively lead to the entire network. The network consists of 50 layers. This has been depicted in Fig. 2. In order to fine-tune the network, the output of the base model is passed to our own newly created layer head consisting of a global average pooling layer, two fully connected layers (fc-1 & fc-2, having 512 and 256 neurons respectively, with ReLU activation function and dropout during learning to overcome the overfitting) and finally a softmax layer to perform classification.

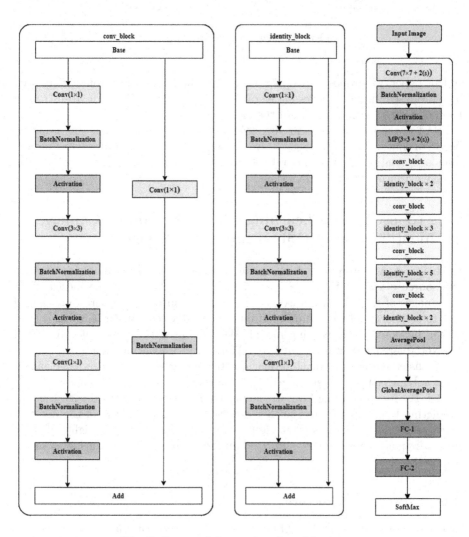

Fig. 2. Proposed deep network architecture

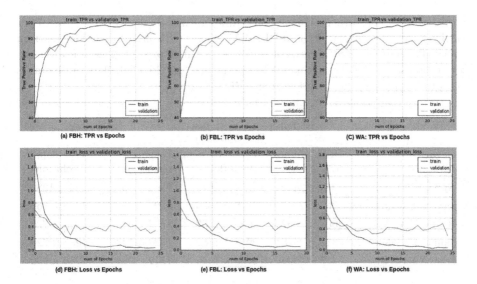

Fig. 3. True positive rate and loss plot wrt epochs

2.2 Network Parameters

Here, we have used Adam optimizer as optimization algorithm and categorical cross-entropy as loss function. This loss function is used when there is single label categorization that is the output can belong to one class only. The cross-entropy function can be mathematically modelled as follows:

$$Cross - entropy = -\sum_{c=1}^{M} y_{o,c} \log(p_{o,c}) \tag{1}$$

where, M is the total number of classes, y is the binary indicator (0 or 1) indicating whether or not, the class lebel c is the correct classification for observation o, and p is the predicted probability that observation o belongs to class c.

3   Experiments, Results and Discussion

In this section, first we explain the experimental setup, then the performance of our model followed by comparison of our proposed model with state-of-the-art.

3.1   Experimental Setup

For the evaluation of the experiments, we use images from Vision dataset [5]. The dataset consists of images captured from 35 smartphones/tablets belonging to 11 different brands. The native images were shared through Facebook, in both high (FBH) and low (FBL) quality, and through Whatsapp (WA). For this work, we conduct our experiments on 5 different mobile devices, 150 images per device for each category (FBH, FBL, WA), listed in Table 1. We divide the train and validation set into a ratio of 80:20. All results presented here are on the validation set. All the experiments are performed on Google Colab and Keras is used to implement the deep learning API.

Table 1. Our dataset.

Device	Original image resolution	Facebook high resolution	Facebook low resolution	Whatsapp resolution
Apple iPhone 5	3264 × 2448	1536 × 2048	720 × 960	960 × 1280
Samsung Galaxy S3	3264 × 2448	2048 × 1536	960 × 720	1280 × 960
Redmi Note 3	4608 × 2592	2048 × 1152	1152 × 648	1280 × 720
Samsung Galaxy S5	5312 × 2988	2048 × 1152	1328 × 747	1280 × 720
Sony Xperia Z1	5248 × 3936	2048 × 1536	1312 × 984	1280 × 960

3.2   Performance Evaluation

In this work, we have used a batch size of 64 and hence it takes $N/64$ iterations to complete an epoch, where N is the total number of training images. The image block size is chosen as 512×512 and we have evaluated the model for 25 epochs for FBH and WA images and 20 epochs for FBL images.

We compute the accuracy, F1-score, precision, and recall in terms of the numbers of True Positive (a true positive is an outcome where the model correctly predicts the positive class), True Negative (a true negative is an outcome where the model correctly predicts the negative class), False Positive (a false positive is an outcome where the model incorrectly predicts the positive class), and False Negative (a false negative is an outcome where the model incorrectly predicts the negative class). Table 2 depicts the accuracy, loss, F1-score, precision, and recall for each category of OSN compressed images.

Figure 3 shows the train and validation True Positive Rate (TPR) with respect to number of epochs, and loss with respect to number of epochs for Facebook high (FBH) and low (FBL) resolution, and Whatsapp (WA) respectively.

Table 2. Experimental result.

Image category	Accuracy	Loss	F1-score	Precision	Recall
FBH	97.06%	0.3314	0.9267	0.9267	0.9267
FBL	96.26%	0.4466	0.9067	0.9067	0.9067
WA	96.26%	0.2963	0.9067	0.9067	0.9067

3.3 Comparison

We compare the performance of the proposed deep learning model for Facebook and Whatsapp images source classification, with the state-of-the-art. The results of the comparison are presented in Table 3. We observe that the CAGIF technique [8] is able to classify the image sources with an accuracy of 87.36%, 81.04% and 87.2%, respectively for FBH, FBL, and WA. The state-of-the-art PRNU based fingerprinting technique [7] also suffers due to the compression caused by OSN upload; its source detection accuracy is only 78.31% in the case of FBH. The recent deep learning based model [9] produced a classification accuracy of 94.93% for FBH on our dataset compared to an accuracy of 97.06% by the proposed approach.

Table 3. Performance comparison of proposed method with state–of–the–art.

Camera model identification method	FBH accuracy (%)	FBL accuracy (%)	WA accuracy (%)
PRNU [7]	78.31	79.35	87.08
CAGIF [8]	87.36	81.04	87.2
Sameer et al. [9]	94.93	94.53	94.13
Proposed model	97.06	96.26	96.26

4   Conclusion and Future Work

Source Camera Identification of OSN images is the need of the hour and a challenging task. Due to manipulation of images and compression by OSNs and the advancement of counter forensic, the fingerprint based technique is vulnerable and shows inaccuracy in mapping the OSN images.

In this work, we address the problem of source camera identification for OSN compressed smartphone images, and propose a deep network architecture to address the above problem. The experimental results depict a significant performance of the proposed method in comparison to the state–of–the–art. Further, we would like to test the robustness of the proposed model to various other online social networks, including Twitter and Instagram and for the images compressed by other tools or softwares as our future research.

References

1. Kharrazi, M., Sencar, H.T., Memon, N.: Blind source camera identification. In: 2004 International Conference on Image Processing, ICIP 2004, vol. 1, pp. 709–712. IEEE (2004)
2. Lukas, J., Fridrich, J., Goljan, M.: Digital camera identification from sensor pattern noise. IEEE Trans. Inf. Forensics Secur. **1**(2), 205–214 (2006)

3. Dirik, A.E., Sencar, H.T., Memon, N.: Analysis of seam-carving-based anonymization of images against prnu noise pattern-based source attribution. IEEE Trans. Inf.
   Forensics Secur. **9**(12), 2277–2290 (2014)
4. Karaküçük, A., Dirik, A.E.: Adaptive photo-response non-uniformity noise removal
   against image source attribution. Digit. Investig. **12**, 66–76 (2015)
5. Shullani, D., et al.: VISION: a video and image dataset for source identification.
   EURASIP J. Info. Secur. **2017**, 15 (2017). https://doi.org/10.1186/s13635-017-
   0067-2
6. He, K., Zhang, X., Ren, S., Sun, J.: Deep residual learning for image recognition. In:
   Proceedings of the IEEE Conference on Computer Vision and Pattern Recognition,
   pp. 770–778 (2016)
7. Chen, M., Fridrich, J., Goljan, M., Lukás, J.: Determining image origin and integrity
   using sensor noise. IEEE Trans. Inf. Forensics Secur. **3**(1), 74–90 (2008)
8. Zeng, H., Kang, X.: Fast source camera identification using content adaptive guided
   image filter. J. Forensic Sci. **61**(2), 520–526 (2016)
9. Sameer, V.U., Dali, I., Naskar, R.: A deep learning based digital forensic solution
   to blind source identification of Facebook images. In: Ganapathy, V., Jaeger, T.,
   Shyamasundar, R.K. (eds.) ICISS 2018. LNCS, vol. 11281, pp. 291–303. Springer,
   Cham (2018). https://doi.org/10.1007/978-3-030-05171-6_15

Cryptography

Cheating Detectable Ramp Secret Sharing with Optimal Cheating Resiliency

Jyotirmoy Pramanik[1]([✉])(iD), Sabyasachi Dutta[2], Partha Sarathi Roy[3](iD), and Avishek Adhikari[4](iD)

[1] Department of Mathematics, Taki Government College, Taki 743429, India
jyotirmoy.pramanik2@gmail.com
[2] Department of Computer Science, University of Calgary, 2500 University Drive, Calgary, NW T2N1N4, Canada
saby.math@gmail.com
[3] School of Computing and Information Technology, University of Wollongong, Northfields Avenue, Wollongong, NSW 2522, Australia
royparthasarathi0@gmail.com
[4] Department of Mathematics, Presidency University, 86, 1, College Street, Kolkata 700073, India
avishek.adh@gmail.com

Abstract. A (k, L, n) ramp secret sharing scheme allows a dealer to share a secret vector with a lesser share size compared to threshold secret sharing schemes. In this work, we formalize the definition of cheating in ramp secret sharing schemes and propose two constructions. The proposed constructions of ramp secret sharing scheme are capable of cheating detection even if $n-1$ out of n participants conspire against the single honest participant and try to convince him of a valid but incorrect secret. This is the strongest possible adversarial setup known as the CDV^{n-1} model of cheating. Moreover, we consider arbitrary secret distribution on the space of secrets. To the best of our knowledge, we are the first to address cheating in ramp setup against $n-1$ cheaters. Both the constructions proposed in this work are optimal cheating resilient against a centralized adversary with unbounded computational resources.

Keywords: Information theoretic security · Secret sharing · Detection · Optimal cheating resiliency

1 Introduction

Introduced by Shamir and Blakley independently in [50] and [9], secret sharing is a very well studied, as well as practically implemented, primitive. Due to its ample applications in secure multiparty computation [8,16,27], threshold cryptography [21,25], private information retrieval [19,28] and many other primitives, secret sharing has gained humongous popularity in the past four decades.

The problem dealt in secret sharing was to 'share' a piece of information into n *shares* in a way that certain shares together qualify to recover the secret

© Springer Nature Switzerland AG 2020
S. Kanhere et al. (Eds.): ICISS 2020, LNCS 12553, pp. 169–184, 2020.
https://doi.org/10.1007/978-3-030-65610-2_11

whereas other combinations of shares are forbidden. A subset $A \in 2^{\mathcal{P}}$, where $2^{\mathcal{P}}$ denotes the power set of the set of participants $\mathcal{P}$, is said to be *qualified* if the participants in A are able to pool their shares of the secret s and determine s completely and uniquely from that. A subset $A \in 2^{\mathcal{P}}$ is said to be *forbidden* if they can gain no more information about 's' than what they already know from the probability distribution of the space of potential secrets. A secret sharing scheme consists of a share generation protocol ShareGen and a reconstruction protocol Reconst. An impartial party, called *Dealer*, invokes the ShareGen protocol and is assumed to behave honestly. Dishonest dealers exist in literature and are usually considered in a costlier variant of secret sharing called *Verifiable Secret Sharing* [47]. Since, ramp secret sharing schemes mainly aim towards cost cutting in share distribution, we consider honest dealers only. Reconst protocol is initiated by a few (or all, depending on the context) reconstructing participants in absence of the dealer to recover the shared information.

Shamir introduced *threshold secret sharing* in [50]. Shamir's secret sharing scheme, though being a remarkable concept, was not secure against *active adversaries* who may modify their shares during reconstruction of secrets. This might lead to the reconstruction of a false secret and honest participants could easily be duped. Tompa and Woll [51] resolved this matter by introducing a relatively *smaller* secret space inside the underlying field of secret sharing. Cheating in secret sharing has been, since then, addressed in many other works [1,4,13,14,23,38,39,41,46,48,49].

Ramp Secret Sharing Schemes [10,33,42,53]. These are practical cost efficient versions of usual secret sharing schemes with a reasonable trade-off in security. Yamamoto [53] introduced (k, L, n) ramp secret sharing schemes which are able to share an information X so that every shareholder receives a subinformation of size $1/L$ of the original information which is why ramp schemes are very efficient. The *privacy threshold* and *reconstruction threshold* in this scheme are $k - L$ and k respectively, i.e. there is a *nontrivial gap* between the thresholds which captures the flavour of ramp secret sharing schemes. However, if $k - t$ shareholders ($1 \leq t \leq L - 1$) pool their subinformations, they may gain information about the information shared with an ambiguity of $(t/L)H(X)$. Blundo et al. shared *multiple secrets* via ramp schemes in [12]. Okada and Kurosawa [43], and Blundo et al. [11] derived lower bounds for size of shares (subinformations). Ogata and Kurosawa [40] gave necessary and sufficient condition on the existence of ramp secret sharing scheme along with a construction attain both the combinatorial type bound and an entropy type bound that they provide. They also introduced verifiable ramp secret sharing scheme. Crescenzo [20] gave tight bounds for multi secret sharing scheme. A ramp secret sharing scheme is either *strong* or *weak*, where strong ramp secret sharing schemes do not leak any explicit information about the secret even if there is some information leakage due to some forbidden shares, whereas the latter makes no such promise. Iwamoto and Yamamoto [29] showed that given a secret sharing scheme on general access structure, a strong ramp secret sharing scheme can always be constructed. They also showed that Shamir [50] based threshold ramp secret sharing schemes are not always strong. In terms of linearity, ramp secret sharing scheme can be either *linear* or *nonlinear*. Yoshida and Fujiwara [54] provided efficient construction for nonlinear function ramp threshold secret sharing scheme where $H(V_i) < H(S)$. Chen et al. [17] introduced construction of strongly multiplicative ramp schemes from high degree rational points on algebraic curves. Strong security of McEliece and Sarwate [33] and Chen et al. [17] ramp schemes were proved in [37] and [32] respectively. Chen et al. [18] gave constructions for multiplicative and strongly multiplicative linear ramp secret sharing schemes. Zhang and Matsumoto [55] introduced quantum strongly secure ramp secret sharing schemes. Nakamura et al. [35,36] constructed (k, L, n) ramp secret sharing schemes prohibiting substitution and impersonation attacks with number of forged shares a satisfying $1 \leq a \leq k - 1$. Asymptotic behaviour of partial leakage and partial reconstruction of ramp secret sharing schemes is studied by Geil et al. in [26]. Evolving ramp secret sharing schemes were studied in [6,7]. Cascudo et al. [15] improved bounds on threshold gap in ramp secret sharing schemes. Lin et al. [31] introduced threshold changeable ramp secret sharing schemes. Agematsu and Obana [3] modified the verification function of [36] to obtain (almost) optimal results for $(2, 2, n)$ ramp secret sharing schemes where the authors use the product of the two secrets as a verification function. However this verification function cannot be used to any arbitrary ramp secret sharing scheme. Pramanik and Adhikari introduced cheater identifiable ramp secret sharing schemes in [44].

1.1   Our Contribution

In this work, we introduce ramp secret sharing schemes capable of sharing a secret vector secure against at most $n - 1$ cheaters, which is an improvement to [35], [36] and [3] defending only up to $k - 1$ cheaters. Moreover, both the schemes that we present are in the so called CDV^{n-1} *model* of threshold secret sharing [4] in which the adversary (who controls $n-1$ participants) may learn the secret(s), making it the strongest cheating model and hence, our constructions are optimally cheating resilient. In addition, to the best of our knowledge, this is the first work to consider arbitrary distribution of secrets, as opposed to uniform distribution of secrets considered in the OKS model [41] in all the ramp secret sharing schemes with cheating detection [3,35,36]. To elaborate, in CDV^{n-1} model, the cheaters know the secret(s) being shared, resulting in a bias which they may try to use to force the honest participant to recover a *false but valid* secret. To be specific, we have the following results (the results are formally presented with with proofs in Theorems 1 and 2 respectively).

Result 1 (Informal). *There exists a $(k, k + l, n)$ ramp secret sharing scheme which is able to detect cheating, by a coalition of up to $n - 1$ computationally unbounded participants who may know the secrets beforehand, except for a negligible probability $\leq \frac{(D^l-1)(k+l-1)}{p-(l+n-1)}$; share size of the ith participant is*
$$|\mathcal{S}|^{2/l} > \left(l + n - 1 + \frac{(D^l-1)(k+l-1)}{\varepsilon}\right)^{2/l}, \ i = 1, 2, \ldots, n.$$

Result 2 (Informal). *There exists a $(k, k + l, n)$ ramp secret sharing scheme which is able to detect cheating, by a coalition of up to $n - 1$ computationally unbounded participants who may know the secrets beforehand, except for a negligible probability $\leq \frac{(k+l-1)}{p-(l+n-1)}$; share size of the ith participant is $|\mathcal{S}|^{3/l} > \left(l + n - 1 + \frac{k+l-1}{\varepsilon}\right)^{3/l}$, $i = 1, 2, \ldots, n$.*

Both the constructions are efficient. We summarize the results in Table 1.

Table 1. Comparison Table for cheating detectable (k, L, n)-ramp secret sharing schemes

Scheme	#(Cheaters)	Distribution on Secret Space	Cheating Model
[35]	$< k$	Uniform	OKS
[36]	$< k$	Uniform	OKS
[3]	$< k$	Uniform	OKS
Proposed	$< n$	Arbitrary	CDV^{n-1}
Proposed	$< n$	Arbitrary	CDV^{n-1}

Organization of the Paper: In this work, we give constructions for two cheating detectable secret sharing schemes in ramp setup. A brief summary of ramp secret sharing schemes and a few relevant results are given in *Sect. 2.1*. In *Sect. 3*, we formalize the definition of cheating in ramp setup through a game between a centralized adversary controlling up to $n - 1$ cheaters and the challenger. We give a construction for ramp secret sharing scheme capable of cheating detection in Sect. 3.1. This construction achieves a share size $|V_i| = |\mathcal{S}|^{2/l}$. This is the first scheme, to the best of our knowledge, that addresses cheating detection in the CDV^{n-1} model with arbitrary secret distribution in ramp setup which means our scheme attains optimal cheater resiliency. In Sect. 3.2, we give another construction for the same with share size $|V_i| = |\mathcal{S}|^{3/l}$. We then discuss the parametric restrictions under which either scheme performs better than the other in Sect. 3.3. Finally, in Sect. 4, we leave a few open problems.

Notation: Throughout the manuscript, we shall loosely use the notation $[n]$ to denote the set of indices $\{1, 2, \ldots, n\}$ or the set of participants $\{P_1, P_2, \ldots, P_n\}$, wherever these do not conflict.

2 Preliminaries

Let us begin with a few relevant definitions and results first.

An access structure consists of precisely the combination of participants who have access to the secret. A secret sharing scheme consists of two protocols, namely, a share generation protocol called ShareGen, and a reconstruction protocol, called Reconst. Given a secret $s \in \mathcal{S}$ and an access structure Γ on the set of participants $\mathcal{P}$, let Π be a secret sharing scheme realizing Γ. A *share* v_i for the i-th participant P_i ($i = 1, 2, \ldots, n$) is an encoding of the secret which, when accumulated with other shares from a qualified set, can obtain the secret back, whereas accumulation with participants from a forbidden subset yields nothing that the probability distribution of the secret does not already convey. In other words, joint distribution of shares of different secrets are indistinguishable for forbidden set of participants.

The formal definition of a perfect secret sharing scheme is as follows.

Definition 1 Secret Sharing Scheme [5]). *A secret sharing scheme Π for an access structure Γ consists of a pair of algorithms (ShareGen, Reconst). ShareGen is a probabilistic algorithm that gets as input a secret m (from a domain of secrets S) and number of parties n, and generates n shares $(sh_1, \ldots, sh_n) \longleftarrow$ ShareGen(m). Reconst is a deterministic algorithm that gets as input the shares of a subset B of parties and outputs a string. The requirements for defining a secret sharing scheme are as follow:*

1. *(Correctness) For every secret $m \in S$ and every qualified set $B \in \Gamma$, it must hold that $Pr[\text{Reconst}(\{sh_i\}_{i \in B}, B) = m] = 1$.*
2. *(Perfect Secrecy) For every forbidden set $F \notin \Gamma$ and for any two distinct secrets $m_0 \neq m_1$ in S, it must hold that following two distributions*

$$\{\text{ShareGen}(m_0)_i\}_{i \in F} \text{ and } \{\text{ShareGen}(m_1)_i\}_{i \in F} \text{ are identical.}$$

In (k, n) threshold secret sharing [50], the dealer chooses a random polynomial $f(x)$ (from $\mathbb{F}_p[x]$) of degree $\leq k - 1$ with the secret to be shared as its constant term. The ith participant ($i \in [n]$) is handed over $f(i)$ as his share. It immediately follows that any k shares are enough to recover the secret. On the other hand, $k - 1$ or lesser number of shares can guess the secret with a probability bounded above by $Pr[s \leftarrow \mathcal{S}]$, which, also, is the probability of guessing the secret with zero shares at disposal. All the computations are done in a field of size $p > n$. Shamir's construction for (k, n) threshold secret sharing can be modified to share a secret vector with a reasonable loss in security but achieving smaller share size than the secret size. We discuss this in the following section. For the algebraic intrinsicalities involved in this paper, one may refer [2].

2.1 Ramp Secret Sharing

Ramp secret sharing schemes or nonperfect secret sharing schemes [10,33,42,53] are a practical variant of usual threshold secret sharing schemes. What separates ramp secret sharing schemes from usual threshold schemes is a 'gap' between the *privacy threshold* (p) and *reconstruction threshold* (r). Also, nothing can be said about those subsets with size between privacy threshold and reconstruction threshold. As an interesting application of ramp secret sharing, a secret vector can be shared in one go without overburdening the shares of participants [53]. However, there is a partial leakage of information in the ramp setup. A ramp secret sharing scheme Ramp is also a two-parted protocol, namely, ShareGen

(the share generation protocol) and Reconst (the secret reconstruction protocol).
Given two positive integers r, p with $p \lneqq r$, a *ramp access structure* consists of
three pairwise disjoint subsets $\mathcal{Q}, \mathcal{F}, \mathcal{I} \subset 2^{\mathcal{P}}$ such that:

1. $\mathcal{Q} \sqcup \mathcal{F} \sqcup \mathcal{I} = 2^{\mathcal{P}}$.
2. (*Qualified Sets*) $A \in \mathcal{Q}$, if $|A| \geq r$; in this case, $Pr[\mathsf{Reconst}(\{\mathsf{sh}_i\}_{i \in A}, A) = m] = 1$.
3. (*Forbidden Sets*) $A \in \mathcal{F}$, if $|A| \leq p$; in this case, $Pr[\mathsf{Reconst}(\{\mathsf{sh}_i\}_{i \in A}, A) = m] = Pr[m \leftarrow \mathcal{S}]$, $\mathcal{S}$ being the secret space.
4. (*Intermediate Sets*) $A \in \mathcal{I}$ if $p + 1 \leq |A| \leq r - 1$; in this case, $1 \gneqq Pr[\mathsf{Reconst}(\{\mathsf{sh}_i\}_{i \in A}, A) = m] \gneqq Pr[s \leftarrow \mathcal{S}]$

A (k, L, n) ramp secret sharing scheme Ramp = (ShareGen, Reconst) can be
formally defined as:

Definition 2 ((k, L, n) Ramp Secret Sharing). *In a (k, L, n) ramp secret
sharing scheme Ramp = (ShareGen, Reconst) sharing secret $\boldsymbol{s} = (s_0, s_1, \ldots, s_{l-1})$
on a set of participants $\mathcal{P}$ of size n, qualified sets are of size $L (= k+l)$ or larger;
forbidden sets are of size k or smaller. Formally, for a subset A of participants,*

(i) $Pr[\mathsf{Reconst}(\{sh_i\}_{i \in A}, A) = (s_0, s_1, \ldots, s_{l-1}) \mid |A| \geq L] = 1$,
(ii) $Pr[\mathsf{Reconst}(\{sh_i\}_{i \in A}, A) = (s_0, s_1, \ldots, s_{l-1}) \mid |A| \leq k] = Pr[(s_0, s_1, \ldots, s_{l-1}) \leftarrow \mathcal{S}^l]$,
(iii) $Pr[\mathsf{Reconst}(\{sh_i\}_{i \in A}, A) = (s_0, s_1, \ldots, s_{l-1}) \mid k + 1 \leq |A| \leq L - 1] = |\mathcal{S}|^{|A|-k} \cdot Pr[(s_0, s_1, \ldots, s_{l-1}) \leftarrow \mathcal{S}^l]$.

- **A Construction of Ramp Secret Sharing Scheme** [28]
  We recall a ramp scheme from [28] which shares a secret vector in an
space efficient manner. The share generation algorithm ShareGen takes as inputs
$\boldsymbol{s} = (s_0, s_1, \ldots, s_{l-1})$, number of participants n, thresholds $k, L = k+l (\leq n)$ and
outputs a list of n shares $v_1, v_2, \ldots, v_n$. The reconstruction algorithm Reconst
takes $m (\geq k + l)$ shares as input and outputs $\boldsymbol{s'}$.

The following results follow immediately.

Proposition 1. *Each participant receives a share of size $p = |\mathcal{S}|^{1/l}$.*

Proposition 2. *1. On a collusion of $k + l$ (reconstruction threshold) or more
participants, $\boldsymbol{s}$ is reconstructed with certainty, i.e. $Pr[\mathsf{Reconst} \rightarrow \boldsymbol{s'} = \boldsymbol{s}] = 1$
but k (privacy threshold) or less participants guess $\boldsymbol{s}$ with a probability $\dfrac{1}{p^l}$.*
*2. A collusion of $k + j$ participants $(j = 1, 2, \ldots, l - 1)$ can guess the list of
secrets with a probability $\dfrac{1}{p^{l-j}}$.*

Proposition 3. *The degree of freedom of the share generating polynomial is
$k + l$.*

ShareGen :

1. Let all the s_i's be represented as elements from the field $\mathbb{Z}_p$, p being a prime number.
2. Let $F(x)$ be a random polynomial of degree at most $k + l - 1$ which passes through the points $(0, s_0), (1, s_1), \ldots, (l - 1, s_{l-1})$.
3. The Dealer chooses n pairwise distinct points $\alpha_1, \alpha_2, \ldots, \alpha_n$ uniformly at random from $\mathbb{Z}_p \setminus \{0, 1, \ldots, l-1\}$ and publishes on a public bulletin board as the *public IDS* of the participants.
4. Dealer provides the i-th participant with, his share, $v_i = F(\alpha_i)$, $i = 1, 2, \ldots, n$, each through a private and secure channel.

Reconst : On input of m ($\geq k + l$) shares $\{v_{j_i}\}_{i=1}^{m}$, the reconstructing parties jointly reconstruct a unique polynomial $F'(x)$ of degree $k + l - 1$ passing through $\{(\alpha_{j_i}, v_{j_i})\}_{i=1}^{m}$ and output, $s' = (F'(0), F'(1), \ldots, F'(l-1))$.

Fig. 1. Ramp scheme from[28]

Note that, the properties described in Propositions 1, 2 and 3 are specific to the ramp secret sharing scheme described above.

• **An attack on the scheme described in** Fig. 1: The scheme described in Fig. 1 is not impervious to attack. In fact, a single cheating participant may, should he choose, convince other reconstructing parties of an incorrect but valid secret vector. Consider the following simple attack similar to [51] on a $(2, 4, n)$ ramp secret sharing scheme: Suppose the share generation polynomial $F(x) = a_0 + a_1x + a_2x^2 + a_3x^3$ shares the secret vector (a_0, a_1). The cheating participant P_{i_1} chooses an error polynomial $\Delta(x) = b_0 + b_1x + b_2x^2 + b_3x^3$ such that $\Delta(\alpha_{i_2}) = \Delta(\alpha_{i_3}) = \Delta(\alpha_{i_4}) = 0$ and $\Delta(0) = \delta_0$, where δ_0 is the error the cheater wishes to induce into a_0 and $\alpha_{i_1}, \alpha_{i_2}, \alpha_{i_3}$ and α_{i_4} respectively denote the IDs of the reconstructing parties $P_{i_1}, P_{i_2}, P_{i_3}$ and P_{i_4}. Using Lagrange's interpolation [52], it follows that, $\Delta(x) = -(\alpha_{i_2}\alpha_{i_3}\alpha_{i_4})^{-1}\delta_0[x^3 - (\sum \alpha_{i_j})x^2 + (\sum \alpha_{i_j}\alpha_{i_k})x - \alpha_{i_2}\alpha_{i_3}\alpha_{i_4}]$. Instead of submitting, his actual share $F(\alpha_{i_1})$, P_{i_1} submits as his forged share $F(\alpha_{i_1}) + \Delta(\alpha_{i_1})$. Note that, by construction of $\Delta(x)$, it follows that, in spite of other participants submitting their actual shares, they jointly reconstruct an incorrect polynomial $G(x) = F(x) + \Delta(x)$. The reconstructed secrets in this case would be $(a'_0, a'_1) = (a_0 + \delta_0, \ a_1 - \{\alpha_{i_2}\alpha_{i_3}\alpha_{i_4}\}^{-1}\delta_0\{\sum \alpha_{i_j}\alpha_{i_k}\})$.

2.2 Cheating Model

Before beginning with cheating detection, let us fix the cheating model first. There are two standard cheating models concerning secret sharing with cheating detection, namely, the CDV model and the OKS model. The CDV model of adversasrial setup, named after the authors of [14], allows the $k-1$ cheaters to have access to the secret(s), yet secures tampering attacks to the secrets, as long as the cheaters don't have any advantage guessing the honest participant's share from the collective information that they possess. The OKS model, named after the authors of [41], does not aid the $k-1$ cheaters with the secret(s). Later, in [4], the author modified the former model to CDV^{n-1}, which considers a single participant to be honest only. This is a fairly strong model of cheating where a single honest party is about to be cheated by $n-1$ remaining participants who, also, have access to the secret(s). [3,35,36] consider ramp secret sharing schemes secure against OKS cheaters. In this paper, we consider the cheaters to be in CDV^{n-1} model which is a much stronger adversarial setup.

3 Ramp Secret Sharing with Cheating Detection

The ramp secret sharing scheme described in Fig. 1 is not secure against active adversaries who may modify shares before submission in the reconstruction phase. With a very high probability, this might lead to the reconstruction of an incorrect secret for honest participants whereas the cheater(s) get the correct secret. Let, $s = (s_0, s_1, \ldots, s_{l-1})$ denote the vector of original secret and $s' = (s'_0, s'_1, \ldots, s'_{l-1})$ denote that of reconstructed secret due to cheating. Note that, *successful cheating* occurs if $s' \in V^l$ and $s' \neq s$, where $V \subseteq S$ denotes the sub-collection of valid secrets in the space S of secrets, where V is pre-defined and fixed.

Modelling the Adversary: Suppose, $\mathcal{A} = (\mathcal{A}_1, \mathcal{A}_2)$ denotes a centralized adversary who can choose and corrupt up to $n-1$ out of the n participants involved, where $\mathcal{A}_1$ and $\mathcal{A}_2$ are two probabilistic Turing machines. In other words, $\mathcal{A}$ may choose whom he wishes to cheat and influence all the others. We also assume that $\mathcal{A}$ knows the share generating polynomial $F(x)$ but he shall not know the share of the targeted honest participant. This is the most powerful adversarial setup possible with n participants. Suppose there are $k+l$ participants available during reconstruction. $\mathcal{A}_1$ outputs $k+l-1$ participants (under his influence) out of the $k+l$ participants and $\mathcal{A}_2$ outputs the honest participant i_{k+l} and modifies the shares of the others. We demonstrate the following game Game(Ramp, $\mathcal{A}$) in Fig. 2 between the adversary and the scheme to demonstrate the adversarial advantage.

Let us denote the cheating probability by $\epsilon(\mathsf{Ramp}, \mathcal{A})$. Formally,

$$\epsilon(\mathsf{Ramp}, \mathcal{A}) = Pr[\mathsf{Reconst}(\{\mathsf{sh}_i\}_{i \in [k+l]}, [k+l]) = s' \mid s' \in V^l \land s' \neq s].$$

Game(Ramp, $\mathcal{A}$)

$s \leftarrow \mathcal{S}^l$ // *according to the probability distribution over $\mathcal{S}^l$*
$(v_1, \ldots, v_n) \leftarrow$ ShareGen(s, k, n)
$\{i_1, i_2, \cdots, i_{k+l-1}\} \leftarrow \mathcal{A}_1(s);$
$(v'_{i_1}, \ldots, v'_{i_{k+l-1}}, i_{k+l}) \leftarrow \mathcal{A}_2(v_{i_1}, \ldots, v_{i_{k+l-1}}, v_{i_{k+l+1}}, \ldots, v_{i_n}, s)$

Fig. 2. Game between Ramp and $\mathcal{A}$.

Definition 3 (Secure Ramp Secret Sharing Scheme). *A ramp secret sharing scheme* Ramp $=$ (ShareGen, Reconst) *is called ε-secure with respect to* Game(Ramp, $\mathcal{A}$), *if ϵ(Ramp, $\mathcal{A}$) $\leq \varepsilon$, where $\mathcal{A}$ controls $n - 1$ cheaters.*

We now present two constructions for ramp secret sharing capable of cheating detection.

3.1 Construction - I

In this section, we propose a construction (Fig. 3) for cheating detectable $(k, k + l, n)$-ramp secret sharing scheme. The cheating model is same as in Definition 3. Let $\varepsilon > 0$. Suppose $s_0, s_1, \ldots, s_{l-1} \in V \subsetneq \mathbb{Z}_p$, where $V = \{0, 1, \ldots, D - 1\}$ denotes the valid secret range[1] and $\mathbb{Z}_p$ denotes the field of integers modulo p, p being a prime number such that

$$p > l + n - 1 + \frac{(D^l - 1)(k + l - 1)}{\varepsilon}. \tag{1}$$

If every reconstructed component $s'_i \in V$, then $s' = (s'_1, \ldots, s'_{l-1})$ is accepted to be a correct secret by an honest participant.

Theorem 1. *The construction described in Fig. 3 admits an information theoretically secure ramp scheme with reconstruction threshold $k + l$ and privacy threshold k . Moreover, the scheme is able to detect cheating, except for a negligible probability ϵ(Ramp, $\mathcal{A}$) $\leq \frac{(D^l-1)(k+l-1)}{p-(l+n-1)} < \varepsilon$. Also, the ith participant holds a share of size $|\mathcal{V}_i| = p^2 = |\mathcal{S}|^{2/l} > \left(l + n - 1 + \frac{(D^l-1)(k+l-1)}{\varepsilon}\right)^{2/l}$.*

Proof: *Correctness and Perfect Secrecy:* The correctness and perfect secrecy follow from properties of polynomial interpolation. In short, if one pools $k + l$ points from an $k + l - 1$ degree polynomial, he can uniquely determine the polynomial using Lagrange's interpolation over finite fields. On the contrary, if k or less points are available, dimension of the solution space of system of linear equations with $k + l$ unknowns and k equations would be l and hence, the probability of guessing the correct polynomial would be $\frac{1}{p^l}$. In presence of $k + j$ $(j = 1, 2, \ldots, l - 1)$ points, this probability becomes $\frac{1}{p^{l-j}}$.

---

[1] V can be chosen to be any subset of $\mathbb{Z}_p$ of size D.

ShareGen : Input $(s_0, s_1, \ldots, s_{l-1}) \in \mathbb{Z}_p^l$;
Output a list of shares $v_1, v_2, \ldots, v_n$ as follows:

1. Let, $x_l, x_{l+1}, \ldots, x_{k+l-1}$ be k points from $\mathbb{Z}_p$ chosen uniformly at random and $F(x)$ denote the unique polynomial of degree at most $k + l - 1$ which passes through the points $(0, s_0), (1, s_1), \ldots, (l-1, s_{l-1}), (l, x_l), (l+1, x_{l+1}), \ldots, (k+l-1, x_{k+l-1})$.
2. The Dealer chooses n pairwise distinct points $\alpha_1, \alpha_2, \ldots, \alpha_n$ uniformly at random from $\mathbb{Z}_p \setminus \{0, 1, \ldots, l-1\}$. Here α_i shall denote the *private id* of the i-th participant P_i, $i = 1, 2, \ldots, n$.
3. Dealer provides the i-th participant, his share, $v_i = (\alpha_i, F(\alpha_i))$, $i = 1, 2, \ldots, n$, each through a private and secure channel.

Reconst : On input of $m(\geq k + l)$ shares $\{v'_{j_i}\}_{i=1}^m$

1. Reconstructing parties reconstruct the unique polynomial $F'(x)$ passing through $\{v'_{j_i}\}_{i=1}^m$ and hence, $s'_0 = F'(0), s'_1 = F'(1), \ldots, s'_{l-1} = F'(l-1)$.
2. **Cheating Detection** :
   - for t = 0 to $l - 1$:
   -     if $s'_t \notin V$:
   -         **output** $\perp$
   -         **break**
   - else :
   -     **output** $(s'_0, s'_1, \ldots, s'_{l-1})$.

Fig. 3. Construction of cheating detectable ramp scheme in the CDV^{n-1} model.

Cheating Detection: Suppose, without loss of generality, that P_n is the only honest participant in the scheme. Also, it is reasonable to assume that P_n is one of the reconstructing participants, else there would be no point of cheating. We show that the cheaters can successfully dupe P_n with at least one valid but incorrect coordinate of the secret vector with probability at most $\frac{(D^l-1)(k+l-1)}{p-(l+n-1)} < \varepsilon$.

$\mathcal{A}$ chooses $k+l-1$ participants under his influence and modifies their shares to $(\alpha'_{i_1}, \beta'_{i_1}), (\alpha'_{i_2}, \beta'_{i_2}), \ldots, (\alpha'_{i_{k+l-1}}, \beta'_{i_{k+l-1}})$. Suppose, $F'(x)$ denotes the unique polynomial of degree $k+l-1$ passing through the $k+l-1$ modified points and one honest point.

For a successful cheating it is imperative that $F(\alpha_n) = F'(\alpha_n)$, where, (in $\mathcal{A}$'s view) α_n is uniformly random over $\mathbb{Z}_p \setminus \{0, 1, \ldots, l-1, \alpha_1, \alpha_2, \ldots, \alpha_{n-1}\}$. $F(x)$ and $F'(x)$ being two distinct polynomials of degree $k+l-1$, can have at most $k+l-1$ common points. Then for every $s' \neq s$, the cheating succeeds with a probability $\dfrac{k+l-1}{p-(l+n-1)}$. For all possible valid but incorrect secrets s', the cheating probability is at most, $\epsilon(\mathsf{Ramp}, \mathcal{A}) \leq \dfrac{(D^l-1)(k+l-1)}{p-(l+n-1)} < \varepsilon$.

Each participant receives 2 field elements from $\mathbb{Z}_p = |\mathcal{S}|^{1/l}$, as share. Hence, the share size of the ith participant is given by $|\mathcal{V}_i| > \left(l+n-1+\dfrac{(D^l-1)(k+l-1)}{\varepsilon}\right)^{2/l}$, $i = 1, 2, \ldots, n$. ∎

Remark: The proof described above was done considering uniform secret distribution, however, the technique used can be used to avail similar result for arbitrary secret distribution.

3.2 Construction - II

In this section, we present another construction for ramp secret sharing scheme capable of cheating detection. This scheme is secure against $n-1$ colluding cheaters who may know the secret beforehand. In Fig. 4 we give a concrete construction of a cheating detectable $(k, k+l, n)$- ramp scheme in the CDV^{n-1} model.

Theorem 2. *The construction described in Fig. 4 admits an information theoretically secure ramp scheme with reconstruction threshold $k+l$ and privacy threshold k. Moreover, the scheme is able to detect cheating, except for a negligible probability $\epsilon(\mathsf{Ramp}, \mathcal{A}) \leq \dfrac{(k+l-1)}{p-(l+n-1)} < \varepsilon$. Share size of the ith participant is given by $|\mathcal{V}_i| = p^3 = |\mathcal{S}|^{3/l} > \left(l+n-1+\dfrac{k+l-1}{\varepsilon}\right)^{3/l}$, $i = 1, 2, \ldots, n$.*

Proof: *Correctness and Perfect Secrecy:* Correctness and perfect secrecy proofs are similar to Theorem 1 and, hence, are omitted. We only show that the cheating probability is negligible.

Cheating Detection: Let us suppose, without loss of generality, P_n be the only honest participant in this scenario. Without loss of generality, say, $\mathcal{A}$ modifies shares of $P_1, P_2, \ldots, P_{k+l-1}$ to (α'_i, f'_i, g'_i), $i \in [k+l-1]$. Suppose, the points $\{(\alpha'_i, f'_i) \mid i = 1, 2, \ldots, k+l-1, n\}$ and $\{(\alpha'_i, g'_i) \mid i = 1, 2, \ldots, k+l-1, n\}$ yield to the unique polynomials $F'(x)$ and $G'(x)$ respectively, of degree $\leq k+l-1$ each. Successful undetected cheating takes place if $F'(t) = G'(t)$, for all $t = 0, 1, \ldots, l-1$ but $(F'(0), \ldots, F'(l-1)) = s' \neq s$. In other words, the honest participant will not detect the cheating, only if, the cheaters under the influence of $\mathcal{A}$ must have $F'(\alpha_n) = F(\alpha_n)$ satisfied. Now, from $\mathcal{A}$'s point of view, α_n is a random point from $\mathbb{Z}_p \setminus \{0, 1, \ldots, l-1, \alpha_1, \alpha_2, \ldots, \alpha_{n-1}\}$. Moreover, the two polynomials $F'(x)$ and $F(x)$, both being separate polynomials of degree (at most) $k+l-1$, may intersect at, at most, $k+l-1$ points. So, the cheating probability for some fixed set of secrets is bounded above by $\dfrac{k+l-1}{p-(l+n-1)}$.

ShareGen :
Input $(s_0, s_1, \ldots, s_{l-1}) \in \mathbb{Z}_p^l$;
Outputs a list of shares $v_1, v_2, \ldots, v_n$ as:

1. The dealer generates two random polynomials of degree (at most) $k+l-1$, namely $F(x)$ and $G(x)$, with $F(0) = G(0) = s_0$, $F(1) = G(1) = s_1, \ldots, F(l-1) = G(l-1) = s_{l-1}$.
2. The Dealer chooses n pairwise disjoint points $\alpha_1, \alpha_2, \ldots, \alpha_n$ uniformly at random from $\mathbb{Z}_p \setminus \{0, 1, \ldots, l-1\}$; α_i shall denote the *private id* of the ith participant P_i, $i \in [n]$.
3. Dealer provides the ith participant, his share, $v_i = (\alpha_i, F(\alpha_i), G(\alpha_i))$, $i \in [n]$, each through a private and secure channel.

Reconst : On input of $m(\geq k+l)$ shares $\{v'_{j_i}\}_{i=1}^m$

1. Reconstructing parties reconstruct the unique polynomials $F'(x)$ and $G'(x)$ passing through $\{v'_{j_i}\}_{i=1}^m$.
2. **Cheating Detection** :
   - for t = 0 to $l-1$:
     - if $F'(t) \neq G'(t)$:
       - **output** $\perp$
       - **break**
   - else :
     - **output** $(F'(0), F'(1), \ldots, F'(l-1))$.

Fig. 4. A simple construction of cheating detectable ramp scheme in the CDV^{n-1} model.

It follows that, for $\epsilon(\mathsf{Ramp}, \mathcal{A}) < \varepsilon$ to hold, the following inequality must satisfy: $p > l + n - 1 + \frac{(k+l-1)}{\varepsilon}$. Each participant receives 3 field elements from $\mathbb{Z}_p = |\mathcal{S}|^{1/l}$, as share. Hence, the share size of the ith participant is given by $|\mathcal{V}_i| > \left(l + n - 1 + \frac{k+l-1}{\varepsilon}\right)^{3/l}$, $i = 1, 2, \ldots, n$. ∎

Remark: The proof described above was done considering uniform secret distribution, however, the technique used can be used to avail similar result for arbitrary secret distribution.

3.3   Few Words on Share Size

Construction I exhibits a share size of $|\mathcal{S}|^{2/l}$ i.e. it requires 2 field elements to share l field elements of secret. It follows from the cheating probability of the scheme that (Eq. 1) $p > l + n - 1 + \frac{(D^l - 1)(k+l-1)}{\varepsilon}$. On the other hand, Construction II exhibits a share size of $|\mathcal{S}|^{3/l}$ i.e. it requires 3 field elements to do the same, where the field size $p > l + n - 1 + \frac{k+l-1}{\varepsilon}$. Apparently, Construction I requires lesser field elements, however, the field size required in Construction II is much smaller. Let us consider the following equation:

$$(a + (D_0^l - 1)b)^2 = (a + b)^3, \quad where \ a = l + n - 1, \ b = \frac{k+l-1}{\varepsilon}$$
$$\Rightarrow a + (D_0^l - 1)b = (a + b)^{3/2}$$
$$\Rightarrow D_0^l - 1 = \frac{(a+b)^{3/2} - a}{b}$$
$$\Rightarrow D_0 = \left(\frac{(a+b)^{3/2} - a}{b} + 1 \right)^{1/l} = \left(\frac{\left(l+n-1+\frac{k+l-1}{\varepsilon} \right)^{3/2} - (l+n-1)}{\frac{k+l-1}{\varepsilon}} + 1 \right)^{1/l}$$

To sum up, if all the other parameters are same, Construction I produces better share size than Construction II if and only if $D < D_0$, i.e. for lesser number of possible valid secrets.

4 Conclusion

The papers [3], [35] and [36] that deal with cheating detection in ramp secret sharing can tolerate at most $k-1$ cheaters. In addition to that, all of these works consider uniform secret distribution and the adversary is in the OKS model where the cheaters are not allowed to know the secret beforehand. As an improvement, the two constructions that we present in this work are secure against $n - 1$ cheaters who conspire against one honest participant and try to convince him of a secret which is valid but incorrect (in other words, CDV^{n-1} model). Distribution of secrets is considered to be arbitrary. Both the constructions are information theoretically secure and do not assume any computational restrictions for the cheaters and achieve optimal cheater resiliency against the $n - 1$ CDV cheaters. A summarized comparison of the constructions with other relevant works is available in Table 1. Further studies like cheating variants of evolving secret sharing [6,7,22,24,30,45] schemes where share size is grows over time but in ramp setup are left as open problems. Introducing variants of new paradigms such as in [34] might be interesting.

Acknowledgement. The research of the fourth author is partially supported by DST-SERB Project MATRICS vide Sanction Order: MTR/2019/001573. In the end, authors would like to thank the annonymous reviewers who brought forward suggestions which improved this paper.

References

1. Adhikari, A., Morozov, K., Obana, S., Roy, P.S., Sakurai, K., Xu, R.: Efficient threshold secret sharing schemes secure against rushing cheaters. ICITS **2016**, 3–23 (2016). https://doi.org/10.1007/978-3-319-49175-2_1
2. Adhikari, M.R., Adhikari, A.: Basic Modern Algebra with Applications. Springer, Cham (2014). https://doi.org/10.1007/978-81-322-1599-8
3. Agematsu, T., Obana, S.: Almost optimal cheating-detectable (2, 2, n) ramp secret sharing scheme. CANDAR **2019**, 1–9 (2019). https://doi.org/10.1109/CANDAR. 2019.00009

4. Araki, T.: Efficient (k, n) threshold secret sharing schemes secure against cheating from n-1 cheaters. ACISP **2007**, 133–142 (2007). https://doi.org/10.1007/978-3-540-73458-1_11

5. Beimel, A.: Secret-sharing schemes: a survey. In: Coding and Cryptology - Third International Workshop, IWCC 2011, Qingdao, China, May 30-June 3, 2011. Proceedings, pp. 11–46 (2011). https://doi.org/10.1007/978-3-642-20901-7_2

6. Beimel, A., Othman, H.: Evolving ramp secret-sharing schemes. SCN **2018**, 313–332 (2018). https://doi.org/10.1007/978-3-319-98113-0_17

7. Beimel, A., Othman, H.: Evolving ramp secret sharing with a small gap. In: EUROCRYPT 2020 Part I, pp. 529–555 (2020). https://doi.org/10.1007/978-3-030-45721-1_19

8. Ben-Or, M., Goldwasser, S., Wigderson, A.: Completeness theorems for non-cryptographic fault-tolerant distributed computation (extended abstract). STOC **1988**, 1–10 (1988). https://doi.org/10.1145/62212.62213

9. Blakley, G.R.: Safeguarding cryptographic keys. In: International Workshop on Managing Requirements Knowledge (AFIPS), pp. 313–317 (1979). https://doi.org/10.1109/AFIPS.1979.98

10. Blakley, G.R., Meadows, C.A.: Security of ramp schemes. CRYPTO **1984**, 242–268 (1984). https://doi.org/10.1007/3-540-39568-7_20

11. Blundo, C., Santis, A.D., Crescenzo, G.D., Gaggia, A.G., Vaccaro, U.: Multi-secret sharing schemes. CRYPTO **1994**, 150–163 (1994). https://doi.org/10.1007/3-540-48658-5_17

12. Blundo, C., Santis, A.D., Vaccaro, U.: Efficient sharing of many secrets. STACS **1993**, 692–703 (1993). https://doi.org/10.1007/3-540-56503-5_68

13. Cabello, S., Padró, C., Sáez, G.: Secret sharing schemes with detection of cheaters for a general access structure. Des. Codes Cryptography 25(2), 175–188 (2002)

14. Carpentieri, M., Santis, A.D., Vaccaro, U.: Size of shares and probability of cheating in threshold schemes. EUROCRYPT **1993**, 118–125 (1993). https://doi.org/10.1007/3-540-48285-7_10

15. Cascudo, I., Gundersen, J.S., Ruano, D.: Improved bounds on the threshold gap in ramp secret sharing. IEEE Trans. Inf. Theory 65(7), 4620–4633 (2019). https://doi.org/10.1109/TIT.2019.2902151

16. Chaum, D., Crépeau, C., Damgård, I.: Multiparty unconditionally secure protocols (extended abstract). STOC **1988**, 11–19 (1988). https://doi.org/10.1145/62212.62214

17. Chen, H., Cramer, R., de Haan, R., Cascudo Pueyo, I.: Strongly multiplicative ramp schemes from high degree rational points on curves. EUROCRYPT **2008**, 451–470 (2008). https://doi.org/10.1007/978-3-540-78967-3_26

18. Chen, Q., Pei, D., Tang, C., Yue, Q., Ji, T.: A note on ramp secret sharing schemes from error-correcting codes. Math. Comput. Model. 57(11–12), 2695–2702 (2013). https://doi.org/10.1016/j.mcm.2011.07.024

19. Chor, B., Goldreich, O., Kushilevitz, E., Sudan, M.: Private information retrieval. SFCS **1995**, 41–50 (1995). https://doi.org/10.1109/SFCS.1995.492461

20. Crescenzo, G.D.: Sharing one secret vs. sharing many secrets. Theor. Comput. Sci. 295, 123–140 (2003). https://doi.org/10.1016/S0304-3975(02)00399-7

21. Desmedt, Y.: Treshold cryptosystems (invited talk). AUSCRYPT **1992**, 3–14 (1992). https://doi.org/10.1007/3-540-57220-1_47

22. Desmedt, Y., Dutta, S., Morozov, K.: Evolving perfect hash families: a combinatorial viewpoint of evolving secret sharing. In: CANS 2019, Proceedings, pp. 291–307 (2019)

23. Dutta, S., Roy, P.S., Adhikari, A., Sakurai, K.: On the robustness of visual cryptographic schemes. In: IWDW 2016, Revised Selected Papers, pp. 251–262 (2016)
24. Dutta, S., Roy, P.S., Fukushima, K., Kiyomoto, S., Sakurai, K.: Secret sharing on evolving multi-level access structure. In: WISA 2019, Revised Selected Papers, pp. 180–191 (2019)
25. Frankel, Y., Desmedt, Y.: Classification of ideal homomorphic threshold schemes over finite abelian groups (extended abstract). EUROCRYPT **1992**, 25–34 (1992). https://doi.org/10.1007/3-540-47555-9_2
26. Geil, O., Martin, S., Martínez-Peñas, U., Matsumoto, R., Ruano, D.: On asymptotically good ramp secret sharing schemes. IEICE Trans. Fundam. Electron. Commun. Comput. Sci. 100-A(12), 2699–2708 (2017). https://doi.org/10.1587/transfun.E100.A.2699
27. Goldreich, O., Micali, S., Wigderson, A.: How to play any mental game or a completeness theorem for protocols with honest majority. STOC **1987**, 218–229 (1987). https://doi.org/10.1145/28395.28420
28. Henry, R.: Polynomial batch codes for efficient IT-PIR. PoPETs **2016**(4), 202–218 (2016). https://doi.org/10.1515/popets-2016-0036
29. Iwamoto, M., Yamamoto, H.: Strongly secure ramp secret sharing schemes. IEEE ISIT **2005**, 1221–1225 (2005). https://doi.org/10.1109/ISIT.2005.1523536
30. Komargodski, I., Naor, M., Yogev, E.: How to share a secret, infinitely. In: TCC 2016-B, Proceedings, Part II, pp. 485–514 (2016)
31. Lin, F., Ling, S., Wang, H., Zeng, N.: Threshold changeable ramp secret sharing. CANS **2019**, 308–327 (2019). https://doi.org/10.1007/978-3-030-31578-8_17
32. Matsumoto, R.: Strong security of the strongly multiplicative ramp secret sharing based on algebraic curves. IEICE Transactions 98-A(7), 1576–1578 (2015). https://doi.org/10.1587/transfun.E98.A.1576
33. McEliece, R.J., Sarwate, D.V.: On sharing secrets and reed-solomon codes. Commun. ACM 24(9), 583–584 (1981). https://doi.org/10.1145/358746.358762
34. Meraouche, I., Dutta, S., Sakurai, K.: 3-party adversarial cryptography. EIDWT **2020**, 247–258 (2020)
35. Nakamura, W., Yamamoto, H., Chan, T.: A ramp threshold secret sharing scheme against cheating by substitution attacks. ISITA **2016**, 340–344 (2016)
36. Nakamura, W., Yamamoto, H., Chan, T.: A cheating-detectable (k, L, n) ramp secret sharing scheme. In: IEICE Transactions 100-A(12), 2709–2719 (2017). https://doi.org/10.1587/transfun.E100.A.2709
37. Nishiara, M., Takizawa, K.: Strongly secure secret sharing scheme with ramp threshold based on shamir's polynomial interpolation scheme. The IEICE Trans. on Fund. of Electr., Comm. and Comp. Sc. (Jp. ed.) A 92(12), 1009–1013 (2009). https://ci.nii.ac.jp/naid/110007483234/en/
38. Obana, S., Tsuchida, K.: Cheating detectable secret sharing schemes supporting an arbitrary finite field. IWSEC **2014**, 88–97 (2014). https://doi.org/10.1007/978-3-319-09843-2_7
39. Ogata, W., Eguchi, H.: Cheating detectable threshold scheme against most powerful cheaters for long secrets. Des. Codes Cryptography 71(3), 527–539 (2014). https://doi.org/10.1007/s10623-012-9756-5
40. Ogata, W., Kurosawa, K.: Some basic properties of general nonperfect secret sharing schemes. J. UCS 4(8), 690–704 (1998). https://doi.org/10.3217/jucs-004-08-0690
41. Ogata, W., Kurosawa, K., Stinson, D.R.: Optimum secret sharing scheme secure against cheating. SIAM J. Discrete Math. 20(1), 79–95 (2006). https://doi.org/10.1137/S0895480100378689

42. Ogata, W., Kurosawa, K., Tsujii, S.: Nonperfect secret sharing schemes. AUSCRYPT **1992**, 56–66 (1992). https://doi.org/10.1007/3-540-57220-1_52

43. Okada, K., Kurosawa, K.: Lower bound on the size of shares of nonperfect secret sharing schemes. ASIACRYPT **1994**, 33–41 (1994). https://doi.org/10.1007/BFb0000422

44. Pramanik, J., Adhikari, A.: Ramp secret sharing with cheater identification in presence of rushing cheaters. Groups Complexity Cryptol. **11**(2), 103–113 (2019). https://doi.org/10.1515/gcc-2019-2006

45. Pramanik, J., Adhikari, A.: Evolving secret sharing with essential participants. Cryptology ePrint Archive, Report 2020/1035 (2020)

46. Pramanik, J., Roy, P.S., Dutta, S., Adhikari, A., Sakurai, K.: Secret sharing schemes on compartmental access structure in presence of cheaters. In: ICISS 2018, Proceedings, pp. 171–188 (2018)

47. Rabin, T., Ben-Or, M.: Verifiable secret sharing and multiparty protocols with honest majority (extended abstract). ACM STC **1989**, 73–85 (1989). https://doi.org/10.1145/73007.73014

48. Roy, P.S., Adhikari, A., Xu, R., Morozov, K., Sakurai, K.: An efficient robust secret sharing scheme with optimal cheater resiliency. In: SPACE 2014, Proceedings, pp. 47–58 (2014)

49. Roy, P.S., Das, A., Adhikari, A.: Computationally secure cheating identifiable multi-secret sharing for general access structure. In: ICDCIT 2015, Proceedings, pp. 278–287 (2015)

50. Shamir, A.: How to share a secret. Commun. ACM **22**(11), 612–613 (1979). https://doi.org/10.1145/359168.359176

51. Tompa, M., Woll, H.: How to share a secret with cheaters. J. Cryptology **1**(2), 133–138 (1988). https://doi.org/10.1007/BF02252871

52. Waring, E.: Problems concerning interpolations. Phil. Trans. R. Soc. Lond. **69**, 59–67 (1779)

53. Yamamoto, H.: On secret sharing systems using (k, l, n) threshold scheme. IEICE Trans. Fundamentals (Japanese Edition), A **68**(9), 945–952 (1985)

54. Yoshida, M., Fujiwara, T.: Secure construction for nonlinear function threshold ramp secret sharing. IEEE ISIT **2007**, 1041–1045 (2007). https://doi.org/10.1109/ISIT.2007.4557361

55. Zhang, P., Matsumoto, R.: Quantum strongly secure ramp secret sharing. Quantum Information Process. **14**(2), 715–729 (2015). https://doi.org/10.1007/s11128-014-0863-2

LiARX: A Lightweight Cipher Based on the LTS Design Strategy of ARX

Saurabh Mishra(iD) and Debanjan Sadhya(✉)(iD)

ABV-Indian Institute of Information Technology and Management Gwalior,
Gwalior, India
saurabhmishra272@gmail.com, debanjan@iiitm.ac.in

Abstract. In recent years, technological advancements have led to the production of hardware devices that have extremely constrained resources (viz. RFID tags and sensors). Ensuring the required security guarantees to these low-end devices is a challenging task since conventional cryptographic mechanisms are not suited in such scenarios. For instance, it is advisable to use the Advanced encryption standard (AES) only for those devices where the availability of computational resources is not a major issue. This and more related factors have led to the emergence of Lightweight cryptography. In this paper, we discuss the recommended design principles for constructing a lightweight cipher. From the available literature, we have specifically focused on the Addition-Rotation-XOR (ARX) based design paradigm for this specific purpose. In this work, we have also argued that why the ARX based Long trail strategy (LTS) is a suitable design component for constructing practical lightweight ciphers. Finally, we have introduced a new lightweight cipher named LiARX which is based on the design recommendations of other ARX based ciphers. We have extensively analyzed and compared the performance of our cipher with some existing S-Box and ARX based lightweight ciphers, thereby proving its practicability.

Keywords: Lightweight cryptography · ARX · LTS · Design strategy

1 Introduction

The emergence of resource-constraint devices has driven the problem of the usability of conventional cryptographic algorithms therein. It is understandable to apply traditional ciphers like AES [6] in general devices where there is no constraint (or not much) on resources. However, it is impracticable to use these in specific devices with significantly less memory and computational resources, such as RFIDs tag, smart cards, sensors, and indicators. This technological shift has led to the need for new cryptographic primitives, which is now known as lightweight cryptographic primitives or ciphers.

Lightweight algorithms are characterized by properties such as smaller block sizes and simpler round function [20]. In comparison to traditional crypto-

© Springer Nature Switzerland AG 2020
S. Kanhere et al. (Eds.): ICISS 2020, LNCS 12553, pp. 185–197, 2020.
https://doi.org/10.1007/978-3-030-65610-2_12

graphic algorithms, these properties make them suitable for extremely low-powered devices. In this paper, we initially present the timeline of development in lightweight cryptography (especially block ciphers). We specifically state the requirements of a lightweight cipher and subsequently examine the existing design techniques which cater to such objectives. Next, we discuss the ARX architecture and its suitability for the construction of lightweight ciphers. Based on our previous observations and general recommendations, we propose the design of a lightweight cipher termed as LiARX. The suitability of LiARX for usage in resource-constrained scenarios is empirically validated via estimating multiple model parameters in simulated environments.

The rest of the sections are organized as follows. The fundamentals of lightweight cryptography are briefly discussed in Sect. 2, which includes general characteristics, constraints, and current developments in this domain. In Sect. 3, the concept of ARX architecture is detailed, which is followed by the cipher design strategies in Sect. 4. We give details about our proposed cipher in Sect. 5, and its empirical analysis is performed in Sect. 6. Finally, Sect. 7 concludes this work while providing future research directions.

2   Lightweight Cryptography

Lightweight cryptography is a branch of cryptography whose objective is to cater to the security requirements of resource-constrained gadgets. It essentially considers the implementation cost of the cipher as the essential criterion. However, the security and performance aspects of the algorithm should also be kept satisfactory under all possible circumstances [9]. Ideally, a compromise between these three properties is desirable, which subsequently depends on the resources of the target devices [27]. We further discuss these requirements in more detail in later sections.

The criteria on which a lightweight cryptographic algorithm is evaluated are mainly performance and resource utilization. The performance factor can be measured in terms of energy consumption and the latency for both hardware and software [20]. In hardware, resources are expressed in terms of the gate area, gate equivalents, or logic blocks. The minimization of the area tends to reduce the power consumption. Alternatively in software, resources can be measured in terms of numbers of registers, RAM storage, and ROM storage. The essential function of RAM is to hold transient values of operations, whereas the ROM is utilized to store any hard-coded data (e.g., round keys and S-Boxes).

2.1   General Characteristics

There are some general characteristics of lightweight ciphers that are recommended during its design phase [22]. Firstly, the essential properties of the algorithm (viz. block size and key length) should be decreased within reasonable limits. Furthermore, it should be attempted to base the lightweight algorithm upon conventional computational elements such as arithmetic and logic operations, and linear or nonlinear transformations. Since these functions are widely used and thoroughly analyzed, their usage can compensate for some forced decrease of the cryptographic strength of the lightweight algorithms. The layers of transformation should also be simplified by decreasing the ROM requirement. Finally, low-cost but effective elements should be used during the actual implementation. Some instances of such elements include data-dependent bit permutations and shift registers.

Changes in design approaches of the existing ciphers are required for constructing their lightweight versions. These factors have consequentially led to some compromises. Resource constraints have forced cryptographers to design lightweight algorithms with comparatively small block sizes and key lengths. This decision consequently makes lightweight ciphers more vulnerable to cryptographic attacks as compared to traditional ciphers. Another problem lies in the possibility of a side-channel attack. As mentioned in the literature, the security of a few lightweight encryption techniques is not investigated against this specific attack form [22].

2.2 Existing Designs

There exist many lightweight ciphers that satisfy the need for resource-constrained devices. These ciphers are primarily classified into two classes. The first class belongs to ciphers which are built by simplifying existing and popular block ciphers. This strategy consequently improves their efficiency and makes them compatible according to the need for lightweight devices. In this class, the initial ciphers were derived from the Data encryption standard (DES) [23]. DESL [19] is a simplified variant of DES, where instead of using eight different S-box, one single S-box is used to decrease ROM storage. In another variant DESXL [16], two extra layers of key whitening are performed (one at the input and one at the output) using a specific subkey. The whitening process is performed to increase resistance against the brute-force key attacks. There is another group of ciphers which are derived by either simplifying AES or using components from AES. Since AES is a cryptographic standard for traditional ciphers, it became a desirable choice to serve as the inspiration. Some of the key lightweight ciphers which were designed based on AES are KLEIN [10], LED [12], and Midori [1].

The second class of lightweight ciphers pertains to those designs which are made from scratch. Among these, PRESENT [4] is an important cipher since it is based on a unique design strategy that is different from other ciphers. It uses 4-bit S-boxes instead of 8-bit S-boxes, which results in significant area saving in hardware implementation. For comparison, the S-box used in PRESENT consumes 28 GE, whereas the S-box used in AES consumes 395 GE [20]. Some other algorithms in this class include RC5 [24], TEA [28], and XTEA [26]. The common property which makes these ciphers suitable for lightweight environments is the presence of simple round structures.

3 ARX

ARX [8], standing for Addition/Rotation/Xor, is a category of symmetric key algorithms that are based solely on the modular addition/bitwise addition, bitwise rotation, and exclusive-OR operations. The only source of non-linearity in ARX based designs arises from the modular addition operation. In contrast, non-linearity in S-Box based ciphers can be attributed to the substitution tables. The choice of using the ARX paradigm is based on the following three observations [8]:

1. Eliminating the look-ups tables of S-box based designs increases the resilience against side-channel attacks.
2. The ARX design decreases the numbers of operations during encryption, thereby allowing particularly fast software implementations.
3. The size of the low-level code describing ARX based algorithms is minimal. This characteristic makes the ARX approach especially appealing for lightweight block ciphers since memory is expensive therein.

To summarize, algorithms built on the ARX architecture are generally faster and smaller than S-box based designs. Furthermore, they have some inherent security features against side-channel attacks since modular addition leaks less information than a look-up table. The lack of S-box also saves a lot of ROM storage, which is crucial in resource constraint devices.

3.1 Current Scenario

Even though the coning of the term 'ARX' is relatively new, the concept of ARX was being used in many ciphers before its naming. The earliest cipher based on the ARX architecture was RC5, which was proposed in 1995. Like most of the ARX ciphers, it was based on the Feistel structure [17]. It is the patented cipher of RSA security, and had served as inspiration for the improved RC6 [25] due to its excellent design criteria. The next significant ARX based cipher was XTEA [26], which was an improvement of a previously made cipher called TEA. It is a 64-bit Feistel cipher with a 128-bit key. It has a distinctive feature that it can be described in the smallest amount of code. This particular property later becomes one of the distinguishing characteristics of every ARX-based cipher. Among more recent works, HIGHT [14], LEA [13], and Chaskey [21] are some major designs. HIGHT is a block cipher of 64-bit block length and 128-bit key length. It is an ARX-based generalized Feistel structure that requires hardware cost nearly the same as AES (3048 GE Versus 3400 GE). However, it is comparatively much faster in performance [20].

The most popular of all ARX-based cipher is arguably the SIMON/SPECK family of ciphers. SPECK [2] has been optimized for performance in software implementations, while its sister algorithm SIMON [2] has been optimized for hardware implementation. Both of these are two-branch Feistel networks but differ by the nature of their Feistel feature. Although NSA tried to make them a standard for lightweight devices, it failed because of their vulnerabilities to differential and linear attacks. Still, a lot of focus has come upon the architecture and properties of ARX due to the high scrutiny of these ciphers.

All the ARX-based ciphers suffer from one open problem: "Is it possible to design an ARX cipher that is provably secure against single-trail differential and linear cryptanalysis by design ?" [8]. Currently, a strategy known as WTS [7] is used in traditional ciphers, but it is not applicable in ARX-based ciphers. For a clear understanding, WTS will be briefly discussed in Subsect. 4.1.

4   Cipher Design Strategies

An efficient cipher design strategy is always required for constructing a cipher that is provably secure against cryptographic attacks. WTS and LTS [8] are two conventional design strategies that cater to such purposes. These are briefly discussed in the following subsections.

4.1   Wide Trail Strategy (WTS)

The WTS is utilized for designing cryptographic cipher with provable bounds against differential and linear attacks. In ciphers designed by the WTS, a relatively large amount of resources is spent in the linear step to provide high multiple-round diffusion but small and efficient S-boxes are utilized in this design. Noticeably, AES is based on this strategy. The name itself comes from the probability 'trails' which are used in differential and linear cryptanalysis; the wider they are, the harder they are to exploit. In WTS, S-box plays an essential and crucial role. However, it cannot be used in ARX-based ciphers due to a lack of S-Boxes therein.

4.2   Long Trail Strategy (LTS)

The notion of LTS was initially proposed in [8]. In their study, the authors provided a strategy for designing ARX-based symmetric key primitives with provable resistance against single trail differential and linear cryptanalysis. It should be noted that the LTS advocates the use of large but weak (ARX-based) S-Boxes together with sparse linear layers. This strategy provides the best case of building a lightweight symmetric key cipher because of the following reasons:

- It provides provable security against single trail differential and linear cryptanalysis, which was one of the oldest open problems in lightweight cryptography
- The lack of look-ups table based S-box in LTS strategy makes it inherently resistance against side-channel attacks
- It allows the designer to check whether a design is vulnerable or not against integral attacks

In LTS, the concepts of MEDCP (Maximum Expected Differential Characteristic Probability) and MELCC (Maximum Expected Linear Characteristic Correlation) [15] are used. These concepts are borrowed from the WTS strategy, and are defined as:

Definition 1. *MEDCP [15]*
The MEDCP of the keyed function $f_{k_i} : x \mapsto f\,(x \oplus k_i)$ iterated over r rounds is defined as follows :

$$MEDCP(f^r) = \max_{(\triangle_0 \to \ldots \triangle_r) \in V_\delta(f)^r} \prod_{i=0}^{r-1} Pr\left[\triangle_i \xrightarrow{d} \triangle_{i+1}\right]$$

The MEDLCC(f^r) is defined analogously. It is always desiarable that MEDCP(f^r) $<< 2^{-n}$ and MELCC(f^r) $<< 2^{-n/2}$ where n is the block size.

The basic structure based of the LTS strategy is illustrated in Fig. 1. In LTS, the encryption consists of s steps, each composed of an ARX layer of r rounds and a linear mixing layer. In the ARX-box layer, each word of the internal state undergoes r rounds of the ARX box.

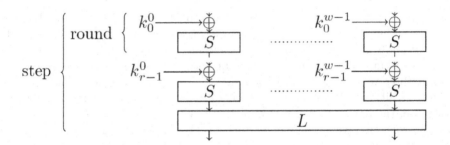

Fig. 1. A cipher structure based on the LTS design strategy.

5   The LiARX Cipher

Based on the LTS design strategy, we introduce a new lightweight cipher termed as LiARX (Lightweight ARX). This design has a 64-bit block size and a 128-bit key size. The 'A' in the design denotes an ARX Box, which is used as the S-box replacement in LTS. The superscript over 'A' indicates the number of times it is iterated in a single step. The step structure of LiARX is illustrated in Fig. 2. In LTS, one single step consists of multiple iterations of ARX-box (known as round), followed by a linear layer. The encryption of LiARX consists of 8 steps. Subsequently, each step is formed of an ARX layer of 3 rounds, followed by a linear mixing layer. In the ARX-box layer, each word of the internal state undergoes three rounds of MARX-2 [3], including key additions. The number of steps and rounds of LiARX has been calculated using the MEDCP and MELCC bounds of LTS. The operations which are required for LiARX are:

- Addition modulo 2^{16} and 2^8, denoted by $\boxplus$,
- 16-bit/8-bit exclusive-or (XOR), denoted $\oplus$, and
- 16-bit/8-bit rotation to the left or right by i, denoted respectively by $x \lll i$, and $x \ggg i$.

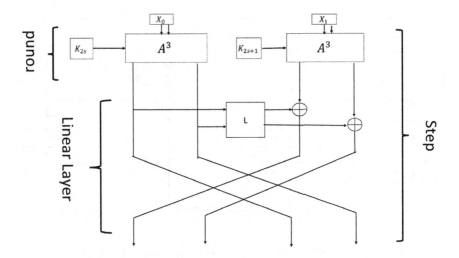

Fig. 2. The step structure of LiARX.

There are three main components of the design, which are (i) MARX-2 (which is used as an ARX box), (ii) Linear Layer, (iii) Key schedule. These structures are individually explained in the following subsections.

5.1   MARX-2

MARX-2 [3] is one of the two recommended ARX boxes that have been thoroughly investigated (other being SPECKEY). It is based on the MIX function of Skein and is a variant of MARX. It has two additional rotation operations that are constructed of two parallel applications of the round of SPECK with 8-bit words. The main advantage of MARX-2 over SPECK32 arises due to the full state key addition at the beginning of every round. This primitive belongs to the class of key-alternating ciphers, a sub-class of Markov ciphers [18], and therefore satisfies the Markov assumption. MARX-2 achieves full diffusion in the same number of rounds as SPECK32 at the expense of two additional rotation operations. The rotation constants of MARX-2 have been chosen by exhaustively searching over all four rotation values (4095 values in total excluding the all-zero choice). The results show that no set of rotation constants exists for which full diffusion can be reached in less than 10 rounds. From the constants that ensure diffusion in 10 rounds, we have selected $(r_1, r_2, r_3, r_4) = (2, 3, 1, 7)$ since for this set we get slightly better DP (differential probabilities) than SPECK32 (2^{-35} vs. 2^{-34}). Furthermore, all the constants from the set are different and are not multiples of each other, which is also considered as a desirable property. Other choices that also result in full diffusion for 10 rounds are: (2, 3, 7, 2), (2, 3, 1, 2) and (5, 5, 2, 7). The MARX-2 design is illustrated in Fig. 3.

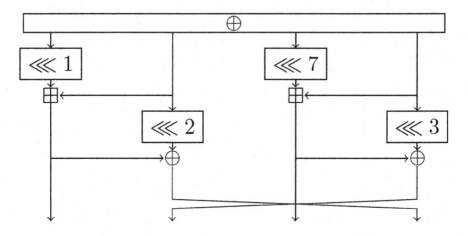

Fig. 3. The MARX-2 architecture (ARX box of LiARX).

5.2 Linear Layer

The Linear layer is a core component in any block cipher design since its design significantly influences both the security and efficiency of the cipher. The linear layer is the primary source of diffusion in cipher design. The LTS strategy advocates the use of large (ARX-based) S-box together with sparse (small but strong) linear layers [8]. In their work, the authors proposed four linear layers after exhaustively checking all possible linear layers for which one could prove the MEDCP and MELCC bounds. The Linear layers are represented in forms of matrices, the constraint being that there must be at most one 1 in each column and at most one 1 in each row. In our work, we selected the best matrices according to one of the following two criteria [8]:

- Minimizing the differential/linear trail probability: We compute the number of steps when the trail probability bound derived by the algorithm is less than 2^{-128} for differential trails and less than 2^{-64} for linear trails.
- Minimizing the number of steps of the integral characteristic found with the division property.

The linear layer used is one of four layers that was proposed in the original LTS. It is used in our design since it only requires one rotation by 8 bits and

3 XORs, which are cheap operations. This layer essentially uses the **L** function based on a Lai-Massey structure, which is borrowed from NOEKEON [5]. The outline of this component is presented in Fig. 4.

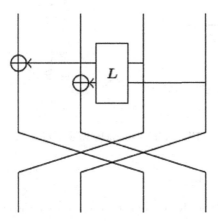

Fig. 4. The Linear Layer of LiARX.

5.3 Key Schedule

Any cipher algorithm consists of many rounds and each of these rounds requires a key since there is only one original key (master key). This master key subsequently contributes to the rest of the keys. A key schedule is an algorithm that calculates the subkeys for these rounds given the key. For the Feistel ciphers, it was observed that those with complex and well-designed key schedules could reach a uniform distribution for the probabilities of differentials and linear hulls faster than those with poorly designed key schedules. The key schedule used in LiARX is based on the generalized Feistel structure and influenced by the design of the key schedule of SPARX-64/128. The components from MARX-2 are reused in this phase for bounding the code size. This final cipher component is presented in Fig. 5.

6 Experiments

The performance of LiARX is calculated by simulating it on FELICS[1]. FELICS is an open-source tool that evaluates cipher performances on a wide range of platforms based on a set of metrics. It also evaluates cipher design in three different scenarios. The devices on which FELICS tests the cipher performance are: (i) 8-bit Atmel AVR ATmega128, and (ii) PC(Personal Computer) System: AMD A8-455M CPU with 6 GB RAM and 64 bit OS. The other relevant details are mentioned as follows.

---

[1] https://www.cryptolux.org/index.php/FELICS.

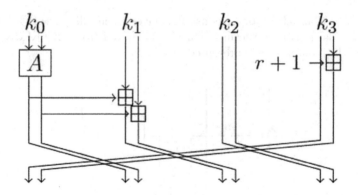

Fig. 5. The key schedule of LiARX.

6.1   Performance Metrics

The performance metrics for evaluating the cipher performance are:

- **Binary Code Size** (in Bytes): The ROM storage which is used for storing recomputed data of the program
- **RAM** (in Bytes): RAM (Random Access Memory) is the internal memory of the CPU for storing data, program, and the program results. It is a read/write memory which stores data until the machine is working
- **Execution time** (in Cycles): It is amount time required to perform the whole encryption process. It is measured in machine cycles

6.2   Scenarios

FELICS checks the performance of any cipher over two important scenarios:

- **Scenario 1: Communication Protocol**- This scenario covers the need for secure communication in sensor networks and between IoT devices. It assumes that the sensitive data is encrypted and decrypted using a lightweight block cipher in CBC mode of operation
- **Scenario 2: Challenge-Handshake Authentication Protocol**- Challenge-handshake authentication covers the need for authentication in the IoT. The scenario assumes an authentication protocol where the block cipher is used in CTR mode to encrypt 128 bits of data

6.3   Results

To establish the lightweight property of LiARX, we have compared its results with those of SPECK and LED [12]. The reason for selecting SPECK is that it is NSA standard for lightweight cryptographic cipher and has an ARX-based architecture (which is a common feature with our cipher). The second cipher that is selected for comparison is LED since it is essentially an S-Box based on the SPN structure. We have presented the results of both the scenarios in Table 1 for AVR. Noticeably, we have included the results in PC hardware only for LiARX in Table 2 since we were unable to simulate LED and SPECK over the aforementioned PC configuration.

Table 1. The AVR results for LiARX

Block Size (Bits)	LiARX			SPECK			LED		
	Time (Cycles)	Code (Bytes)	RAM (Bytes)	Time (Cycles)	Code (Bytes)	RAM (Bytes)	Time (Cycles)	Code (Bytes)	RAM (Bytes)
Scenario 1									
64	243021	2944	422	40666	956	292	2213031	4882	560
Scenario 2									
64	30871	2068	81	2972	484	57	134921	2590	265

Table 2. The PC results for LiARX

Block Size (Bits)	LiARX		
	Time (Cycles)	Code (Bytes)	RAM (Bytes)
Scenario 1			
64	125192	6656	872
Scenario 2			
64	8382	5640	496

It can be observed in Table 1 that the results of LiARX are either nearby or little more than those of SPECK. The metric values are observed to be more in some cases because the round function of LiARX is bigger than that of SPECK. In the other comparison between LiARX and LED, it can be noted that LiARX performs better than LED due to LiARX's ARX based architecture. As discussed in the previous sections, our proposed cipher has many structural advantages over the other two ciphers. The performance of LiARX is also found to be comparatively better than ciphers like TWINE [29], PRESENT [4], RC5-20 [24], Robin [11], and AES [6]. The relevant details can be found at www.cryptolux.org/index. php/FELICS_Block_Ciphers_Brief_Results.

7 Conclusion

Since the number of devices that fall in the category of lightweight devices is going to proliferate, it is necessary to focus on lightweight cipher designs that are efficient for resource-constraint devices. In this paper, we discuss the basic timeline of design development in lightweight ciphers along-with the most critical problems faced. We also argue on the necessity of the ARX architecture for the construction of such ciphers. Subsequently, we discuss new design strategies for ARX with provable bounds (viz. LTS). We also introduce a new lightweight cipher termed LiARX which is based on this strategy. Finally, we empirically vindicate the efficacy of this cipher over two distinct implementation scenarios. In the future extension of this work, we would increase the choices for the ARX-boxes since there are currently only two such boxes that are thoroughly investigated and with proven security.

References

1. Banik, S., et al.: Midori: a block cipher for low energy. In: Iwata, T., Cheon, J.H. (eds.) ASIACRYPT 2015. LNCS, vol. 9453, pp. 411–436. Springer, Heidelberg (2015). https://doi.org/10.1007/978-3-662-48800-3_17
2. Beaulieu, R., Shors, D., Smith, J., Treatman-Clark, S., Weeks, B., Wingers, L.: The SIMON and speck families of lightweight block ciphers. IACR Cryptology ePrint Arch. 2013(1), 404–449 (2013)
3. Biryukov, A., Velichkov, V., Le Corre, Y.: Automatic search for the best trails in ARX: application to block cipher SPECK. In: Peyrin, T. (ed.) FSE 2016. LNCS, vol. 9783, pp. 289–310. Springer, Heidelberg (2016). https://doi.org/10.1007/978-3-662-52993-5_15
4. Bogdanov, A., et al.: PRESENT: an ultra-lightweight block cipher. In: Paillier, P., Verbauwhede, I. (eds.) CHES 2007. LNCS, vol. 4727, pp. 450–466. Springer, Heidelberg (2007). https://doi.org/10.1007/978-3-540-74735-2_31
5. Daemen, J., Peeters, M., Van Assche, G., Rijmen, V.: Nessie proposal: noekeon. In: First Open NESSIE Workshop, pp. 213–230 (2000)
6. Daemen, J., Rijmen, V.: Aes proposal: rijndael. AES submission (1999). http://jda.noekeon.org/
7. Daemen, J., Rijmen, V.: The wide trail design strategy. In: Honary, B. (ed.) Cryptography and Coding 2001. LNCS, vol. 2260, pp. 222–238. Springer, Heidelberg (2001). https://doi.org/10.1007/3-540-45325-3_20
8. Dinu, D., Perrin, L., Udovenko, A., Velichkov, V., Großschädl, J., Biryukov, A.: Design strategies for ARX with provable bounds: SPARX and LAX. In: Cheon, J.H., Takagi, T. (eds.) ASIACRYPT 2016. LNCS, vol. 10031, pp. 484–513. Springer, Heidelberg (2016). https://doi.org/10.1007/978-3-662-53887-6_18
9. Eisenbarth, T., Kumar, S., Paar, C., Poschmann, A., Uhsadel, L.: A survey of lightweight-cryptography implementations. IEEE Des. Test Comput. 24(6), 522–533 (2007)
10. Gong, Z., Nikova, S., Law, Y.W.: KLEIN: a new family of lightweight block ciphers. In: Juels, A., Paar, C. (eds.) RFIDSec 2011. LNCS, vol. 7055, pp. 1–18. Springer, Heidelberg (2012). https://doi.org/10.1007/978-3-642-25286-0_1
11. Grosso, V., Leurent, G., Standaert, F.-X., Varıcı, K.: LS-Designs: bitslice encryption for efficient masked software implementations. In: Cid, C., Rechberger, C. (eds.) FSE 2014. LNCS, vol. 8540, pp. 18–37. Springer, Heidelberg (2015). https://doi.org/10.1007/978-3-662-46706-0_2
12. Guo, J., Peyrin, T., Poschmann, A., Robshaw, M.: The LED block cipher. In: Preneel, B., Takagi, T. (eds.) CHES 2011. LNCS, vol. 6917, pp. 326–341. Springer, Heidelberg (2011). https://doi.org/10.1007/978-3-642-23951-9_22

13. Hong, D., Lee, J.-K., Kim, D.-C., Kwon, D., Ryu, K.H., Lee, D.-G.: LEA: a 128-Bit block cipher for fast encryption on common processors. In: Kim, Y., Lee, H., Perrig, A. (eds.) WISA 2013. LNCS, vol. 8267, pp. 3–27. Springer, Cham (2014). https://doi.org/10.1007/978-3-319-05149-9_1

14. Hong, D., et al.: HIGHT: a new block cipher suitable for low-resource device. In: Goubin, L., Matsui, M. (eds.) CHES 2006. LNCS, vol. 4249, pp. 46–59. Springer, Heidelberg (2006). https://doi.org/10.1007/11894063_4

15. Keliher, L., Sui, J.: Exact maximum expected differential and linear probability for two-round advanced encryption standard. IET Inf. Secur. 1(2), 53–57 (2007)

16. Kilian, J., Rogaway, P.: How to protect DES against exhaustive key search. In: Koblitz, N. (ed.) CRYPTO 1996. LNCS, vol. 1109, pp. 252–267. Springer, Heidelberg (1996). https://doi.org/10.1007/3-540-68697-5_20

17. Knudsen, L.R.: Practically secure feistel ciphers. In: Anderson, R. (ed.) FSE 1993. LNCS, vol. 809, pp. 211–221. Springer, Heidelberg (1994). https://doi.org/10.1007/3-540-58108-1_26

18. Lai, X., Massey, J.L., Murphy, S.: Markov ciphers and differential cryptanalysis. In: Davies, D.W. (ed.) EUROCRYPT 1991. LNCS, vol. 547, pp. 17–38. Springer, Heidelberg (1991). https://doi.org/10.1007/3-540-46416-6_2

19. Leander, G., Paar, C., Poschmann, A., Schramm, K.: New lightweight DES variants. In: Biryukov, A. (ed.) FSE 2007. LNCS, vol. 4593, pp. 196–210. Springer, Heidelberg (2007). https://doi.org/10.1007/978-3-540-74619-5_13

20. McKay, K., Bassham, L., Sönmez Turan, M., Mouha, N.: Report on lightweight cryptography. Technical Report National Institute of Standards and Technology (2016)

21. Mouha, N., Mennink, B., Van Herrewege, A., Watanabe, D., Preneel, B., Verbauwhede, I.: Chaskey: an efficient MAC algorithm for 32-bit microcontrollers. In: Joux, A., Youssef, A. (eds.) SAC 2014. LNCS, vol. 8781, pp. 306–323. Springer, Cham (2014). https://doi.org/10.1007/978-3-319-13051-4_19

22. Panasenko, S., Smagin, S.: Lightweight cryptography: underlying principles and approaches. Int. J. Comput. Theory Eng. 3(4), 516 (2011)

23. Pub F.: Data encryption standard (des). FIPS PUB pp. 46–3 (1999)

24. Rivest, R.L.: The RC5 encryption algorithm. In: Preneel, B. (ed.) FSE 1994. LNCS, vol. 1008, pp. 86–96. Springer, Heidelberg (1995). https://doi.org/10.1007/3-540-60590-8_7

25. Rivest, R.L., Robshaw, M.J., Sidney, R., Yin, Y.L.: The rc6 block cipher. In: in First Advanced Encryption Standard (AES) Conference. Citeseer (1998)

26. Roger, M., Wheeler, D.: Tea extensions. Technical Report, Computer Laboratory, University of Cambridge, Technical Report (1997)

27. Saarinen, M.J.O., Engels, D.W.: A do-it-all-cipher for RFID: design requirements. IACR Cryptology EPrint Arch. 2012, 317 (2012)

28. Shepherd, S.J.: The tiny encryption algorithm. Cryptologia 31(3), 233–245 (2007)

29. Suzaki, T., Minematsu, K., Morioka, S., Kobayashi, E.: TWINE: a lightweight block cipher for multiple platforms. In: Knudsen, L.R., Wu, H. (eds.) SAC 2012. LNCS, vol. 7707, pp. 339–354. Springer, Heidelberg (2013). https://doi.org/10.1007/978-3-642-35999-6_22

Color Visual Cryptography Schemes Using Linear Algebraic Techniques over Rings

Sabyasachi Dutta[1]([✉]), Md Kutubuddin Sardar[2], Avishek Adhikari[3],
Sushmita Ruj[4], and Kouichi Sakurai[5]

[1] University of Calgary, Calgary, Canada
saby.math@gmail.com
[2] University of Calcutta, Kolkata, India
kutubpmath@gmail.com
[3] Presidency University, Kolkata, India
avishek.adh@gmail.com
[4] CSIRO, Data61, Sydney, Australia
sushmita.ruj@gmail.com, sushmita.ruj@csiro.au
[5] Kyushu University, Fukuoka, Japan
sakurai@inf.kyushu-u.ac.jp

Abstract. The research on color Visual Cryptographic Scheme (VCS) is much more difficult than that of the black and white VCS. This is essentially because of the fact that in color VCS, the rule for superimposition of two colors is not that simple as in black and white VCS. It was a long standing open issue whether linear algebraic technique in constructing Black and White visual cryptographic schemes could also be extended for color images. It was thought that such an extension was impossible. However, we resolve this issue by providing color VCS in same color model for the threshold access structures by extending linear algebraic techniques from the binary field $\mathbb{Z}_2$ to finite ring $\mathbb{Z}_c$ of integers modulo c. We first give a construction method based on linear algebra to share a color image for an (n, n)-threshold access structure. Then we give constructions for $(2, n)$-threshold access structures and in general (k, n)-threshold access structures. Existing methodology for constructing color VCS in same color model assumes the existence of black and white VCS, whereas our construction is a direct one. Moreover, we give closed form formulas for pixel expansion which is combinatorially a difficult task. Lastly, we give experimental results and propose a method to reduce pixel expansion.

S. Dutta—is grateful to the NICT, Japan for financial support under the NICT International Exchange Program during 2018-19 when the preliminary draft was prepared.
Md K. Sardar—is thankful to the CSIR, Govt. of India for providing financial support (Award no. 09/028(0975)/2016-EMR-1).
A. Adhikari—Research of A. Adhikari is partially supported by DST-SERB Project MATRICS vide Sanction Order: MTR/2019/001573.

© Springer Nature Switzerland AG 2020
S. Kanhere et al. (Eds.): ICISS 2020, LNCS 12553, pp. 198–217, 2020.
https://doi.org/10.1007/978-3-030-65610-2_13

Keywords: Color visual secret sharing · Linear algebra · Pixel expansion · Relative contrast

1 Introduction

In a visual cryptographic scheme (VCS), on a set of n participants, a dealer who possesses a secret image encodes it into n shares and distributes these shares among n participants. Physically, each of the participants obtain a transparency on which his or her share is photocopied. Only a pre-specified collection of subsets of participants can visually recover the secret image. However, no subset of participants which are outside the above mentioned collection can recover the secret image – in fact, a stronger security condition is achieved viz. such subsets of participants obtain no information about the secret image. Eligible subsets are called "qualified" sets and ineligible subsets are termed as "forbidden" sets.

Main motivation to study visual cryptographic scheme is its simple recovery process. No participation of computing device is needed, the decoding process is done by the human visual system. Visual secret sharing has found its applications into several interesting areas - watermarking [15], application to QR-codes [11] etc. to name a few.

1.1 Related Works

Naor and Shamir [26] proposed the first visual cryptographic scheme and the concept has been further explored in [1,2,6,7,9,10] and extended to general access structures. Some recent works gave efficient constructions for few important and interesting access structures [5,16,17,20,28]. The work of Adhikari et al. [2] introduced an elegant linear algebraic technique to construct basis matrices for a black and white image - one only needs to solve systems of linear equations over the binary field $\mathbb{Z}_2$. The power of the technique was researched and resulted in a number of works - both in OR model [1,16,29,31] and XOR model [17,30] for B/W visual cryptography.

Verheul-Tilborg [33] for the first time, conceptualized color visual cryptography as an extension of the existing B/W visual cryptography model. They provided the model of color visual cryptographic scheme and constructed a color (n, n)-visual cryptographic scheme. Constructing color visual secret sharing depends on the underlying color-superposition principle. In B/W visual cryptography, color superposition principle is easy – two white pixels (when superposed) results in white pixel but if at least one of the two is a black pixel, the result is a black pixel. The situation gets complicated in case of color images – two different colors (when superposed) may result in a completely different third color. There are three major color models [14] conceptualized in the literature – *same color* (SC) model, *no darkening* (ND) model and *general* model. In the SC model, superposition of two different colored pixels is not allowed. However, there is an exception for the annihilator/masking "•" color which is different from the set of ingredient colors. In SC model, superposing two same colored pixels results in a pixel with same color while superposing a colored pixel with "•" results in "•". However in this model the fact of darkening of reconstructed pixel is ignored – when two same colored pixels are superposed then in reality a darker version of that color is obtained. The premise is rather simplistic – superposition of two i colored pixels gives back one i colored pixel. The no-darkening model is similar to the same color model but in this case the problem of darkening is considered – when more than two same colored pixels are superimposed then the resulting pixel is a darker version of the color and therefore, to obtain "non-darkened" reconstructed pixel a colored pixel can only superpose with a white (transparent) pixel. The general model of color-superposition puts no restrictions on superposition principle - the color superposition satisfies real world color superposition principles.

Cimato et al. [13] considered no-darkening model and put forward construction of (k, n)-threshold color visual cryptographic scheme with the help of basis matrices of a $(k - 1, k - 1)$-threshold B/W visual cryptographic scheme. The resulting c-color VCS has a pixel expansion of $c\binom{n}{k}2^{k-2}$ and achieves "maximal contrast". The term maximal contrast loosely means that while recovering a secret pixel of some color i, no other false colored pixel j is reconstructed (see Definition 3). The authors [13] also provided c-color $(2, n)$-VCS with pixel expansion $c(n-1)$. Rijmen et al. [27] was the first to consider the general model of color superposition along with some of the follow up works [3,24]. Generic constructions of $(2, n)$-threshold color visual secret sharing schemes from B/W cryptographic schemes can be obtained using the techniques from [3,24]. A number of works [10,12,33,35] exist in the same color model. The main trick is in the encoding of color pixels – it is done in such a manner that during the implementing "superposition", same color model is satisfied. Verheul et al. [33] constructed c color (n, n)-threshold scheme, $(k, c-1)$-threshold scheme and (k, c)-scheme with the restriction that c is a prime power. For any value of c, Blundo et al. [10] gave constructions of c color $(2, n)$-schemes and (n, n)-schemes. Koga et al. [24] and Yang et al. [35] provided color visual cryptographic schemes for (k, n)-threshold access structures. Color VCS realizing general access structures was proposed in the work of Yang et al. [35]. Recently, Dutta et al. [19] gave a generic construction of color VCS realizing general access structure and an efficient scheme to realize $(k, n)^*$-access structure in the same-color model. Several other color visual cryptographic schemes with extra features have been proposed [21,23,25,32]. Iwamoto [22] introduced a "weaker notion of security" and used techniques of integer linear programming to obtain color VCS. For more literature one can refer to [14].

1.2   Our Contribution

Constructing visual cryptographic schemes using linear algebraic technique has long been proposed in the literature for B&W images [1,2]. It was a long standing open issue whether similar technique can be extended for color images. It was thought that such an extension was impossible. We resolve this issue by providing color VCS for the threshold access structures by extending simple linear algebraic techniques from the binary field $\mathbb{Z}_2$ to finite ring $\mathbb{Z}_c$ of integers modulo c. In this work we consider the same-color model of color VCS. To the best our knowledge, all the generic constructions (except [19]) proposed so far to construct basis matrices for color VCS (in the same-color model) inherently assume the constructions of basis matrices for B&W images. More concretely, construction of basis matrices for color VCS used the basis matrices for B&W images realizing the same access structure. Novelty of our construction is that our methodology does not assume such existence of basis matrices for B&W images. Using our simple linear algebra based technique, one can build color VCS directly. This separates our work from [19] who assumed existence of a class of "basis matrices" to achieve their schemes. Furthermore, we give closed form formulas for pixel expansion which is combinatorially a difficult task. Lastly, we give experimental results and propose a method to reduce pixel expansion.

2 Prerequisites

We describe some basic definitions, fix color-superposition model and state some mathematical results on finite rings that are required for the paper.

2.1 The Color Model

We follow Verheul-Tilborg [33] model of color visual cryptography (CVCS). The model can be perceived as the Same Color model (SC model) of color visual cryptography. In this model, a colored image is an array of pixels each of which may have one of the c different colors $0, 1, \ldots, c-1$.

The color superposition principle is described in the following:
Each secret pixel is divided into m subpixels of color $0, 1, \ldots, c-1$. If some subpixels are placed one top of the other and held to light then a light of color i filters through the stacked subpixels if and only if all the subpixels are color i. Otherwise, no light i.e. *black* color filters through the stacking. The color "*black*" is denoted by • and always is distinguishable from the c colors.

The "generalized OR"(GOR) denoted by $\vee$, of the elements $0, 1, \ldots, c-1$ is defined as follows: $i \vee i = i$ and $i \vee \bullet = \bullet$ for all $i = 0, 1, \ldots, c-1$ and $i \vee j = \bullet$ for all $i \neq j$ where $i, j = 0, 1, \ldots, c-1$.

For any n-dimensional vector V with entries from the set $\{0, 1, \ldots, c-1\}$, $z_i(V)$ denotes the number of coordinates in V equal to i where $i = 0, 1, \ldots, c-1$. For example, if $V = (0, 1, 0, 2, 2)$ with entries from the set $\{0, 1, 2\}$, then $z_0(V) = 2$, $z_1(V) = 1$ and $z_2(V) = 2$.

2.2 Color Visual Cryptographic Scheme

In a (k, n) threshold access structure subsets of size k or more are called "qualified" set and rest are "forbidden" sets which are subsets of size $k-1$ or less. We now define *unconditionally secure* c color (k, n)-threshold visual cryptographic scheme and denote such a scheme by $(k, n)_c$-CVCS where c denotes the number of *true* colors. We require two conditions to be satisfied viz. the "contrast" condition and the "security" condition. The first condition guarantees that secret image is reconstructed by any set of k (or more) participants whereas the second is to ensure that no subset of size less than k can get any information about the image.

For defining $(k, n)_c$-CVCS in concrete terms, we require c *basis* matrices $S^0, S^1, \ldots, S^{c-1}$ where S^b corresponds to the color $b \in \{0, 1, \ldots, c - 1\}$. The entries of these matrices belong to the set of colors $\{0, 1, \ldots, c - 1\}$. To share a secret pixel $b \in \{0, 1, \ldots, c-1\}$, the dealer in the *share generation* phase, chooses the matrix S^b and then applies a random column permutation on the matrix S^b. Share of participant P_i the i-th row of the resulting permuted matrix. To share a c-colored image, dealer repeatedly performs the above process (for every secret pixel) till all the pixels are shared. The formal definition is as follows.

Definition 1. *(adopted from [10, 35]) A $(k, n)_c$-CVCS with pixel expansion m is realized using c many $n \times m$ matrices $S^0, S^1, \ldots, S^{c-1}$ called basis matrices, if there exist two sequences of non-negative numbers $\{h_X\}$ and, $\{l_X\}$ with $l_X < h_X$ such that the following two conditions hold:*

1. *(contrast condition) If $X = \{i_1, i_2, \ldots, i_k\} \subseteq \mathcal{P}$ i.e., if X is a qualified set, then for any $b \in \{0, 1, \ldots, c - 1\}$ the component-wise "GOR" of the rows of S^b indexed by X denoted by S^b_X, satisfies $z_b(S^b_X) \geq h_X$; whereas, for $b' \neq b$ it results in $z_{b'}(S^b_X) \leq l_X$.*
2. *(security condition) If $Y = \{i_1, i_2, \ldots, i_s\} \subset \mathcal{P}$ with $s < k$ then the c many $s \times m$ restricted matrices $S^0[Y], S^1[Y], \ldots, S^{c-1}[Y]$ obtained by restricting $S^0, S^1, \ldots, S^{c-1}$ respectively to rows indexed by $i_1, i_2, \ldots, i_s$ are identical up to column permutations.*

The above definition can be suitably modified for any arbitrary access structure on a set of participants. Although in this paper we do not deal with general access structure, we discuss for sake of completeness. An access structure on a set of parties $\mathcal{P} = \{1, 2, \ldots, n\}$ can be described by the collection of all qualified sets $\mathcal{Q}$ and forbidden sets $\mathcal{F}$. Basis matrices realizing a general access structure $(\mathcal{Q}, \mathcal{F})$ with c many colors are defined as follows.

Definition 2. *(adapted from [35]) A $(\mathcal{Q}, \mathcal{F})_c$-CVCS with pixel expansion m is realized using c many $n \times m$ matrices $S^0, S^1, \ldots, S^{c-1}$ called basis matrices, if there exist two non-negative numbers h, l with $l < h$ such that the following two conditions hold:*

1. *(contrast condition) If $X \in \mathcal{Q}$ i.e., if X is a qualified set, then for any $b \in \{0, 1, \ldots, c - 1\}$ the component-wise "GOR" of the rows of S^b indexed by X, satisfies $z_b(S^b_X) \geq h$; whereas, for $b' \neq b$ it results in $z_{b'}(S^b_X) \leq l$.*
2. *(security condition) If $Y \in \mathcal{F}$ then the c many $s \times m$ restricted matrices $S^0[Y], S^1[Y], \ldots, S^{c-1}[Y]$ obtained by restricting $S^0, S^1, \ldots, S^{c-1}$ respectively to rows indexed by the participants of Y, are identical up to column permutations.*

The *contrast* of reconstructed image in a color VCS [10,33] is defined as $\alpha = \frac{h-l}{h+l}$. The *loss in contrast* is measured by the quantity $\frac{h-l}{m(h+l)}$. On the other hand, [12] define the contrast to be the value $\frac{h-l}{m}$ keeping parity with the well-known definition of contrast given in [26]. A scheme is said to achieve *maximal contrast* if $l = 0$ [10]. In other words, maximal contrast guarantees that while reconstructing a secret pixel of color $i \in \{0, 1, \ldots, c-1\}$ no pixel of color $j(\neq i)$ is recovered. The formal definition is as follows.

Definition 3. *(adopted from [10])* *With same notations described in Definition 2, the contrast is defined as* $\alpha = \frac{h-l}{h+l}$ *for a color visual cryptographic scheme. Furthermore, it is of maximal contrast if* $l = 0$.

2.3 Some Mathematical Results

We state some mathematical definitions and results [4] that will be needed through out this paper.

a. For any positive integer c, $(\mathbb{Z}_c, +, .)$ forms a finite *commutative ring* with *unity*. The addition "$+$" is addition modulo c and the multiplication "$.$" is multiplication modulo c. The elements of the set $\mathbb{Z}_c$ are denoted by $0, 1, \ldots, c-1$.

b. A *non-zero* element $x \in \mathbb{Z}_c$ is called a *zero-divisor* if there exists a *non-zero* element $y \in \mathbb{Z}_c$ such that $x.y = 0$. A *non-zero* element $x \in \mathbb{Z}_c$ is called a *unit* if there exists a *non-zero* element $y \in \mathbb{Z}_c$ such that $x.y = 1$. For example, $4 \in \mathbb{Z}_6$ is a zero-divisor as $4.3 = 0$ and $5 \in \mathbb{Z}_6$ is a unit as $5.5 = 1$.

c. Any non-zero element in $\mathbb{Z}_c$ is either a unit or a zero-divisor.

d. An element $x \in \mathbb{Z}_c$ is a unit if and only if $gcd(x, c) = 1$.

e. Every non-zero element $x \in \mathbb{Z}_c$ is a unit if and only if c is a prime. So when c is prime $\mathbb{Z}_c$ is said to form a *field* i.e. a commutative ring with unity where every non-zero element is unit.

f. Let $A\boldsymbol{x} = \boldsymbol{b}$ be a system of linear equations in n many unknowns $x_1, x_2, \ldots, x_n$ where the entries of the matrix A come from the ring $\mathbb{Z}_c$ and let $\boldsymbol{\alpha}_0 = [\alpha_1, \alpha_2, \ldots, \alpha_n]^t$ be a particular solution to the above system. If $\boldsymbol{\beta} = [\beta_1, \beta_2, \ldots, \beta_n]^t$ be any solution to the homogeneous system $A\boldsymbol{x} = \boldsymbol{0}$ then $\boldsymbol{\alpha}_0 + \boldsymbol{\beta}$ is a solution to $A\boldsymbol{x} = \boldsymbol{b}$.

g. For any prime power p^n there exists a field of size p^n.

3 Main Results

We propose a linear algebraic construction for obtaining basis matrices $S^0, \ldots, S^{c-1}$ for a $(k, n)_c$-CVCS, where $2 \le k \le n$. The methodology though simple, requires several involved results from algebra to prove correctness and security of such sharing scheme. First we give details of the underlying technique.

3.1 Constructing Color VCS from Smaller Schemes

In this section we present a construction for color visual cryptographic schemes using smaller schemes as building blocks. At this point we mention that we are considering the *same-color* model of color superposition to avoid any confusion. Let us consider a color image with c colors labeled by $0, 1, \ldots, c-1$.

Let (Q', F') and (Q'', F'') be two access structures defined on two sets $\mathcal{P}_1$ and $\mathcal{P}_2$ respectively having cardinality n_1 and n_2 respectively, where the symbols have their usual meanings. Suppose there exist a (Q', F') color VCS with pixel expansion m' and a (Q'', F'') color VCS with pixel expansion m''. Also suppose $(R^0, R^1, \ldots, R^{c-1})$ denote the basis matrices for the first scheme and $(T^0, T^1, \ldots, T^{c-1})$ denote the same for the second scheme. We now describe how to construct a color-VCS for the access structure $(Q, F) = (Q' \cup Q'', F' \cap F'')$ on the set of participants $\mathcal{P} = \mathcal{P}_1 \cup \mathcal{P}_1$ containig n elements. Let us write $\mathcal{P} = \{1, 2, \ldots, n\}$.

From the given matrices we construct basis matrices $(S^0, S^1, \ldots, S^{c-1})$ realizing (Q, F) in Algorithm 1.

Algorithm 1 Construction of basis matrices from smaller schemes

---

1: **procedure** PREPARATION OF INTERMEDIATE MATRICES
2: for $\alpha = 0, \ldots, c-1$
3:    for $i = 1, \ldots, n$
4:       if the ith participant is not present in (Q', F')
5:          ith row of matrix $\hat{R}^\alpha$ = all • entries
6:       else it is the row corresponding to the ith party in R^α,
7:
8: for $\alpha = 0, \ldots, c-1$
9:    for $i = 1, \ldots, n$
10:      if the ith participant is not present in (Q'', F'')
11:         ith row of matrix $\hat{T}^\alpha$ = all • entries
12:      else it is the row corresponding to the ith party in T^α,
13:
14: **procedure** CONSTRUCTION OF BASIS MATRICES
15: for color $\alpha = 0, 1, \ldots, c-1$,
16:    construct the matrices $S^\alpha = \hat{R}^\alpha || \hat{T}^\alpha$, where $||$ denotes "concatenation" of
17:    matrices.

We now have the following theorem (a parallel version of it is proved for B & W image in Theorem 4.4 of [6]).

Theorem 1. *Let (Q', F') and (Q'', F'') be two access structures defined on two sets $\mathcal{P}_1$ and $\mathcal{P}_2$ respectively having cardinality n_1 and n_2 respectively. Suppose there exist a (Q', F', m') color VCS and a (Q'', F'', m'') color VCS with basis matrices $(R^0, R^1, \ldots, R^{c-1})$ and $(T^0, T^1, \ldots, T^{c-1})$ respectively. Then Algorithm 1 yields a $(Q' \cup Q'', F' \cap F'', m' + m'')$ color VCS on the set of participants $\mathcal{P} = \mathcal{P}_1 \cup \mathcal{P}_2$.*

The above theorem can be extended to multiple access structures.

Corollary 1. *Let* (Q, F) *be an access structure such that* $Q = Q_1 \cup \ldots \cup Q_r$ *and* $F = F_1 \cap \ldots \cap F_r$. *If there exists* (Q_i, F_i, m_i) *color VCS for all* $i = 1, \ldots, r$ *then using Algorithm 1 repeatedly we get hold of a* (Q, F, m) *color VCS with* $m = m_1 + \cdots + m_r$.

On the basis of Corollary 1 we build our linear algebraic scheme for constructing basis matrices. We first give a high level idea of the entire methodology which consists of three main steps.

1. First, we partition the collection $\mathcal{Q}_{min}$ of *all minimal* qualified sets into groups $G_1, G_2, \ldots, G_t$ such that every group contains precisely two minimal qualified sets ($|G_i| = 2$ for all i), any two groups are disjoint ($G_i \cap G_j = \emptyset$ for $i \neq j$), union of the groups gives back the collection $\mathcal{Q}_{min}$ (i.e. $\cup G_i = \mathcal{Q}_{min}$). Moreover we want this grouping is done in such a way that two minimal qualified sets belonging in the same group have maximum intersection. This step corresponds to the decomposition of the given access structure into smaller access structures as stated in Corollary 1.
2. We associate a variable x_i to participant P_i for every i and formulate system of two linear equations for each group G_j. Thus we will have exactly those many systems of linear equations as the number of groups. For a system we will write all possible n-tuples of solutions of the variables as columns to construct a matrix. Here we emphasize that if a variable x_t is absent in a system we will set $x_t = \bullet$. In this scenario notice that every entry of the t-th row of the above-mentioned matrix is $\bullet$. We do this for every system of linear equations. This step merges the procedure of constructing basis matrices of smaller schemes (whose existence were assumed) in Corollary 1 and the procedure of "preparation of intermediate matrices" in Algorithm 1.
3. In the third step, we concatenate these matrices to get the basis matrices. This step corresponds to the procedure of "construction of basis matrices" of Algorithm 1.

3.2   Construction of $(n, n)_c$-CVCS

Let us assume for the time being that n and c are relatively prime i.e. $gcd(n, c) = 1$. Consider an (n, n)-threshold structure on the set of n many parties. There is only one qualified set namely, the set of participants $\mathcal{P}$ itself. Therefore there is only one group. Let us associate the variable x_i to the i-th participant, where $i = 1, 2, \ldots, n$.

Consider the linear equation over the ring $\mathbb{Z}_c$

$$x_1 + x_2 + \cdots + x_n = a \,\}$$

where $a \in \mathbb{Z}_c$ and $+$ denotes the operation *addition modulo c*.
First we notice that we have a unique $r \in \mathbb{Z}_c$ such that $x_1 = x_2 = \cdots = x_n = r$ satisfying the above equation. This follows from the fact that $nr = a$ has a

unique solution $r = n^{-1}a$ since $(n, r) = 1$ implies n has a multiplicative inverse. It is easy to see that in the equation if we fix the values of any $n - 1$ many variables then the value of the n-th one is automatically fixed. Thus there are c^{n-1} many solutions to the equation. If we write all the solutions as columns to form an $n \times c^{n-1}$ matrix then it has the following properties:

- exactly one column has all entries equal to $r \in \mathbb{Z}_c$,
- rest $c^{n-1} - 1$ columns contain at least two distinct entries from $\mathbb{Z}_c$.

Since the rows of this matrix are the shares of the n parties therefore super-position of all of them will yield the color r. Moreover any submatrix of size $(n - i) \times c^{n-1}$ contains all possible c^{n-i} columns each occurring exactly c^{i-1} times and thus revealing no information about r. Varying a over $\mathbb{Z}_c$ we get all the basis matrices $S^0, S^1, \ldots, S^{c-1}$ to realize an $(n, n)_c$-CVCS.

Theorem 2. *Suppose c and n are relatively prime. Then there exists an $(n, n)_c$-CVCS with pixel expansion c^{n-1} and $h = 1$, $l = 0$.*

Note 1. We note that the construction gives a maximal contrast (*see* Definition 3) color visual cryptographic scheme.

Example 1. Let us construct a $(2, 2)_5$-CVCS on the set of parties $\mathcal{P} = \{1, 2\}$. The five colors are identified as the elements of $\mathbb{Z}_5 = \{0, 1, 2, 3, 4\}$. Only minimal qualified set is $\{1, 2\}$. Following five matrices realize $(2, 2)_5$-CVCS.

$$S^0 = \begin{bmatrix} 0\,1\,2\,3\,4 \\ 0\,4\,3\,2\,1 \end{bmatrix}, \ S^1 = \begin{bmatrix} 0\,1\,2\,3\,4 \\ 2\,1\,0\,4\,3 \end{bmatrix}, \ S^2 = \begin{bmatrix} 0\,1\,2\,3\,4 \\ 4\,3\,2\,1\,0 \end{bmatrix}, \ S^3 = \begin{bmatrix} 0\,1\,2\,3\,4 \\ 1\,0\,4\,3\,2 \end{bmatrix},$$

$$S^4 = \begin{bmatrix} 0\,1\,2\,3\,4 \\ 3\,2\,1\,3\,4 \end{bmatrix} \text{ which are obtained by solving (over } \mathbb{Z}_5 \text{) the equations } x_1 + x_2 =$$

0, $x_1 + x_2 = 2$, $x_1 + x_2 = 4$, $x_1 + x_2 = 1$, $x_1 + x_2 = 3$ respectively.

Remark 1. We emphasize that the fact $gcd(c, n) = 1$ is of immense importance. In the proof we have used that n has a multiplicative inverse in $\mathbb{Z}_c$. When $gcd(c, n) \neq 1$ then our method fails. Suppose we want to construct a $(2, 2)$-CVCS with 4 colors identified as the four elements $\{0, 1, 2, 3\}$ of $\mathbb{Z}_4$. Solving $x_1 + x_2 = 0$ we get $\begin{bmatrix} 0\,1\,2\,3 \\ 0\,3\,2\,1 \end{bmatrix}$ which does not satisfy the contrast condition of Definition 1 because of $[0, 0]^t$ and $[2, 2]^t$ appearing once each. We will discuss a method to fix the problem of non-coprime in Sect. 3.5.

3.3 Construction of $(2, n)_c$-CVCS

Let us now consider the case of $(2, n)$-threshold access structure and we have a secret image with c colors. The colors are identified as the elements of $\mathbb{Z}_c = \{0, 1, \ldots, c - 1\}$. We give a detailed analysis of the construction method and proofs. This technique can essentially be generalized further to construct $(k, n)_c$-CVCS. We again make the following

Assumption: The numbers c and n are relatively prime, i.e. $gcd(2, c) = 1$. We will show why this assumption is necessary for our construction.

Let $\mathcal{P} = \{1, 2, \ldots, n\}$ be the set of participants. Thus $\mathcal{Q}_{min} = \{Q \subset \mathcal{P} : |Q| = 2\}$ which implies $|\mathcal{Q}_{min}| = \binom{n}{2} = \frac{n(n-1)}{2}$. We will denote $\frac{n(n-1)}{2}$ by r. We arrange the elements of $\mathcal{Q}_{min}$ in the **lexicographic** order, say $B_1, B_2, \ldots, B_r$. We will collect these subsets to form groups $\{G\}_i$, such that when r is even

- each group G_i contains exactly two sets B_u, B_w with $|B_u \cap B_w| = 1$
- there are $\frac{r}{2}$ many groups

and when r is odd

- each group G_i for $i = 1, 2, \ldots, \frac{r-1}{2}$ contains exactly two sets B_u, B_w with $|B_u \cap B_w| = 1$
- the last group $G_{\frac{r+1}{2}}$ contains a single set B_r.

Let us attach variable x_i to participant i for $i = 1, 2, \ldots, n$. Let $f_{B_j} = \alpha$ denote the linear equation $\Sigma_{k \in B_j} x_k = \alpha$ over $\mathbb{Z}_c$ where $\alpha \in \mathbb{Z}_c$.
For each group $G_i = \{B_u, B_w\}$ consider the following systems of linear equations over $\mathbb{Z}_c$:

$$\left. \begin{matrix} f_{B_u} = 0 \\ f_{B_w} = 0 \end{matrix} \right\} \text{-i(0)} \ , \ \left. \begin{matrix} f_{B_u} = 1 \\ f_{B_w} = 1 \end{matrix} \right\} \text{-i(1)} \ , \ldots\ldots\ldots\ , \ \left. \begin{matrix} f_{B_u} = c-1 \\ f_{B_w} = c-1 \end{matrix} \right\} \text{-i(c-1)}.$$

When G_i is singleton $\{B_r\}$ then consider

$$f_{B_r} = 0 \ \} \text{-i(0)} \ , \ f_{B_r} = 1 \ \} \text{-i(1)} \ , \ldots\ldots\ldots\ , \ f_{B_r} = c-1 \ \} \text{-i(c-1)}.$$

We solve (for x_i s) these systems and if some variable(s) is(are) absent then we set the value of the variable to be $\bullet$.

Let $M_1^0, M_2^0, \ldots, M_{\lceil \frac{r}{2} \rceil}^0$ be the matrices whose columns are respectively the solutions of equations $1(0), 2(0), \ldots, \lceil \frac{r}{2} \rceil(0)$. Construct $S^0 = M_1^0 || M_2^0 || \ldots || M_{\lceil \frac{r}{2} \rceil}^0$, where $||$ denotes concatenation of the matrices. In general, we solve systems $1(\alpha), 2(\alpha), \ldots, \lceil \frac{r}{2} \rceil(\alpha)$ to get $M_1^{\lceil \frac{c}{2} \rceil \alpha}, M_2^{\lceil \frac{c}{2} \rceil \alpha}, \ldots, M_{\lceil \frac{r}{2} \rceil}^{\lceil \frac{c}{2} \rceil \alpha}$ and then concatenate them to obtain $S^{\lceil \frac{c}{2} \rceil \alpha}$ for every color $\alpha = 0, 1, \ldots, c-1$. We claim that these matrices $S^0, S^1, \ldots, S^{c-1}$ are basis matrices realizing the $(2, n)_c$-CVCS. Proof of the claim is given in Theorem 3. Before that we give a concrete example.

Example 2. Let $\mathcal{P} = \{1, 2, 3\}$ and we have three colors $0, 1, 2$. Thus, $\mathcal{Q}_{min} = \{12, 13, 23\}$, where 12 means the set $\{1, 2\}$ etc. We will sometimes denote a set in this form for brevity, when there is no scope for confusion. We form two groups $G_1 = \{12, 13\}$ and $G_2 = \{23\}$. Consider the following systems of equations over $\mathbb{Z}_3$:

$$\left. \begin{matrix} x_1 + x_2 = 0 \\ x_1 + x_3 = 0 \end{matrix} \right\} \text{-1(0)} \ , \ \left. \begin{matrix} x_1 + x_2 = 1 \\ x_1 + x_3 = 1 \end{matrix} \right\} \text{-1(1)} \ \text{and} \ \left. \begin{matrix} x_1 + x_2 = 2 \\ x_1 + x_3 = 2 \end{matrix} \right\} \text{-1(2).}$$

and

$$x_2 + x_3 = 0 \} -2(0) \ , \ x_2 + x_3 = 1 \} -2(1) \ \text{ and } \ x_2 + x_3 = 2 \} -2(2).$$

Solving 1(0) and 2(0) we get, $S^0 = \begin{bmatrix} 012 & \bullet \bullet \bullet \\ 021 & 012 \\ 021 & 021 \end{bmatrix}$. Notice that the $\bullet$s are present

due to the absence of x_1 in Equation 2(0).

Solving 1(1) and 2(1) we get, $S^2 = \begin{bmatrix} 012 & \bullet \bullet \bullet \\ 102 & 012 \\ 102 & 102 \end{bmatrix}$.

Lastly, solving 1(2) and 2(2) we get, $S^1 = \begin{bmatrix} 012 & \bullet \bullet \bullet \\ 210 & 012 \\ 210 & 210 \end{bmatrix}$.

Theorem 3. *Let the numbers 2 and c are relatively prime, where c denote the number of colors. The matrices $S^0, S^1, \ldots, S^{c-1}$ constructed above are basis matrices realizing a $(2, n)_c$-CVCS. Moreover, the construction has pixel expansion $\lceil \frac{n(n-1)}{4} \rceil c$.*

Proof. First we prove the *security condition* in Definition 1. Let us take a forbidden set $X = \{i\}$ consisting of one single participant $\{i\}$. If we are able to prove that $M_k^0[i]$ and $M_k^j[i]$ are equal upto a column permutation for any $j = 0, 1, \ldots, c - 1$ and for any $k = 1, 2, \ldots, \lceil \frac{r}{2} \rceil$ where $r = \binom{n}{2}$ then it is not hard to see the $S^0[i]$ and $S^j[i]$ are equal upto a column permutation. From this the proof will follow. We recall that the kth blocks are obtained by solving the simultaneous linear equations corresponding to the kth group $G_k = \{B, C\}$, say. Note that if i is not present in group G_k then $M_k^0[i] = [\bullet \bullet \ldots \bullet]_{1 \times c} = M_k^j[i]$ and hence they are equal.

If i is present in $G_k = \{B, C\}$ then $i \in B - C$ or $i \in C - B$ or belongs to both.

Suppose $i \in B - C$, then there exists a party μ such that $\mu \in B \cap C$ (our algorithm ensures that there is always such a party) and another party $\beta \in C - B$. Thus $B = \{i, \mu\}$ and $C = \{\mu, \beta\}$.

Let the equations we solved to obtain M_k^0 and M_k^j be respectively

$$\left. \begin{array}{c} x_i + x_\mu = 0 \\ x_\beta + x_\mu = 0 \end{array} \right\} \text{-k(0)} \quad \text{and} \quad \left. \begin{array}{c} x_i + x_\mu = a \\ x_\beta + x_\mu = a \end{array} \right\} \text{-k(a)}.$$

where $2j = a(mod \ c)$. A particular solution to the system $k(a)$ is given by $x_i = 0 = x_\beta$ and $x_\mu = a$ and every solution to this system is obtained by adding this particular solution to every solution of $k(0)$. That is, there is a particular solution which assigns 0 to the variable x_i and that is all we need. Now it is easy to see that $M_k^0[i]$ and $M_k^j[i]$ are equal upto a column permutation. The case when $i \in C - B$ is handled similarly.

Lastly, when $i \in B \cap C$, it is easy to see that there exist parties $\alpha \in B$ and $\gamma \in C$ so that $B = \{i, \alpha\}$ and $C = \{i, \gamma\}$. Then, $x_\alpha = a = x_\gamma$ and $x_i = 0$ is a particular solution to $k(a)$. Again we can conclude that $M_k^0[i]$ and $M_k^j[i]$ are equal upto a column permutation.

Therefore, in any case we see that $M_k^0[i]$ and $M_k^j[i]$ are equal upto a column permutation for any $j = 0, 1, \ldots, c-1$ and for all $k = 1, 2, \ldots, \lceil \frac{r}{2} \rceil$. This implies that the matrices $S^0[i]$ and $S^j[i]$ are equal upto a column permutation. The proof now follows.

To prove the *contrast condition* let us first choose a minimal qualified set $B = \{i_1, i_2\}$. Let j be any color from the set of colors $\{0, 1, \ldots, c-1\}$. Also let the corresponding matrix S^j is obtained by solving the systems in which the right hand side is equal to the constant a. Thus we know $2j = a \pmod{c}$. Now since B is a minimal qualified set therefore it belongs to a group G_k (possibly) together with another minimal qualified set. Thus the equation $x_{i_1} + x_{i_2} = a$ appears in the system $k(a)$ and solving this system we obtain M_k^j. Note that $x_{i_1} = j = x_{i_2}$ is a solution to this system.

Let us restrict our view to $M_k^j[B]$ which is the restriction of M_k^j to the rows indexed by B. We observe that the column vector $[j \; j]^t$ occurs exactly once in this restricted matrix and no other $[l \; l]^t$ type column occurs in $M_k^j[B]$. The reason for this is the equation $2x = a$ has a unique solution in $\mathbb{Z}_c$ as 2 being relatively prime to c, has a unique multiplicative inverse in $\mathbb{Z}_c$. Moreover the unique solution is j. Thus the G-OR of the rows i_1, i_2, when restricted to the block M_k^j gives *one* j and the rest are equal to •.

On the other hand, it is possible that i_1 and i_2 occur in another group say, $G_t = \{\{i_1, \mu\}, \{i_2, \mu\}\}$. We obtain the block M_t^j by solving the system

$$\left. \begin{array}{c} x_{i_1} + x_\mu = a \\ x_{i_1} + x_\mu = a \end{array} \right\} \underline{\quad} t(a) \; .$$

We notice that in the above system if we fix any value from $\{0, 1, \ldots, c-1\}$ for x_μ then the values of x_{i_1} and x_{i_2} are equal. Thus, we have
$M_t^j[B] = \begin{bmatrix} 0 & 1 & \ldots & c-1 \\ 0 & 1 & \ldots & c-1 \end{bmatrix}$ which shows that the G-OR of the rows i_1, i_2, when restricted to the block M_t^j gives every color α exactly once.

Lastly, if at least one of i_1 and i_2 is absent in any group say, G_s then the absent variable assumes •. Thus, in the block M_s^j at least one of i_1 and i_2-th row has all its entries equal to •. Hence G-OR of i_1 and i_2-th rows when restricted to the block M_s^j gives • in all entries.

Combining the above three cases we can easily see that the G-OR of the two rows of restricted matrix $S^j[\{i_1, i_2\}]$ has at least one more j than any other color $l \in \mathbb{Z}_c - \{j\}$. Thus the contrast condition is satisfied.

We notice that in any system of the linear equations if we fix the value of one variable then the values of other variables are uniquely determined. This gives the pixel expansion of the scheme to be $\lceil \frac{n(n-1)}{4} \rceil c$.

Thus we have a $(2, n)_c$-CVCS when $gcd(2, c) = 1$. □

Remark 2. We note that in light of Remark 1 the assumption $gcd(2, c) = 1$ plays a crucial role in the correctness of construction method. However the grouping technique does not play any role whatsoever in the construction of $(2,n)_c$-CVCS. Our pairing algorithm gives a closed form of pixel expansion and it is the minimum pixel expansion one can get while using the linear algebraic technique. But any type of pairing of the minimal qualified sets will admit a $(2,n)_c$-CVCS, only with higher pixel expansion.

3.4   Construction of $(k,n)_c$-CVCS

Taking cue from Remark 2 we now construct a color visual secret sharing scheme on (k,n)-threshold access structure. Again we assume that $gcd(k,c) = 1$. The method of construction remains the same - we first pair the minimal qualified sets to form groups, form and solve corresponding systems of linear equations and collect the solutions to construct basis matrices. The proofs of correctness and secrecy follow an essentially same line of argument that has been used in Theorem 3.

We note that size of any minimal qualified set is k and therefore every system of linear equations contains $2k$ many variables. If $2k \leq n$ then there is a possibility that these $2k$ variables occurring in a system can be all different. In order to solve such a system of linear equations we need to fix the values of $2k - 2$ variables which results in c^{2k-2} many solutions for that system.

Theorem 4. *If $gcd(k,c) = 1$, $2 \leq k \leq n$ and m denotes the pixel expansion of a $(k,n)_c$-CVCS then $m \leq \lceil \frac{l}{2} \rceil c^{2k-2}$, where $l = \binom{n}{k}$.*

If we can adopt a technique for grouping such that in every group the pair of minimal qualified sets have $k - 1$ common participants then we have a $(k,n)_c$-CVCS with much better pixel expansion. Such a pairing technique is possible, see [8]. We now have the following theorem.

Theorem 5. *If $gcd(k,c) = 1$ and $2 \leq k \leq n$ then we have a $(k,n)_c$-CVCS with pixel expansion $\lceil \frac{l}{2} \rceil c^{k-1}$, where $l = \binom{n}{k}$.*

3.5   Modification of the Technique

We have noticed that the condition $gcd(k,c) = 1$ plays a crucial role in the construction where k denotes the threshold value and c is the number of colors. In fact, the methodology fails if c,k are not relatively prime (*see* Remark 1). To overcome the difficulty when the numbers are not relatively prime, we can introduce some *dummy* colors $c, \ldots, r$ such that r is the least positive integer which is greater than c and also relatively prime with k. We can now work with the ring $\mathbb{Z}_r$ of colors where the last $r - c$ colors are dummy. Basis matrices for each of the first c colors can now be constructed using linear algebraic technique. Then we get rid of the dummy colors by replacing them with •. It can be easily checked that after this replacement the resulting matrices constitute the basis matrices realizing the original $(k,n)_c$-CVCS according to Definition 1.

To gain clarity into the above discussion we describe construction of basis matrices of a $(3,4)$-CVCS with 3 colors $\{0,1,2\}$. As we have observed earlier, number of colors and the threshold value are not relatively prime. We will introduce one *dummy* color to make number of colors and threshold value relatively prime. Thus, the new color set can be thought of as $\mathbb{Z}_4 = \{0,1,2,3\}$. Following the same (usual) notations, the system of equations over $\mathbb{Z}_4$

$$\left.\begin{array}{l} x_1 + x_2 + x_3 = 0 \\ x_1 + x_2 + x_4 = 0 \end{array}\right\}{-1(0)}, \quad \left.\begin{array}{l} x_1 + x_2 + x_3 = 1 \\ x_1 + x_2 + x_4 = 1 \end{array}\right\}{-1(1)} \quad \& \quad \left.\begin{array}{l} x_1 + x_2 + x_3 = 2 \\ x_1 + x_2 + x_4 = 2 \end{array}\right\}{-1(2)} \ .$$

and

$$\left.\begin{array}{l} x_1 + x_3 + x_4 = 0 \\ x_2 + x_3 + x_4 = 0 \end{array}\right\}{-2(0)}, \quad \left.\begin{array}{l} x_1 + x_3 + x_4 = 1 \\ x_2 + x_3 + x_4 = 1 \end{array}\right\}{-2(1)} \quad \& \quad \left.\begin{array}{l} x_1 + x_3 + x_4 = 2 \\ x_2 + x_3 + x_4 = 2 \end{array}\right\}{-2(2)} \ .$$

Solving the above systems over $\mathbb{Z}_4$ and using the concatenation technique (Subsect. 3.1) we get

$$U^0 = \begin{bmatrix} 0000 \ 1111 \ 2222 \ 3333 \ 0321 \ 3210 \ 2103 \ 1032 \\ 0123 \ 0123 \ 0123 \ 0123 \ 0321 \ 3210 \ 2103 \ 1032 \\ 0321 \ 3210 \ 2103 \ 1032 \ 0123 \ 0123 \ 0123 \ 0123 \\ 0321 \ 3210 \ 2103 \ 1032 \ 0000 \ 1111 \ 2222 \ 3333 \end{bmatrix},$$

$$U^1 = \begin{bmatrix} 3333 \ 0000 \ 1111 \ 2222 \ 0321 \ 3210 \ 2103 \ 1032 \\ 0123 \ 0123 \ 0123 \ 0123 \ 0321 \ 3210 \ 2103 \ 1032 \\ 0321 \ 3210 \ 2103 \ 1032 \ 0123 \ 0123 \ 0123 \ 0123 \\ 0321 \ 3210 \ 2103 \ 1032 \ 3333 \ 0000 \ 1111 \ 2222 \end{bmatrix},$$

$$U^2 = \begin{bmatrix} 2222 \ 3333 \ 1111 \ 0000 \ 0321 \ 3210 \ 2103 \ 1032 \\ 0123 \ 0123 \ 0123 \ 0123 \ 0321 \ 3210 \ 2103 \ 1032 \\ 0321 \ 3210 \ 2103 \ 1032 \ 0123 \ 0123 \ 0123 \ 0123 \\ 0321 \ 3210 \ 2103 \ 1032 \ 2222 \ 3333 \ 1111 \ 0000 \end{bmatrix}.$$

We observe that U^0, U^1, U^2 are the basis matrices for the colors $0, 1, 2$ respectively when we consider $(3,4)_4$-CVCS with 4 colors. But in the original image the fourth color 3 was not present. It is the dummy color that we have introduced. Therefore we replace this dummy color by • to obtain the following three matrices. It is now easy to check that the following three are basis matrices realizing a $(3,4)_3$-CVCS.

$$S^0 = \begin{bmatrix} 0000 \ 1111 \ 2222 \ \bullet\bullet\bullet\bullet \ 0\bullet21 \ \bullet210 \ 210\bullet \ 10\bullet2 \\ 012\bullet \ 012\bullet \ 012\bullet \ 012\bullet \ 0\bullet21 \ \bullet210 \ 210\bullet \ 10\bullet2 \\ 0\bullet21 \ \bullet210 \ 210\bullet \ 10\bullet2 \ 012\bullet \ 012\bullet \ 012\bullet \ 012\bullet \\ 0\bullet21 \ \bullet210 \ 210\bullet \ 10\bullet2 \ 0000 \ 1111 \ 2222 \ \bullet\bullet\bullet\bullet \end{bmatrix},$$

$$S^1 = \begin{bmatrix} \bullet\bullet\bullet\bullet \ 0000 \ 1111 \ 2222 \ 0\bullet21 \ \bullet210 \ 210\bullet \ 10\bullet2 \\ 012\bullet \ 012\bullet \ 012\bullet \ 012\bullet \ 0\bullet21 \ \bullet210 \ 210\bullet \ 10\bullet2 \\ 0\bullet21 \ \bullet210 \ 210\bullet \ 10\bullet2 \ 012\bullet \ 012\bullet \ 012\bullet \ 012\bullet \\ 0\bullet21 \ \bullet210 \ 210\bullet \ 10\bullet2 \ \bullet\bullet\bullet\bullet \ 0000 \ 1111 \ 2222 \end{bmatrix},$$

$$S^2 = \begin{bmatrix} 2222 & \bullet\bullet\bullet\bullet & 1111 & 0000 & 0\bullet21 & \bullet210 & 210\bullet & 10\bullet2 \\ 012\bullet & 012\bullet & 012\bullet & 012\bullet & 0\bullet21 & \bullet210 & 210\bullet & 10\bullet2 \\ 0\bullet21 & \bullet210 & 210\bullet & 10\bullet2 & 012\bullet & 012\bullet & 012\bullet & 012\bullet \\ 0\bullet21 & \bullet210 & 210\bullet & 10\bullet2 & 2222 & \bullet\bullet\bullet\bullet & 1111 & 0000 \end{bmatrix}.$$

4   Discussions and Experimental Results

In this section we discuss some experimental results and consider the problem of reducing share size.

In Fig. 1 we implement a $(2,2)$-threshold visual cryptographic scheme for a color image. The secret image is a picture with three colors and we use the construction technique shown in Subsect. 3.2. We observe that since the scheme is of maximal contrast, corresponding to one secret pixel three subpixels are reconstructed - one true color pixel and two $\bullet$. Presence of two $\bullet$'s makes the reconstructed image dark.

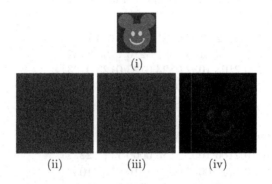

(i)

(ii)   (iii)   (iv)

Fig. 1. $(2,2)$-CVCS with 3 colors using Subsect. 3.2 (i) secret image, (ii)–(iii) shares of P_1, P_2 respectively, (iv) GOR(share1, share2) (Color figure online)

In Fig. 2 we implement a $(2,3)$-threshold visual cryptographic scheme using the construction technique described in Example 2.

The main issue with deterministic GOR based color visual cryptographic scheme is its pixel expansion which is the share size of the scheme. Same problem occurs in the deterministic OR based black and white visual cryptographic scheme. To reduce share size, Yang [34] introduced a novel idea for B&W visual cryptographic scheme. Instead of distributing rows of a basis matrix to the participants as their shares, the dealer chooses randomly one column from a basis matrix and distribute the corresponding entries to the parties. Although the pixel expansion is reduced to 1, which implies the share size is equal to secret image size, but the deterministic recovery of the secret pixel is hampered. An error probability of correct reconstruction of secret pixel is automatically introduced. For black and white image there are only two choices for every reconstructed

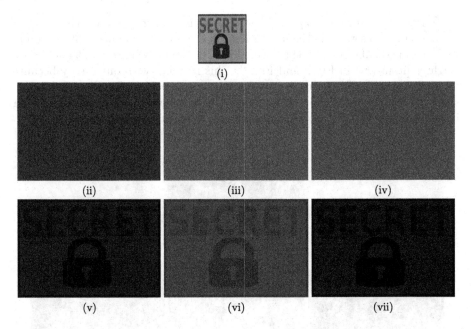

Fig. 2. $(2,3)$-CVCS with 3 colors using Subsect. 3.3 (i) secret image, (ii)-(iv) shares of P_1, P_2, P_3 respectively, (v) GOR(share1, share2), (vi) GOR(share2, share3), (vii) GOR(share1, share2, share3)

pixel- either black or white and this can be directly translated to "either correct or incorrect". The problem with color visual secret sharing is more tricky. Although the meaning of "correct reconstruction" of a colored pixel remains the same but "incorrect reconstruction" now perhaps includes more options.

Let us consider the basis matrix S^0 of Example 2. The discussion for S^1, S^2 will be similar. First let us focus on shares of P_2, P_3. If a column from S^0 is randomly selected and the entries are given as shares then incorrect reconstruction can happen in three different manner- reconstruction of • or 1 or 2. If a • is observed then it is not possible to guess the actual color of the corresponding pixel but if 1 or 2 is reconstructed then there is problem of misinterpreting the true color of the original pixel. It is easily seen that the probability of reconstructing color 1 is $\frac{1}{6}$ and that of color 2 is also $\frac{1}{6}$. However, probability of reconstructing true color 0 is higher viz. $\frac{2}{6}$. On the other hand, if we consider the shares of P_1, P_2 it can be easily seen that there is no possibility of misinterpretation of the recovered color - either it is the pixel of color 0 or •. In other words, these two shares satisfy the conditions of maximal contrast (see Definition 3).

In Fig. 3 we implement a probabilistic color visual cryptographic scheme using the basis matrices given in Example 2 and then choosing columns of S^c randomly to share a pixel of color c. The recovered images from the shares of P_2 and P_3 are brighter [item (vi) in Fig. 2 and Fig. 3]. This matches with our theory because for the shares P_2, P_3 the recovery of • is less (probable). On the other hand, share of P_1 contributes more •s into the recovered images and thereby resulting in more darker versions of recovered images [(v) & (vii) of Fig. 2 and Fig. 3].

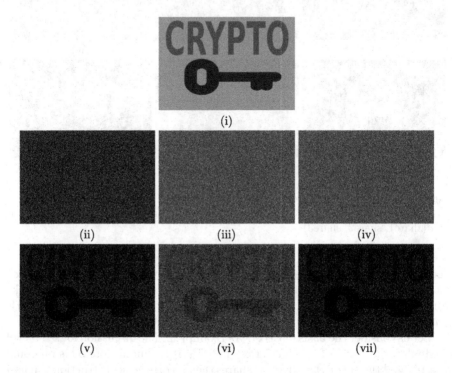

Fig. 3. $(2,3)$-PCVCS with 3 colors using Subsect. 3.3 (i) secret image, (ii)-(iv) shares of P_1, P_2, P_3 respectively, (v) GOR(share1, share2), (vi) GOR(share2, share3), (vii) GOR(share1, share2, share3) (Color figure online)

4.1 Comparison

In Table 1 and Table 2 we compare our results (from Sect. 3) with the existing works of Yang-Laih [35] and Verheul-Tilborg [33].

Table 1. Comparison of pixel expansions among our proposed scheme, Yang et al. [35] & Verheul-Tilborg [33] with three colors.

Schemes	Pixel expansion		
	Our	Yang-Laih[35]	Verheul-Tilborg [33]
(2,2)	3	5	9
(2,3)	6	8	12
(2,4)	9	11	15
(3,3)	16	12	27
(3,4)	32	18	75
(4,4)	27	23	81

Table 2. Comparison of pixel expansions among our proposed scheme, Yang et al. [35] & Verheul-Tilborg [33] with four colors.

Schemes	Pixel expansion		
	Our	Yang-Laih [35]	Verheul-Tilborg [33]
(2,2)	5	7	12
(2,3)	10	11	12
(2,4)	15	15	15
(3,3)	16	13	48
(3,4)	32	24	75
(4,4)	125	31	142

5 Conclusion

We have given a linear algebraic method for constructing basis matrices realizing color visual cryptographic scheme for threshold access structures. Using the same technique to construct general access structures have some inherent difficulties e.g. the number of colors and number of parties in every minimal qualified set have to be relatively prime. Introducing *dummy* colors we may fix the problem but that will incur in huge pixel expansion. Efficient solution to this question can be a direction for further research.

References

1. Adhikari, A.: Linear algebraic techniques to construct monochrome visual cryptographic schemes for general access structure and its applications to color images. Des. Codes Crypt. **73**(3), 865–895 (2013). https://doi.org/10.1007/s10623-013-9832-5

2. Adhikari, A., Dutta, T.K., Roy, B.: A new black and white visual cryptographic scheme for general access structures. In: Canteaut, A., Viswanathan, K. (eds.) INDOCRYPT 2004. LNCS, vol. 3348, pp. 399–413. Springer, Heidelberg (2004). https://doi.org/10.1007/978-3-540-30556-9_31
3. Adhikari, A., Sikdar, S.: A new $(2,n)$-visual threshold scheme for color images. In: Johansson, T., Maitra, S. (eds.) INDOCRYPT 2003. LNCS, vol. 2904, pp. 148–161. Springer, Heidelberg (2003). https://doi.org/10.1007/978-3-540-24582-7_11
4. Adhikari, M.R., Adhikari, A.: Basic Modern Algebra with Applications. Springer, New Delhi (2014). https://doi.org/10.1007/978-81-322-1599-8_9
5. Arumugam, S., Lakshmanan, R., Nagar, A.K.: On $(k,n)^*$-visual cryptography scheme. Des. Codes Crypt. **71**(1), 153–162 (2014). https://doi.org/10.1007/s10623-012-9722-2
6. Ateniese, G., Blundo, C., Santis, A.D., Stinson, D.R.: Visual Cryptography for General Access Structures. Inf. Comput. **129**, 86–106 (1996)
7. Ateniese, G., Blundo, C., De Santis, A., Stinson, D.R.: Constructions and bounds for visual cryptography. In: Meyer, F., Monien, B. (eds.) ICALP 1996. LNCS, vol. 1099, pp. 416–428. Springer, Heidelberg (1996). https://doi.org/10.1007/3-540-61440-0_147
8. Bitner, J.R., Ehrlich, G., Reingold, E.M.: Efficient generation of the binary reflected Gray code. Commun. ACM **19**(9), 517–521 (1976)
9. Blundo, C., D'arco, P., Santis, A.D., Stinson, D.R.: Contrast optimal threshold visual cryptography. SIAM J. Discrete Math. **16**(2), 224–261 (2003)
10. Blundo, C., Bonis, A.D., Santis, A.D.: Improved schemes for visual cryptography. Des. Codes Crypt. **24**(3), 255–278 (2001)
11. Cheng, Y., Fu, Z., Yu, B.: Improved visual secret sharing scheme for QR code applications. IEEE Trans. Inf. Forensics Secur. **13**(9), 2393–2403 (2018)
12. Cimato, S., Prisco, R.D., Santis, A.D.: Optimal colored threshold visual cryptography schemes. Des. Codes Crypt. **35**(3), 311–335 (2005). https://doi.org/10.1007/s10623-003-6741-z
13. Cimato, S., Prisco, R.D., Santis, A.D.: Colored visual cryptography without color darkening. Theor. Comput. Sci. **374**(1–3), 261–276 (2007)
14. Cimato, S., Yang, C.N.: Visual Cryptography and Secret Image Sharing. Taylor & Francis, CRC Press (2011)
15. Cimato, S., Yang, J.C.N., Wu, C.-C.: Visual cryptography based watermarking. In: Shi, Y.Q., Liu, F., Yan, W. (eds.) Transactions on Data Hiding and Multimedia Security IX. LNCS, vol. 8363, pp. 91–109. Springer, Heidelberg (2014). https://doi.org/10.1007/978-3-642-55046-1_6
16. Dutta, S., Rohit, R.S., Adhikari, A.: Constructions and analysis of some efficient $t-(k,n)^*$-visual cryptographic schemes using linear algebraic techniques. Des. Codes Crypt. **80**(1), 165–196 (2016)
17. Dutta, S., Adhikari, A.: XOR based non-monotone $t-(k,n)^*$ -visual cryptographic schemes using linear algebra. ICICS **2014**, 230–242 (2014)
18. Dutta, S., Adhikari, A.: Contrast optimal XOR based visual cryptographic schemes. In: Shikata, J. (ed.) ICITS 2017. LNCS, vol. 10681, pp. 58–72. Springer, Cham (2017). https://doi.org/10.1007/978-3-319-72089-0_4
19. Dutta, S., Adhikari, A., Ruj, S.: Maximal contrast color visual secret sharing schemes. Des. Codes Crypt. **87**(7), 1699–1711 (2018). https://doi.org/10.1007/s10623-018-0570-6
20. Guo, T., Liu, F., Wu, C.K., Ren, Y.W., Wang, W.: On (k,n) visual cryptography scheme with t essential parties. In: Padró, C. (ed.) ICITS 2013. LNCS, vol. 8317, pp. 56–68. Springer, Cham (2014). https://doi.org/10.1007/978-3-319-04268-8_4

21. Hou, Y.-C.: Visual cryptography for color images. Pattern Recogn. **36**(7), 1619–1629 (2003)
22. Iwamoto, M.: A weak security notion for visual secret sharing schemes. IEEE Trans. Inf. Forensics Secur. **7**(2), 372–382 (2012)
23. Jin, D., Yan, W.-Q., Kankanhalli, M.S.: Progressive color visual cryptography. J. Electron. Imaging **14**(3), 033019 (2005)
24. Koga, H., Yamamoto, H.: Proposal of a lattice-based visual secret sharing scheme for color and gray-scale images. IEICE Trans. Fund. Electron. Commun. Comput. Sci. **81**(6), 1262–1269 (1998)
25. Liu, F., Wu, C.K., Lin, X.J.: Colour visual cryptography schemes. IET Inf. Secur. **2**(4), 151–165 (2008)
26. Naor, M., Shamir, A.: Visual cryptography. In: De Santis, A. (ed.) EUROCRYPT 1994. LNCS, vol. 950, pp. 1–12. Springer, Heidelberg (1995). https://doi.org/10.1007/BFb0053419
27. Rijmen, V., Preneel, B.: Efficient colour visual encryption or Shared colors of benetton. EUROCRYPT 1996 Rump Section (1996). http://www.iacr.org/conference/ec96/rump/preneel.ps.gz
28. Praveen, K., Rajeev, K., Sethumadhavan, M.: On the extensions of $(k, n)^*$-visual cryptographic schemes. In: Martínez Pérez, G., Thampi, S.M., Ko, R., Shu, L. (eds.) SNDS 2014. CCIS, vol. 420, pp. 231–238. Springer, Heidelberg (2014). https://doi.org/10.1007/978-3-642-54525-2_21
29. Shen, G., Liu, F., Fu, Z., Yu, B.: New insight into linear algebraic technique to construct visual cryptography scheme for general access structure. Multimedia Tools Appl. **76**(12), 14511–14533 (2017)
30. Shen, G., Liu, F., Fu, Z., Yu, B.: Perfect contrast XOR-based visual cryptography schemes via linear algebra. Des. Codes Crypt. **85**(1), 15–37 (2016). https://doi.org/10.1007/s10623-016-0285-5
31. Shen, G., Liu, F., Fu, Z., Yu, B.: Visual cryptograms of random grids via linear algebra. Multimedia Tools Appl. **77**(10), 12871–12899 (2017). https://doi.org/10.1007/s11042-017-4921-5
32. Shyu, S.J.: Efficient visual secret sharing scheme for color images. Pattern Recogn. **39**(5), 866–880 (2006)
33. Verheul, E.R., Tilborg, H.C.A.: Constructions and properties of k out of n visual secret sharing schemes. Des. Codes Crypt. **11**(2), 179–196 (1997). https://doi.org/10.1023/A:1008280705142
34. Yang, C.-N.: New visual secret sharing schemes using probabilistic method. Pattern Recogn. Lett. **25**, 481–494 (2004)
35. Yang, C.-N., Laih, C.-S.: New colored visual secret sharing schemes. Des. Codes Crypt. **20**(3), 325–336 (2000)

Systems Security

Secure Calculation for Position Information of IoT Device with Few Communication and Small Secret Information

Hidema Tanaka[✉] and Keisuke Fukushima

National Defense Academy, Japan, 1-10-20 Hashirimizu, Yokosuka, Kanagawa
239-8686, Japan
hidema@nda.ac.jp

Abstract. Since IoT devices have small computing power and limited
battery size, it is desirable that the number of communications be as
small as possible. To solve such a request, we propose a calculation
method based on triangulation. The feature of our method is that the
number of communications is one round trip, and sufficient computational security is realized with small entropy secret information using
W-OTS+ and HMAC. In this paper, "small entropy" means a 8-digit
integer (about 24 [bit]) that can be memorized by humans. We show an
example calculation and analyze the relationship between accuracy of
position measurement and security. From the results, we conclude that
our method has sufficient security and enough practicality using small
entropy secret information.

Keywords: Position information · Hash function · W-OTS+ · HMAC

1 Introduction

1.1 Background

The recent spread of IoT devices is remarkable. Along with this, wireless communication infrastructures are being expanded around the world, including the
evolution to 5G mobile phone networks, provision of public Wi-Fi services, and
the development of Bluetooth standards [3]. Position measurement such as GPS,
Quasi-Zenith Satellite and equipments such as iBeacon [9] has become an always
available service. Not only that, even in buildings or underground where these
satellites can not be captured, position information services using Wi-Fi access
points and mobile phone network are common. As a result, businesses and hobby
that combine IoT devices and position information are expanding, and new service development is also expected. Some of them are unmanned and automated
social infrastructure, such as unmanned vehicles and home delivery services by
drone. In addition, installation of security camera, environment measurement

S. Kanhere et al. (Eds.): ICISS 2020, LNCS 12553, pp. 221–240, 2020.
https://doi.org/10.1007/978-3-030-65610-2_14

sensor, digital signage, guidance of sightseeing spot, etc. are familiar usage situation. Thus, the importance of the combination of IoT devices and position information is increasing dramatically.

The conventional research on such technology from the viewpoint of security is mainly protection of user's privacy information, device authentication and side channel attack countermeasure implementation. There are two major security problems.

Problem1. Forgery of position information (e.g. Pokemon GO cheat play)
Problem2. Improper use of position information (e.g. Monitoring behavior using
   smartphone's position information)

These are discussed independently in almost previous researches. Problem1 is caused because all position information is represented by value of matrix, and is open to public. Therefore, any position information can be used by everyone. The mechanism by which Iranian was able to capture U.S. military drone RQ-170 in 2011 is also based on this fact [4]. For intentional forgery, it is generally detected whether or not an incorrect position is used based on the appropriateness of the movement distance per unit time. However, the vulnerability is also pointed out in the mechanism in GPS itself, and it is difficult to simply perform forgery detection [12]. There are very few countermeasures against this problem, and for example, the method of [15] has been proposed.

Problem2 is a typical privacy problem, and it is possible to solve with the application of a cryptographic protocol. Furthermore, although it is considered that Problem1 can be solved by using some signature methods, we could not find existing research that has been explicitly discussed. For many crypto-researchers, it is considered that Problem1 and 2 can be solved by a combination of existing crypto techniques. However these solutions will have the following inconvenient facts.

- Large size of secret information
- High computational costs such as homomorphic applications
- Large number of communications

In particular, having a large number of communications has a large impact on battery consumption. Because battery performance is proportional to its size, it undermines the benefits of small size.

Furthermore, although the discussion mainly focuses on protection of user's privacy, the development of usage of IoT devices has also evolved into a method for managing multiple IoT devices. The existing discussions so far can not be considered as contributions to such future needs. For example, there are tags for preventing lost items (such as wallets) using RFID and identification of lost places. In such a case, only the owner needs to know the position information of the device, and it is necessary that the position information of the device is not forged. However, it is expected that the implementation of typical cryptographically secure protocols will be difficult, and as a result, there may be a drawback that the use situation. Alternatively, it may be an operation assuming TTP (to be used by joining a server operating a service), and it may not lead to a smart solution "only between the user and the device". In this paper, we apply triangulation as a calculation of position information and apply a method to identify without directly treating it. Our proposed method requires computational cost to specify the position (user side), but it reduces the computational cost and the number of communication to transmit its position (device side).

1.2 Communication Types and Security

The communication environment used by IoT devices can be classified into the following three types.

- Mobile phone communication
- Wi-Fi access
- Proximity communication such as Bluetooth

Although mobile phone communication and Wi-Fi access have a large difference in the reach of radio waves, we treat them equally as "Wi-Fi based IoT". Wi-Fi based IoT is characterized in that it can establish "secure communication of full spec (full spec security)". We see it as

$$\text{mutual authentication} \rightarrow \text{key exchange} \rightarrow \text{encryption}$$

communication process. While public key cryptography requires additional access to PKI, we focus on secret key cryptography based protocols in this paper. As a result, Wi-Fi based IoT is possible to establish full spec security, but the number of communication increases. Therefore, it is limited to the use environment which can be applied.

On the other hand, in the case of proximity communication such as Bluetooth (Bluetooth-based IoT), since the host and IoT device are limited to the reach of the user, the phases of mutual authentication and key exchange can be omitted. Furthermore, since the type of data to be processed is also limited, input secret information is characterized as being very short (small entropy). Since the number of calculations and communication for establishing secure communication can be reduced, the device itself can be miniaturized by battery operation.

From these facts, it is clear that Wi-Fi based IoT is desirable from the viewpoint of security, but from the convenience of IoT, Bluetooth-based can be expected to be applied and developed. In order to establish strict secure communication, three-way protocol has to be repeated between the host and the IoT device. In the case of general electronic devices, the power consumption required for communication is much larger than the internal processing.

1.3 Our Purpose

The purpose of our research is to combine the advantages of Wi-Fi based IoT and Bluetooth-based, and we propose a method to realize the following.

1. Small entropy secret information

2. Perform mutual authentication and secret communication simultaneously
3. Few communication (one round trip)
4. Low battery

In particular, the use of small entropy secret information is advantageous in side-channel attack countermeasure implementation. However, it is theoretically impossible to simultaneously satisfy the following conditions.

- Establish communication with "full spec security"
- Use small entropy secret information

In this paper, we show that the application of triangulation to the calculation of position information can satisfy the above requirements only by using hash function. In encryption technology (e.g. 128-bit block cipher), a small key size means that exhaustive search is possible for attacker. On the other hand, hash function has only a pre-image attack to estimate the input. While the input data and the key are clearly separated and processed in the encryption method, it is possible to explosively increase the amount of inverse calculation cost, because it is easy to process mixed input of the key and data in hash function. In order to make the best use of this mechanism, we take W-OTS+ and HMAC in this paper, and assume a 8-digit integer (about 24 [bit]) as small entropy secret information.

On the other hand, the following points can be expected against our proposed method. "When initializing an IoT device, for example, why entering a 128-bit key and using MAC is not enough?" The following consideration is given to this question.

a) Compared to random secret value of 128 [bit] or more, human beings can easily store 8-digit integers, so the setting can be changed to ad-hoc, and the number of digits can be increased if necessary. For example, when IoT devices are used by many users and secret information is changed each time, easily memorized values can contribute to ease of management.
b) Enables flexible operation according to a predetermined SOP (Standard Operating Procedure), especially when humans directly operate the IoT device. For example, the SOP corresponding to the communication date and time may be determined (e.g. Day31: Hour12: Minute 47 → 05, 05, 52 (5 is added to each value)). In such a case, randomness can be realized only by human operations, which contributes to the ease of operation.

The latter is particularly effective in the use of IoT devices in the military (e.g. measuring the position of a unit etc.). Also, for example, a combination of block cipher and MAC can realize general-purpose and high-security communication, but it is excessive security performance when handling only position information.

In this paper, we set Verifier and Player, and give the following roles.

Verifier: Manage the position of IoT devices and users (hereinafter referred to as Player). Initially give them secret information (a 8-digit integer).
Player: Show own position information Verifier.

We assume that Verifier knows Player's position roughly (city, area, etc., limited area). We also assume that Attacker can eavesdrop and forge their communications under an insecure communication environment. Verifier operates a server and is feasible to calculate a large amount of computation. Player is battery-powered and has small computing power. Based on this assumption, we aim to satisfy the following security requirements.

– Player communicates its position information only Verifier.
– Player's position information can not be forged.
– Attacker can not impersonate Verifier or Player.

Our paper is structured as follows. Section 2 gives an overview of W-OTS+ and HMAC, which are the basis of our idea. However, the detailed specifications are omitted, we show the outline necessary for the proposed method. Section 3 shows the proposed method. Section 4 discusses the effects of actual operation. In particular, the validity of using a 8-digit integer will be described from the viewpoint of measurement accuracy of position information. Section 5 shows an example calculation. Section 6 presents security evaluation and indicates that the security requirements described above are hold. Conclusions are given in Sect. 7.

2   Preliminaries

2.1   W-OTS+

W-OTS+ is an Winternitz type one time signature scheme [8]. In this paper, we show the outline and omit the details. W-OTS+ is parameterized by security parameter $n \in \mathbb{N}$, message length m and Winternitz parameter $w \in \mathbb{N}$, $w > 1$. From these parameters, we determine followings.

$$\ell_1 = \left\lceil \frac{m}{\log(w)} \right\rceil, \quad \ell_2 = \left\lfloor \frac{\log(\ell_1(w-1))}{\log(w)} \right\rfloor + 1, \quad \ell = \ell_1 + \ell_2 \qquad (2.1)$$

From the definition, we should use a family of functions $\mathcal{F}_n : \{f_k : \{0,1\}^n \to \{0,1\}^n | k \in \mathcal{K}_n\}$ with key space $\mathcal{K}_n$, however, we use cryptographic hash function $h(\cdot)$. Original W-OTS+ uses random element r, in this paper, we omit it in this section. The proposed method does not use random elements as well as the original calculation, but gives randomness as another security measure, so it can be secure even if the original random element is omitted (see Sect. 3.3). From secret key $\mathsf{sk} = (\mathsf{sk}_0, \mathsf{sk}_1, \ldots, \mathsf{sk}_{\ell-1})$, verification key pk is defined as follows.

$$\mathsf{pk} = (h^{w-1}(\mathsf{sk}_0), h^{w-1}(\mathsf{sk}_1), \ldots, h^{w-1}(\mathsf{sk}_{\ell-1})), \qquad (2.2)$$

where $h^n(\cdot)$ denotes n times iteration of hash function $h(\cdot)$.

For m [bit] message M, W-OTS+ generates a base w representation of M : $M = (M_0, M_1, \ldots, M_{\ell_1-1})$ where $M_i \in \{0, 1, \ldots, w-1\}$. The checksum is defined as follows.

$$C = \sum_{i=0}^{\ell_1-1} (w - 1 - M_i) \qquad (2.3)$$

The value of C is also a base w represented as $C : C = (C_0, C_1, \ldots, C_{\ell_2-1})$ where $C_i \in \{0, 1, \ldots, w-1\}$. Then we determine $B = (b_0, b_1, \ldots, b_{\ell-1}) = (M_0, \ldots, M_{\ell_1-1}, C_0, \ldots, C_{\ell_2-1})$ and calculate signature σ as follows.

$$\sigma = (\sigma_0, \sigma_1, \ldots, \sigma_{\ell-1}) = (h^{b_0}(\mathsf{sk_0}), h^{b_1}(\mathsf{sk_1}), \ldots, h^{b_{\ell-1}}(\mathsf{sk_{\ell-1}})) \quad (2.4)$$

Verifier who gets message M, signature σ and verification key pk, checks following.

$$\mathsf{pk} \overset{?}{=} (h^{w-1-b_0}(\sigma_0), h^{w-1-b_1}(\sigma_1), \ldots, h^{w-1-b_{\ell-1}}(\sigma_{\ell-1})) \quad (2.5)$$

In this paper, we especially focus on "base w representation" and "calculation of checksum C". We do not use verification key pk in original purpose, however, modify the signature verification scheme. In particular, W-OTS+ opens the value of w, however, it is used as the secret information in our method.

2.2 HMAC

HMAC is a keyed hash message authentication code using any cryptographic hash functions [1]. It is defined as follows.

$$HMAC(k, M) = h(k' \oplus opad || h(k' \oplus ipad) || M), \quad (2.6)$$

where k denotes a secret key and k' denotes another secret key derived from k. The values of $opad$ and $ipad$ denote outer padding and inner padding which are defined as one-block-long hexadecimal constants. From the definition of HMAC, k' is derived by padding k to the right with extra zeroes to the input block size of the hash function, or by hashing k if it is longer than that block size. However, for simplicity, we treat $k' = k$ in the followings, because we assume that size of k is not larger than the input block size of hash function. In addition, since considerable attack against HMAC is brute force search for the secret key k, security of HMAC depends on only the size of secret key k. Therefore, the condition of $k' = k$ does not reduce the essential security of HMAC.

3 Proposed Method

3.1 Preparation Phase

The basic idea of our method is based on triangulation and is only to use hash function. However, in order to establish secure communication between Verifier and Player, it is necessary to apply secret information with small entropy. In this paper, we define such small entropy as the amount of information that human can memorize easily. We assume that it is a 8-digit integer.

Player and Verifier share $w_i, (i = 0, 1, 2)$ and random element r beforehand. We assume that each size of w_i is 2-digit integer. These should be stored in the device or memorized by human Player. Our proposed method starts from Player making a request to Verifier.

Table 1. Equator radius a and Polar radius b

	a [m]	b [m]
Bessel ellipsoid	6,377,397.155	6,356,079.000 000
GRS80 [7]	6,378,137.000	6,356,752.314 140
WGS84 [18]	6,378,137.000	6,356,752.314 245

3.2 Commitment Phase

Let $p(x, y)$ be the position information of Player. The distance d_i between $p(x,y)$ and a temporal position $t_i(x_i, y_i)$ where Verifier selects randomly, can be calculated using Hubeny formula as follows ($i = 0, 1, 2$).

$$d_i = \left\lceil \sqrt{(d_y M)^2 + (d_x N \cos \mu_y)^2} \right\rceil \tag{3.1}$$

It is developed from Vincenty formula [16]. In this formula each parameter defined as follows.

$$d_x = x - x_i, \quad d_y = y - y_i \tag{3.2}$$

$$\mu_y = \frac{y + y_i}{2} \tag{3.3}$$

We use following constants based on physical observation.

$$\begin{aligned}\text{Meridian curvature radius} \quad & M = a(1 - e^2)/W^3 \\ \text{Prime vertical radius of curvature} \quad & N = a/W,\end{aligned} \tag{3.4}$$

where

$$W = (1 - e^2 \sin^2 \mu_y)^{1/2}, \tag{3.5}$$

$$e = \{(a^2 - b^2)/a^2\}^{1/2}. \tag{3.6}$$

Note that "a" denotes Equator radius and "b" denotes Polar radius. These values differ depending on the measurement, and there are several standard values for determine of position information. Table 1 shows examples. There are many web services of distance measurement using this mechanism (e.g. [2]).

Using secret information w_i, Player calculates followings.

$$\begin{cases} m_i = d_i \bmod w_i \\ c_i = w_i - 1 - m_i \end{cases} \tag{3.7}$$

These calculations are almost same as generation of message blocks and checksum of W-OTS+. In the same way as W-OTS+, we need to set the initial values which is equivalent roles of the secret key of W-OTS+. In the case of W-OTS+, if $b_i = 0$, $\sigma_i = \mathsf{sk}_i$ from Eq. (2.4), then the partial information of secret key is open. However, since it is used as one time signature scheme, such situation does not become security weakness. On the other hand, our method is not one time usage, we need to hide the value of $p(x, y)$ as the secret information. Therefore, in this paper, we generate the randomized initial values $\delta_{a,i}$ and $\delta_{b,i}$ using HMAC.

$$\begin{cases} \delta_{a,i} = h(w_i||h(x||x_i)||y) & \rightarrow \quad \sigma_{a,i} = h^{m_i}(\delta_{a,i}) \\ \delta_{b,i} = h(w_i||h(y||y_i)||x) & \rightarrow \quad \sigma_{b,i} = h^{c_i}(\delta_{b,i}). \end{cases} \quad (3.8)$$

As a result, Player has commitment $\sigma_{a,i}$, $\sigma_{b,i}$ and m_i, and sends them Verifier. Note that Player should send only m_i as commitment unlike W-OTS+. If both m_i and c_i are send, the value of w_i can easily be calculated using eq.(3.7). Furthermore, since $0 \leq m_i < w_i$, it is possible to estimate w_i if Attacker can observe communications multiple times. To prevent this, prepare a 2-digit integer r as random element. In Sect. 2.1, the random element r used in the original W-OTS + is omitted, but in the same meaning, randomization is performed so that the value of m_i is not directly communicated.

$$\bar{m}_i = m_i \oplus r \quad (3.9)$$

The procedure of Commitment phase is summarized as follows (see Fig. 1).

[**Procedure of Commitment phase**]

Step-0. Player requests authentication.
Step-1. Verifier selects random position information $t_i(x_i, y_i)$,$(i = 0, 1, 2)$ and sends them to Player.
Step-2. For $i = 0, 1, 2$, Player calculates d_i and generates $\bar{m}_i$, $\sigma_{a,i}$ and $\sigma_{b,i}$ and send them to Verifier.
Step-3. Verifier receives commitments.

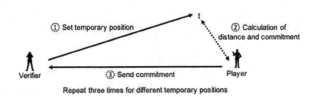

Fig. 1. Outline of commitment phase

3.3   Verification Phase

After receiving commitment, Verifier estimates distance $\tilde{d}_i$ as follows.

$$\tilde{d}_i = n_i \times w_i + (\bar{m}_i \oplus r), \quad (3.10)$$

where n_i denotes integer coefficient ($n_i \geq 0$). Then Verifier can create concentric circles with radius $\tilde{d}_i$ centered on $t_i(x_i, y_i)$. Let C_{i,n_i} be one of such circles. From

Commitment phase, Verifier gets three kinds of concentric circles and finds out many intersections (see Fig.2). Among them, the intersections of three circles C_{0,n_0}, C_{1,n_1} and C_{2,n_2} are candidates of position of Player $p(x,y)$. Let $\tilde{p}_i(\tilde{x},\tilde{y})$ be position of such candidate. From Eq. (3.7) and Eq. (3.8), true value holds followings;

$$\sigma_{a,i} = h^{m_i}(h(w_i||h(\tilde{x}||x_i)||\tilde{y})) \tag{3.11}$$

and

$$\sigma_{b,i} = h^{w_i-1-m_i}(h(w_i||h(\tilde{y}||y_i)||\tilde{x})). \tag{3.12}$$

As a result, Verifier can identify the correct position information of Player.

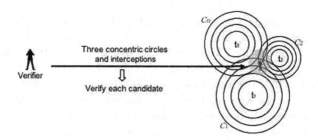

Fig. 2. Outline of verification phase

4   Effectiveness in Practical Operations

4.1   Accuracy and Computational Cost

Since the distance d_i is calculated as Eq. (3.1), it is very difficult for the value of $p(x,y)$ to be accurate. Therefore, Verifier estimates it from the method described in Sect. 3.3 and confirms using Eq. (3.11) and Eq. (3.12). In addition, we can hardly expect that the intersections of the three circles can be expressed properly as overlapping points. Thus, Verifier searches for the subspace $\mathcal{S}$ having the smallest area surrounded by three circles (see Fig.3). In the area of $\mathcal{S}$, there are some candidates for the range of possible values within significant figures of a number (accuracy). Therefore, Verifier checks them using Eq. (3.11). If there is no candidate which holds Eq. (3.11), he searches for the next subspace $\mathcal{S}$ where is the second smallest area, and repeats check calculations, or repeats the procedure of Commitment phase again.

Such trial and error and the number of retries depend on the accuracy which means the number of significant figures of the value for representing the position information. In the case of "degrees/minutes/sec" representation, which is a general latitude and longitude representation method, accuracy can be adjusted in seconds. For example,

· Latitude: 35° 35 min 45 s north; Longitude: 135° 28 min 55 s east,

has 13 digits of significant figure, and

· 44°59'247 N; 145°12'893 E,

has 15 digits of significant figure. On the other hand, in the world geodetic system (WGS) which is standard on GPS and the Internet map services, the effective figure is 17 digits (56 [bit] in double precision). For example,

· 40.711523, -74.013271

Obviously, the larger the significant figure (high accuracy), the more exponentially the number of candidates included in S increases. This also depends on the unit for calculating the distance d_i. In the case of WGS, accuracy can be expected within few centimeters. If the value of d_i is set in units of meters, there are at most 10,000 candidates around 1.0 [m^2] of S. In order to reduce the number of useless trial and error, it is necessary to determine the distance unit in advance assuming the accuracy of position information. On the other hand, imposing large number of candidates and detailed calculations on Attacker, it is possible to increase the computational cost for attack and improve security. However, since the accuracy of the position information differs depending on the size and purpose of Player itself, appropriate setting is necessary.

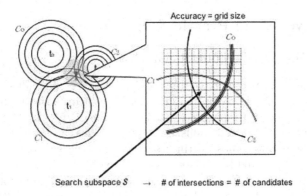

Fig. 3. Accuracy and number of candidates

4.2 Influence of Size of Entropy

The size of secret information shared beforehand is determined by the size of w_i. If giving priority to reducing the entropy size, even with a single digit value of w_i can provide sufficient security (Detailed analysis is shown in Sect. 6). However in this case, the number of trial and error for Verifier becomes very huge. For example, in the case of $w_i = 1$, the number of trial and error becomes the maximum with requiring almost same cost as exhaustive search. Therefore, w_i of small entropy is advantageous in handling small size of secret information, but it has drawback of increasing Verifier's computational cost.

On the other hand, it is disadvantageous to set w_i with large entropy. There are two major disadvantageous points. One is to handle large size of secret information itself. It becomes a size that can not be memorized by humans, and operations become more difficult and complicated. The other is that the value of n_i in Eq. (3.9) is approximately 0 or 1 when w_i is large. Therefore, it is easier for Attacker to predict the position of Player (Note that it is premised that the estimation of random element r succeeded). Attacker who does not know the value of w_i is difficult to obtain accurate Player position by trial and error as shown in Sect. 3.3 and Sect. 4.1. However, since the commitment from Player is open to public, Attacker will be able to make decisions of search subspace S as easy as Verifier (Detailed analysis is shown in Sect. 6.2). Therefore, w_i with large entropy does not contribute to security improvement.

Considering those above, we need to determine the value of w_i is minimum necessary. To satisfy such request, we need also check the measurement error of position and consider the influence of communication environment.

4.3   How to Determine the Value of w_i

For IoT devices, wireless communication is the main communication method. However, for example Wi-Fi access, wireless connection is certainly established between the access point and Player, but the destination is wired connection. Therefore, it is possible for Attacker to estimate a certain position information of Player from the followings.

- Radio source from Player
- Area covered by the base station of mobile phone
- IP address of Player
- RTT(Round Trip Time) or Latency of communication

Since the output power of radio waves used in a typical mobile phone is about 0.6 [w], the range of 3–5 [km] radius can be easily supplemented without special measurement or equipments. Google My Location [6] and Skyhook [14] applies their position information of base station and Wi-Fi access points. In such cases, it can provide 200–1000 [m] of accuracy by mobile phone, and 10–20 [m] by Wi-Fi. Obviously, Attacker can determine the search area S if the base station used by Player is detected. When such highly accurate measurement is possible, the required error is within 1–20 [cm] (estimated almost $1/1000$–$1/100$). Therefore the value of d_i is estimated within a few centimeters to 1 [m]. Since the security of our proposed method depends on the difficulty of predicting the value of n_i, for example, we expect that n_i becomes $3 \leq n_i \leq 32$. Then $w_i = 4(\simeq 100/32) - -34(\simeq 100/3)$ will be necessary minimum by the calculation skipping examinations of the unit conversion and characteristics of modulo operation.

Although it is not always possible for Attacker to obtain the IP address of Player directly by monitoring packets, the IP addresses of routers and servers on the path can be easily known and the position of Player can be estimated based on these information. Such information services already exist on the web, and IP location finder [10] and IP address location lookup [11] are well known. In this case, unlike the radio observation mentioned above, it is advantageous for Attacker to be able to obtain the position information even from a remote place. Using the method shown in [17], it is possible to perform measurement with an error of 690 [m] at the maximum although it requires many communications data. Considering the same as above, the required error is about 7 [cm] and $w_i = 3(\simeq 70/32) - -24(\simeq 70/3)$ will be necessary minimum.

In this way, since the range of $\mathcal{S}$ is limited from the communication environment to be used. In addition, from Sect. 4.1 and Sect. 4.2, we can conclude that it is necessary to determine the value of w_i considering the accuracy and unit of distance d_i. As a result, we expect that $4 \leq w_i \leq 34$ is appropriate from some trial calculations mentioned above. Note that the values of w_i can be set to be different from each other. Therefore, it is considered that by combining small and large values, it is possible to achieve both high accuracy and reduction of trial and error. To realize such requirements and highly accurate calculations while making it difficult for Attacker to predict the value of w_i, it is necessary to widen the range of values that it can take. From some calculations, we conclude that $4 \leq w_i \leq 34$ will be sufficient for these requirements. Therefore, we conclude that w_i is about 6 [bit], and ex-ored random element r is also 6 [bit].

By the way, regardless of radio observations or monitoring of packets, the above attack is almost impossible unless it is premised that communication is performed multiple times in the same communication environment. In the "full spec secure" communication, the above conditions are unfortunately satisfied. On the other hand, since our proposed method is only one time of calculation, we can expect that such attack is not realistic. In addition, radio observation is very difficult under the condition of one round trip. Therefore, we can conclude that the fact that the number of communications is small is effective not only for power consumption but also for improving security.

5   Example Calculation

5.1   Procedure

Let us suppose Player exists in somewhere in Liberty island in Upper New York Bay, in the United States. And we suppose that Verifier also knows this fact. Beforehand, Verifier and Player shared the secret information $(w_0, w_1, w_2) = (5, 7, 11)$ and random element, and they have decided in advance to calculate the accuracy in centimeters and the value of d_i in meters (Step-0). In the following, the calculation of random element r is omitted for simplicity. Verifier uses general PC for calculation and Player uses GPS for measurement of position information. We also assume that there is no error in communication and measurement.

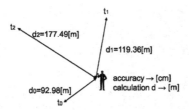

Fig. 4. Calculation of d_i

In the Commitment phase, at first, Verifier chooses following three temporary position randomly and sends them to Player (Step-1).

$$t_0 = (40.689308, -74.045631)$$
$$t_1 = (40.690202, -74.044031)$$
$$t_2 = (40.690020, -74.046343)$$

Then Player can measure each distance d_i as follows. Note that the unit of d_i is meters (see Fig.4).

$$d_0 = 92.98[\mathrm{m}] \rightarrow 93[\mathrm{m}]$$
$$d_1 = 119.36[\mathrm{m}] \rightarrow 120[\mathrm{m}]$$
$$d_2 = 177.49[\mathrm{m}] \rightarrow 178[\mathrm{m}]$$

From these values, Player calculate each m_i as follows.

$$m_0 = 93 \bmod 5 = 3$$
$$m_1 = 120 \bmod 7 = 1$$
$$m_2 = 178 \bmod 11 = 2$$

Using $(m_0, m_1, m_2) = (3, 1, 2)$, Player generates commitments and sends Verifier (Step-2).

In the Verification phase, Verifier searches for subspace S changing (n_0, n_1, n_2). When $(n_0, n_1, n_2) = (18, 17, 16)$, Verifier found the minimum area of S (see Fig.5). In the case of accuracy in centimeters, the number of candidates is 270,861 in the area. Therefore, Verifier needs to perform about 2^{18} times of trial and error, however, on a general PC, this calculation can be completed in a second (Step-3). In our computing environment (CPU:intel Core i7 2[GHz], MEM:8[GB]), this process took about 0.2 s under the condition of using SHA-256. The proposed method performs hash function calculation up to 34 times for W-OTS+ and twice for HMAC. Since this is done for three types of values, up to 108 hash function calculations are required. In this example, since there is a candidate of 2^{18}, a hash function calculation of about 2^{24} is performed in the worst case. In our computer environment, this worst case calculation took about 1.2 s. As a result, Verifier gets following.

$$p(x, y) = (40.689198, -74.044539)$$

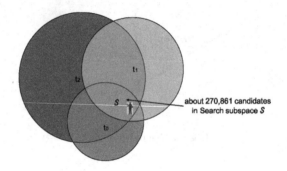

Fig. 5. Search result of subspace S

In the case of accuracy in meters, only 29 candidates in the area. Although the computational cost for Verifier will be very small, it is thought that Attacker prediction will be easier. On the other hand, if the computational cost is small, mobile tracking is possible and the scenario of threat will be changed. A brief discussion is given in Sect. 6, but in detailed discussion and analysis of such a case is our future work.

5.2   Evaluation of Efficiency

Assuming that hash function is 256 [bit] value, we analyze the amount of data to be transmitted by the proposed method and the number of communications.

Verifier →Player: temporary position 56 [bit] × 3 = 168 [bit] (one way)

Player →Verifier: ($\bar{m}_i$ (18 [bit]) + $\sigma_{a,i}$ (256 [bit]) + $\sigma_{b,i}$ (256 [bit])) × 3 = 1590 [bit] (one way)

Therefore, the total data amount is 168 + 1590 = 1758 [bit], and one round trip communcation.

Next, we estimate using the "full spec secure" communication described in Sect. 1.2. Mutual authentication assumes that Challenge and response using random numbers are mutually executed, and then Diffie-Hellman key sharing is performed. And then, encrypted communication is assumed as a 128-bit block cipher using a key length of 256 [bit]. Note that this condition suggests that our proposed method uses 256 [bit] hash function and the improvement in security is considered as much as possible.

Challenge and response (twice time): (128 [bit] random value × 2) × 2 = 512 [bit] (2 round trip)

Diffie-Hellman key sharing: 256 [bit] random value $\times$ 2 = 512 [bit] (one round trip)

Player $\rightarrow$ Verifier: Encrypted data 128 [bit] (one way)

Therefore, the total data amount is 1280 [bit], and the number of communications is 3.5 at most. However, it should be noted that this is a naive result, as a more efficient approach can be considered for mutual authentication. Comparing these results, the total data amount can be neglected from the viewpoint of recent wireless communication speeds and packet size. On the other hand, there is a large difference in the number of times of communication, and a significant difference occurs in the power consumption difference.

Also, Player of the proposed method performs hash function calculation up to 34 times for W-OTS+ and twice for HMAC. Since this is done for three different values, up to 108 hash function calculations are required. On the other hand, Player of full spec secure communication performs block encryption calculation once by creating encrypted data twice by Challenge and response. In addition, Player performs a single exponentiation for key exchange. Although the difference in power consumption is large compared with the simple case, it is difficult to think that a large difference will occur because IoT devices will use lightweight block ciphers and lightweight hash functions. Implementation comparison is our future work.

6   Security Evaluations

6.1   Threat Scenario

In this section, we discuss security of our proposed method. We assume that Attacker does not know the position information of Player $p(x, y)$, w_i and random element r but can obtain and forge communication data without error. The computer resources that Attacker can use are limited to $O(2^{60})$ considering realistic processing performance. Under these assumptions, we consider following threat scenarios to hold the security requirements shown in Sect. 1.3.

Inverse calculation of position information of Player: In this scenario, Attacker tries to determine the position information of Player from commitment. If inverse calculation is impossible, this situation is equivalent to the fact that Player has been communicated only Verifier. However, Attacker who can perform exhaustive search can always succeed this attack.

Forgery attack of commitment: In this scenario, Attacker aims to have Verifier calculates different position information. Attacker who can also perform an exhaustive search can always succeed in forgery.

Impersonate attack of Player/Verifier: Attacker impersonates Player or Verifier. In the case of impersonating Player, it aims to forge the position information of authorized Player. In the case of impersonating Verifier, it aims to obtain position information of Player more effectively.

In the followings, we discuss security against each threat scenario. However, assuming that Attacker succeeds in predicting the random element r for simplicity, the condition that m_i is obtained to the attacker is given. In order to execute the attack while predicting random element r, 2^6 kinds of candidates exist, and $\sigma_{a,i}$ and $\sigma_{b,i}$ can be used to identify the correct value. Therefore, in the worst case, the calculation amount of 2^6 times amount shown below is required. On the condition of the attacker's advantage, we evaluate the security without including the amount of calculation necessary for the above estimation.

6.2   Inverse Calculation of Position Information of Player

Attacker can predict the random element r and obtain the commitments m_i, $\sigma_{a,i}$ and $\sigma_{b,i}$. From Eq. (3.8), Attacker can also know $\sigma_{a,i}$ is an output of m_i times of iterations of hash function. Therefore, if Attacker can succeed m_i times of pre-image attack, he can determine the initial value $\delta_{a,i}$. We assume that $h(\cdot)$ is cryptographic secure hash function such as SHA-256 [5], it is well known that this attack requires exhaustive search in general. Therefore in case of using SHA-256, Attacker needs $O(2^{256})$ of computational cost. Note that Attacker who does not know the value of w_i, can not calculate $\sigma_{b,i}$ because he can not determine c_i (see Eq. (3.7)). The value of $\delta_{a,i}$ and $\delta_{b,i}$ can be regarded as the output of HMAC. In other words, eq.(3.8) can be regarded as HMAC processing of x_i (or y_i) using keys x and y instead of exor-ed key k with *opad* and *ipad*. Therefore it is impossible to realize $\delta_{a,i} \rightarrow (x, y)$ using known (x_i, y_i) by realistic computational resources. As a result, we can conclude that our proposed method is secure against this condition of threat scenario. And such security also does not depend on the size of w_i. Therefore we can conclude the secret information with small entropy can provide sufficient computational security for our proposed method.

On the other hand, when Attacker can success to predict the value of $p(x, y)$, he can take another strategy. Particularly, when Attacker can success the specification of the area $\mathcal{S}$, its computational cost for attack is equal to one of Verifier. Two strategies to specify the area $\mathcal{S}$ are considered.

1) **Estimating n_i and w_i from m_i and $t_i(x_i, y_i)$**
From eq.(3.9), Attacker also generates any concentric circles with any radius centered $t_i(x_i, y_i)$. If Player exists inside a triangle whose vertices are t_0, t_1 and t_2, he can limit the search area. Let $C_{i,max}$ be a circle whose radius is the longest distance among temporary position t_i and $t_{\backslash i}$. Then Attacker can get the maximum area of $\tilde{\mathcal{S}}$ surrounding by three circles $C_{0,max}$, $C_{1,max}$ and $C_{2,max}$. Attacker can identify if possible position information of Player in $\tilde{\mathcal{S}}$ can be searched by brute force. If Player does not exist inside such triangle, Attacker fails to limit the search area. The necessary amount of calculation cost should be considered together with the following next strategy.

2) Restricting the possible positions of Player based on radio source and IP address

This strategy can limit the possible area more efficiently than above. In fact, there are factors such as the measurement error of radio waves and the success or failure of IP address acquisition, related to the attack success. However, we assume that Attacker is advantageous except that it relates to calculation cost. Assuming WGS, the amount of unknowns for Attacker is estimates as follows.

$$3 \times w_i(6 \text{ [bit]}) + \text{WGS}(56 \text{ [bit]}) = 74 \text{ [bit]} \tag{6.1}$$

If it is impossible to estimate w_i and the amount of computation that Attacker can use is limited to $O(2^{60})$, we can conclude that it is impossible to specify even if the information of 14 [bit] can be known by Attacker. Since WGS has a value of 17 digits, this estimation means that the value of 4 digits could be known by Attacker. The calculation cost that a general PC can process in one hour is about $O(2^{40})$, if it is aimed to keep position information secret for about an hour, even if Attacker can know about 34 [bit] (almost 10 digits), it is secure against this treat scenario.

Using the example shown in Sect. 5, even if

$$p(x,y) = (40.\text{xxxxxx}, -74.\text{xxxxxx})$$

is known to Attacker, it is secure under the condition of limit of computational complexity under $O(2^{60})$. In this case, it is almost the same as knowing that Player is in Liberty island. If

$$p(x,y) = (40.689\text{xxx}, -74.044\text{xxx})$$

is known to Attacker, he will estimate that Player exists nearly a triangle whose vertices are t_0, t_1 and t_2. (In fact, Player is outside of the triangle, but attacker will be able to see that Player is near the Statue of Liberty.) On the premise that Player moves within one hour, sufficient security can be realized. As a result, if there are 2^{40} or more candidates in area $\tilde{S}$, we can conclude that our proposed method has sufficient security.

6.3   Forgery Attack of Commitment

Attacker can always make forged commitments $\hat{m}_i$ and $\hat{\sigma}_{a,i}$ easily as follows.

$$\hat{m}_i = m_i + z \tag{6.2}$$

$$\hat{\sigma}_{a,i} = h^z(\sigma_{a,i}) \tag{6.3}$$

However, if $\hat{m}_i \geq w_i$, it is obviously easy to detect the forgery by Verifier. And Verifier also can detect forgery using c_i and Eq. (3.8). On the other hand, even if Attacker can get true value of w_i, he never success forgery attack because the security of our proposed method is based on W-OTS+. In order to success forgery attack against c_i with knowledge of the value of w_i, it is necessary to succeed pre-image attack against hash function $h(\cdot)$ to make forged commitments $\hat{m}_i$. For example $z = 1$,

$$\hat{m}_i = m_i + 1 \qquad (6.4)$$
$$\hat{c}_i = w_i - 1 - \hat{m}_i = c_i - 1 \qquad (6.5)$$

Then Attacker needs to calculate $\hat{\sigma}_{b,i} = h^{\hat{c}_i}(\delta_{b,i}) = h^{-1}(\sigma_{b,i})$. As the result, if hash function $h(\cdot)$ is cryptographically secure, we can conclude that our method is secure against forgery attack. The disadvantage of this scheme is that it can not be done unless Verifier has completed estimation of the position information of Player. Improvement of this problem is also our future work.

6.4   Impersonation Attack of Player/Verifier

The purpose of impersonation of Player is to forge the position information of authorized Player. Since position information is public data, any position information can be used. However, since Attacker who does not know the value of w_i can not calculate the initial values $\delta_{a,i}$ and $\delta_{b,i}$ (see eq.(3.8)), he can not generate valid commitments. Attacker estimating w_i and Verifier calculate followings each other.

$$\begin{cases} \hat{m}_i = d_i \mod \hat{w}_i \\ \delta_{a,i} = h(w_i||h(x||x_i)||y) \\ \hat{\delta}_{a,i} = h(\hat{w}_i||h(x||x_i)||y) \end{cases} \qquad (6.6)$$

Note that $\hat{m}_i$ denotes forged commitment using estimated $\hat{w}_i$. But the information which Verifier uses is only true w_i, he calculates using only this value.

$$h^{\hat{m}_i}(\delta_{a,i}) = h^{\hat{m}_i}(\hat{\delta}_{a,i}) \qquad (6.7)$$

Since the size of w_i is 6 [bit], if hash function $h(\cdot)$ has found collision among about 64 different inputs, Eq. (6.6) holds. Or Eq. (6.7) is hold if collision search is succeeded in $\hat{m}_i$ times of iteration. These conditions can not be hold in cryptographic secure hash function, we can conclude that our method is secure against impersonation attack of Player.

The purpose of impersonation of Verifier is to obtain more advantageous position information from authorized Player. However, even in this case, Attacker does not know the value of w_i, so it does not differ from the situations pointed above. As a result, Attacker can not make any advantageous situation, we can also conclude that our method is secure against impersonation attack of Verifier.

6.5   Importance of Random Element r

In the above, we omit the effectiveness of random element r and analyze the attack using information obtained from only one round trip communication. However, if Attacker knows the value of r, the value of w_i can be determined, if Player can be observed each time the position changes. Since $4 \le w_i \le 34$, the condition of $4 \le m_i(= \bar{m}_i \oplus r) \le 34$ also holds. Therefore, Attacker can determine

w_i from the maximum value of m_i. This requires a minimum of 64 $(=4^3)$ and maximum of 39,304($=34^3$) times of successful observations. As mentioned in Sect. 4.3, such eavesdrop is physically very difficult.

In addition, since Player and Verifier can choose r within $0x00 \leq r \leq 0x3f$, there are some candidates of true random element which holds $4 \leq (\bar{m}_i \oplus r) \leq 34$. As a result, Attacker needs to execute attack procedure multiple times.

Furthermore, since the values of w_i and r are very small entropy (total 24[bit]), they are easy to change and do not complicate operations. We can conclude that r contributes greatly improvement of security.

7 Conclusions

We propose a calculation method suitable for position information of IoT devices. The purpose is to reduce the number of communications and the power consumption, and we applied small entropy secret information and the existing hash function signature scheme to achieve this purpose. As shown in Sect. 6, the proposed method shows that the security requirements defined in Sect. 1.3 can achieve practical computational security with a 8-digit integer. We also succeeded in realizing some kind of mutual authentication between Verifier and Player. Detailed analysis and evaluation from the view point of authentication scheme is our future work.

Actual operability is estimated by computer simulation. Therefore, the determination method of sub space $\mathcal{S}$ by Verifier and the range setting in the value of w_i are based on calculation under ideal conditions. In particular, the method of determining sub space $\mathcal{S}$ is simply determined by the size of the area (in order of small number of candidates). Fortunately in our computer simulations, this decision take almost no time, but we need to improve it to handle the worst case. Similarly, when applied to mobiles described in Sect. 5.1 and Sect. 6.2, the analysis of the relationship between the setting of w_i and the measurement accuracy is our future work. Furthermore, in actual operation, since measurement errors and communication errors occur, it is necessary to confirm by hardware implementation.

It has become common that recent digital map information is also provided with altitude and depth. Therefore, although three circles are used in the proposed method, if it is developed into three spheres, our proposed method can be developed into position information including height and depth. However, errors in the measurement of altitude and depth by IoT devices are large. Therefore, it is expected that the processing by the mixture of values with different numbers of measurement errors is necessary. If advanced measurement and mobile application become possible, for example, detailed and real-time drone management will be ready and the scope of the proposed method will be further expanded.

Acknowldgement. This work was supported by JSPS KAKENHI Grant Number 17K06455.

References

1. Bellare, M., Canetti, R., Krawczyk, H.: Keying hash functions for message authentication. In: Koblitz, N. (ed.) CRYPTO 1996. LNCS, vol. 1109, pp. 1–15. Springer, Heidelberg (1996). https://doi.org/10.1007/3-540-68697-5_1
2. Advanced Google Maps Distance Calculator. https://www.daftlogic.com/projects-advanced-google-maps-distance-calculator.htm
3. Bluetooth SIG. https://www.bluetooth.com
4. The Christian Science: Exclusive: Iran hijacked US drone, says Iranian engineer. https://www.csmonitor.com/World/Middle-East/2011/1215/Exclusive-Iran-hijacked-US-drone-says-Iranian-engineer
5. Gilbert, H., Handschuh, H.: Security analysis of SHA-256 and sisters. In: Matsui, M., Zuccherato, R.J. (eds.) SAC 2003. LNCS, vol. 3006, pp. 175–193. Springer, Heidelberg (2004). https://doi.org/10.1007/978-3-540-24654-1_13
6. Google maps with my location. http://www.google.com/mobile/gmm/mylocation/index.html
7. Geodetic Reference System 1980 (GRS80), Bulletin Geodesique, Vol 54:3, 1980. Republished (with corrections) in Moritz, H., 2000,"Geodetic Reference System 1980," J. Geod. **74**(1), pp. 128–162
8. Hülsing, A.: W-OTS+ – shorter signatures for hash-based signature schemes. In: Youssef, A., Nitaj, A., Hassanien, A.E. (eds.) AFRICACRYPT 2013. LNCS, vol. 7918, pp. 173–188. Springer, Heidelberg (2013). https://doi.org/10.1007/978-3-642-38553-7_10
9. Apple: iBeacon. https://developer.apple.com/ibeacon/
10. IP location finder. https://www.iplocation.net
11. IP address location lookup. http://www.ipfingerprints.com
12. Kuusniemi, H., Lohan, E.S., Järvinen, K., et al.: Information security of location estimation increasing trustworthiness. ESA NAVITEC 2016. https://www.researchgate.net/publication/313288754_INFORMATION_SECURITY_OF_LOCATION_ESTIMATION_-_INCREASING_TRUSTWORTHINESS
13. Meltdown and Spectre -Vulnerabilities in modern computers leak passwords and sensitive data. https://meltdownattack.com
14. Skyhook. http://www.skyhookwireless.com/
15. Tanaka, H., Wang, L., Ichikawa, R., Iwama, T., Koyama, Y.: Position authentication using homomorphic encryption. IEICE Trans. Inf. Syst. **96**(8), 1913–1924 (2013)
16. Vincenty, T.: Direct and inverse solutions of geodesics on the ellipsoid with application of nested equations. Surv. Rev. **23**(176), 88–93 (1975)
17. Wang, Y., Burgener, D., Flores, M., Kuzmanovic, A., Huang, C.: Towards street-level client-independent IP geolocation. In: 8th USENIX Symposium on Networked Systems Design and Implementation (NSDI 2011). https://www.usenix.org/legacy/events/nsdi11/tech/full_papers/Wang_Yong.pdf
18. World Geodetic System 1984 (WGS 84). https://cddis.nasa.gov/926/egm96/doc/S11.HTML

Attacks on Android-Based Smartphones and Impact of Vendor Customization on Android OS Security

Sudesh Kumar$^{(\boxtimes)}$, Lakshmi Jayant Kittur , and Alwyn Roshan Pais

Information Security Research Lab,
Department of Computer Science and Engineering,
National Institute of Technology Karnataka, Surathkal,
Mangalore, Karnataka, India
sudesh1611@gmail.com , kittur.lakshmi@gmail.com, alwyn.pais@gmail.com

Abstract. Smartphones are ubiquitous today, and they contain a large amount of personal and sensitive information. It is, therefore, essential to secure the underlying operating system. Android is the dominant operating system among the smartphone market; therefore, it is critical to uphold the security standards of Android. Android smartphone manufacturers and third-party custom ROM developers modify the operating system heavily to differentiate themselves among the competitors. The modifications done by the Smartphone manufacturers and third-party custom ROM developers posses a threat to the smartphone user's privacy and make the Android OS vulnerable to advanced persistent threat (APT) attacks. This paper demonstrates that Smartphone manufacturers and third-party custom ROM developers can bypass Android's security mechanisms and breach the user's privacy without getting detected by the user by modifying parts of Android OS except for the kernel. In particular, this paper shows methods by which APT attacks can be performed on the Android 10's Camera subsystem to capture pictures from the camera and upload them to a remote server without the user's knowledge.

Keywords: Android 10 · Advanced persistent threat · Camera · AOSP · Privacy · Smartphone manufacturers · Android security · Operating system · OEMs · Backdoor · Custom ROM developer

1 Introduction

Smartphones have become a part of modern life. They are populated with a large amount of sensitive information. Android is an open-source operating system that is released as the Android Open Source Project (AOSP). It is estimated that more than one billion devices worldwide run on Android [6]. Android is a Linux kernel-based operating system. To make sure that Android and user's data both are secure, Android uses different techniques provided by Linux kernel like process isolation, application permissions, secured inter-process communication.

© Springer Nature Switzerland AG 2020
S. Kanhere et al. (Eds.): ICISS 2020, LNCS 12553, pp. 241–252, 2020.
https://doi.org/10.1007/978-3-030-65610-2_15

Android smartphone manufacturers, also called Android Original Equipment Manufacturers (OEMs), are the companies that manufacture Android smartphones. Most of these vendors modify Android OS according to their needs. Third-party custom ROM developers modify the Android OS to provide features and functionalities that are not provided by stock Android OS. The Linux kernel associated with Android is released under the copyleft GNU General Public License version 2, allowing anyone to modify and redistribute Android kernel as long as they make modified kernel's source code public. On the other hand, Android OS's source code is licensed under the non-copyleft Apache License version 2.0, allowing anyone to modify and redistribute the Android OS without making the source code of modified Android OS public. This possesses a huge risk to users' privacy who are using these devices because Smartphone manufacturers and third-party custom ROM developers can easily introduce backdoors and bypass the security mechanisms placed by Android to protect user's privacy. In this paper, we demonstrate methods by which Advanced Persistent Threat (APT) attacks can be performed on Android OS to install backdoors by modifying Android parts other than the kernel. In particular, we performed an APT attack on the Camera subsystem to capture pictures from the camera and upload them to a remote server without getting detected by the user in whatsoever manner.

The rest of the paper is organized as follows. In Sect. 2, literature survey on existing work is presented. In Sect. 3, we have presented a brief overview of the Android 10 camera subsystem and discussed the security mechanisms of Android 10 and the camera subsystem that are critical in protecting user's privacy. In Sect. 4, we have discussed how the security mechanisms listed in Sect. 3 can be bypassed along with the proof of work. Finally, in the last section, the conclusion is presented.

2   Literature Survey

This section will briefly discuss research work that has been carried out related to the Android OS modification and android Smartphone manufacturers. Farhang et al. [7] showed that the vendors do not invest in security quality for naive users, and these users do not bother much about security issues that may be present in the smartphone. Smartphone manufacturers add their own customizations to the stock Android which helps them to stand out among their competitors. However, vendors do not always invest their time and money in Android's security quality while customizing.

Wu et al. [11] presented the different security issues that are introduced due to vendor customizations. They presented a three-stage analysis consisting of provenance analysis, permission usage analysis, and vulnerability analysis. In the provenance analysis, they classify apps in categories of AOSP apps, vendor apps, and third-party apps. The permission usage analysis identifies those pre-loaded apps that request more permissions than they actually need. Finally, the vulnerability analysis checks if permission re-delegation attacks can be introduced through the pre-loaded apps. Permission re-delegation means that an app that does not have particular permission to perform a sensitive task gets the required task performed by the app with the required permission [8]. The privilege tasks may involve opening a camera or reading text messages.

Karthick et al. [9] discussed how the app permissions could misuse the Shared User ID. They also discussed how the two-factor authentication might fail if the spyware gets access to read and write messages by over-claiming the permissions for the application. Anto et al. [4] presented the method of implementing kernel-modification advanced persistent threat attack (APT) in the GT S-6102 kernel. To launch an APT attack, an attacker has to download the android kernel source code from the internet, add required malicious functionality to it, like recording voices without the user's knowledge. The attacker can then change the original android kernel with the malicious one and bypass the original kernel's security mechanisms. Anto et al. [4] also presented a method of detecting such an APT attack using control flow analysis of the kernel code. However, implementing an APT attack on Android kernel is impossible for the Smartphone manufacturers because they are obliged to make the source code of the kernel public. Hence, in this paper, we have presented a way to perform an APT attack by only modifying parts other than the kernel.

3   Android and Camera Subsystem Security

Camera is one of the those sensors on a smartphone that is used quite often. Over the past years, there have been many incidents where there was a breach of user's privacy through the camera. In Android 10, Google made many changes to make the camera as secure as possible. In this section, we will discuss the Android 10 Camera subsystem and its security mechanisms.

3.1   Android's Camera Architecture

Android 10's Camera subsystem consists of Camera API v2, a native C++ implementation of Camera API v2, Camera HAL (Hardware Abstraction Layer), and camera drivers. Figure 1 shows the layered architecture of the Android 10's Camera subsystem. Camera API v2 is implemented as Java classes in the Java API Framework layer of Android software stack. HAL defines standard interfaces that must be implemented by camera hardware manufacturers in the form of camera drivers so that apps can operate camera hardware efficiently.

3.2   Android Camera's Security Mechanisms

In this subsection, we list various defense mechanisms that Android has placed to prevent anyone to access camera in illegitimate way. These mechanisms also prevent anyone to perform APT attacks on the camera.

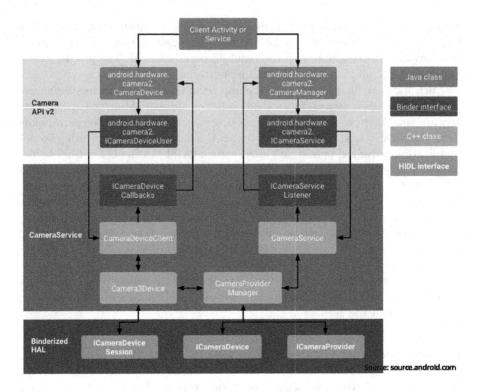

Fig. 1. Camera architecture [2]

Camera Permission. The Permission mechanism is a crucial security feature of Android. In Android, every resource (e.g., Camera, GPS) is represented by a Linux group and given a particular Group ID. Every app is represented by a Linux User and given a specific and unique User ID[5]. If an app wants to access a particular resource, then that app's User ID must be the owner of that resource or a member of that particular resource's Group ID. The Linux kernel enforces these rules at the kernel level by using SELinux policies. An app is given a unique User ID at the time of installation, and it never changes during the lifetime of an app. Android exposes these functionalities, granting and revoking permission of resources, through Permission Manager to apps at the Application Layer. Every permission is given a protection level that depends on the risk it can cause to user's privacy. Usually, resources that might expose the user's private information like Contacts, Camera are given "dangerous" protection levels. The user needs to grant dangerous permissions to the app explicitly.

If an app wants to access a resource, then that permission must be added to the manifest file of that app at the time of application development. If an app requests a permission that is not mentioned in the app's manifest file, then Android throws Security Exception and terminates that app immediately without entertaining that request. Android 10 and above uses run-time permissions.

In run-time permission, the user sees a system dialog that contains the permission group that the app is requesting. User can allow or deny that request, and depending on the user's response, Android system grants or not grants request to the app.

On Android 10 and above, an app needs to add "android.permission. CAMERA" permission to its manifest file to access the Camera. Camera permission has dangerous protection level; therefore, it is granted at run-time only and that also if the user allows. Apart from this, if at any time user wants to see the permissions that are requested by an app, the user can see them in the system's setting app. *adb:Android Debug Bridge* is a utility tool that can be used to see the logs as well as live events that are happening right now [1]. User can also use the adb command tool to see an app's permissions. Without getting camera permission, we cannot capture the picture.

No Camera in Background. Starting from Android 9, an app that is running in the background is not allowed to access the camera [3]. If an app running in the background tries to access the camera, Android disables the camera for that app and stops it immediately. An app for which the camera is disabled can not issue the request to use the camera. An app that is running in the foreground or is part of a foreground process can only access the camera. An app is said to be running in the foreground if it is actively being displayed on the screen. A foreground process is a service that does not have visible activity, but the user is actively aware of it through an ongoing notification in the status bar, which cannot be dismissed. This restriction is also applied to other important sensors like mic to protect the user's privacy.

Compulsory Rendering of Preview. This is another security feature of camera API. An app must start preview of camera before it can request for picture capture [10]. If an app calls capture function before starting preview then system throws error and application is stopped. The preview must be rendered on screen, it can't be null. This feature ensures that a user is aware when the camera is active.

Logs. The moment Android boots up, logging is started. Logging is used for debugging in Android, but it can also be used to see what is happening inside the android system on the process level. As mentioned before, *adb:Android Debug Bridge*, which anyone can download on any operating system, can be used to see the logs as well as live events that are happening right now. Camera API is no exception to this; everything in Camera is logged heavily. Therefore, logs are a simple but effective tool for people with some technical knowledge to see if anything suspicious is going with the Camera subsystem.

For logging, different macros and functions are used, common ones are ALOGI, ALOGV, ALOGE, ALOGW, logDeviceRemoved(), etc. We developed a small android application to get Camera subsystem logs and check if logging works or not in Android. After running that application, it was seen that our camera activity is being logged. Therefore, to stealthily click picture, we have to modify Android OS such that only our camera activities are not logged at all.

Because of all the security restrictions mentioned above that are imposed by Android, it is difficult to perform an APT attack to capture a picture from Camera without the user noticing it. In the next section, we will see how these security restrictions can be bypassed to fulfill our objective i.e., breaching the user's privacy without getting detected by the user by modifying Android's source code.

4   Circumventing Android's Camera Security

In this section, we will present implementation details and proof of a working solution that can bypass all the security restrictions mentioned in the previous section and capture pictures through Camera without getting detected by the user.

4.1   Granting Critical Permissions Without Prompting User

As described in the previous section, Android's Permission Granting and Revoking mechanism is highly robust and secure. The complete process of granting permission to an app is represented in Fig. 2 and 3. As shown in Fig. 2 and 3, an app starts this process of requesting permission at the application layer and ends at the kernel layer where the permission is granted. It can also be seen that at every level, there are security checks placed so that only legitimate requests are handled. These checks ensure that the permission being requested should already be mentioned in the manifest file of that app, and if permission is mentioned in the manifest file, then the user can see that permission in the Settings app. These checks also ensure that only the system packages that have permission to "Grant Permissions" handle these requests. These checks also ensure that whenever permission is requested, the user is prompted with a dialog to allow or deny that permission. Permission is granted if and only if user clicks allow. One possible solution to overcome these restrictions is to modify the kernel itself, but that can not be done since the Android Kernel is released under the GNU GPLv2 license, which mandates to open source the changes made to the kernel. By going through the modified kernel's source code, it can be easily verified that we circumvented the default Permission mechanism of Android. Therefore, we modified Android's other parts to build another mechanism to grant permissions.

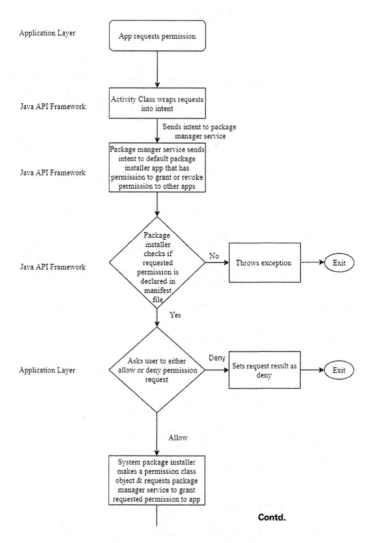

Fig. 2. Android's Permission Granting Mechanism

Our mechanism is similar to Android's default permission mechanism and exists along with Android's default permission mechanism except for one significant change that our permission mechanism does not contain the security restrictions imposed by the default permission mechanism. To ensure that only the apps we allow use our permission mechanism and all other apps use Android's default permission mechanism, our app passes a secret key along with the permission request. If the app's secret key matches the key used by our permission mechanism, then permission is granted without any security checks, the user is not prompted at all, and no information is logged regarding granting of this permission anywhere. If the secret key is not present with the permission request

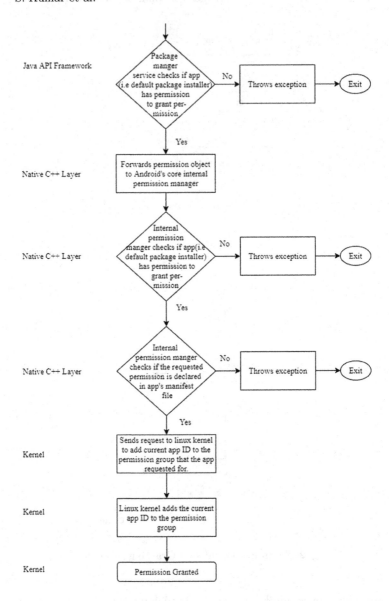

Fig. 3. Android's Permission Granting Mechanism

or secret key is not correct, then that request uses Android's default permission mechanism. Revoking permission also follows the same procedure as granting permission follows. Therefore, we can grant permission of an app with our modified Android OS without bringing anything to the user's notice in whatsoever manner.

We made a video (https://youtu.be/N1OP0wPzgSc) to show that our solution to circumvent Android 10's permission mechanism without being detected works as described above. For proof, we made two simple camera apps that capture pictures like a regular camera app would. The only difference between the two is that the first app uses Android's default permission mechanism, whereas the second app uses our modified permission mechanism. In the video, it can be seen that the first app prompts the user to grant camera permission to open the Camera, and in the settings app, camera permission is shown as permission for the first app. However, if we see permissions for the second app, no permission is requested by the app. Also, the second app does not prompt the user to grant permission for anything but it is still able to open the Camera. Hence, proving that our solution to bypass Android 10's permission mechanism works without being detected by the user.

By implementing another permission pipeline, we performed an APT attack on the Android. We can grant not only the camera permission but also other critical permissions like storage, contacts, call, etc. without the user's knowledge. In this second video demonstration (https://youtu.be/gA9uuEoWv3U), it can be seen that our solution works as expected.

4.2 Capture Picture from Background

To capture pictures from the background, we need to overcome two restrictions applied by Android. First, capture a picture without rendering a preview window and second, open camera from background.

There are mainly two ways to click pictures without rendering the preview on screen. One method is to make the preview window so small that the user cannot see the preview window. If we make windows size 0 px by 0 px, then system will throw an exception, therefore, minimum size of video can be 1 px by 1 px. Although the preview is almost impossible to be seen with naked eyes but technically, the preview is still being rendered on the screen; therefore, it is not a perfect solution. The correct solution is to direct the output of the camera to a dummy TextureView surface instead of directing it to the screen. A TextureView is used to display streaming content like video and OpenGL scene. One major benefit of using TextureView is that if it is rendered in software, i.e., a surface that does not exist, then TextureView will draw nothing. The beauty of this solution is that it does not require us to modify Android OS; we implement this solution in our app at the time of developing the app.

To understand how Android recognizes whether an app is running in the background or not, we need to understand how Android prioritize apps running in different states. An application that is running visible to the user is given the highest priority. The second priority is given to the application that is running as foreground processes. A foreground process is a service that does not have visible activity, but the user is actively aware of it through an ongoing notification in the status bar, which can not be dismissed. The lowest priority is given to the processes that are running in the background. A process having low priority means that it will get critical resources like CPU and RAM, less often as compared to the processes having higher priority.

Android uses the priority mechanism to find out if the app that is trying to open the camera is running in the foreground or background. When an app requests to open the camera, Android starts a timer and gives the process a simple task to perform. If the process does not complete the task within the time limit, Android disables the camera for that app and throws "Camera Disabled Exception" and immediately stops further processing of the request to open the camera. Since the app running in the background has low priority; therefore, it will not get enough CPU cycles to complete the task, and Android will stop it from opening the camera. This mechanism works most of the time, but it is not perfect because there are times when the total number of processes running is low, then even background processes get enough CPU cycles to complete the task, and Android allows the camera to be opened. CameraService is Android's core process that handles Android's Camera operations and communicates directly with the Camera HAL layer. We modified the CameraService code such that our app does not need to perform the above-described task even if it is running in the background. To show that this solution works, we made a video (https://youtu.be/cwdYWb484-o) in which it is demonstrated that an app can open the camera in the background, click pictures without displaying any preview and send those pictures to a remote server without user's knowledge.

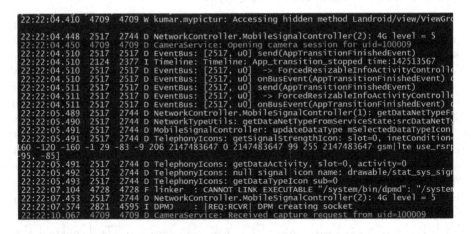

Fig. 4. Logs before modifications

4.3   Disabling Logs

We ran a camera app multiple times and noted different code segments where logging happens. Figure 4 shows some of these logs. To get around the logging of our app's activity, we modified the CameraService and some other services such that our app's activity is not logged. Figure 5 shows logs after modification, and it can be seen that no logs from our app appeared anywhere. In this section, we presented methods to implant an APT attack in Android OS to breach the

```
22:57:03.135  9313  9313 W kumar.mypictur: Accessing hidden method Landroid/view/ViewGroup;->make
22:57:03.273  2517  2517 D EventBus: [2517, u0] send(AppTransitionFinishedEvent)
22:57:03.273  2517  2517 D EventBus: [2517, u0]  -> ForcedResizableInfoActivityController [0x5a7a
22:57:03.273  2517  2517 D EventBus: [2517, u0] onBusEvent(AppTransitionFinishedEvent) duration:
22:57:03.273  2517  2517 D EventBus: [2517, u0] send(AppTransitionFinishedEvent)
22:57:03.274  2517  2517 D EventBus: [2517, u0]  -> ForcedResizableInfoActivityController [0x5a7a
22:57:03.274  2517  2517 D EventBus: [2517, u0] onBusEvent(AppTransitionFinishedEvent) duration:
22:57:03.274  2124  2377 I Timeline: Timeline: App_transition_stopped time:144612948
22:57:04.737  2517  2744 D NetworkController.MobileSignalController(1): 4G level = 5
22:57:04.955  2821  4595 I DPMJ      : |REQ:RCVR| DPM creating socket
22:57:05.658  2124  2420 D NtpTrustedTime: currentTimeMillis() cache hit
22:57:05.682  2124  2420 D NtpTrustedTime: currentTimeMillis() cache hit
22:57:05.684  4004  4469 I TrafficManageService: mina mTrafficStatsReceiver onReceive
22:57:07.671  9345  9345 F linker    : CANNOT LINK EXECUTABLE "/system/bin/dpmd": "/system/lib64/li
22:57:07.741  2517  2744 D NetworkController.MobileSignalController(1): 4G level = 5
22:57:08.428  2517  2744 D NetworkController.MobileSignalController(1): getDataNetTypeFromService
22:57:08.428  2517  2744 D NetworkTypeUtils: getDataNetTypeFromServiceState:srcDataNetType = 13,
22:57:08.431  2517  2744 D MobileSignalController: updateDataType mSelectedDataTypeIcon[0]=213123
```

Fig. 5. Logs after modifications

user's privacy by modifying Android's source code and without getting detected in whatsoever manner.

The APT attack discussed in this paper can only be detected by analyzing the source code of the modified Android OS. But, some non-technical solutions can be adopted by governing authorities to prevent these kinds of APT attacks. Governing authorities can frame policies and make laws to protect their people's data. The policies or laws should clearly state who can collect the data, from whom data can be collected, what kind of data can be collected and who has access to it.

5   Conclusions

Android is a mature operating system. It is anticipated that most of the core structure and functionalities of Android will remain the same in future releases. Since Android is an open-source operating system, anyone can see the source code, which makes everyone trust the Android operating system. This openness is a crucial factor that sets Android apart from other closed-source operating systems like Windows, macOS, and iOS. However, in the hands of smartphone manufacturers, it is like any other operating system in terms of openness because they do not make their modified Android's source code public. Android smartphone manufacturers and third-party custom ROM developers modify the Android OS according to their needs, and nothing is stopping them from mangling with Android's security mechanisms. In this paper, we showed that it is very easy for Android smartphone manufacturers and third-party custom ROM developers to perform APT attacks. We demonstrated that it is possible to implant an APT attack to capture a photo from the smartphone's camera and upload it to a remote server without the user's knowledge by modifying parts of the Android operating system other than the kernel. This possesses huge concerns on the privacy of users in countries like India where, there is no specific legislation to protect its citizens' data, and the majority of the smartphone sold are from companies that are from outside.

References

1. Hathy, A.: Android debug bridge. https://www.digitalocean.com/community/tutorials/how-to-build-android-roms-on-ubuntu-16-04. Accessed 5 Dec 2019
2. Android: Android camera architecture. https://source.android.com/devices/camera. Accessed 15 May 2020
3. Android: No camera and mic for idle UIDs in android p. https://android-review.googlesource.com/c/platform/system/sepolicy/+/588493. Accessed 13 Dec 2019
4. Anto, A., Rao, R.S., Pais, A.R.: Kernel modification APT attack detection in android. In: Thampi, S.M., Martínez Pérez, G., Westphall, C.B., Hu, J., Fan, C.I., Gómez Mármol, F. (eds.) SSCC 2017. CCIS, vol. 746, pp. 236–249. Springer, Singapore (2017). https://doi.org/10.1007/978-981-10-6898-0_20
5. Chan, B.: Android groups and permissions. https://pierrchen.blogspot.com/2016/09/an-walk-through-of-android-uidgid-based.html?m=1. Accessed 04 Nov 2019
6. Chau, M., Reith, R.: Worldwide smartphone shipment OS market share. https://www.idc.com/promo/smartphone-market-share/os. Accessed 20 Apr 2020
7. Farhang, S., Laszka, A., Grossklags, J.: An economic study of the effect of android platform fragmentation on security updates. In: Meiklejohn, S., Sako, K. (eds.) FC 2018. LNCS, vol. 10957, pp. 119–137. Springer, Heidelberg (2018). https://doi.org/10.1007/978-3-662-58387-6_7
8. Felt, A.P., Wang, H.J., Moshchuk, A., Hanna, S., Chin, E.: Permission redelegation: attacks and defenses. In: USENIX Security Symposium, vol. 30, p. 88 (2011)
9. Karthick, S., Binu, S.: Android security issues and solutions. In: 2017 International Conference on Innovative Mechanisms for Industry Applications (ICIMIA), pp. 686–689. IEEE (2017)
10. Wahltinez, O.: Understanding android camera capture sessions and requests. https://medium.com/androiddevelopers/understanding-android-camera-capture-sessions-and-requests-4e54d9150295. Accessed 13 Jan 2020
11. Wu, L., Grace, M., Zhou, Y., Wu, C., Jiang, X.: The impact of vendor customizations on android security. In: Proceedings of the 2013 ACM SIGSAC Conference on Computer & Communications Security, pp. 623–634 (2013)

Detection of Malign and Benign PE Files Using Texture Analysis

Vinita Verma[1]([✉]) [ID], Sunil K. Muttoo[1] [ID], and V. B. Singh[2] [ID]

[1] Department of Computer Science, University of Delhi, Delhi, India
vinitaducs@gmail.com, drskmuttoo@gmail.com
[2] Department of Computer Science, Delhi College of Arts and Commerce, University of Delhi, Delhi, India
vbsinghdcacdu@gmail.com

Abstract. With the unlimited growth of malware and the abundant and often reckless downloading of files from the internet, it is crucial to have an efficient method that can also be scalable and fast for detecting malware on a popular operating system, Microsoft Windows. Unlike static or dynamic detection that involves disassembling the code or time-intensive execution, statistical analysis that operates directly on binary content has a distinct advantage in speed and scalability. However, high feature dimensionality and high feature extraction cost increase the complexity of the algorithm and training model as well. Higher false negatives is another major limitation in detection. To address these challenges, this paper presents binary texture analysis extended from our work [22] by deriving new statistical texture features to detect over 10,000 Windows Portable Executable (PE) files into malign and benign ones. The same features [22] extracted over PE files (both DLLs and EXEs) have yielded good accuracy but the False Negative Rate (FNR) was still high. However, new features have enhanced the analysis and thus distinguishability between benign and malign files. Relative to state-of-the-art texture-based methods, the proposed method has used smaller feature dimensionality extracted at a lower cost, and with that, it has significantly reduced FNR to 0.4% while achieving an accuracy of 99.61%. The result is also compared with other malicious file detectors. The method thus has improved the other parameters than accuracy which are vital to the overall efficiency of the detection method.

Keywords: PE files · Binary texture analysis · Malware detection · Ensemble learning

1 Introduction

The most popular desktop operating system is Microsoft Windows with over 70% market share worldwide since 2009 per Global Stats [1]. Being popular, Windows operating system has been an easy wide target for malware intrusion, making it crucial to detect malicious files. The techniques used for detection include static and dynamic analyses. Static analysis disassembles the code to determine any malign operation. However, this approach is limited by code obfuscation that packs, compresses, and encrypts the

© Springer Nature Switzerland AG 2020
S. Kanhere et al. (Eds.): ICISS 2020, LNCS 12553, pp. 253–266, 2020.
https://doi.org/10.1007/978-3-030-65610-2_16

malicious file to evade detection, making reverse engineering and thus static analysis expensive and complex. Static detection usually analyzes opcodes [2], control flow graphs [3], function call frequency [4], or API calls [5, 6]. A social graph of PE files [7] has analyzed the file relations. The detection has also been performed using the PE header [8]. On the other hand, dynamic analysis executes the code in a virtual environment to trace any malicious action. This detection however is time- and resource-consuming with behavior often constrained in the running environment. It involves analysis based on API call sequence [9–13] and system-call-based graph models [14–16].

Another approach is a statistical analysis that uses binary content to derive statistical features without code disassembly or execution. The reuse of code to produce new malware variants reserves statistical and structural properties at the binary level. This byte-level similarity produces visual similarity in terms of texture and layout among the malware variants. Motivated by this analysis, we proposed binary texture analysis [22] classifying malicious executables into respective malware families. This paper extends our previous approach by extracting additional new statistical texture features to classify Windows PE files into benign and malign ones.

The rest of the paper is structured as follows. Section 2 discusses the related work. Section 3 describes the format of PE files. Section 4 presents the methodology for the proposed technique. The classification results are analyzed in Sect. 5, and Sect. 6 presents the conclusion.

2   Related Work

The binary files have been converted into images and entropy graphs [17] for classifying malware into their respective families. Another visual analysis for identifying malware families transformed the malware binary information into image matrices [18]. This matrix similarity-based detection used opcodes as binary information. Another byte-level-based detection transformed the executables into images, followed by extracting micro-patterns using the local binary pattern (LBP) method [19]. The method has also been applied to the opcodes to detect malware and benign executables. Three different sets of features: 6 Intensity-based, 16 Wavelet-based and 512 Gabor-based texture features [20] have been extracted from the executables converted into images. The 534 features resulted in an accuracy of 95% for detecting malicious and benign samples. Collective features have yielded a better result than Intensity and Wavelet features combined or Gabor-based features alone. Another Gabor-based detection method extracted 512 GIST descriptors [21] from clean and malign PE files. It used extremely randomized trees, achieving about 96% accuracy and 97.51% recall rate. The static analysis of PE files has derived features from the PE header, file structure [25], and the PE optional header [26]. Other static methods over PE files have used byte n-grams [27], opcode sequences [28], malicious sequential pattern [29], function call frequency [30] and string patterns [31]. Behavioral analysis has derived API sequences from the PE file execution [32]. It resulted in 98.5% accuracy. To enhance the detection, hybrid analysis [33–36] has been proposed over the PE files.

Binary texture analysis for benign and malign PE file detection presented in this paper has used relatively 41 texture statistics extracted in an average time of 38 ms without code disassembly or execution. This has attributed to the speed, scalability, and lesser complexity of the proposed method showing better classification performance.

3 PE File Format

PE format is a file format for DLLs, executables, and object codes in the Windows operating system. The file structure contains several headers and sections. The file layout is specified by the PE file header that uses information such as the number of sections in the file, time-date stamp representing the time the file was created, type of target machine to run the file, and size of the optional header. The optional header holds other information such as the PE file size on runtime, a field indicating whether the executable is 32-bit or 64-bit and data directories to find components like imported functions in the file. Addresses where the file will be memory-mapped and where the loader will begin execution are also stored in the optional header. Following this header are the section headers containing the real and virtual size of corresponding sections, their virtual address in memory, and the access rights. The sections the file includes are the .txt section which holds executable code with execute/read access, the .data section holding initialized data including global variables, and the .bss section holding uninitialized data, both with read/write access. The .rdata section contains read-only data such as literal strings or constants with read-only access. The resource container .rsrc section with read-only access contains resources such as icons, images used in the application's UI with their size.

4 Method Proposed

Inspired by our method [22] that identified malware families of the executables, we extend our work in this paper to detect benign and malicious Windows PE files. Our previous approach is motivated by the idea that due to the reuse of code, the same family malware variants show similar statistical and structural properties at the binary level. Thus, statistical texture features were extracted after converting executables into images. The method effectively classified variants into their families. This paper explores the potential of this method to detect benign and malign Windows files. Unlike our method that used datasets of entirely malicious executables from different families, this paper uses a dataset of benign and malign PE files including both DLLs and EXEs. We first extracted the same features [22] over the files in this paper. However, it didn't achieve an effective result in terms of FNR which is an important objective of this paper. We found that additional features have enhanced the texture analysis of PE files, thereby improving distinguishability and relatively reducing FNR effectively. The results have been discussed in Sect. 5. This can be attributed to the intent of the files to be classified. All family executables have malicious intent. However, the same features may not be sufficient when non-malicious files (both DLLs and EXEs) are also added. According to Haralick [23], the texture of an image is well described by the spatial relationship between the gray levels, given by second-order statistical features. This paper extracts six different second-order texture statistics beyond the features [22] to enhance statistical and structural based detection between clean ware and malware, involving three steps:

Step 1: The file content is read byte-by-byte into pixels of a grayscale image. The file size determines the height of the image and the width is fixed as follows in Table 1. The image is preprocessed through histogram equalization that uniformly distributes the gray levels. It is then scaled to 64 × 64 pixels to reduce further computations.

Step 2: This follows extracting the features from the image. Gray levels of an image refer to the bytes of file content in the context of this paper. First-order statistical features [22] describing the spatial distribution of gray levels or the code bytes in PE file-converted image I, are extracted as follows:

1. Mean (μ): This gives an average gray level or byte value using Eq. 1.

$$\mu = \frac{1}{M \times N} \sum_{i=1}^{M} \sum_{j=1}^{N} I(i,j) \tag{1}$$

2. Standard Deviation (StD): This measures the deviation in byte values from the mean per Eq. 2.

$$StD = \sqrt{\frac{1}{M \times N - 1} \sum_{i=1}^{M} \sum_{j=1}^{N} (I(i,j) - \mu)^2} \tag{2}$$

3. Skewness: This identifies a lack of symmetry in the binary code distribution using Eq. 3. For an absolute symmetrical distribution, the value is 0.

$$skewness = \frac{\frac{1}{M \times N} \sum_{i=1}^{M} \sum_{j=1}^{N} (I(i,j) - \mu)^3}{StD^3} \tag{3}$$

4. Kurtosis: Using Eq. 4, this measure determines whether the distribution contains extreme byte values.

$$kurtosis = \frac{\frac{1}{M \times N} \sum_{i=1}^{M} \sum_{j=1}^{N} (I(i,j) - \mu)^4}{StD^4} \tag{4}$$

5. First-Order Entropy: This calculates disorder within the distribution using Eq. 5 and Eq. 6.

$$entropy = - \sum_{i=0}^{255} h(i) \log h(i), \tag{5}$$

$$h(i) = \frac{number\ of\ times\ gray\ level\ or\ byte\ value\ i\ occurs\ within\ the\ image}{M \times N} \tag{6}$$

6. First-Order Energy: This statistic is evaluated per Eq. 7.

$$energy = \sum_{i=0}^{255} h(i)^2 \tag{7}$$

7. 10th Percentile ($prct_{10}$): This measure is more robust to outliers which separates 10% byte values lesser than and 90% higher than $prct_{10}$ in the distribution, evaluated using Eq. 8.

$$prct_{10} = prctile(I, 10) \tag{8}$$

8. 90th Percentile ($prct_{90}$): 90% of the byte values are less than and 10% are more than $prct_{90}$ in the distribution. The value is given by Eq. 9.

$$prct_{90} = prctile(I, 90) \tag{9}$$

9. Inter Quartile Range (IQR): This provides the interval comprising the central 50% byte values via Eq. 10.

$$IQR = prct_{75} - prct_{25} \tag{10}$$

10. Median: File content or the code bytes have approximate even distribution in case median and mean are the same.
11. Mean Absolute Deviation (MAD): This provides the average absolute distance of the byte values from the mean, measured using Eq. 11.

$$MAD = \frac{\sum_{i=1}^{M} \sum_{j=1}^{N} |I(i,j) - \mu|}{M \times N} \tag{11}$$

12. Median Absolute Deviation (MedAD): Resilient to outliers, this measure calculates the median of absolute deviation of the byte values from the median of distribution using Eq. 12.

$$MedAD = median(|I(i,j) - median(I)|) \tag{12}$$

13. Coefficient of Variation (CV): Eq. 13 provides this standard measure of variation used for comparison between the binary code distributions.

$$CV = \frac{StD}{\mu} \tag{13}$$

14. Minimum byte value: This is given by min (I).
15. Maximum byte value: This is calculated as max (I).
16. Quartile Coefficient of Dispersion (QCD): This measure compares two or more distributions and is robust to outliers as given in Eq. 14.

$$QCD = \frac{prct_{75} - prct_{25}}{prct_{75} + prct_{25}} \qquad (14)$$

17. Root Mean Square (RMS): This value is also known as quadratic mean, calculated through Eq. 15.

$$RMS = \sqrt{\frac{\sum_{i=1}^{M} \sum_{j=1}^{N} I(i,j)^2}{M \times N}} \qquad (15)$$

18. Variance: This evaluates the variation in byte value distribution using Eq. 16.

$$variance = \frac{1}{M \times N - 1} \sum_{i=1}^{M} \sum_{j=1}^{N} (I(i,j) - \mu)^2 \qquad (16)$$

19. Range: This uses Eq. 17 to identify the interval size characterizing the entire distribution.

$$range = max(I) - min(I) \qquad (17)$$

Following the first-order features that use discrete values to describe the distribution of byte values, second-order statistical features are extracted which use joint probability distribution of the gray levels/code bytes to depict the spatial relationship between the values. This information is specified using a Gray-Level Co-occurrence Matrix (GLCM) [23]. An element of GLCM specifies the frequency of the co-occurrence of gray levels separated by a distance d in direction θ within an image. In the method presented, the image I is quantized to L = 32 levels sufficient to generate the matrix. Four GLCM matrices, each of size 32 × 32 pixels are created from the image, corresponding to θ = 0°, 45°, 90°, and 135° between the adjacent byte values using d = 1. Second-order texture features [22] along with new texture statistics are extracted from each of the normalized matrix p as follows:

1. Contrast: As provided in Eq. 18, this measure calculates variation between the neighboring bytes of the code.

$$contrast = \sum_{i=1}^{L} \sum_{j=1}^{L} |i - j|^2 p(i,j) \qquad (18)$$

2. Joint Average (μ_j): Eq. 19 provides the mean byte value co-occurrence.

$$\mu_j = \sum_{i=1}^{L} \sum_{j=1}^{L} ip(i,j) \tag{19}$$

3. Autocorrelation: This statistic determines the periodicity of the texture with the period given by the space between adjacent texture elements. For a coarse texture, the value declines slowly whereas the function will drop off rapidly for a fine texture. The feature value is calculated using Eq. 20.

$$autocorrelation = \sum_{i=1}^{L} \sum_{j=1}^{L} ijp(i,j) \tag{20}$$

4. Cluster Tendency: It identifies whether the distribution contains any inherent grouping structure via Eq. 21.

$$cluster\ tendency = \sum_{i=1}^{L} \sum_{j=1}^{L} \left(i + j - 2\mu_j\right)^2 p(i,j) \tag{21}$$

5. Uniformity: Eq. 22 provides this measure of uniformity in the distribution.

$$uniformity = \sum_{i=1}^{L} \sum_{j=1}^{L} p(i,j)^2 \tag{22}$$

6. Sum of Squares or Joint Variance (σ^2): This calculates the variance of the joint probability distribution of the code bytes per Eq. 23.

$$\sigma^2 = \sum_{i=1}^{L} \sum_{j=1}^{L} \left(i - \mu_j\right)^2 p(i,j) \tag{23}$$

7. Joint Maximum: This corresponds to the most frequent co-occurrence of bytes, calculated as max (p).
8. Correlation: This is a measure of linear dependence between the neighboring byte values, given by Eq. 24.

$$correlation = \sum_{i=1}^{L} \sum_{j=1}^{L} \frac{\left(i - \mu_j\right)\left(j - \mu_j\right)p(i,j)}{\sigma^2} \tag{24}$$

9. Homogeneity: Eq. 25 calculates this measure of homogeneity within the co-occurrence distribution.

$$homogeneity = \sum_{i=1}^{L} \sum_{j=1}^{L} \frac{p(i,j)}{1 + ((i-j)/L)^2} \tag{25}$$

10. Joint Entropy: This uses Eq. 26 to evaluate randomness within the joint probability distribution of byte values.

$$joint\ entropy = -\sum_{i=1}^{L} \sum_{j=1}^{L} p(i,j) \log p(i,j) \qquad (26)$$

11. Cluster Shade: It is a measure of skewness or asymmetry in the joint probability distribution. The higher the value, the greater is the asymmetry about the mean, calculated via Eq. 27.

$$cluster\ shade = \sum_{i=1}^{L} \sum_{j=1}^{L} (i+j-2\mu_j)^3 p(i,j) \qquad (27)$$

These eleven features are calculated over four different directions. Thus, we calculate the two functions, standard deviation and mean which are invariant under rotation, over the four directions for each feature, resulting in twenty-two second-order texture statistics. Both the order are concatenated, rendering 41 statistical texture features. The procedure is illustrated in Fig. 1.

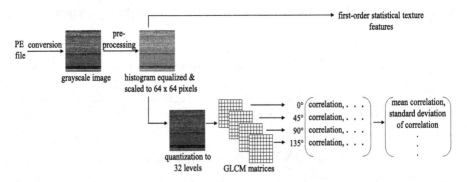

Fig. 1. procedure to extract statistical texture features

Step 3: This performs classification using random forest ensemble classifier using K-fold cross-validation, where K = 10.

Table 1. Image height for different file sizes

Size of the file	Height of the image
<10 kB	32
(10–30) kB	64
(30–60) kB	128
(60–100) kB	256
(100–200) kB	384
(200–500) kB	512
(500–1000) kB	768
>1000 kB	1024

5 Experiment and Results

The dataset used in this paper consists of 10,882 PE files, both DLLs and EXEs comprising an equal number of benign and malign samples. Benign files have been collected from the root directory of the Windows operating system and malign ones from a malware repository [24]. All the files are for 32-bit architecture. Benign files are of size 2 KB – 21,658 KB and the malign ones have a size distribution of 7 KB – 2,643 KB. The malware samples are both packed and unpacked belonging to twenty-five different families, with the samples packed with UPX packer. Also, the code section of some samples is encrypted. The samples have been converted into grayscale images followed by extracting the features using the procedure mentioned in Sect. 4. A small-dimensional feature set comprising of 41 statistical texture features is attained, thereby decreasing the training model complexity. This is followed by 10-fold cross-validation using a random forest classifier. To evaluate the performance of the proposed method, other texture-based detection methods [19–21] have been applied to our dataset since their datasets could not be traced. The comparative analysis is presented in Table 2. The table shows that relatively our method has significantly reduced FNR to 0.0040 (0.4%) using a substantial reduction in feature dimensionality. Moreover, the time for extracting first- and

Table 2. A comparative analysis of the proposed method with other texture-based methods

	Intensity + wavelet + gabor [20]	GIST [21]	LBP [19]	Proposed method
Feature dimensionality	534	512	590	**41**
Feature extraction time(s)	8.7652	0.054	8.0788	**0.0377**

(*continued*)

Table 2. (*continued*)

	Intensity + wavelet + gabor [20]	GIST [21]	LBP [19]	Proposed method
Accuracy	95.62%	96.45%	98.56%	**99.61%**
Precision	96.74%	99.93%	97.77%	**99.63%**
Recall	94.42%	92.95%	99.46%	**99.60%**
F1 measure	95.57%	96.32%	98.61%	**99.61%**
False negative rate	0.0558	0.0705	0.0054	**0.0040**

second-order statistical features used in the proposed method is 0.0377 s, which is lesser than that for Gabor, Wavelet, and Intensity-based features [20], GIST [21], and LBP features [19].

Our focus is on reducing FNR besides improving the speed since many existing works have already improved accuracy. Method [19] has resulted in a low FNR of 0.54%. The same features [22] and 41 features both have attained an accuracy of over 99%. However, [22] resulted in FNR of 0.5% which shows a reduction in this metric by 7.4% relative to [19]. On other hand, our method yielding 0.4% FNR shows a reduction of 26% compared to that of [19]. A comparison of our method with other static, dynamic, and hybrid analysis-based PE malicious file detectors [25–36] is shown in Table 3. The table shows that relatively, our method has resulted in a pretty high accuracy of 99.61% without any disassembly or code execution.

Table 3. A comparative analysis of our method with other PE malicious file detection methods

Method	Dataset of PE files (#samples)	Features extracted	Accuracy
Static [30]	2,460 malign, 627 benign	Suspicious section count, function call frequency	98.35%
Static [25]	1,230 malign, 1,230 benign	PE header, file structure-based.	95.59%
Static [26]	338 malign, 214 benign	PE optional header-based.	97.25%
Static + dynamic [33]	72,317 malign, 17,683 benign	(Byte + byte entropy) histogram, (section, imports, exports, file, header) information, strings, API call sequences	97.3%
Dynamic [32]	120 malign, 150 benign	A distinct set of API sequences	98.5%
Static [29]	8,847 malign, 1,460 benign	Malicious instruction sequences	95.25%
Static [27]	5,500 malign, 5,455 benign	Byte n-grams	94.67%
Static + dynamic [34]	617 malign, 1,310 benign	Byte frequency, API call sequences	94.70%
Static [28]	3,000 malign, 3,000 benign	Opcode sequences	~96%
Static + dynamic [35]	3,548 malign, 1,628 benign	strings, DLLs, API calls, assembly instruction	98%

(*continued*)

Table 3. (*continued*)

Method	Dataset of PE files (#samples)	Features extracted	Accuracy
Static + dynamic [36]	100,000 malign, 100,000 benign	Three contexts (static, dynamic, instruction) based.	96.7%
Static [31]	D1 (small dataset): 651 malign, 1,303 benign D2 (large): 15,079 malign, 25,986 benign	Raw bytes or (byte n-grams, PE imports, section names, string patterns)	D1: 99.03% D2: 98.69%
Our method	5,441 malign, 5,441 benign	Statistical texture features	99.61%

Another performance indicator, the Receiver Operating Characteristic (ROC) curve, is a graphical plot between the False Positive Rate (FPR) on the x-axis and True Positive Rate (TPR) on the y-axis at several thresholds. The best prediction yields a point at the upper-left corner, the coordinate (0,1) of ROC space, representing no false positives and no false negatives. The area under the curve (AUC) ranges in value from 0 to 1 and is a good estimate of the classification performance. The larger the AUC, the higher the performance. Figure 2 shows ROC curves corresponding to the classification results under each fold for the proposed method. We have changed the scale to make the curves readable. The curves are nearer to the upper-left corner as shown in Fig. 2, resulting in the AUCs closer to 1. This indicates the efficiency of the proposed method for malware detection.

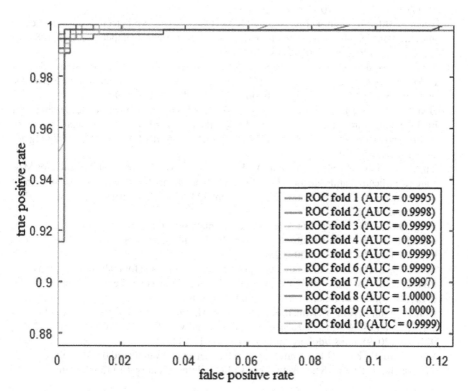

Fig. 2. ROC curves for 10-fold cross-validation for the proposed method

6 Conclusion

This paper has presented a cost- and time-effective method for detecting benign and malicious Windows PE files. The proposed method performs binary texture analysis, extracting statistical texture features representing the code structure without any disassembly, unpacking, decryption, or code execution. Relative to state-of-the-art methods, the proposed method has used a lesser number of features derived at low cost, and with that, it has substantially decreased the False Negative Rate to 0.4% and attained an accuracy over 99%. The method has shown considerable potential for detecting clean ware and malware. The proposed analysis has an advantage of speed, scalability, and complexity, enhancing the overall efficiency of the detection method.

Acknowledgments. All the authors have contributed to the work without any conflict of interest. The authors in particular thank VirusShare.com for providing access to their malware repository, and to the publisher of [22] to include the author's rights that enable us to extend our work. To specify, the study has not received any grant from any funding agencies.

References

1. Global Stats. https://gs.statcounter.com/. Accessed 18 June 2020
2. Manavi, F., Hamzeh, A.: A new method for malware detection using opcode visualization. In: 2017 Artificial Intelligence and Signal Processing Conference (AISP), pp. 96–102. IEEE (2017). https://doi.org/10.1109/aisp.2017.8324117
3. Nguyen, M.H., Nguyen, D.Le., Nguyen, X.M., Quan, T.T.: Auto-detection of sophisticated malware using lazy-binding control flow graph and deep learning. Comput. Secur. **76**, 128–155 (2018). https://doi.org/10.1016/j.cose.2018.02.006
4. Saini, A., Gandotra, E., Bansal, D., Sofat, S.: Classification of PE files using static analysis. In: Proceedings of the 7th International Conference on Security of Information and Networks, pp. 429–433. ACM (2014). https://doi.org/10.1145/2659651.2659679
5. Hou, S., Chen, L., Tas, E., Demihovskiy, I., Ye, Y.: Cluster-oriented ensemble classifiers for intelligent malware detection. In: Proceedings of the 2015 IEEE 9th International Conference on Semantic Computing (IEEE ICSC 2015), pp. 189–196. IEEE (2015). https://doi.org/10.1109/icosc.2015.7050805
6. Uppal, D., Sinha, R., Mehra, V., Jain, V.: Exploring behavioral aspects of API calls for Malware identification and categorization. In: 2014 International Conference on Computational Intelligence and Communication Networks, pp. 824–828. IEEE (2014). https://doi.org/10.1109/cicn.2014.176
7. Jiang, Q., Liu, N., Zhang, W.: A feature representation method of social graph for malware detection. In: 2013 Fourth Global Congress on Intelligent Systems, pp. 139–143. IEEE (2013). https://doi.org/10.1109/gcis.2013.28
8. Khorsand, Z., Hamzeh, A.: A novel compression-based approach for malware detection using PE header. In: The 5th Conference on Information and Knowledge Technology, pp. 127–133. IEEE (2013). https://doi.org/10.1109/ikt.2013.6620051
9. Kim, H., Kim, J., Kim, Y., Kim, I., Kim, K.J., Kim, H.: Improvement of malware detection and classification using API call sequence alignment and visualization. Cluster Comput. **22**(1), 921–929 (2019). https://doi.org/10.1007/s10586-017-1110-2
10. Ki, Y., Kim, E., Kim, H.K.: A novel approach to detect malware based on API call sequence analysis. Int. J. Distrib. Sens. Networks **11** (2015). https://doi.org/10.1155/2015/659101

11. Cao, Y., Miao, Q., Liu, J., Gao, L.: Abstracting minimal security-relevant behaviors for malware analysis. J. Comput. Virol. Hacking Techniq. **9**(4), 193–204 (2013). https://doi.org/10.1007/s11416-013-0186-3

12. Galal, H.S., Mahdy, Y.B., Atiea, M.A.: Behavior-based features model for malware detection. J. Comput. Virol. Hacking Techniq. **12**(2), 59–67 (2016). https://doi.org/10.1007/s11416-015-0244-0

13. Tian, R., Islam, R., Batten, L., Versteeg, S.: Differentiating malware from cleanware using behavioural analysis. In: 2010 5th International Conference on Malicious and Unwanted Software. pp. 23–30. IEEE (2010). https://doi.org/10.1109/malware.2010.5665796

14. Nikolopoulos, S.D., Polenakis, I.: A graph-based model for malware detection and classification using system-call groups. J. Comput. Virol. Hacking Techniq. **13**(1), 29–46 (2017). https://doi.org/10.1007/s11416-016-0267-1

15. Park, Y., Reeves, D., Mulukutla, V., Sundaravel, B.: Fast malware classification by automated behavioral graph matching. In: Proceedings of the Sixth Annual Workshop on Cyber Security and Information Intelligence Research, pp. 1–4. ACM (2010). https://doi.org/10.1145/1852666.1852716

16. Imran, M., Afzal, M.T., Qadir, M.A.: Using hidden markov model for dynamic malware analysis: first impressions. In: 2015 12th International Conference on Fuzzy Systems and Knowledge Discovery (FSKD), pp. 816–821. IEEE (2015). https://doi.org/10.1109/fskd.2015.7382048

17. Han, K.S., Lim, J.H., Kang, B., Im, E.G.: Malware analysis using visualized images and entropy graphs. Int. J. Inf. Secur. **14**(1), 1–14 (2015). https://doi.org/10.1007/s10207-014-0242-0

18. Han, K., Lim, J.H., Im, E.G.: Malware analysis method using visualization of binary files. In: Proceedings of the 2013 Research in Adaptive and Convergent Systems, RACS 2013. pp. 317–321. ACM (2013). https://doi.org/10.1145/2513228.2513294

19. Hashemi, H., Hamzeh, A.: Visual malware detection using local malicious pattern. J. Comput. Virol. Hacking Techniq. **15**(1), 1–14 (2019). https://doi.org/10.1007/s11416-018-0314-1

20. Kancherla, K., Mukkamala, S.: Image visualization based malware detection. In: 2013 IEEE Symposium on Computational Intelligence in Cyber Security (CICS), pp. 40–44. IEEE (2013). https://doi.org/10.1109/cicybs.2013.6597204

21. Zhou, X., Pang, J., Liang, G.: Image classification for malware detection using extremely randomized trees. In: 2017 11th IEEE International Conference on Anti-counterfeiting, Security, and Identification (ASID), pp. 54–59. IEEE (2017). https://doi.org/10.1109/icasid.2017.8285743

22. Verma, V., Muttoo, S.K., Singh, V.B.: Multiclass malware classification via first- and second-order texture statistics. Comput. Secur. **97** (2020). https://doi.org/10.1016/j.cose.2020.101895

23. Haralick, R.M., Shanmugam, K., Dinstein, I.: Textural features for image classification. IEEE Trans. Syst. Man. Cybern. SMC-3, 610–621 (1973). https://doi.org/10.1109/tsmc.1973.4309314

24. Malware Repository. https://virusshare.com/. Accessed 22 Jan 2020

25. Rezaei, T., Hamze, A.: An efficient approach for malware detection using PE header specifications. In: 2020 6th International Conference on Web Research (ICWR), pp. 234–239. IEEE (2020). https://doi.org/10.1109/icwr49608.2020.9122312

26. Belaoued, M., Mazouzi, S.: A real-time PE-malware detection system based on CHI-square test and PE-file features. In: Computer Science and Its Applications, CIIA 2015. IFIP AICT, pp. 416–425 (2015). https://doi.org/10.1007/978-3-319-19578-0_34

27. Li, B., Zhang, Y., Yao, J., Yin, T.: MDBA: Detecting Malware based on Bytes N-Gram with Association Mining. In: 2019 26th International Conference on Telecommunications (ICT), pp. 227–232. IEEE (2019). https://doi.org/10.1109/ict.2019.8798828

28. Ding, Y., Chen, S., Xu, J.: Application of Deep Belief Networks for opcode based malware detection. In: 2016 International Joint Conference on Neural Networks (IJCNN), pp. 3901–3908. IEEE (2016). https://doi.org/10.1109/ijcnn.2016.7727705
29. Fan, Y., Ye, Y., Chen, L.: Malicious sequential pattern mining for automatic malware detection. Expert Syst. Appl. **52**, 16–25 (2016). https://doi.org/10.1016/j.eswa.2016.01.002
30. Saini, A., Gandotra, E., Bansal, D., Sofat, S.: Classification of PE files using static analysis. In: Proceedings of the 7th International Conference on Security of Information and Networks, pp. 429–433. ACM (2014). https://doi.org/10.1145/2659651.2659679
31. Yang, L., Liu, J.: TuningMalconv: malware detection with not just raw bytes. IEEE Access. **8**, 140915–140922 (2020). https://doi.org/10.1109/ACCESS.2020.3014245
32. Uppal, D., Sinha, R., Mehra, V., Jain, V.: Malware detection and classification based on extraction of API sequences. In: 2014 International Conference on Advances in Computing, Communications and Informatics (ICACCI), pp. 2337–2342. IEEE (2014). https://doi.org/10.1109/icacci.2014.6968547
33. Zhou, H.: Malware detection with neural network using combined features. In: CNCERT 2018, CCIS, pp. 96–106 (2019). https://doi.org/10.1007/978-981-13-6621-5_8
34. Huang, X., Ma, L., Yang, W., Zhong, Y.: A method for windows malware detection based on deep learning. J. Signal Process. Syst. (2020). https://doi.org/10.1007/s11265-020-01588-1
35. Zhao, J., Zhang, S., Liu, B., B.C.: Malware detection using machine learning based on the combination of dynamic and static features. In: 2018 27th International Conference on Computer Communication and Networks (ICCCN). IEEE (2018). https://doi.org/10.1109/icccn.2018.8487459
36. Saleh, M., Li, T., Xu, S.: Multi-context features for detecting malicious programs. J. Comput. Virol. Hacking Techniq. **14**(2), 181–193 (2018). https://doi.org/10.1007/s11416-017-0304-8

Estimating the Cost of Cybersecurity Activities with CAspeA: A Case Study and Comparative Analysis

Rafał Leszczyna[1](✉)(iD) and Adrian Litwin[2]

[1] Faculty of Management and Economics, Gdańsk University of Technology,
Narutowicza 11/12, 80-233 Gdańsk, Poland
rafal.leszczyna@pg.edu.pl
[2] Homerun, Singel 542, 1017 AZ Amsterdam, The Netherlands

Abstract. Contemporary approaches to the estimation of cybersecurity costs in organisations tend to focus on the cost of incidents or technological investments. However, there are other, less transparent costs related to cybersecurity management that need to be properly recognised in order to get a complete picture. These costs are associated with everyday activities and the time spent by employees on cybersecurity-related actions. Such costs constitute a substantial component of cybersecurity expenditures, but because they become evident only during scrupulous analyses, often they are neglected. This paper presents new developments on CAspeA – a method which enables estimating the cost of these activities based on a model derived from the Activity-Based Costing (ABC) and the NIST SP 800-53 guidelines. The application of the method is illustrated by a case study of a civil engineering enterprise. The method's evaluation based on comparative analysis in respect to SQUARE is described.

Keywords: Cybersecurity management · Organisational management · Business management · Cost · Estimation · Computer security · Information security

1 Introduction

With the dynamically evolving threat landscape, the number of organisations forced to bear the costs associated with cybersecurity incidents is inevitably raising. According to the study of Accenture Security and Ponemon Institute [1], during the last five years, the average number of security breaches (in the study defined as 'successful cyberattacks that cause business disruptions') increased 67%[1]. The attacks cost enterprises on average 13 million US dollars (USD) each year [1] which corresponds to the costs' increase of 12% in the last five years. The expenses are associated with interruptions in performing business operations,

---

[1] The study covered 355 organisations worldwide from various economic sectors.

© Springer Nature Switzerland AG 2020
S. Kanhere et al. (Eds.): ICISS 2020, LNCS 12553, pp. 267–287, 2020.
https://doi.org/10.1007/978-3-030-65610-2_17

loss of data, loss of revenue and damaged information system assets. The cost of data loss represents the largest cost component (5,9 million USD).

On the other hand, enterprises which decided to acquire security intelligence and threat sharing systems noted around 2 million USD on technology savings. Also, investments in cybersecurity automation, AI and machine learning resulted in around 2 million USD of savings. At the same time, expenditures on advanced perimeter controls have not brought in the expected financial returns [1]. Proper decisions in cybersecurity investments are crucial for the operation of contemporary enterprises. The investments compete for funds with other areas of company activities and thus they require rational economic justifications [2]. To plan effective cybersecurity strategies [3], practical tools for measuring the cost of cybersecurity are demanded [4].

In response to this demand, CAsPeA – the *C*ost *A*ssessment of *P*ersonnel Activities in Information Security Management (https://zie.pg.edu.pl/cybsec/caspea) was introduced [5–8]. The method enables evaluations of the costs of employees' effort and time spent on cybersecurity-related actions during their daily work. These costs regard, for instance, participation in cybersecurity training and awareness sessions, setting up protections for devices and applications, or adopting organisational cybersecurity policies and procedures. Such costs constitute a substantial component of cybersecurity spendings, but because they become evident only during scrupulous analyses, often they are neglected.

This paper presents the recent developments on the method. After a brief discussion of the relevant terminology (Sect. 2) and the analysis of related studies (Sect. 3), the key characteristics of CAsPeA are presented (Sect. 4). The method's application based on a case study of a civil engineering company is described in Sect. 5. The main goal of the case study is to demonstrate the straightforwardness of CAsPeA-based estimations. As a part of the method's evaluation, CAsPeA was subject to a comparative analysis with respect to SQUARE. The analysis is presented in Sect. 6. The paper concludes with closing remarks.

2   Costs of Cybersecurity

Costs of cybersecurity management can be defined as *the evaluated use of resources in monetary terms* [9,10]. These costs are associated with various types of measures and activities that are aimed at reducing cybersecurity risks, including technical as well as organisational. They embrace [10]:

- the costs caused by information security incidents,
- costs of information security management,
- costs of security controls,
- and the costs of capital induced by information security risks.

In the Detica's research [11], classification of costs associated with cybercrime is presented, which distinguishes between:

- *costs in anticipation of cybercrime* that include the costs of security controls, insurance costs, and the costs of compliance with security standards,

- *costs as a consequence of cybercrime* comprising direct losses, such as disaster recovery costs and indirect losses related for instance to reduced competitiveness,
- *costs in response to cybercrime*, for instance, compensation payments to victims, fines imposed by regulatory bodies or the costs of legal or forensic conducts,
- *indirect costs associated with cybercrime*, including the costs resulting from damage of reputation, loss of trust of customers or reduced public sector revenues.

Anderson et al. [12] propose an alternative framework for categorising the costs of cybercrime presented in Fig. 1.

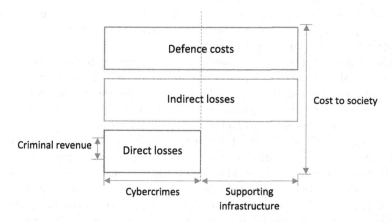

Fig. 1. Framework for categorising the costs of cybercrime. Source [12].

3   Related Work

The studies of the cost of cyber-crime focus on the identification of reliable data on cyber incidents and their structured analysis [11–14]. For instance, Riek et al. [15] developed an instrument to measure the costs of cyber-crime for consumers that incorporates the findings of earlier studies in this domain and applied it to obtain data in six European countries. Farahmand et al. [16] discussed the criteria for categorising enterprise information assets and provided a three-dimensional scheme for probabilistic evaluation of the impact of security threats.

Sawik [17] studied the problem of the optimal selection of cybersecurity measures to reduce the impact of information flow disruptions in enterprises' supply chains given a constrained budget. Various Stochastic Mixed Integer Programming models were applied to the analyses. Cybersecurity investments with nonlinear budget constraints were researched by Daniele and Scrimali [18] and Nagurney et al. [19]. A dynamic model of security investments that acknowledges the trade-off between confidentiality and availability of information was introduced by Ioannidis et al. [20]. Another dynamic model is described by Tatsumi and Goto [21]. In 2010 Böhme et al. [22] presented a model which extends the iterated weakest link (IWL) model with penetration testing.

Among the studies on cyber-insurance, Bandyopadhyay and Mookerjee [23] constructed a model for deriving the overall optimal decision to purchase cyber-insurance based on the determination of the impact of secondary loss in structuring the use of cyber-insurance and backward analysis of multiple incident scenarios. Bartolini et al. [24] analysed the processes performed by insurance companies that aim at evaluating an enterprise's cybersecurity risk level. Pal et al. [25] developed a model for deriving optimal cyber-insurance contracts which considers two types of cyber-insurance agency strategies: welfare maximising or profit maximising [25]. Shetty et al. [26] devised a model to study the effects of cyber-insurance on user security and their welfare in which a probability of a successful attack depends on the individual security of a user and on the network security (independent of the user).

Other interesting economics-based security studies include the work of Havakhor et al. [27] who investigated the capital market's response to an organisation's cybersecurity investments. The study demonstrated that properly communicating cybersecurity investments to investors would likely reduce information asymmetries surrounding enterprises' risks and result in the cost of capital reduction. Rodrigues et al. [28] proposed a framework for evaluating the economic impact of cybersecurity measures in distributed ecosystems with several participants. The framework provides models for cost estimations and the mapping of relations between interdependent systems and their components. Chessa et al. [29] proposed a cooperative game-theoretic approach to quantify the value of personal data in networks. Robinson et al. [30] presented an application of stated preference discrete choice experiments (SPDCEs) to analyse and quantify the security and privacy preferences and views of individuals.

Cost calculators are straightforward applications for deriving rough cost figures based on the input data characterising a given organisation e.g. the number of users, the number of servers or the cost of electricity, training, bandwidth etc. Publicly available cost calculators include Data Breach Risk Calculator of the Ponemon Institute and IBM [31], CyberTab [32], Websense Hosted Email Security Calculator [33] and Small Business Risk Calculator [34]. In addition, it is popular to apply widely recognised financial metrics including the Rate of Return, maximum Net Present Value or the Return on Investment [4,35] to analyse the results of the estimations.

As far as the methods for calculating the costs related to implementing security controls are concerned only few proposals have been developed including I-CAMP [36], I-CAMP II [37], SAEM [38] or SQUARE [39]. Cyber Incident Cost Assessment (CICA) is also mentioned in the literature, but its documentation is unavailable. The methods' descriptions can be found, for instance, in [5,10,35,40,41]. Radziwill and Benton [42] developed a mapping between the NIST Cybersecurity Framework (CSF) and the costs of quality that can be adopted by organisations that apply the framework to plan, manage, and improve their cybersecurity operations. In addition, the mapping enables linking elements in accounting systems that are associated with cybersecurity operations and risk management to a quality cost model.

The Cost/Benefit Analysis-based framework developed by the System Quality Requirements Engineering (SQUARE) Team from Software Engineering Institute (SEI) [39] is a method that earned interest of researchers and practitioners [6,43–46]. The method estimates the costs of computer security-related projects conducted in small enterprises based on threat categories that are publicly available from national surveys. For each category of threats, costs, benefits, baseline risks, and residual risks can be estimated assuming average yearly probabilities of categorised threats and averaged extent of financial loss resulting from the exposure to threats in the categories [39]. The results of SQUARE calculations can be used to obtain the *cost of mitigation of a vulnerability* which Zineddine specifies as [47]:

$$cv_j = \lambda C L\nu_j - \mu C S\nu_{ij} \tag{1}$$

$$\lambda + \mu = 1 \tag{2}$$

where $CL\nu_j$ is the cost of damage resulting from the exploitation of the vulnerability v_i. $CL\nu_j$ can be calculated based on the SQUARE findings. $CS\nu_{ij}$ is the cost of alleviating the vulnerability v_i. λ and ν are coefficients that can be arbitrarily set, within the range depicted in (2), by an organisation depending on the targeted level of security. In Sect. 6 a comparative analysis of CAsPeA in respect to SQUARE is presented.

The analysis of the related work revealed that the studies and methods focus on cybersecurity investments into technical or organisational cybersecurity controls and financial losses resulting from security breaches. The costs are investigated individually or introduced into a cost-benefit analysis. Also, they are studied at different levels, from micro- to macroeconomic. However, the insight into the costing component associated with personnel activities related to cybersecurity management in companies and organisations has been missing.

4   Method Description

CAsPeA – *C*ost *A*ssessment of *P*ersonnel *A*ctivities in Information Security Management (https://zie.pg.edu.pl/cybsec/caspea) – is a method that complements the portfolio of the available methods for estimating the cost of cybersecurity management by enabling the estimation of the costs of human effort and time spent on cybersecurity-related actions during their daily work [5–8]. These costs regard, for instance, employees' participation in cybersecurity training, managing secure configurations of utilised hardware and software or reading cybersecurity policy documents. Such costs constitute a substantial component of cybersecurity spendings, but because they become evident only during scrupulous analyses, often they are neglected. By enabling their estimations, the method should provide a more complete view of the costs of cybersecurity. In the following text, the highlights of the methods are provided. More detailed descriptions can be found in [5–8].

To enable the calculations, the Activity-Based Costing (ABC) system was selected and adapted to the costing model [5–8]. The advantage of the ABC is that it recognises activities (human or machine operations) as fundamental objects that induce costs in enterprises. In CAsPeA, the total cost in organisation is calculated as a sum of costs of all activities performed in an enterprise. Then, to derive the costs of activities, proper cost centres must be assigned to them using relevant cost drivers. Duration driver in the form of working time expressed in hours was chosen as the activity cost driver.

For the reference list of the activities to be included in the model, NIST SP's 800-53 list of security controls was selected after a thorough literature analysis. The list embraces multiple cybersecurity areas that altogether comprehensively address the organisational cybersecurity context. Examples of the areas include the *AT Awareness and Training*, *CM Configuration Management* or *PS Personnel Security* [48]. Another strength of the document is that it is fully compatible with ISO/IEC 27001 (see the mapping between the documents in Appendix H, Table H-1 of NIST SP 800-53) – the most recognised cybersecurity standard worldwide.

The method enables estimations based on a baseline set of input data that characterise an organisation such as the number of employees that utilise computer devices, average hourly pay rates of personnel that performs or is responsible for security activities or hire/termination rate/promotion/demotion/transfer rates. Minimum, maximum, average and usual duration times are assigned to the cost drivers and the posts of personnel performing or responsible for relevant cybersecurity activities (e.g. IT administrators, users or Human Resources Management professionals) associated with resource cost drivers.

Based on the input data, the total cost of staff activities related to information security management, the cost of exclusive IT security professionals' activities, the minimum amount of work time of information security professionals indispensable for assuring sufficient level of information security in an organisation and the related minimum required quantity of information security professionals are calculated. Each of the parameters is represented by its minimum, maximum, average and the usual value.

To facilitate calculations, a spreadsheet was developed and updated periodically. It comprises four worksheets that correspond to subsequent steps of the assessment process. The *Organisation data* worksheet (see Fig. 2) enables entering all required input data, such as the number of employees, human resources metrics or hourly pay rates. The worksheets *List of activities* (see Fig. 3) and *Cost of information security professionals* comprise formulae for calculation of the total cost of activities. In the *Assessment results worksheet* (see Fig. 4) the outcomes of the assessment are presented.

	A	B	C	
1	Number of users	46		
2	Planned number of information security professionals	0		
3	Hire rate	10%		
4	Termination rate	10%		
5	Promotion/demotion/transfer rate	10%		
6	Mobile devices usage index	25%		
7	Average number of outsiders having access to the system	5		
8				
9	Resource cost drivers	Average hourly gross pay rate [euro]		
10	Information security professionals	8.9		
11	IT administrators	4.4		
12	Human Resources Management professionals	4.6		
13	Users	4.16		
14	Senior-level executives or managers	7.6		
15	Physical security officers	4.87		
16	Physical security officers guards	2.23		
17	Budget Planning and Control professionals	5.65		
18				

‹ ›   **1. Organisation data** ... ⊕

Fig. 2. The *Organisation data* worksheet provides fields for all the required input data, such as the number of employees, human resources metrics, or hourly pay rates.

5 Case Study

This section illustrates the application of CAsPeA in a case study of a civil engineering company that specialises in designing public and private sector objects including hospitals, industrial and technological facilities or shopping centres. The designs represent various types of structures and buildings in practically all branches of industry, and vary from complex endeavours that cover all functions and components of completely new facilities (starting from their 'founding stone') to the projects that focus on enhancing or reorganising existing constructions. Figure 5 presents the structure of the IT system of the enterprise. The main goal of this case study is to demonstrate how straightforward is the process of estimating the costs with CAsPeA.

5.1 Input Data

The company employs 48 workers including:

- executives (2),
- secretaries (2),
- accountants (3),
- architects (38),
- auxiliary staff (1),
- cleaning staff (2).

274   R. Leszczyna and A. Litwin

Fig. 3. The worksheet *List of activities* comprise formulae for calculation of the total cost of information security management activities.

Fig. 4. The *Assessment results* worksheet shows the outcome of the cost assessment.

In the first step of the cost assessment process, the number of employees who can use the information system was determined. In the company the majority of the workers had their personal working stations apart from the cleaning staff. Thus, 46 employees were authorised to use the information system. Further data required for the calculation of cost estimates were as follows:

- percentage of personnel hired in the current year (hire rate) – 10%,
- percentage of workers that terminated their employment in the current year (termination rate) – 10%,
- the rate of employees' promotions, demotions and transfers – 10%,
- mobile devices usage index (i_{mdui}) – 25%,
- the approximate number of external users authorised to access the organisation's information system – 5.

The average hourly gross pay rates necessary to estimate the total cost of information security activities were based on the data from Sedlak&Sedlak consulting[2] and converted to US dollars (USD) from Polish Złoty with a rounded average exchange rate equal to 4[3]. Roughly, the rate can be also used to interpret the values in Euro. The input data are presented in Fig. 2.

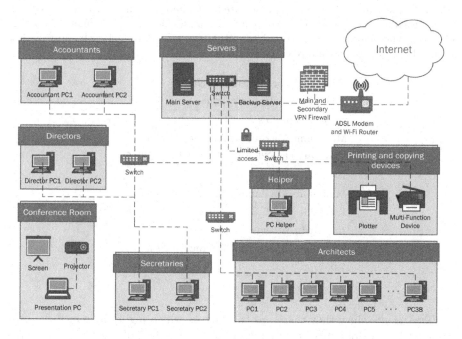

Fig. 5. Information system of the civil engineering design company

5.2   Results

The obtained cost estimates are presented in Tables 1 and 2.

---

[2] Available at http://www.wynagrodzenia.pl/. Last access: 10.10.2020.
[3] Source: www.exchangerates.org.uk/USD-EUR-exchange-rate-history.html.   Last access: 10.10.2020.

Table 1. The estimate of the total yearly cost of activities associated with information security management in the enterprise, depending on whether Physical Access Monitoring and Control (PAMC) activities are included/excluded. The values were converted to US dollars (USD) from Polish Złoty with a rounded average exchange rate equal to 4.

Total cost of activities [USD]			
Excluding PAMC			
Minimum	Maximum	Average	*Usual*
10,075.69	70,656.62	40,366.16	*24,464.70*
Including PAMC			
Minimum	Maximum	Average	*Usual*
21,031.81	210,991.83	116,011.82	*39,686.95*

Table 2. Estimates of parameters associated with information security professionals: cost of their activities, the number of required working hours, and the required number of posts. The values were converted to US dollars (USD) from Polish Złoty with a rounded average exchange rate equal to 4.

Estimated parameters associated with IT security professionals			
Cost of activities [USD]			
Minimum	Maximum	Average	*Usual*
9,062.29	65,035.58	37,048.93	*22,608.66*
Required working hours			
Minimum	Maximum	Average	*Usual*
1,018.23	7,307.37	4,162.80	*2,540.30*
Required positions			
Minimum	Maximum	Average	*Usual*
1.0	4.0	2.5	*1.5*

The results show that there are two factors which highly influence the estimated total cost of cybersecurity management. The first of them is whether the organisation already manages its physical security. Then, if it does, the second question regards the extent to which the cost of the management is attributed to information security.

If an organisation already manages its physical security and monitoring and control of physical access to the information system, then the estimated total cost of activities is around 24,465 US dollars (USD) during a year (see Table 1). This estimate is coherent with an expectation of the cost of security management in the system of this scale. It is worth to note that the major part (around 92%) of the cost is associated with the activities performed by information security professionals (see Table 2), and only around 1,856 USD will be spent on the activities of other employees. The evaluation indicates also that for managing information security in the company, employing one information security professional is sufficient.

A significantly different situation occurs when the organisation starts to consider its physical security only after evaluating the decision of the establishment of information security management and associates the physical security just with the protection of its information assets. Then, the estimated cost boosts significantly, and it reaches the value of approximately 39,687 USD (see Table 1). This is due to the fact, that in this case, the activities linked with physical security become dominant. Precisely, the activities connected to PE-3 Physical Access Control and PE-6 Monitoring Physical Access security components, are expensive. The cost of the activities reached as much as 15,222 USD, which corresponds to around 38% of the total activities cost.

Such a high cost of physical access control and monitoring activities stems from the fact that the activities require the continuous presence of guards and security specialists. To estimate the cost, the following assumptions were made:

- Information system physical access control requires the continuous presence of a security guard for 12 h (from 8:00 am to 8:00 pm) in weekdays (on average 250 days during a year).
- Information system physical access monitoring is part of the entire monitoring of the organisation headquarters and requires on average one tenth its time. The headquarters are monitored 24 h a day, each day of a year. The monitoring requires the continuous presence of at least one guard or security professional.

In this perspective, the yearly cost of activities associated with the establishment and maintenance of information security may constitute a significant position in the organisation's budget, depending on the turnover. This fact would need to be taken into careful consideration in the organisation tactical planning. At the same time, it must be borne in mind that at the other end lies much higher cost, which the organisation will have to meet in the event of failure caused by a successful computer attack.

Other estimates that refer to the total cost of work of IT security professionals, namely the minimum amount of work time of information security professionals indispensable for assuring sufficient level of information security in the organisation and the related number of information security professionals – remain the same as they are independent of physical security (Table 2). It is worth to note that in everyday practice the first scenario is much more common than the second, as most organisations protect their physical resources, whether on their own or by delegating this task to security agencies.

For the organisation, the estimated cost is acceptable. The performed estimation provides an incentive for extending the existing cybersecurity level.

6 Comparative Analysis with SQUARE

As a part of the method's evaluation, CAsPeA was subject to a comparative analysis with respect to SQUARE (see Sect. 3) based on two existing small and medium enterprises that operate in the global and national (Polish) market: a boatyard and an IT support company.

The boatyard designs and builds customised luxury sailing and power catamarans and super-yachts from 17 to 60 m (60 to 200 feet). The company operates on the world market carrying out orders from individual clients. It specialises in the unit production, where the projects and their implementation are always accommodated to the requirements of an orderer. The company very intensively utilises information technologies during yacht design and in production management. Additionally, the entire documentation is stored in the electronic form and printed only on demand. Thus, for the company, it is paramount to assure the security of the data.

The IT support company provides IT support for a publishing group which is one of the largest publishers in Poland. The company creates and maintains a wide portfolio of internet applications. The most popular of them is an advertisement service recognised in all country regions and the internet issue of one of the oldest journals. The internet traffic reaches as much as a few million page hits daily for each service. The company databases store hundreds of thousands of personal data.

6.1   Input Data

The boatyard employs in total around 200 workers. The number is approximated because the quantity of production personnel varies depending on the actual production needs. In the boatyard, the production personnel, which constitutes the majority of the workforce has a very limited (practically null) access to the system, while the system users are management, designers and engineers. Further analysis reveals that 35 workers are authorised to use the information system.

Additional data required for the calculation of cost estimates were as follows: HR - hire rate – 34,29%, TR - termination rate – 28,57%, PDTR - promotion/-demotion/transfer rate – 8,57%, i_{mdui} – mobile devices usage index – 25,71%, approximate number of people outside of the organisation who have access to the organisation's IT system – 6. The data are summarised in the Table 3.

Table 3. Input data for the boatyard.

Indicator	Value
Number of users	35
Planned number of information security professionals	0
HR - hire rate	34.29%
TR - termination rate	28.57%
PDTR - promotion/demotion/transfer rate	8.57%
i_{mdui}	25.71%
Approximate number of outsiders with access to the organisation's IT system	6

The average hourly gross pay rates necessary to estimate the total cost of information security activities were estimated based on the data from Sedlak&Sedlak consulting[4]. The analogous input data for the IT support company are presented in the Table 4.

Table 4. Input data for the IT support company.

Indicator	Value
Number of employees	104
Number of users	95
Planned number of information security professionals	1
HR - hire rate	24.21%
TR - termination rate	26.32%
PDTR - promotion/demotion/transfer rate	32.63%
i_{mdui}	42.11%
Approximate number of outsiders with access to the organisation's IT system	30

6.2   Results Obtained with CAsPeA

Boatyard. Based on the input data presented in Table 3, the estimates summarised in Table 5 and Table 6 were obtained[5]. The cost estimates are reasonable for a company which in average sells 3–5 yachts a year for the price varying between 700,000–6,000,000 Euro (around 800,000–7,000,000 US dollars).

Table 5. The estimate of the total yearly cost of activities associated with cybersecurity management for the boatyard. The values were converted to USD from Polish Złoty with a rounded average exchange rate equal to 4.

Total cost of activities [USD]			
Minimum	Maximum	Average	*Usual*
18,861.60	198,967.79	108,914.70	*34,715.46*

---

[4] Available at http://www.wynagrodzenia.pl/.
[5] The values were converted to US dollars (USD) from Polish Złoty with a rounded average exchange rate equal to 4. Roughly, the rate can be also used to interpret the values in Euro.

IT Support Company. The cost values estimated for the IT support company are presented in Table 7 and Table 8. The cost figures acquired with CAsPeA are adherent to the operational reality of the IT support company. With a yearly revenues at the level of millions of USD, the average values of the cost seem to be affordable.

Table 6. Estimates of parameters associated with cybersecurity professionals for the boatyard. The values were converted to US dollars from Polish Złoty with a rounded average exchange rate equal to 4.

Estimated parameters associated with IT security professionals			
Cost of activities [USD]			
Minimum	Maximum	Average	Usual
6,622.23	50,719.39	28,670.81	17,214.45
Required working hours			
Minimum	Maximum	Average	Usual
741.69	5,680.57	3,211.13	1928.02
Required positions			
Minimum	Maximum	Average	Usual
0.5	3.0	2.0	1.0

Table 7. The estimate of the total yearly cost of activities associated with cybersecurity management in the IT support company. The values were converted to US dollars from Polish Złoty with a rounded average exchange rate equal to 4.

Total cost of activities [USD]			
Minimum	Maximum	Average	Usual
21,221.10	244,726.62	132,973.86	39,026.87

6.3   Results Obtained with SQUARE

The same data as for CAsPeA, supplemented with the costs of implementation and a prognosis of a number of incidents of each threat category were used for the input for the SQUARE estimation.

Boatyard. The security cost estimation resulted in selecting four most attractive, by means of cost-benefit ratio, scenarios for the implementation of security measures in the company. The highest priority was assigned to the scenarios aiming at protecting from malware, social engineering and cyber-extortion, because these attacks are among the biggest threats to the computer systems of companies (see Table 9).

It is worth to note the relatively high cost-benefit indicators (higher than for the IT support company). This is primarily due to the assumed lower implementation costs, lesser geographical distribution and the number of security staff. Also, there is no need for additional security officer positions or the extension of duties since the implementation of the projects is relatively straightforward.

The IT Support Company. Similarly as in the previous case, four security implementations projects were determined based on SQUARE analysis of a total cost around 12,000 US dollars (USD) yearly. The company can save on them up to 900,000 USD a year, which results from potential avoiding security incidents and the associated costs of the damages and their restoration. Also in this case, the highest priority was assigned to the projects aiming at protecting from malware, social engineering and cyber-extortion. The results are presented in Table 10.

Table 8. Estimates of parameters associated with cybersecurity professionals for the IT support company. The values were converted to US dollars from Polish Złoty with a rounded average exchange rate equal to 4.

Estimated parameters associated with IT security professionals			
Cost of activities [USD]			
Minimum	Maximum	Average	*Usual*
8,104.62	90,897.56	49,501.09	*20,141.04*
Required working hours			
Minimum	Maximum	Average	*Usual*
907.723	10,180.53	5,544.12	*2,255.80*
Required positions			
Minimum	Maximum	Average	*Usual*
0.5	5.5	3.0	*1.5*

6.4 Results Analysis

The analysis reveals significant differences between the maximum and usual estimated cost values. This result can be connected to the observation of Xie [39] that for the enterprises which normally do not perform cybersecurity activities, even very small investments and thoughtful organisational changes bring influential benefits. The upper limit for the security investments does not exist [35]. According to the law of diminishing returns, with the increase of IT security spendings, the marginal benefit achieved from them will be decreasing. There is an opinion among the experts [49], that as it is impossible to reach perfect security no matter how big are the efforts, the security expenses should be kept

Table 9. Yearly cybersecurity costs' estimates obtained with SQUARE for four protection scenarios (associated with threat categories) of the boatyard. The values were converted to US dollars from Polish Złoty with a rounded average exchange rate equal to 4.

Category of Threats	Category of Preventions	Benefit [USD]	Total Implementation Costs [USD]	Benefit to Cost Value (B/C)	Net Project Value [USD]	Total Value of Unprotected System [USD]	Total Value of Protected System [USD]
Social engineering and cyber-extortion	Training and procedures	107,616.65	4,000.00	26.90	103,616.65	-75,744.44	31,872.22
Viruses, worms, spyware, spam	Anti-malware	519,034.68	2,000.00	259,52	517,034.68	-59,670.52	459,364.16
Phishing, identity theft	Use of Data Certification Schemas	32,010.11	2,250.00	14,23	29,760.11	-7,898.84	24,111.26
Botnets, unauthorised use	Network traffic monitoring tools	23,335.00	1000.00	23,33	22,335.00	-2,228.16	21,106.84

Table 10. Yearly cybersecurity costs' estimates obtained with SQUARE for four protection scenarios (associated with threat categories) of the IT support company. The values were converted to US dollars from Polish Złoty with a rounded average exchange rate equal to 4.

Category of Threats	Category of Preventions	Benefit [USD]	Total Implementation Costs [USD]	Benefit to Cost Value (B/C)	Net Project Value [USD]	Total Value of Unprotected System [USD]	Total Value of Protected System [USD]
Social engineering and cyber-extortion	Training and procedures	107,616.65	6,500.00	16.56	101,416.65	-78,244.44	29,372.22
Viruses, worms, spyware, spam	Anti-malware	519,034.68	3,000.00	173.01	516,034.68	-60,670.52	458,364.16
Unauthorised access	Firewalls, software updates, IDS	33,350.06	2,000.00	16.68	31,350.06	-4,128.73	29,221.33
Theft of mobile devices	Hard disks encryption	32,380.01	1,000.00	32.38	31,380.01	-2,001.44	30,378.56

rational. A good boundary can be defined by potential financial losses due to a security breach.

SQUARE is scenario-oriented. It supports identifying the most profitable ways of protecting an organisation from cybersecurity threats. Thus, the main output of the method are the cost values and financial determinants of different defence scenarios connected to threat categories. CAsPeA, on the other hand, focuses on obtaining the total cost of all human activities related to achieving 'general' cybersecurity level (i.e. protection from various threat types) in an organisation. In this context, the CAsPeA calculation spreadsheet (presented in Sect. 4) turns out to be inflexible to accommodate different scenarios of cybersecurity provision. Currently, modifications are possible only by explicitly altering the spreadsheet formulas. Enriching the method with a module that enables such estimations would provide an added value and would enable better alignment with SQUARE (e.g. allowing for comparison of results).

The estimations obtained with SQUARE are highly influenced by the input data – the bypass rate and the probability of incident occurrence when there are no security measures in place (basis risk) as well as the expected annual loss for each threat category. For both, CAsPeA and SQUARE estimations, the amount of the costs matches the companies' financial capacities. The results are realistic and based on the broad knowledge security incidents and the protection methods. The overall feedback received during the analysis was that both methods could support the organisations' investment decision processes. At the same time, it becomes evident that the methods diverge in scope. CAsPeA concentrates on the cost of the NIST SP 800-53-indicated activities involved in providing IT security (human factor), while SQUARE is threat category-driven. Also, at the moment, CAsPeA does not contain the entire cost-benefit analysis apparatus is it lacks the 'benefit' part of the cost-benefit equation. Thus, the best option is to use the methods in a complementary manner.

7   Conclusions

The paper presented the recent developments on CAsPeA – a method for the assessment of the cost of employees' activities connected with the establishment and the operation of cybersecurity management system. The use of the method was illustrated in a case study of a civil engineering company. The study demonstrated that CAsPeA can effectively support the decision process of an enterprise with regard to the investments into information security. Applying CAsPeA requires only a few straightforward steps and parameters to obtain rough estimations. Additionally, the study evidenced that physical security can become a dominant component in the cost cybersecurity management and thus it should be appropriately considered. In the particular application, the cost estimated with CAsPeA turned out to be acceptable for the organisation and provided an incentive for extending their existing cybersecurity level. This can be a certain prognostic for other companies considering investments in their cybersecurity management systems.

As a part of the method's evaluation, a comparative analysis of CAsPeA and SQUARE was performed. The study was separate from the case study and regarded applying both solutions to evaluate the costs in two enterprises: a boat-yard and an IT support company. The analysis showed that the methods should not be taken as alternatives but as complementary solutions. SQUARE guides through the entire cost-benefit analysis process but focuses on particular protection scenarios without detailed consideration of the human factor. CAsPeA, on the other hand, provides estimations for all activities involved in the cybersecurity management and is human actions-centric but misses the 'benefit' part of the cost-benefit analysis. These observations gave additional insight into where CAsPeA can be improved. For instance, extending the method with a module that enables flexible definitions of investment scenarios or covering the entire cost-benefit analysis are prospective development directions. Other further studies include:

- enhancing CAsPeA with activities linked to the security controls of the secondary and tertiary NIST SP 800-53 baselines,
- developing a dedicated version based on ISO/IEC 27001,
- performing a comparative analysis with the ISO/IEC 27001-based version,
- including technical cybersecurity controls into the CAsPeA estimations,
- researching the applicability of CAsPeA in various contexts (e.g. entrepreneurial sectors) and analysing its fitness and accuracy (e.g. for instance depending on the sector).

References

1. Accenture and Ponemon Institute: The cost of cybercrime: ninth annual cost of cybercrime study. Technical report (2019)
2. Gordon, L.A., Loeb, M.: Return on information security investments: myths vs. realities. J. Strateg. Financ. **84**, 26–32 (2002)
3. Chapman, T.A., Reithel, B.J.: Perceptions of cybersecurity readiness among workgroup IT managers. J. Comput. Inf. Syst. 1–12 (2020). https://doi.org/10.1080/08874417.2019.1703224
4. Sonnenreich, W., Albanese, J., Stout, B.: Return on security investment (ROSI): a practical quantitative model. J. Res. Pract. Inf. Technol. **38**, 55–66 (2006)
5. Leszczyna, R.: Cost of cybersecurity management. Cybersecurity in the Electricity Sector, pp. 127–147. Springer, Cham (2019). https://doi.org/10.1007/978-3-030-19538-0_5
6. Leszczyna, R.: Approaching secure industrial control systems. IET Inf. Secur. **9**(1), 81–89 (2015)
7. Leszczyna, R.: Cost assessment of computer security activities. Comput. Fraud Secur. **2013**(7), 11–16 (2013)
8. Rafał, L.: Metoda szacowania kosztu zarządzania bezpieczeństwem informacji i przykład jej zastosowania w zakładzie opieki zdrowotnej. Zeszyty Kolegium Analiz Ekonomicznych (2017)
9. Martin, K.: Controlling der information security. In: Dieter, B.R., Ralf (eds.) Praxiswissen IT-Sicherheit: Praxishandbuch fur Aufbau, Zertifizierung und Betrieb, chapter 03710. TÜV Media, 19 edn. (2011)

10. Brecht, M., Nowey, T.: A closer look at information security costs. In: Böhme, R. (ed.) The Economics of Information Security and Privacy, pp. 3–24. Springer, Heidelberg (2013). https://doi.org/10.1007/978-3-642-39498-0_1
11. Detica and Office of Cyber Security and Information Assurance: The cost of cyber crime. Technical report (2011)
12. Anderson, R., et al.: Measuring the cost of cybercrime. In: Böhme, R. (ed.) The Economics of Information Security and Privacy, pp. 265–300. Springer, Heidelberg (2013). https://doi.org/10.1007/978-3-642-39498-0_12
13. Moore, T., Clayton, R., Anderson, R.: The economics of online crime. J. Econ. Perspect. **23**(3), 3–20 (2009)
14. Campbell, K., Gordon, L.A., Loeb, M.P., Zhou, L.: The economic cost of publicly announced information security breaches: empirical evidence from the stock market. J. Comput. Secur. **11**, 431–448 (2003)
15. Riek, M., Böhme, R., Ciere, M., Gañán, C., van Eeten, M.: Estimating the costs of consumer-facing cybercrime: a tailored instrument and representative data for six EU countries (2016)
16. Farahmand, F., Navathe, S.B., Sharp, G.P., Enslow, P.H.: Evaluating damages caused by information systems security incidents. In: Camp, L.J., Lewis, S. (eds.) Economics of Information Security. Advances in Information Security, vol. 12. Springer, Boston (2004). https://doi.org/10.1007/1-4020-8090-5_7
17. Sawik, T.: Selection of cybersecurity safeguards portfolio. Supply Chain Disruption Management. ISORMS, vol. 291, pp. 427–448. Springer, Cham (2020). https://doi.org/10.1007/978-3-030-44814-1_15
18. Daniele, P., Scrimali, L.: Strong nash equilibria for cybersecurity investments with nonlinear budget constraints. In: Daniele, P., Scrimali, L. (eds.) New Trends in Emerging Complex Real Life Problems. ASS, vol. 1, pp. 199–207. Springer, Cham (2018). https://doi.org/10.1007/978-3-030-00473-6_22
19. Nagurney, A., Daniele, P., Shukla, S.: A supply chain network game theory model of cybersecurity investments with nonlinear budget constraints. Ann. Oper. Res. **248**, 405–427 (2016). https://doi.org/10.1007/s10479-016-2209-1
20. Ioannidis, C., Pym, D., Williams, J.: Investments and trade-offs in the economics of information security. In: Dingledine, R., Golle, P. (eds.) FC 2009. LNCS, vol. 5628, pp. 148–166. Springer, Heidelberg (2009). https://doi.org/10.1007/978-3-642-03549-4_9
21. Tatsumi, K., Goto, M.: Optimal timing of information security investment: a real options approach. In: Moore, T., Pym, D., Ioannidis, C. (eds.) Economics of Information Security and Privacy, pp. 211–228. Springer, Boston (2010). https://doi.org/10.1007/978-1-4419-6967-5_11
22. Böhme, R., Félegyházi, M.: Optimal information security investment with penetration testing. In: Alpcan, T., Buttyán, L., Baras, J.S. (eds.) GameSec 2010. LNCS, vol. 6442, pp. 21–37. Springer, Heidelberg (2010). https://doi.org/10.1007/978-3-642-17197-0_2
23. Bandyopadhyay, T., Mookerjee, V.: A model to analyze the challenge of using cyber insurance. Inf. Syst. Front. **21**(2), 301–325 (2017). https://doi.org/10.1007/s10796-017-9737-3
24. Bartolini, D.N., Benavente-Peces, C., Ahrens, A.: Using risk assessments to assess insurability in the context of cyber insurance. In: Obaidat, M.S., Cabello, E. (eds.) ICETE 2017. CCIS, vol. 990, pp. 337–345. Springer, Cham (2019). https://doi.org/10.1007/978-3-030-11039-0_16
25. Pal, R., Golubchik, L.: On the economics of information security. ACM SIGMETRICS Perform. Eval. Rev. **38**(2), 51 (2010)

26. Shetty, N., Schwartz, G., Felegyhazi, M., Walrand, J.: Competitive cyber-insurance and internet security. In: Moore, T., Pym, D., Ioannidis, C. (eds.) Economics of Information Security and Privacy. CCIS, pp. 229–247. Springer, Boston (2010). https://doi.org/10.1007/978-1-4419-6967-5_12

27. Havakhor, T., Rahman, M., Zhang, T.: Cybersecurity investments and the cost of capital. SSRN Electron. J. (2020). https://doi.org/10.2139/ssrn.3553470

28. Rodrigues, B., Franco, M., Parangi, G., Stiller, B.: SEConomy: a framework for the economic assessment of cybersecurity. In: Djemame, K., Altmann, J., Bañares, J.Á., Agmon Ben-Yehuda, O., Naldi, M. (eds.) GECON 2019. LNCS, vol. 11819, pp. 154–166. Springer, Cham (2019). https://doi.org/10.1007/978-3-030-36027-6_13

29. Chessa, M., Loiseau, P.: A cooperative game-theoretic approach to quantify the value of personal data in networks (2016)

30. Robinson, N., Potoglou, D., Kim, C., Burge, P., Warnes, R.: Security at what cost? In: Moore, T., Shenoi, S. (eds.) ICCIP 2010. IAICT, vol. 342, pp. 3–15. Springer, Heidelberg (2010). https://doi.org/10.1007/978-3-642-16806-2_1

31. Ponemon Institue and IBM: Data breach risk calculator. Website (2016)

32. The Economist Intelligence Unit: CyberTab: free tool estimates damages from attacks (2014)

33. Websense: TCO calculator: websense hosted email security calculator. Website (2016)

34. Symantec: Small business risk calculator. Website (2016)

35. Su, X.: An overview of economic approaches to information security management. Technical report, University of Twente (2006)

36. Rezmierski, V., Deering, S., Fazio, A., Ziobro, S.: Incident cost analysis and modeling project. Final Report. Technical report, Committee on Institutional Cooperation Chief Information Officers Committee (1998)

37. Rezmierski, V., Carroll, A., Hine, J.: Incident cost analysis and modeling project II. Final Report. Technical report, Committee on Institutional Cooperation Chief Information Officers Committee (2000)

38. Butler, S.A.: Security attribute evaluation method: a cost-benefit approach. In: Proceedings of the 24th International Conference on Software Engineering - ICSE 2002, p. 232. ACM Press, New York (2002)

39. Xie, N., Mead, N.R.: SQUARE project: cost/benefit analysis framework for information security improvement projects in small companies. Technical report, Carnegie Mellon University (2004)

40. Anderson, R., Moore, T.: Information security economics – and beyond. In: Menezes, A. (ed.) CRYPTO 2007. LNCS, vol. 4622, pp. 68–91. Springer, Heidelberg (2007). https://doi.org/10.1007/978-3-540-74143-5_5

41. Mercuri, R.T.: Analyzing security costs. Commun. ACM 46(6), 15–18 (2003)

42. Radziwill, N.M., Benton, M.C.: Cybersecurity cost of quality: managing the costs of cybersecurity risk management. Softw. Qual. Prof. 19(3), 25–43 (2017)

43. Heitzenrater, C.D., Simpson, A.: Policy, statistics and questions: reflections on UK cyber security disclosures. J. Cybersecur. 2, 43–56 (2016)

44. Akbari Roumani, M., Fung, C., Rai, S., Xie, H.: Value analysis of cyber security based on attack types. ITMSOC: Trans. Innov. Bus. Eng. 1, 34–39 (2016)

45. Mallios, Y., Bauer, L., Kaynar, D., Martinelli, F., Morisset, C.: Probabilistic cost enforcement of security policies. J. Comput. Secur. 23, 759–787 (2015)

46. Yang, Y., Jing, D., Wang, Q.: Shaping the effort of developing secure software. Procedia Comput. Sci. 44, 609–618 (2015)

47. Zineddine, M.: Vulnerabilities and mitigation techniques toning in the cloud: a cost and vulnerabilities coverage optimization approach using Cuckoo search algorithm with Lévy flights. Comput. Secur. **48**, 1–18 (2015)
48. National Institute of Standards and Technology (NIST): NIST SP 800-53 Rev. 4 Recommended Security Controls for Federal Information Systems and Organizations. U.S. Government Printing Office (2013)
49. Dittrich, D.A.: Developing an effective incident cost analysis mechanism. Internet (2002)

Author Index

Printed in the United States
By Bookmasters